MODERN
BRITISH
HISTORY ★ A
Garland
Series

Edited by
PETER STANSKY and
LESLIE HUME

THE PREROGATIVE OF ASYLUMDOM ★ Social, Cultural, and Administrative Aspects of the Institutional Treatment of the Insane in Nineteenth-Century Britain

D. J. Mellett

Garland Publishing, Inc.
New York & London ★ 1982

Library of Congress Cataloging in Publication Data

Mellett, D. J. (David J.), 1947–
The prerogative of asylumdom.

(Modern British history ; 14)
Originally presented as the author's thesis (doctoral—University of Cambridge, 1977)
Bibliography: p.
Includes index.
1. Mentally ill—Care and treatment—Great Britain—History. 2. Psychiatric hospitals—Great Britain—History. 3. Mental health laws—Great Britain—History.
I. Title. II. Series.
RC450.G7M44 1982 362.2′0941 81-48363
ISBN 0-8240-5159-9

All volumes in this series are printed on acid-free, 250-year-life paper.
Printed in the United States of America

FOR MY PARENTS.

CONTENTS

PREFACE

Canaan, Leigh,
Greater Manchester,
April, 1981.

This monograph is a shortened, but otherwise unrevised version of a doctoral dissertation submitted to the University of Cambridge in 1977. The research on which it is based was carried out in Cambridge from 1969 to 1972, financed by a research studentship award from the Department of Education and Science.

When the research was begun, the area of mental health was largely neglected by historians, and existing analyses by psychiatrists or historians of the social services tended to offer hermeneutically discrete discussions of the identification and treatment of mental illness in styles which assumed the validity of present-day categories, without examining their historical relativity. It appeared that a somewhat less uncritical approach was called for, one which would try to provide materials for a social history of mental illness by examining the dynamics of the evolution of modern categories: by considering as products of history not only the lunatic asylums, but the categories they imposed, the uses to which they were put, and the problems for which they were created.

Since the dissertation was written, our knowledge and understanding of some of the issues and problems involved have been considerably enlarged by Andrew Scull's Museum of Madness (London 1979), a work which is in many ways complementary to the present study, though its discussion proceeds from a somewhat different set of ideological perspectives, predominantly those founded in 'anti-psychiatry'. Several recent articles indicate a widening, as well as a deepening interest in this area of research, notably: William F. Bynum, 'Rationales for Therapy in British Psychiatry 1780 - 1835' in Medical History vol 18 (1974); P. McCandless, 'Liberty and Lunacy: the Victorians and wrongful confinement' in Journal of Social History vol 10 (1978) and 'Build! Build! The controversy over the care of the chronic insane in England 1855-70' in Bulletin of the History of Medicine vol. 53 (1979); M.A. Shepherd, 'Lunacy and Labour' in Bulletin of the Society for the Study of Labour History vol. 34 (1977); John K. Walton, 'Lunacy in the Industrial Revolution: a study of asylum admissions in Lancashire 1848-50' in Journal of Social History vol. 12 (1980); Elaine Showalter, 'Victorian Women and Insanity' in Victorian Studies vol. 23 (1980).

The influence of Foucault has produced some highly theoretical interventions in this and related areas: Robert Castel, L'Ordre Psychiatrique (Paris 1976) and a reveiw of this work - Peter Miller, 'The Territory of the Psychiatrist' in Ideology and Consciousness vol. 7 (1980) - are, perhaps, the most accessible examples.

A recent symposium at the Wellcome Institute (September 1980) evidenced the breadth of historians' current interest in mental illness - Anne Digby's 'Moral Treatment at the Retreat 1796-1846' (xeroxed paper, Wellcome Institute) being the paper most directly relevant to the study which follows - whilst a paper prepared by D.M. Jones for a Manchester History Workshop (November 1980) offers a long view of developments in Lancashire: 'The custody and care of the mentally ill in Lancashire' in J.V. Pickstone, ed., Health, Disease and Medicine in Lancashire 1750-1950 (UMIST Occasional Publications, No. 2).

I wish to thank Professor J.R. Vincent for directing my attention to this area of research; Dr. Derek Beales, my supervisor, for patient criticism; Mrs. Olive Keidan, who acted as supervisor whilst I was based at Liverpool University working on Lancashire sources. For advice and criticism at various stages, I wish to thank: Mrs. G.E. Brennan, Mr. John Brogan, Miss P.J. Brown, Mr. John Cassidy, Miss M.R. Glover, Dr. D.I. Harker, Dr. Brian Harrison, Professor Roy MacLeod, Dr. William Parry-Jones, Dr. C.M. Vaillant and Mr. K.P. Wren.

The staff of the University Library, Cambridge, the Liverpool Medical Institution and the John Rylands Library, Manchester, deserve special mention for their kind assistance. My thanks, too, to staff at the Public Record Office, the Lancashire County Record Office, Preston, the Brown Library, Liverpool and the Central Library, Manchester.

Parts of chapter six were included in 'Bureaucracy and Mental Illness: the Commissioners in Lunacy 1845-90' in Medical History (July 1981).

David J. Mellett.

ABBREVIATIONS

ALFS	Alleged Lunatic's Friend Society
AMOAHI	Association of Medical Officers in Asylums and Hospitals for the Insane.
Am.J.Med.Sc.	*American Journal of Medical Science*
Am.J.Psych.	*American Journal of Psychiatry*
Am.J.Insanity	*American Journal of Insanity*
Am.Soc.R.	*American Sociological Review*
B.J.S.	*British Journal of Sociology*
B.M.J.	*British Medical Journal*
Bull.Hist.Med.	*Bulletin of the History of Medicine*
CRO	County Record Office
DNB	*Dictionary of National Biography*
E.H.R.	*English Historical Review*
Ec.H.R.	*Economic History Review*
F.M.J.	*Folk Music Journal*
F.S.J.	*Folk Song Journal*
H.J.	*Historical Journal*
J.Ec.H.	*Journal of Economic History*
J.Hist.Med.&All.Sc.	*Journal of the History of Medicine and Allied Sciences*
J.M.Sc.	*Journal of Mental Science*
L.A.B.	Lancashire Asylums Board
L.G.B.	Local Government Board
LLRA	Lunacy Law Reform Association
MACA	Mental After Care Association
MO	Medical Officer
PRO	Public Record Office
Proc.R.S.Med.	*Proceedings of the Royal Society of Medicine*
R.C.P.	Royal College of Physicians
T.R.H.S.	Transactions of the Royal Historical Society.

LIST OF TABLES

INTRODUCTION

During the nineteenth century, dramatic changes took place in the theory and practice of psychiatry, in response to, and mirroring economic, social, political and intellectual developments in western Europe and the United States. The main purpose of the present study is to provide materials towards a social history of mental illness in Britain (1) by analysing two key features of nineteenth-century theory and practice: (i) the emergence of the asylum as the ideal first-resort solution to problems created by mental illness and (ii) the administration of legislation specifically directed towards the insane. Discussion of these related responses to madness occupies the bulk of the study. A necessary contextual framework, in the form of analysis of ways in which insanity was identified, is provided by prefatory discussion of the perceived nature of mental illness, and by interwoven analysis of medical, legal and social factors in the growth of the asylum system.

The timespan covered is a long one, and in most cases, the terminal dating attached to chapters is somewhat arbitrary: rigid terminal dating is inapplicable to much of the subject matter. The reason for such a long, and at times unwieldy timespan is simply the necessity of fixing outside dates for the genesis of the asylum-ideal as an acceptable facet of social policy, and for its development into a taken-for-granted premise in all dealings with the insane. The consolidating lunacy legislation of 1890 provides an obvious ending; a beginning is more difficult. Converging legal, medical, administrative and social factors do not fall into conveniently identical periods of evolution. Accordingly, I have adopted 1790 as a starting point in the first three chapters, though there is some backtracking to mid-century for particular lines of institutional and medical development. The two sections dealing with administrative history are more straightforward: starting dates are those of the inception of Metropolitan and national lunacy inspectorates respectively; end-point is again determined by the 1890 legislation which consolidated the role of the Commissioners in Lunacy.

Throughout, most attention is given to pauper lunatics and to institutions catering for them. This is because, firstly, there were more pauper than non-pauper lunatics; secondly, their care and control involved criteria other than that of perceived madness; thirdly, two sets of legal and administrative machinery were involved in that care and control, thus affording opportunities for interdepartmental comparisons; fourthly, the history of provision for private patients has already been excellently documented. (2)

By far the greatest amount of evidence used comes from Lancashire and London. The reasons are, again, quite straightforward. Firstly, total numbers of certified and confined insane were greater in these two areas. Secondly, they possessed the biggest asylums, and had more- both public and private - than other parts of the country. Thirdly, the medical complement of the central inspectorate displayed a heavy bias towards physicians whose experience had been gained in Lancashire and the Metropolis. (3)

Initially, the dissertation was planned as an exercise in administrative history, with the Lunacy Commission (which retains a key role in the study) providing the focal point of a study of lunacy legislation in Victorian England. However, it became obvious at an early stage that the asylum was crucial to the evolution of lunacy law, and was central to the purpose of the Lunacy Commission, dictating its organisation and function. Earlier studies appeared to take the asylum for granted (4) or, in the case of Foucault, offered interpretations which, however brilliant, reached only into the realm of ideas. (5) Therefore, an attempt was made to investigate the origins and nature of the asylum from as many perspectives as possible, and the asylum itself, as idea and as physical reality, took on the role of focus for the various strands of investigation into the ways in which madmen were perceived and treated in the nineteenth century. This in turn led to a reconsideration of the status and organisation of nineteenth-century psychiatry, especially as a dynamic element in the creation of attitudes to insanity. The asylum was here seen to be a causal force in the development of Victorian psychiatry, and assumed, therefore, a many-sided historical significance which determined its centrality to the dissertation on more than a merely structural level.

The materials for the study almost selected themselves from the vast amounts of sources available. Heaviest concentration has been on those representing medical, legal, administrative and social aspects of the asylum. Practically, this entailed exhaustive use of manuscript and printed materials relating to the Lunacy Commission, printed reports from asylum medical staffs; textbooks, monographs and articles written by those most directly concerned in the evolution and maintenance of the asylum system; reports from official and private investigations into the operation of asylums - individually or collectively; extensive recourse to external sources giving as broad a range of attitudes as possible to the asylum system. Given the breadth and diversity of the subject, and the length of time covered, there has been an obvious element of selectivity in the topics highlighted. The basis for selection has been the extent to which possible avenues of investigation lead to an understanding of the links between institutional, medical, legal and administrative dimensions of the lunatic asylum, and of the economic, social and cultural factors determining those dimensions.

The asylum, as the central feature of the study, affords a unifying theme to issues selected for detailed analysis and has dictated the organisation of materials. The asylum is first considered in both its physical and ideological aspects, and its reciprocal relationships with psychiatry next explored (Chapters two, three, and four). Chapter five offers a brief indication of the range of popular images of madness, and of popular reaction to the official response procedures. These procedures receive detailed examination in the two following chapters: Chapter six is a contribution to the history of government growth in the nineteenth century; Chapter seven is an attempt to focus the accumulated interpretations developed in the dissertation onto the workhouse and the status of the pauper lunatic, since this was where diverse identification codes and response procedures converged.

CHAPTER ONE

PERSPECTIVES.

The study of mental disorder has been approached through a variety of disciplines: principally, theology, law, medicine and anthropology. During the past three-quarters of a century, the primacy of medically-orientated methodologies has been asserted: clinical psychology, psychiatry, psychopharmacology. Historical studies have spasmodically appeared - from psychiatrists and from academics engaged in social administration - offering tangential or micro-analytical consideration of many of the issues discussed below; yet much of this writing, and especially that immediately relative to the English experience, offers simply an evaluation of the past in terms of its approximation to present day psychiatric or administrative orthodoxy, or produces a simplistic and episodic 'history of psychiatry', wherein the thought and practice of selected luminaries are isolated and examined as to the ways in which they point to future advances. (1) In addition, there is a broad range of popularisations of twentieth-century progress which reiterates these impressionistic, reflexive interpretations, (2) and perpetuates an entire mythology of clinical and therapeutic evolution. Originating in the third quarter of the nineteenth century, in the writings of men heavily committed to the adolescent asylum system and to a firmly medical model of insanity, this mythology has been most recently rehearsed by Kathleen Jones. Lunacy, Law and Conscience, 1774 - 1845 (London 1955) and Mental Health and Social Policy, 1845 - 1959 (London 1960), written when the mental treatment laws were in process of revision, display an overt willingness to adopt the sentiments and categories of sources. (3) Relying on later nineteenth-century publications by the spokesmen of the medico-psychological Establishment, Jones sees the past two-hundred years as evidencing a continuous, if erratic, progress towards a true medically-orientated awareness of the nature of mental disorder, and towards a valid, medical organization of responses to the disordered. Her bias is intensified by her taking for granted what one would expect her to prove - most markedly in offering a critique of social policy in terms of the letter of the law, instead of in its actual working. Zealously following the ponderous Daniel Hack Tuke, (4) Jones presents a totally unhistorical picture by unquestioningly listing 'reforms' which have contributed towards an implicitly predestined progress.

Baldly stated, this progress is dated from an eighteenth century Dark Age, randomly illumined by humane physicians and intuitive philanthropists, whose disciples, in the years after 1800, fought apathy, fear, vested interest and asinine legalism to lay the foundations of modern psychiatric theory and hospital practice, which, despite setbacks, came to maturity in the second quarter of the twentieth century. (5)

Still firmly attached to a medical model of mental disorder, psychiatric historians Hunter and Macalpine (6) and Parry-Jones, (7) have through careful scholarship, exposed the inaccuracy of traditional views of eighteenth and nineteenth-century theory and practice. Parry-Jones especially has indicated the power of critical investigation to undermine the longest held of misapprehensions. His study of private madhouses - conventionally seen as representing the worst elements of the 'bad old psychiatry' - has shown both the social importance of the private asylum and the positive clinical and therapeutic contributions made by owners. Denis Leigh's biographical studies have done similar service for individual alienists, notably the much maligned John Haslam, by putting their work in its historical perspective, (8) whilst annotated reprints of texts from the nineteenth century and earlier, by Hunter and Macalpine and Bateson, (9) have shown the importance of approaching earlier writers with a proper historical sense, instead of glibly translating them into a present-day mode.

Of recent years sociologists and cultural anthropologists have intervened to ask the kinds of questions that medical specialists have largely ignored. The latter, following their classical tradition, have mostly been concerned with the description of pathological signs and symptoms, and post-Freudian systems have generally seen the etiology of mental illness as a product of individual psychological mechanism. But no empirically tested theory of mental illness emerged and it was left to post-war (mainly American) sociologists to treat mental disorder as a profitable field for enquiry and to investigate the importance of social and cultural variables in the shaping of such disorder. (10)

The biggest shift in perspective has come about by questioning the basic assumption of traditional psychiatry. The increasingly popular trend has been to locate the phenomenon of mental disorder in the larger area of deviant behaviour. Emphasis is upon the processes by which individuals become identified as deviant, and upon the responses (legal, social, and medical) consequent to the identification. Reflecting the influence of the transactionalist theories of Lemert, (11) Howard Becker's definition of deviance has entered the sociological canon:

> Social groups create deviance by making the rules whose infraction constitutes deviance, and by applying those rules to particular people and labelling them as outsiders...
>
> ... deviance is not a quality of the act a person commits, but rather a consequence of the application by others of rules and sanctions to an offender. The deviant is one to whom the label has successfully been applied; deviant behaviour is behaviour that people so label. (12)

The institutional, legal and administrative dimensions involved have been discussed from a similar methodological standpoint by Goffman and Kittrie. (13) Viewed in these terms, mental illness becomes a consequence of labelling processes which are as much, if not more, the result of audience reaction as of an actor's symptoms or function. Deviance patterns labelled as mental illnesses or disorders are thus personality disorders, or simply 'problems of living'. Since the social structure of a group affects the development of a member's personality, the causal force of sociocultural factors in labelled insanities is stressed. There is no inherent necessity to dismiss clinical psychiatry as irrelevent here, and it may be allowed that there must be a constitutional basis for many behaviours in this spectrum of deviance - in psychoses, for example. (14) Yet the array of genetic and biochemical factors, in all their complexity, does not ensure that predisposing physiological factors will combine with specific precipitating factors to produce a form of mental illness. Other, sociological factors must operate. Scheff has attempted to show (15) that the causes of mental illness careers are a part of the social system in which they occur. Mental illness is no longer internalized in the individual's psychological makeup, but externalized as a specific mode of societal reaction to a kind of deviation that admits of no other satisfactory explicit identification. This Scheff terms 'residual deviance'. Once the labelling is complete, a stabilised relationship is confirmed between society and the deviant: the latter's role is set, and he is encouraged to conform to expected deviant performances. A minority of psychiatric opinion goes further and argues that the entire 'illness' concept should be dropped.

Szasz (16) has contended that so-called mental illnesses are in no way disease entities, but exclusively social evaluations incorporating ethical and legal criteria. Szasz is concerned to undermine the validity of the secondary, medical, identification process (17) and he attempts to divest the profession of all its diagnostic and prescriptive roles. Using the vocabulary of game-theory (18) he points to mental illness as just one form of interpersonal strategy, and goes beyond Scheff in suggesting this as a causal force in the identification process instead of as a mere perpetuation of the label's validity. Only as a metaphor, argues Szasz, can mental illness be a disease, and it is both immoral and dangerous in social terms to act as if there were a real disease. (19)

Szasz's historical analysis offers the image of contemporary institutional psychiatry as one outcome of progressive scientific takeovers of the means of social control. In his model, the modern psychiatric Establishment occupies the same strategic function as the Inquisition, with the madman replacing the witch, heretic or Jew as scapegoat for defensively-minded, socially-advantaged groups. (20) This view is shared by the followers of R.D. Laing, whose radical therapy movement has gained wide support, not least through its astute use of the mass media. (21) Greatly influenced by Sartre, Laing, Cooper, (22) Esterson, (23) and others have communicated a political model of madness which threatens western bourgeois social structures at the root: in the family. (24) Ironically, these attacks on the professional Establishment are bolstered by appeals to the writers' own professional credentials. (25)

Exclusive concentration on intrinsic factors, whether

physical or abstract, has elevated the position of the professional alienist above that which his secondary role in the identification of madness would otherwise have allowed. (26) Even modern formulations which open the door to extrinsic factors have been professional in origin and application. The socio-economic implications of 'professionalism' serve as a warning against unquestioned acceptance of its tenets as 'objective' or 'scientific', and it is precisely this point which Szasz's polemical scholarship expounds. (27)

There is a middle ground of psychiatric opinion, committed to a medical model of insanity, which attempts to integrate sociological criteria with traditional clinical perspectives. Much of this opinion is merely an updated and sophisticated development of theories produced by the disillusioned psychiatry of the 1880s and 1890s. (28) Psychiatric disorder is here seen as a reaction or adaptation to the environment, limited by constitutions and biological determinants. (29) Consequently, environmental disruption can become an exciting factor in the shaping of a mental illness career:

> ... culture change can be quite devastating to the mental equilibrium of group members. Where the change is rapid and pervasive, many discontinuities develop. ... Certain roles once matched by compensation become intolerable. Traditional values no longer serve as adequate guidelines ... (30)

It is not simply that social disintegration causes mental illness, but rather that there is a complex inter-relationship between cultural change, social disintegration and psychiatric disorder. Latent psychiatric disorder surfaces when cultural change in a community produces a degree of social disintegration. (31)

Clearly, this could afford a useful model for discussing the period 1790 - 1890, which witnessed accelerating degrees of cultural and social change with perceived acceleration of social disintegration and a heightened incidence of labelled insanity. Moreover, since contemporary scientific and technological achievements, together with trends in social and political organization, are 'the direct, logistic development of forces set in motion in the Britain of George III' (32) the application of these modern psychiatric dicta to their genetic roots would be very appropriate. However, Leighton's view rests on the assumption that mental illness is <u>latent within a community</u>, tacitly ignoring that ascribed disorder might be <u>created</u> by the dynamics of change within the community, or even that the ascription itself might be a symptom of change within the community. The evaluation of behaviours as symptoms of mental 'illness', takes place within a group setting, but individuals belong to and function in more than one group context. Behaviours tolerated in a person's primary group may not be tolerated by members in his secondary groups. (33) Where the latter have authority to label, their values and standards constitute the sole criteria for ascribing deviance. It is a possibility, then, that change in this latter context will have a generative function in creating such deviance, that changes of diverse nature in different groups will have an exaggerating effect and provoke reassessment of labelling processes and of the organization of authority groups' responses.

During the eighteenth-century 'take-off' into economic growth, (34) what the Leightons term 'culture change' operated widely throughout society. The nature and structure of English society were an integral shaping force of economic change (35) and in turn that society was structurally altered. (36) In the course of this alteration, syncopated, geographically varied and disparate within the various sections of the increasingly class-determined social structure, English society received a range of culture-shocks mediated by steam technology, urbanisation and population growth. (37) In the hardening of the liberal capitalism which carried the economy into self-sustaining growth, social and political strategies emerged to enable the more advantaged groups to cope with the effects of these shocks on their own members, or on members of different or rival groups. Sophisticated identification processes for madness, and reformed responses to the mad formed one such strategy.

From the third quarter of the eighteenth century, the operators of normalcy codes - i.e. members of politically and/or economically dominant social groups - in England, as in western Europe and the United States, discovered an avowedly objective criterion in the nascent psychiatry operating within the self-consciously aspiring medical profession. (38) During the course of the century under review there were modifications to the class composition of these operators - chiefly in the form of broadening the bases for admission to decision-making processes and of introducing new, professional executives. (39) Throughout, normalcy was seen as behaviours consonant with the patterns attuned to the working out of the bourgeois interpretation of a vaguely-grasped 'protestant' capitalistic ethic, at the core of which was an adherence to the principle of self-determination and an ambivalent faith in an essentially hierarchical society. The adjudicators of normalcy were spokesmen for this ethic: those whose position evidenced their belief in, and ability to profit by its cultural codes: justices of the peace, clergymen, lawyers, the newly-accepted professional class of doctors, and the successful traders, businessmen and farmers who made up boards of poor law unions and asylum visiting committees.

Identification of the madman, in the nineteenth century as in the twentieth, initially took place either in his primary group, where the pertinent criteria were the extent to which the person failed to fulfil primary social roles (familial or economic) and the extent to which he violated the group's norms and important values; or where authority structures from secondary groups impinged on a primary group's autonomy, where the criteria reflected different tolerance levels and were complicated by political and social ideologies. In neither case was the medical specialist the primary adjudicator. Given the class structure with its complex banks of authority-deference patterns, (40) individuals in the least advantaged groups within a class tended to be recipients of successful labelling, especially from an external source. (41) And for primary or secondary identification, the only operable test was an individual's behaviour. At the end of the century, Charles Mercier (42) could point only to a man's conduct as evidence of his sanity or otherwise: 'However disordered a person's mind may be, he is not regarded as insane unless and until he gives evidence of his insanity by some overt act.' (43) Conduct was defined broadly in Spencerian terms as 'the active or dynamic adjustment of self to circumstances', a part of which consisted of 'maintenance of proper social and political relations.' (44) In this context a man was expected to be able to adjust to his particular social environment and to adopt a particular social role in his capacity as a unit in maintaining the relations of the whole society. Mercier suggests that the assessment of an individual's conduct lay solely in the 'approval and good opinion of those with whom he consorts.' In practice, however, the final arbiters were only rarely the consorts of the assessed, as the majority confined as mad were pauper lunatics. Some grounds for confinement would scarcely have been considered valid by the peers of the individuals confined: the superintendent of the Devon County Asylum, for example, in 1858, had to accept an aged female pauper on the strength of observations noted on the admission order by a Dr. Madden, and these consisted of her use of 'improper and foul expressions' such as 'bloody hell.' (45)

The assessors of behaviour and their professional aides were more at ease when concerned with members of their own classes. Yet even here there were pitfalls. Where, for example, was the line to be drawn between eccentricity and madness? According to John Bucknill (46) it was simply a matter of degree. Hack Tuke (47) hedged round the question by positing a list of variables which, had he in practice accepted at full value, would have precluded his ever making a diagnosis. (48) Alleged peculiarities, argued Tuke, could never be separated from the individual, and in estimating any man's conduct, account must be taken of his education, race, environment, religion and social position. Astutely, Tuke noted the temporal element: yesterday's madness might be today's eccentricity and become tomorrow's norm:

> Before the present fashion of wearing the beard was introduced, we knew a gentleman whose practice of allowing the hair to grow on the face was accepted as one among indications of insanity. The same remarks apply to the action of anyone who has the courage to wear a more wholesome article of dress than his fellows. (49)

Similarly, there were class codes which might colour any diagnosis: for a peasant to sit at his cottage door, slippered and pipesmoking, was normal; in a Harley Street Physician, such behaviour would indicate at least eccentricity. (50) Yet in nineteenth-century England, it was only those of like status to the physician who could run the risk of the eccentricity-label's being applied. As John Stuart Mill perceived: 'Persons require to possess a title, or some other badge or rank ... to be able to indulge somewhat in the luxury of doing what they like without detriment to their estimation.' (51) A sobering thought indeed, when alienists were indicating that 'estimation' was the principal criterion in assessing a man's sanity.

That there should be a risk attached to the indulgences referred to by Mill was inevitable. Social life inevitably leads to the introduction of social controls, and there is no need to adopt the extremism of Szasz or Laing in order to locate the roots of psychiatry and psychiatric hospitals in attempts to broaden social controls. (52) Indeed, organic causality in the creation of behavioural disorders may even be linked to a similarly organically-located origin of social normality. Assuming there is in humanity a biological need to identify with one's fellows, which operates as a primary cause in the evolution of societies, it is possible to hark back to Darwin in arguing that 'group selection', of shared genetic materials initiates biologically-based cultural processes, whereby the preservation of common genes is socially sought through the observation of similarity of behaviour in group members. In its sociocultural expression, 'group selection' can become an observable phenomenon in relationships between group members, especially if heightened by the elevation of intolerance of difference as a necessary cultural ideal. (53) Deliberate cultural exaggeration of inherited components of behaviour favouring group selection can be seen to lead to a society's desire to bring deviance back to the norm. (54) From this perspective, behaviours classified as mental illnesses, whether provably caused by organic lesion, biochemical imbalance, or otherwise, constitute a challenge to society. The symptoms of aberrant behaviour, perceived as threats to the behavioural order of society, and perceived as similar in labelled deviants of disparate classification, afford societies the opportunity of treating criminals, heretics, madmen, political or cultural dissidents in similar fashions. In clear-cut cases - epilepsy, brain syphillis, etc. - the 'illness' label attached to some deviant behaviours had in the nineteenth century, and still retains, some real meaning. However, definitions were (and are) stretched to cover radically different aberrant behaviours, and for reasons of social control rather than for mental healing. (55)

The recipient of the deviance label varies, obviously, in different societies. Equally obviously, particular economic, social and political institutions create particular groups of candidates for specific labels. The madness label in mid-twentieth-century Russia and the United States has consistently been successfully applied to overt critics of those states' respective systems of government and social values. (56) In nineteenth-century Britain, the recipients of the madness label were similarly decided on by the operation of identification codes which were ideologically rather than medically based. It is not contended that the operators of identification codes were consciously or cynically using psychiatry to disguise political oppression or cultural control, as have some modern totalitarian regimes. But it was those who might unwittingly threaten some of the group-selection values of a developing industrial-capitalist society who were diagnosed and institutionalized: working people, poor people, immigrants, women. As will be shown below, the asylum, originally designed for aberrant members of the middling ranks of society, gradually became a public house of detention for people who acted oddly, or who had no place to go: alcoholics, geriatrics, depressives, paranoids. In other words, not the stereotyped lunatics of earlier periods, but pathetic victims of daily life in a brutalising society filled the wards of Victorian asylums.

The denizens of asylums, madhouses and workhouse lunatic wards in nineteenth-century Britain were detained unwillingly. In this respect they bear comparison with mid-twentieth-century inmates of American or Russian mental hospitals, where involuntary confinement of the mentally ill is normal, more than with contemporary Britain, where voluntary, short-stay hospitalization is the norm. For this reason, American psychiatrists and sociologists have concentrated on the phenomenon of institutionalization more than their British counterparts, and their models offer the student of contemporary British forms little of value in terms of methodology or interpretation. They can, however, help to illuminate nineteenth-century forms of psychiatric care and control.

Contemporary criticisms of the asylum as used in totalitarian states see the root problem as abuse of valid medical practice by 'bad' bureaucratic practices - Medvedev's A Question of Madness and the widely-popularised outpourings of Alexander Solzhenitsyn are typical. Conversely, Szasz argues that all involuntary hospitalization constitutes 'spiritual murder' whether those confined are sane or mad. (57) The reasoning behind this assertion consists not only of a questioning of accepted views as to the nature of mental illness, as outlined above, but also of a persuasive analysis of the close connections between state power and psychiatric power, which concludes simply that 'all psychiatry in totalitarian countries, and all institutional psychiatry in non-totalitarian ones, is in the service of the state.' Psychiatric intervention is thus 'initiated, continued and terminated at the will of the institutional psychiatrist and his superiors,' and constitutes 'a type of client-expert relationship in which, ostensibly, something is done for the client, while actually, something is done to him.' The police power of the state is thus a back-up to the imposition of the psychiatrist's services on an unwilling client, who is so placed as to be unable legally to reject them. (58)

The origins of the extension of state power over the mentally disordered are traceable to the 'parens patriae' role of medieval monarchs, based on economically orientated desires to control feudal property rights, and developed over four centuries through a slow process of the transfer of welfare functions from feudal lords, through medieval guilds, the Church and localised philanthropy, to the state of the nineteenth and twentieth centuries. (59) As part of the wider range of public health and welfare strategies, mental health provisions followed the line of development outlined by Sigerist:

> In the western world two trends developed side by side from the 16th to the beginning of the nineteenth century. In countries with absolute governments, such as France, Prussia, Austria, Russia, the administration of public health was centralised and paternalistic, while such initiative was left to the local authorities in democratic countries where the prevailing philosophy was that of liberalism, such as England. (60)

From the second quarter of the nineteenth century, however, the state power in England became more involved in welfare provisions, and the 'parens patriae' role became increasingly played out in the field of mental health and elsewhere. The comments of Charles Reich on the particular instance of public assistance in America are applicable to the recipients of paternal interference in nineteenth-century Britain:

> The law of social welfare grew up on the theory that welfare is a 'gratuity' furnished by the state,and thus may be made subject to whatever conditions the state sees fit to impose. A corollary legal theory holds that since all forms of welfare represent the expenditure of public funds, the public may properly interest itself in these funds even after they have reached the hands of the beneficiaries. With these justifications at hand, recipients have been subjected to many forms of procedure and control not imposed on other citizens, ... But the poor are all too easily regulated. They are an irresistible temptation to moralists, who want not only to assist but to 'improve' by imposing virtue. They are ... necessarily caught up in the workings of large organizations which by their nature are rigid and dehumanizing. (61)

The insane in nineteenth-century Britain, like the mentally ill in twentieth-century America, can be seen as recipients of the moral, economic, social and medical prescriptions of what Kittrie has called the 'therapeutic state.' (62) The 'therapeutic state' is defined as one in which apparently descriptive scientific terms (for example, 'mental illness' or 'alcoholic') replace moral judgement, and in which the application of science to government social welfare programmes results in the imposition of 'beneficial' services compulsorily on the recipient, who is deemed to be in some way incompetent. Compulsory institutionalization, and the involuntary commitment and treatment of the mentally ill and mentally defective, epileptics, alcoholics, drug addicts, juvenile delinquents and psychopaths, are offered as obvious areas of operation for the therapeutic state. (63) The ostensible purpose of such strategies, writes Kittrie, 'is radically different from those of the traditional criminal law,' but 'the social sanctions utilized often remain as severe as those applied by the criminal process. The subject of these proceedings is not punished or burdened with a criminal record, but he may be incarcerated for a long and often indeterminate period. In addition, his return to society from a nonpenal institution is not necessarily any easier, and frequently is less predictable, than return from prison.' (64) The moral overtones which remain, are seen as the result of a necessary imposition of restraints on those whose moral existence is suspended by impaired will-power. 'Thus the need for social defence against those who exert little free will of their own, combined with the belief in scientific cure and with the state's traditional right and duty to extend "parens patriae" functions' are seen as the germinating factors of the new therapeutic state 'which has assumed jurisdiction to compel treatment of the unpunishables under the "parens patriae" power.' (65)

Kittrie's model is designed to explain contemporary American social controls, but the salient components outlined above provide an apt framework for considering the development of asylums and lunacy laws in nineteenth-century Britain. The history of mental health provision is somewhat different from other public health strategies in Victorian Britain: the latter offered services to the willing recipient, making them examples of embryo programmes of what Kittrie terms the 'public welfare state'; the lunacy laws were more authoritarian, and could be exercised on deviant individuals for the public good, with little or no consideration for their own choices or their particular needs. The model of the therapeutic state, though receiving no further explicit discussion, forms an essential scaffolding for the structure and organisation of chapters 2, 3 and 4, which analyse the evolution of the institutional, and the scientific (medical) contexts of one territory in the therapeutic state, that of asylumdom. (66)

CHAPTER TWO

THE INSTITUTIONAL CONTEXT OF ASYLUMDOM 1790 - 1890

Before the eighteenth century, there was virtually no formulated theory of insanity, nor any social strategies for dealing with the insane. Primarily, this was because the mentally-disordered presented no particular problem. Until the later eighteenth century, population growth was negligible and population density tended to be low. The vast majority of communities were predominantly rural, and instances of insanity tended to be treated informally, on familial or community bases: the numerical insufficiency of the insane precluded the erection of special institutions and obviated the need for special sets of relationships between the sane community and the deviant. Only where a madman appeared to threaten public order was there a need for protective measures. Only where disorder could not be contained economically within the family unit was there need for intervention by the community.

I

For the most part, cases involving the insane tended to arise from the workings of the poor law, the vagrancy laws, or, in extreme cases, the criminal law. The only special provision for the insane, before the mid-eighteenth century, was to be found in Bethlem Hospital or in private madhouses. Bethlem, deriving from a monastic establishment founded in 1247, and used as a receptacle for the acutely insane from 1337, was financed by public subscription and bequests, and by the eighteenth century was a wealthy institution. Patients were liable for their own maintenance, except for paupers who were paid for by their parishes. (1) Private madhouses, run for profit, were common from at least 1700, (2) but were, by their nature, limited in their usage to the more affluent sections of society.

After 1750, however, the practice of confining the insane became more common: demographic change was the forcing factor, and personal care, under clerical, medical or private supervision became an impracticable tactic. Significantly, it was in London and the larger towns, where high proportions of nonresidents and transients were found, that institutional provision for the insane followed swiftly similar provision for the idle and the sick. In the half century before the county asylum movement got under way, lunatic hospitals were opened by public subscription in Norwich (1713), London (1751), Newcastle (1764), Manchester (1766), York (1777) and Liverpool (1795). (3) At the same time, the insane were elsewhere, and especially in rural areas, likely to be herded together with other deviants into general welfare or corrective institutions: bridewells, gaols, or poorhouses such as Crabbe sombrely described in 'The Village' (1783):

Parents, who knew no children's love, dwell there!
Heartbroken matrons on their joyless bed,

Forsaken wives, and mothers never wed;
Dejected widows with unheeded tears,
And crippled age with more than childhood fears;
The lame, the blind, and, far the happiest they!
The moping idiot, and the madman gay.

A complementary mixture of private charity and public welfare speeded up the creation of special institutions in the century after 1750 at a rate which far outstripped progress in socio-economic or medical theory. (4)

The limits of the 'specialisation' of the institutions were broad, and in this respect Britain was in line with western Europe and the United States. The heterogeneity of the almshouse in Colonial America reflected the antecedent English workhouse. (5) Similarly, there was a blurred distinction between public welfare and private charity, (6) and their co-operation produced the first special institutions for the insane in the same quarter century. (7) Insane asylums in western Europe and Britain developed out of, and sometimes as a part of general hospitals. (8) Seventeenth-century France and early nineteenth-century Germany evolved institution-types which attempted broadly-based social catchments: in both cases, the centralizing paternalism of the state shaped the objects of its concern. (9) As George Rosen has pointed out, these establishments were inaugurated 'to protect society and to prevent the disintegration of its institutions.' (10) The regulations governing the Bicêtre and the Salpetrière, asylums strategic in the advancement of European psychiatric orthodoxy, provided, in 1680, that

> children of artisans and other poor inhabitants of Paris up to the age of twenty-five, who used their parents badly or who refused to work through laziness, or, in the case of girls, who were debauched, or in evident danger of being debauched, should be shut up, the boys in the Bicêtre, the girls in the Salpetrière ... on the complaint of the parents, ... or of near relatives, or the parish priest. (11)

In Britain, the absence of direct state control in the early stages of asylum growth marked a difference from Continental experiences. Yet the purely philanthropic origins of the asylums, and the unfettered private enterprise of the madhouses, did not bestow immunity from the operation of a straitjacketed institutional psychiatry which was culturally, rather than scientfically based. In the beginning, however, the undeniably philanthropic motivation of the institutions' founders had important results for the theoretical dimensions of the asylum.

David Roberts has written of a 'wave of humanitarianism' whose 'intellectual tributaries were many, ranging from the logical reflections of the Scottish moral philosophers to the generous sentiments of the Lake poets, from Broad Church sensibility ... to the Quakers.' (12) It was a humanitarianism coloured by introverted pietism as well as by the outgoing, though scarcely benevolent, radicalism deriving from Price and Priestley. And however varied the springs, the activities of aroused conscience produced remarkably similar results.

The Bethel Hospital at Norwich was founded and endowed by one woman, Mrs. Mary Chapman, in gratitude for her own unimpaired reason and out of compassion for 'distrest lunaticks'. (13) The object of the founders of the Manchester Lunatic Hospital was partly 'to provide for these miserable objects (ie poor lunatics) being carefully attended and tenderly treated', and partly to relieve the pressures, physical and financial, placed on the Infirmary wards by the presence of unsegregated madmen. (14) Jones has seen this as 'part of ... (a) comprehensive scheme for the treatment of mental and bodily illness in patients of means', but the subscribers' aims were less grandiose and more directly humane. (15) No doubt the scandal-mongering of the Gentleman's Magazine, with exposés of private madhouse treatment, did focus attention at a critical time, as Jones suggests, but the Infirmary's trustees stressed the stimulus given by knowledge of plans to open a lunatic hospital in Newcastle, and the inconvenience and expense of existing arrangements. (16)

Despite its salutary influence on the trustees of Manchester Infirmary, St. Luke's Hospital in Newcastle disappointed its founders, and was so ill-conducted as to provoke citizens to promote a new public asylum for paupers. (17) In York, sectarian response to a similar disappointment had far-reaching results for the theory and practice of asylum organization in Britain and abroad, most importantly in providing a new and potent symbol: the York Retreat; and most influentially in legitimising the concept of 'moral treatment'.

York Asylum had opened in 1777, product of a campaign begun five years earlier. An initial subscription of £2,500 had been directed towards the erection of a building for those insane 'being either parish poor or belonging to distressed and indigent families.' The subsequent asylum regime decided to admit a certain number of 'opulent' patients at a rate suitable to aid in defraying the cost of 'relieving the necessitous' and stopped gratuitous attendance by the physician, Dr. Hunter, who prevailed upon the Asylum committee to permit his receipt of 'suitable fees'.

Several prominent citizens, including Earl Fitzwilliam, (18) protested that a public charity was being converted into a private hotel. As the poet Mason proclaimed, in his polemic Animadversions on the Present State of the York Lunatic Asylum, 'No subscriptions would have been forthcoming if the object of the asylum had been to relieve the relations of the affluent from discharging their obligations ...' (19) The establishment had been constructed to remedy a deficiency in the law:

> were parishes under a legal necessity to relieve their lunatic paupers to the extent of their wants, to afford

> them medical assistance and other suitable accommodation, then persons in low and indigent circumstances might be preferred in this charity to parish lunatics, but, at present, unless their lunacy extend to outrage and danger their parishes are under no obligation to maintain them but as ordinary paupers. (20)

On Hunter's death, in 1809, his pupil, Charles Best inherited control of the institution, and buttressed his position in 1813 by adopting a rule which virtually forbade all external observation. (21) In October of that year, a West Riding magistrate, Godfrey Higgins, (22) was notified of the ill-treatment of a parish patient in the asylum, and his energetic pursual of the case attracted public attention to the asylum. This was of short-term significance, however, compared with an indirect attack on Best's asylum from another quarter. The death of a Quaker in the asylum was the immediate cause of William Tuke's (23) determination to promote 'an institution ... where there should be no concealment and where the patients should be treated with all the kindness which their condition allows.' (24)

II

Whatever William Tuke's intention, his 'retired habitation' became an instant focus of reforming zeal. (25) Tuke himself had a healthy distrust of the medical profession (26) and contrived to eliminate all connotations of hospital or asylum. Tuke retained control for the first five years of the Retreat's existence, employing a visiting physician whose empirical approach resulted in the gradual displacement of restraint and harsh drugs. (27) Samuel Tuke's account (28) of the establishment's origins indicated the ideological roots of the 'moral management' system. The very name 'Retreat' was designed 'to convey the idea of ... a place in which the unhappy might obtain a refuge; a quiet haven in which the shattered bark might find the means of reparation or of safety.' (29) After Tuke relinquished direct involvement, the family-based conformation of the establishment was continued by the appointment of a non-medical superintendent, whose marriage to the female superintendent completed the identification, in a long-lasting partnership (1797 - 1823). (30) At a time when York and Bethlem (31) Asylums were providing lurid tales of brutalisation, the Quakers were publicly airing the discovery that some lunatics could be treated almost completely like human beings. (32) The journals were not slow to seize upon the triumph of virtue, since it proffered still further opportunities to lament the vicious generality of life. Sydney Smith was more intelligently enthusiastic than most:

> The great principle on which it (the Retreat) appears to be conducted is that of kindness to the patients. It does not appear to them (the managers), because a man is mad upon one particular subject, that he is to be considered in a state of complete mental degradation, or insensible to the feelings of kindness and gratitude

> ... (A)n example has been set of courage, patience and kindness which cannot be too highly commended or too widely diffused, and which, we are convinced, will gradually bring into repute a milder and better method of treating the insane. (33)

This enthusiasm was infectious. The Retreat became a Mecca for philanthropists and a temple to English humanitarianism: even American Indian warriors, appearing at a London theatre, were brought north to see the shrine. (34) Despite its exclusive nature and unique reality of community, the Quaker establishment offered a universal message: Smith's emphatic 'kindness', which was most effective as a contrast to brutality in madhouses and neglect in the community. The 'kindness', however, was heavily imbued with the Quaker ethic and the institution itself symbolised the Society's bidding for moral leadership in a state which deprived its members of political aspiration. (35) This fact distinguishes Tuke from Pinel, though contemporaries, in Europe and America, tended to see Paris and York as twin pillars of reform.

Pinel's radical empiricism, deriving ultimately from Locke, immediately from Condillac, (36) led him into innovatory psychiatric therapeutics, rather than into excursions into psychiatric theory. His 'liberation' of the madman into institutional humanity resulted partly from the social transformations attendant on the French Revolution, partly from a basic pragmatism which tried traditional therapeutics - such as restraints, bleeding, corporal punishments - and found them wanting. Pinel's humanitarianism, then, derived from a source totally different from Tuke's, and his long-term aims were social rather than spiritual. Like Tuke, however, Pinel stressed 'moral treatment' - succinctly defined by his greatest pupil, Esquirol, as 'the application of the faculty of intelligence and of emotions in the treatment of mental alienation.' (37) And both men stressed the indispensable role of the institution in providing the necessary authority-base for such 'application'. (38)

The rationale for founding therapeutic institutions was clearly non-medical, both in England and on the Continent. (39) The pervasive influence of Pinel and Tuke meant that psychiatry would develop within the asylum setting: 'kindness' and 'moral management' could hardly exist outside the institution. Yet the institution had prior existence, at least as a type: with social, cultural, even political (40) facets. Pinel in France, Tuke in England, Rush in America, Chiarugi in Italy, were reformers, not creators, grafting social or spiritual purpose on to receptacles of control. In short time, medical dimensions were superadded, or replaced, taking their form from the altered type and reinforcing its original justification: 'kindness' was granted a scientific objectivity; the asylum was granted a universality.

David Rothman's analysis of 'The Discovery of the Asylum' offers a divergent view. His somewhat unevenly-argued thesis, at times overdependent on logical legerdemain and disingenuous imprecision, posits that the 'asylum solution' for problems of deviance in post-Jacksonian America was based on a far-reaching critique of contemporary society, faced with new challenges to its political, social and cultural structures. Rothman indicates European and British parallels and highlights responses to insanity in his overall thesis, which can profitably be considered, for present purposes, in terms of this one crucial component.

In the decades after 1820, American society adopted institutionalization as the first-resort solution to problems of deviance and dependence, replacing traditional Colonial practice where such institutions as had existed were places of last resort. Rothman attempts to locate the various manifestations of asylumdom in America as

> first and foremost a vigorous attempt to promote the stability of the society at a moment when traditional ideas and practices seemed outmoded, constricted and ineffective. The almshouses, the orphan asylum, the penitentiary ... the insane asylum all represented an effort to ensure the cohesion of the community in new and changing circumstances. Legislators, philanthropists, and local officials, as well as students of poverty, crime and insanity, were convinced that the nation was facing unprecedented dangers and unprecedented opportunities. (41)

It was thought that the asylum could restore the necessary balance to the new republic whilst solving an age-old problem.

Rothman interprets the growth of institutionalization as something like the physical expression of a quasi-Utopian dream, spiritually akin to Owenism. The generality of social and psychiatric historians are castigated for assuming the inevitability of the asylum solution - a perspective which is 'bad logic and bad history', taking for granted what ought to be the focus of investigation. (42) One senses the importance of what is intended as a generalized criticism of writers who list 'reforms' unquestioningly, or see all progress in terms of series of pre-destined 'discoveries', yet in this instance his jibes seem unjust. Why the asylum and not something else? asks Rothman. But he offers no alternative other than rejected traditions. Indeed, it is difficult to envisage an alternative, and certainly no involved person, on either side of the Atlantic, offered other solutions for consideration between 1820 and 1870. Proponents of the asylum system had to combat apathy and parsimony, not a rival system. It is unfortunate that Rothman links all asylum-type institutions to the same posited origin, for this masks essential differences in function and purpose, and allows the confusion of native American with imported European influences. Admittedly, we must try to see the growth of the care and treatment of the insane in as wide a context as possible, and must, therefore, look to the particular realities and mores obtaining in specific communities. However, even if not 'bad history' it is surely inadequate history to seek to root into a particular social system, and moreover, in a socio-cultural critique deriving from emotional and intellectual dissatisfaction with the actualities of that system, a phenomenon contemporaneous and similar in several societies disparate in terms of that critique. And to adduce the very uniqueness of the particular as explanatory evidence for the shared experience of the general is definitely 'bad logic'.

The analysis of the growth of insane asylums is particularly prone to bouts of this strange kind of chauvinism. Whilst allowing that American understanding of the nature of insanity derived from European models, Rothman insists on at least a quantitative change of the transplants, (43) and he extends this to the institution form. This argument is largely made up of assertion and at no point does Rothman indicate the continuing similarities with transatlantic forms.

The fundamental similarity was faith in the institution. Throughout the nineteenth century the asylum was the sine qua non of psychiatric progress, though its precise function might change: custodial, curative, controlling. And the asylum-ethos, in America and England alike, remained closely linked to the Quaker ideal of the Retreat, in very practical terms until the 1820's (44) and in spiritual terms thereafter.

Alternative adaptations of the same institution-type further elevated the status of the Retreat by contrast. Best's 'crime' at York Asylum had been the conversion of a public charity into a private profit-making enterprise. Most contemporary provision for the insane was in private asylums - 'madhouses' run for profit which were easy targets for a scandal-mongering press. Eighteenth-century journalists pointed to the widespread use of madhouses as convenient depositories for unwanted spouses or relatives: private prisons inhabited by the sane victims of the unscrupulous. With depressing regularity, from the 1760's onwards, exposés and demands for government regulation blackened the image of the entrepreneur in the 'trade of lunacy', and psychiatric historians have tended to accept the contemporary censures. (45)

It is not immediately to the point to discuss the accuracy or otherwise of these images, (46) but their acceptance added to the innate attractions of the idea of 'moral management'. A further dimension was added to the institution-ideal by the development of the county asylums from the first decade of the nineteenth century. Led by Sir George Onesiphorous Paul, prison reformer, Benthamite, and, in 1806, High Sheriff of Gloucestershire, (47) a movement was organised to pressure the state to provide custom-built institutions for the criminal lunatic and the pauper insane, where their mental condition, rather than their legal or economic status, would be the arbiter of treatment. (48) That treatment, of necessity, was to be the antithesis of the neglect currently shown towards the insane within the community or within the confines of undifferentiated bridewells and gaols, (49) and was to be modelled on Tuke's system, suitably adapted for paupers. (50)

Medical dimensions were immediately added, as Paul, at the time of his initial campaigning on behalf of the insane, was President of the Stroud Society for providing medical attention to the poor, and tended to see the lunacy problem as one component. (51) From the first, then, the nineteenth-century asylum was moulded in a pattern of development dictated by socio-religious norms (Tuke/Pinel) and characterised by a medical specialism reflexively added to a pre-existing institution-model by lay administrators.

The reliance of evolutionary psychiatry on the institution was a crucial factor in the shaping of nineteenth-century theories and therapies. In England, the influential William Battie, first physician to St. Luke's in the Metropolis, based his theorising on his experiences of institution cases. The trend continued throughout the Georgian age and through the nineteenth century: the works of John Haslam, (52) John Conolly (53) and Henry Maudsley (54) derived from similar environments in this respect. Pinel and Esquirol in France, Benjamin Rush, Pliny Earle and Isaac Ray in the United States, (55) theorised and organized from perspectives common to both sides of the Atlantic and located in the variegated nature of the asylum 'patients'. In Germany, the ideal of state-controlled, medically-orientated institutions was consciously stated: Prince Karl August von Hardenburg, in 1805, argued that

> the state must concern itself with all institutions for those with damaged minds, both for the betterment of the unfortunates and for the advancement of science. In this important and difficult field of medicine only unrelenting efforts will enable us to carve out advances for the good of suffering mankind. Perfection can only be achieved in such institutions ... (56)

If the ideal of state-control was slower to gain acceptance in England, the commitment to a medical model of insanity was equally strong. That model, however, was based on analysis of the patient careers of those confined for reasons which, as often as not, expressed 'the ritualised affirmation of the dominant social ethic'. (57) The poor, the physically disabled, the morally degenerate, were threats to social order, and their confinement, like that of the mad, was a convenient tactic of social control. Their confinement <u>with</u> the mad blurred distinctions and permitted the expedient of confinement to be elevated to the level of a scientifically-determined strategy. At the same time, this committed medico-psychological progress to a societally-based institution-model. (58)

The necessity of confinement for the insane had become axiomatic by 1800. William Battie, wrote the first English psychiatric textbook in 1757. There he laid down the rationale for institutionalization of the insane which remained substantially unaltered throughout the next one hundred and fifty years. In madness, wrote Battie,

> The Regimen ... is perhaps of more importance than in any distemper. It was the saying of a very eminent practitioner in such cases that management did much more than medicine; and repeated experience has convinced me that confinement alone is sometimes sufficient, but always so necessary, that without it every method hitherto devised for the cure of Madness would be ineffectual.
> Madness ... requires the patient's being removed from all objects that act forcibly on the nerves, and excite too lively a perception of things ...
> The visits ... of affecting friends as well as enemies ... ought strictly to be forbidden.
> On the same account the place of confinement should be at some distance from home ... (59)

The trustees of the Manchester Infirmary had highlighted the need of 'Poor Lunaticks who only wanted a proper place for their Reception, and a suitable guard upon their Persons and Consciences,' (60) whilst a lay commentator considered the Liverpool Lunatic Hospital an obvious necessity. (61) Medical opinion was committed early, (62) and the influential George Man Burrows (63) voiced what was to become the standard Victorian psychiatric canon:

> There is no general maxim in the treatment of insanity wherein medical practitioners, ancient or modern, foreign or domestic are so unanimous as that of separating the patient from all customary association, his family, and his home; and there is none wherein the advice of the faculty is so commonly and successfully opposed. Thus cases which in the early stages are comparatively manageable, obedient to medical discipline, and commonly curable, are rendered obstinate, tedious, unnecessarily expensive, and too often incurable. Few of the medical profession require arguments or proof to convince them of the great utility of separation ... (64)

John Haslam was more open-minded on the issue:

> From long established practice, there has been usual association between BEING MAD, and confinement in a MADHOUSE. That insanity is a disease, which for its cure, and also for the prevention of mischief, ordinarily requires seclusion, must be admitted; and in many instances, that persons so confined, enjoy a larger portion of comfort than they could attain by being at large is equally certain. Still it is my opinion that confinement is too indiscriminately recommended and persisted in ...
>
> That many persons of deranged intellect are at liberty, and for some years have been permitted to be so, who have conducted themselves in a quiet and harmless manner, is well known. Perhaps when insanity exists without a desire to harm others or themselves, there can be no necessity or even justification for seclusion. But the difficulty is in predicting what

> will be the conduct of a person whose intellect is deranged; he may be harmless one month and disposed to violence the next ...

However, he went on to argue that non-confinement could be a positive therapeutic aid, since in many instances, 'an intercourse with the world has dispelled those hallucinations which a protracted confinement, in all probability, would have added to and confirmed.' (65)

Haslam's influence in England, however, was minimal in his own lifetime, (66) and in practical terms, the winning over of Government and the magistracy to the orthodox medical view became the aim of psychiatrists in both public and private sectors. By mid-century, so far as the organs of central government were concerned, they had become successful, and the centrality of the asylum, in <u>legal</u> as well as medical strategies, ensured its unique position in shaping Victorian attitudes towards madness and the mad.

III

As the environment for 'moral management' the asylum took on an ethical dimension which transcended its ostensibly medical purpose. Skultans (67) has argued unconvincingly that 'moral' in this context, as in the context of 'moral insanity,' should be taken as 'a rough nineteenth-century equivalent of the contemporary term "psychological"' and consigns the ethical connotation to a subsidiary rank. Yet even the most superficial reading of her sources for the period before 1870 refutes her. What she sees as a facet of nascent psychology was more a facet of the particular morality of dominant socio-economic groups in a particular time and place.

Foucault's brilliant analysis of the Enlightenment responses to the madman argues that asylum practice was a purely moral tactic: from the beginning the asylum was

> a structure that formed a kind of microcosm in which were symbolized the massive structures of bourgeois society and its values: Family-Child relations, centred on the theme of paternal authority: Transgression-Punishment relations, centred on the theme of immediate justice; Madness-Disorder relations, centred on the theme of social and moral order. It is from these that the doctor derives his power to cure. (68)

The paternalism mentioned by Foucault was the essence of the Tukes' system at York. The Retreat's reputation was founded upon the avowed success of responding to the insane in a manner that cast the madman in the role of a child and the superintendent in the role of the father. The Swiss physician, Delarive, visiting the Retreat in 1798, commented enthusiastically on the adoption and enforcement of these roles:

> Vous voyez, que dans le traitement moral on ne considère pas les fous comme absolument privés de raison, c'est à

> dire comme inaccesible aux motifs de crainte, d'espérance, de sentiment et d'honneur, on les considère plutôt, ce semble, comme des enfans (sic) qui ont un superflu de force et qui en faisoient un emploi dangereux. (69)

This was not a process analogous to the juridical attribution of minority to the insane, which was simply a convenient fiction for establishing trusteeship. The importance of the Retreat's organization lay in the powers innate in the patriarchal image. The 'liberty' and humanity which contemporaries eulogised have blinded more than one modern historian to the realities of the system.

Samuel Tuke's Description is so well known that the implications of many of its statements are seldom analysed. Even the immediate cause of the Retreat's foundation is bracketed within the loose categorization of humanitarian reform, as though Roberts' 'wave' (70) were not of such a heterogeneous composition. What is often lost sight of is the simple fact that the house was a Quaker foundation for Quakers. Tuke was explicit in his account of the initial motivation:

> ... there has ... been particular occasion to observe the great loss, which individuals of our society have sustained, by being put under the care of those who are not only strangers to our principles, but by whom they are frequently mixed with other patients, who may indulge themselves in ill language, and other exceptionable practices. This often seems to leave an unprofitable effect upon the patients' minds after they are restored to the use of their reason, alienating them from those religious attachments which they had before experienced; and sometimes even corrupting them with vicious habits to which they had been strangers. (71)

The institution, then, was to function as a means of religious and moral segregation and its operative norms were to be defined in terms of the Quaker ethic. Behind the regimen lay the assumption that religion was at once a controlling factor and a curative agent. Inculcated religious principles, argued Tuke, exercised a 'restraining power' over the insane mind. In addition, the society of persons 'of similar habits and opinions' was considered a stimulus to recovery during 'convalescent' stages. Not simply segregation, the system practiced at the Retreat portrayed concern with establishing a special kind of religiously-based morality applicable to the segregated. This morality was essentially an intensification of the Society's ethos, and stressed the relationship between wrongdoing and retribution in a manner specifically orientated to the position of the madman. Within the surrogate family the patient was subjected to external pressures of a moral nature in order to inculcate 'self-restraint'. The means of coercion were always on hand (72) as an incentive to obey the rules of the household. Tuke's regime was attempting to force responsibility on the madman for his actions, a responsibility founded upon the anxieties arising from instilled religious awareness. Physical liberty was the reward for the exhibition of compliance to moral restraints, and those restraints were the core of the system. Medical 'cures' were not consciously sought in the first instance, (73) the watchwords were 'management' and 'control', ideals efficiently achieved by the exercise of paternalistic authority employing a scheme of incentives and deterrents which were based on the assumption that the validity of 'right' and the invalidity of 'wrong' behaviours would thus be communicated. The 'liberty' was founded upon the efficacy of threats: 'The principle of fear, which is rarely decreased by insanity, is considered of great importance in the management of the patients.' (74) The 'salutary effect' of this principle was further underlined by reference to its 'great use in the education of children, whose imperfect knowledge and judgement, occasion them to be less influenced by other motives,' thereby re-asserting the madman/child identification. (75)

The principle of fear was identified as one of the principles of nature. So too were those religious principles inculcated in early life. The organization of these two principles into a joint assault mechanism on the anti-nature of madness (76) was the ultimate rationale of the Tukes' moral management.

Pinel's experimentation had produced a similar brand of moral policing (77) independently worked out from a radically different base. The widespread acceptance of their solution formed the intellectual and social milieu within which the ideals of asylumdom were worked out. Moral management, however, was a loosely defined therapy: its acceptance by the medical faculty necessarily changed William Tuke's vision into something intentionally more clinical; its application to patients outside the Quaker fraternity meant that its religious base had to be malleable; its location in institutions differing from the Retreat in terms of size, management and intake made it susceptible to the influence of external social and economic forces. The results were most marked in the treatment of the pauper insane.

IV

Sir Andrew Halliday (78) was a firm adherent of the institution principle, yet voiced the concern that the insane should have a 'regulated intercourse with the world.' In practical terms, he seems to have meant an approximation to activity in 'the world' rather than direct contact. Significantly, though a medical man, Halliday stressed the function of the asylum in terms of 'watching over' the patients, giving 'cure' only secondary mention. (79) 'Employment' was considered 'the best aid' to treatment and Halliday indicated that this should help determine the construction of asylums. The work-centred treatments of William Ellis (80) at Wakefield Asylum received praise, whilst Halliday maintained that

> The greatest objection to the generality of the public asylums in England is their want of space for different workshops, and of a sufficient quantity of ground on which the patients can be employed in agricultural labour ... (81)

Ellis, first at Wakefield, and later, at Hanwell, was imbued with the therapeutic and financial values of putting inmates to work. Answering an attack on the efficiency of moral treatment in large asylums, Ellis put forward his experience at Wakefield:

> Among the lower classes of the people, it will generally be found that useful occupation in the pursuits that they have been most accustomed to is their best amusement, and such employment the most salutary mode of recreation that can be resorted to. One of the principal objects kept in view, in the direction of this Asylum, has been to obtain for the patients constant and regular employment for that purpose, not only farming and gardening, but all trades have been forced into the service; we have spinners, weavers, tailors, shoemakers, brewers, bakers, blacksmiths, joiners, painters, bricklayers, and stonemasons, all employed. All the clothing for the patients is manufactured and made by themselves; we bake our own bread, brew our own beer, and nearly one half of both male and female patients are constantly engaged in some kind of labour. The moment there is any appearance of convalescence, the patient is enticed to occupy himself with his usual healthy pursuits ... and besides the great and evident benefit which such a system has in the recovery of the patients themselves, it is a source of great saving to the institution; for notwithstanding that we have for many years received only seven shillings a week for each pauper, a fund has accumulated which by the end of the year will exceed three thousand pounds. (82)

The concern to set pauper lunatics to work was more redolent of standard poor law policy than of twentieth-century conceptions of work-therapy. (83) For most of the nineteenth century pauperism was widely attributed to idleness and dissoluteness. Insane paupers partook of this religio-moral stigmatization as well as of that of madness. The weakness of will inherent in current conceptions of insanity intensified the desire to counteract weakness/idleness with wholesome moral remedies, amongst which work for work's sake figured prominently. In workhouses and post-1834 union houses, work, even if unproductive or financially unprofitable, was required of the physically able. (84) The ideal of the asylum was to regenerate (in social terms) the insane patient: cure meant returning the insane to conformity with external values and lifestyles. These values were imposed on the lower classes from above: the complex of social, economic and religious attitudes, once simplistically styled the 'protestant ethic', stressed self-determination and success, the latter confirming righteousness and necessitating work. Lack of success, in socio-economic terms, therefore, implied unrighteousness and unwillingness to work: hence the economy-orientated workhouse could be morally justified. If a person were reduced to workhouse entry, work would supply the necessary regenerative moral boost. The pauper lunatic lacked not only socio-economic success, but also self-determination: the way to the latter lay through discipline which could be engendered by a work-situation. For the insane poor, therefore, employment possessed a double value.

Thomas Eccleston, Superintendent of Rainhill Asylum, Lancashire, thought that 'occupation' was the 'only humane and common sense method of dealing with insanity' so far as paupers were concerned. Results showed that

> Patients who before their admission had stubbornly refused employment, and had been in the constant habit of passing their time either smoking in gloomy airing-courts ... or annoying their fellow patients, are now actively engaged in occupation, and respectful in their demeanour. (85)

Clearly, acceptance of a work-role by a pauper patient proclaimed his deferential acceptance of the authority of the asylum director and staff. 'Respectfulness' was essential in a recipient of moral management, as in a child towards its elders.

The discipline of work necessitated some degree of self-restraint and of wilful obedience to external authority. It therefore fitted perfectly into the county asylums' approximations to Tuke/Pinel models: self-restraint was moral management's alternative to mechanical restraints or drugs. In practice, however, the results were not so clear-cut. John Conolly, as physician to Hanwell, had inherited Ellis's work-orientated system, and was conscious of its potential misuse. Employment could be of great value in relieving the monotony of confinement, he admitted, but there were signs of undesirable workhouse patterns developing:

> As regards county asylums, there is now a great disposition in the officers to set every patient to work as soon as he is admitted; sometimes very improperly, and when, perhaps, work has made the poor creature mad. (86)

The officers' position was uncomfortable. As medical men they were convinced of the pathological nature of insanity and of the curative purpose of the asylum. Yet in practice, their treatment-programmes were perforce largely non-medical, and their patients on the whole not susceptible of medical cure, even in their own eyes. After a brief interlude of optimism at the beginning of the nineteenth century, as to the medical curability of madness, (87) asylum superintendents found it increasingly necessary to keep reminding themselves, as well as the public and the government, of the function of the lunatic asylum. Conolly, for example, began his treatise on asylum construction and management with the assertion that

> ... a lunatic asylum is intended to be not merely a place of security but a place of cure ... The recovery of the curable, the improvement of the incurable, the comfort and happiness of all the patients, should ... be steadily kept in view. (88)

The physical structure of most asylums both belied and counteracted this purpose, whilst the officers themselves occasionally let slip that they considered their institutions as 'refuges' rather than hospitals. (89) Most public asylums betrayed the ideology from which they originated: 'In most of the old asylums the architects appear to have regard solely to the safe-keeping of the in-mates,' wrote Conolly, whilst his own Hanwell was described by the Lancet's Mortimer-Granville as'a vast straggling building, in which the characteristics of a prison, a self-advertising charitable institution, and some ambitious piece of Poor Law architecture struggle for prominence.' (90)

V

The structure of pauper asylums was geared to their purpose of the 'care and control' of the insane poor. Despite the fact that restoration and cure had motivated psychiatrists from the late eighteenth century, there was little chance of the medical purpose's being fulfilled by local authorities anxious to keep ratepayers complaisant. To cure the curable and to 'improve' or 'comfort' the incurable lunatic were two sides of the same coin to the alienist. But to responsible lay officialdom, insanity was merely a confinable condition irrespective of gradation: the standard criteria for the particulars of confinement were convenience and cost. Asylums tended to be built in response to increased needs for institution-provision which existing receptacles could not absorb. Only rarely did a new asylum exceed in capacity immediate needs, (91) and newly-opened institutions were swiftly filled, usually with high proportions of chronic and incurable cases.

The county of Surrey provides an archetypal example of conflicting purposes. Surrey's first asylum was opened in 1841. (92) Three years later, the county was using Bethlem and St. Luke's as its curative establishments, and the county asylum as a house for chronic lunatics, despite the magistrates' claim to be administering the funds at their disposal 'with strict economy, at the same time keeping in view the highest object of effecting the cure of patients.' (93) Metropolitan Commissioners in Lunacy visited the institution in 1843: they found only 37 potentially curable cases out of the asylum's 385 inmates. (94) They lamented the situation further the following year:

> ... the number in the asylum on 1st January, 1844, was 382, of whom 362 were reported incurable. We inquired at the asylum if any steps had been taken

> by the visiting magistrates to secure recent cases being sent there, but we were informed that no measures had been adopted for that purpose; and we fear that the condition of Surrey, with an excellent asylum, will soon, as regards the cure of its insane poor, be similar to that of Middlesex, unless patients be sent to the asylum in the early period of their disorder and some plan be devised for disposing of such of the incurable cases as it may be necessary in the event to remove. (95)

By 1845, Springfield, though increased in capacity to 400 beds, was having to refuse parish applications on behalf of females, as the wards were filled with rejects from Bethlem and St. Luke's. In January, 1846, the visiting committee approached the Commissioners in Lunacy to request permission to enlarge their facilities:

> ... the present asylum contains more than four hundred patients, being all that it can accommodate, ... admission is at this time required for not fewer than two hundred and ninety eight other patients, who are in workhouses, contrary to the existing law, or are confined, at great inconvenience and additional cost to the parishes to which they belong in the several asylums in and about the metropolis ... (Of) the numbers ... in the asylum, there are only about thirteen of whom there is any reasonable hope of recovery; and the visiting justices have reason to believe that of the two hundred and ninety eight requiring admission, nearly the whole are afflicted with those forms of the malady which have seldom been found to yield to medical treatment ... there is little prospect of any increase in the number of curable patients in the asylum ... (96)

In this situation, the authorities silently dropped their concern with 'higher objects' and proposed that

> the asylum is practically an establishment for chronic cases, and as such, it is proposed, may with propriety be extended by the addition of suitable buildings, so as to contain all the pauper lunatics in the county ...

Despite their own opposition to over-extended institutions (97) the Commissioners in Lunacy, conscious of the urgency of the need, did not press too hard, and merely modified the proposals for two extra wings.

Further enlargements were necessary by 1853, and in the following year there were attempts to return harmless patients to the workhouses, a move which had 'not entirely met with the approbation of the Commissioners in Lunacy.' However, the union house officials sent back the insane paupers who disrupted the running of workhouses lacking in special provision. (98) A second asylum was opened at Brookwood (June 1867), but was not sufficiently large for the county's 1866-67 requirements. By 1869, there were some 869 more pauper lunatics in Surrey than the two county establishments could accommodate, (99) and private houses, cashing in on the county's necessity, raised their charges. The problem facing the Surrey magistrates was reducible to four main heads: firstly, the need for a cure-orientated establishment for efficient, and swift, treatment:secondly, the increased attention of public authorities to placing their insane charges immediately in that curative asylum; thirdly, the removal elsewhere of all insane cases that had reached the chronic stage; and finally, care to ensure that the curative establishment was large enough to accommodate all the recent curable cases, not merely as existing, but as might be projected from the past rate of increase. All these considerations were presented incessantly by the Commissioners in Lunacy and by two generations of psychiatric monographs. The Surrey magistracy failed to grasp any of them, (100) Only one-fifth of Brookwood's initial intake was deemed curable. The new asylum was thus immediately turned into what Mortimer-Granville called a 'house of ease' for Springfield. Indeed, there was no serious economic or social planning - simply a desire to relieve pressure. The architect of Brookwood averred, in defence of the poor rate of curable admissions, that the asylum had been designed for only a one-fifth curability intake. (101)

Many contributory factors underlay Surrey's lack of proper planning. Mortimer-Granville indicated one reason for the chaotic state of Springfield:

> It was not in human nature for the committee of Wandsworth to confess that a better asylum might be provided, and express their willingness to be used as an establishment for the safe custody and succour of incurable cases. They must extend, improve, embellish, and, to speak frankly, waste money in trying to mend that which was not only past mending, but ... in all senses obsolete. (102)

Not only Surrey was guilty: 'The universality of this wrong-headedness is its only excuse.' In words that might appeal to contemporary economic considerations, Mortimer-Granville argued that

> No outlay can be too large that produces for the services of the public and the ratepayers an agency capable of resisting the encroachments of insanity and rescuing breadwinners from its toils. (103)

Unfortunately, the medical/curative aim was not always consistent with the economic/curative aim. John Bucknill gave an instance of Mortimer-Granville's argument being turned on its head:

> Not long ago we were examining a union-house, no worse than others, in company with the guardians, and observing a recent, and as we thought curable, lunatic in detention

> there, we expostulated, and advised that he should be sent forthwith to an asylum for treatment; but the deputy chairman remarked to us that the man was old and infirm, and that even if he were cured he would have to be maintained out of the rates. Being a used-up labourer, he was not worth the expense of being cured. (104)

Cost-cutting was another motive for extending existing asylums. The creation of a large establishment would clearly save money in running costs (administration, staffing, provisions etc. would be cheaper for one vast institution than for several smaller ones) as well as in construction costs. Surrey's experiences were similar to those of Middlesex, Lancashire and Yorkshire, counties with large and growing populations and a heavy incidence of diagnosed insanity. In all these areas, the pattern outlined for Surrey was substantially the same. Overlarge institutions evolved, despite the desires of asylums' superintendents and very much against the wishes of the Commissioners in Lunacy. The latter, in 1857, pointed out that

> It has always been the opinion of this Board that asylums beyond a certain size are objectionable. They forfeit the advantage which nothing can replace, whether in general management or the treatment of disease, of individual and responsible supervision ... The more extended they become, the more abridged their means of cure. (105)

Ideologically, both Commissioners in Lunacy and the psychiatric Establishment were concerned with what they identified as medical treatment for a disease, even where that treatment, in practice, was properly identified as moral. Local authorities had completely different notions as to what constituted medical necessity: the Poor Law mentality was scathingly delineated by the medical faculty:

> Lunatics are not regarded as patients under medical treatment <u>for their insanity</u>. They are mad people, to be kept in safe custody and when they happen to <u>fall sick</u> placed under medical treatment. (106)

The visiting committee of Hanwell Asylum gave point to this assertion. In 1864, they refused to comply with the Lunacy Commissioners' urgings to increase the medical staff in the female department, and argued in their own defence that

> It must be obvious to those who superintend great pauper lunatic asylums like that at Hanwell, there always are many cases of a character and description which usually require little more than the general supervision of the medical officers. (107)

The tangential effects of committee-designed and regulated establishments, operating on the extended scale of Hanwell, Springfield, Lancaster Moor, or Rainhill, were as disturbing to the medical profession as the more direct consequences outlined above. An anonymous article in the British Medical Journal in 1871 succinctly analysed the retrogressive situation engendered by such institutions:

> Vast asylums are vast philanthropic mistakes. They have helped to develop unphilanthropic delusions in the mind of the general public, and have produced a stagnation in the study of so called mental disease most injurious to the science of medicine. The citizen of the world and the student of medicine from the contemplation of those mentally afflicted have been debarred. The former regards lunacy as something so horrible and dangerous that its victims must be pushed, like the leper of old, beyond the gates of the city; the latter has been shut off from the study of an everyday disease by the mystery which has been made to overshadow it.

Directly-involved professionals were less absolute in their condemnation. G. Robertson saw nothing wrong with large asylums in principle: Lancashire and the West Riding provided instances of institutions catering for over a thousand inmates. Colney Hatch and Hanwell deserved adverse criticism, not on account of their size, but because of their management. Unlike other large institutions, the Middlesex asylums were not controlled by a medical governor, but by a lay committee. (108) The fault lay in particular systems, not in asylumdom itself.

Robertson went on to express a pride in the British system which reflected the generality of asylum doctors' opinion. Despite their defects, the public asylums were unrivalled as an advance in the care of the insane, and their extension, by means of enlarging existing buildings, erecting detached blocks on the same site, or building cottages on the estate, was seen as eminently desirable. That all of these expedients were workable was instanced at Prestwich, Worcestershire and Warwickshire Asylums (enlargement);at Devon, Chester and Essex Asylums (detached blocks); and Devon again (cottages). (109) Satisfaction with the asylum system, and with the laws governing it, was also evident amongst the Commissioners in Lunacy. Secretary Charles Palmer Phillips could see nothing but perfection in the laws as enforced by the Board in the 1870's and illustrated the Commissioners' unshaken faith in the detention of all the insane in asylums. (110) As he was pleased to admit, 'the tradition of a public office is a very persistent force ...'

Not all central officials shared this prejudice. The Lord Chancellor's Visitors in Lunacy, inspectors of those found lunatic by inquisition, (111) were opposed to the 'incarceration' of any lunatic in an asylum, if due protection and/or employment might be available outside. Sir Charles Lockhart-Robinson (112) confessed that he

> could never have believed that patients who were such

> confirmed lunatics could be treated in private families in the way that Chancery lunatics are, if I had not personally watched these cases. (113)

Since the law required Chancery Visitors to inspect lunatics 'so-found' who were under domestic treatment, four times a year, and those removed to asylums only once a year, this testimony was all the more impressive: opposition to dogmatic asylumdom entailed a fourfold increase in the Visitor's duties.

By far the majority of confined lunatics, however, were paupers, and here the views of Lunacy Commissioners and Poor Law authorities were decisive. 'Asylums are the Commissioners' panacea,' wrote a hostile critic in the British and Foreign Medical and Chirurgical Review (114) and the Board's insistence on institution-based specialised accommodation was fundamentally important in shaping the course of asylumdom. Originally, this attitude was based on the medical orthodoxy of the early nineteenth century, and reflected the optimistic faith in the curability of insanity-as-disease which contemporary psychiatric opinion was fostering. (115) The urge to secure facilitated admission-procedures for early treatment, therefore, had sound theoretical foundations. During the 'sixties and 'seventies, experts tended to retain a strong belief in the essentially curable nature of insanity, if caught sufficiently early. Samuel Gaskell, (116) by then a Lunacy Commissioner, expatiated on the 'mischief' (suicides, murders, assaults etc.) which could occur through delayed admission, (117) whilst Robert Boyd, (118) in his Presidential Address to the RCP, rehearsed the early-treatment rationale with the off-hand eloquence that came from long-practised appeals. (119) At the end of the century, attacks on the Consolidating Lunacy Act (120) stressed the role of 'that early treatment which is so important in cases of mental disease.' (121)

VI

The effect of such emphases was to generate a dualistic approach to the care of the insane, with 'curable' viewed and treated differently from 'incurable' or 'chronic'. The concern of asylums with 'cure-rates' must inevitably have led to selective admission (cf Bethlem) had the law permitted, and did lead to medical pressure for asylums of different sizes, constructions and managements, to suit the polarised conceptions of potential inmates. There were some reactions to such stark divisions, however. Algernon Chapman, Superintendent of the Hereford County Asylum, attacked the idea that early treatment was a necessary safeguard against incurability:

> ... it would be more correct to say that these chronic cases were never acute, and had not a beginning when there was a chance of recovery, and for this reason, that the mass of these ... cases are congenital idiots and imbeciles, cases of senile dementia, and of various forms of progressive brain disease. (122)

At Lancaster Moor, David Cassidy remarked on the 'futility of making artificial distinctions between the curable and incurable insane,' and urged a reassessment of the asylum's true role:

> ... the care and alleviation of the condition of the general body of the insane is at least as important a function of Asylums as the so-called 'cure' of a small percentage of cases, few of whom remain permanently cured ... (123)

The growing doctrinaire movement for special hospitals for 'curables' frightened him: the select few might be helped, but the needs of the majority would be disfavoured. (124) In any case, the whole argument for a new type of institution rested on the assumption that there were high proportions of potentially curable cases barred from necessary treatment by legal or adminstrative blocks. Further, it presumed that the means of cure were to hand. The existence of large classes of artificially-delayed curables or of potentially curable lunatics' being ill-served by existing asylum-provision (125) was open to question. (126)

Especially in the larger county asylums, there was an awareness that the curative function had, for whatever reasons, become virtually lost. But that had never been the sole function. Complaints about workhouses transmitting their excess chronic cases to choke county asylums, whilst understandable in terms of the formal ideology of asylumdom, ignored the fundamental justification of the system. Special controlled provision for the insane, if justifiable medically or legally, had to apply to all those assigned to that category. The epileptics, paralytics, idiots and senile dements who figured so largely in asylum admissions were no less 'patients whose condition necessitates the greatest care and attention' than the curable. 'An Asylum', wrote the Superintendent of Prestwich Asylum in 1879, 'is doing as good work in providing shelter and protection, ... in ministering to the wants of those unfortunates, as in treating more hopeful cases.' (127) Perhaps statements like that reflected the acceptance of reality elevated to a principle, but, given the <u>fact</u> of asylumdom and the belief in its fundamental correctness, the physical development of the asylum, and the practical working-out of madness-identification codes and the segregation-process, inevitably produced a situation in which that was the only principle available. So far as the Commissioners in Lunacy had been able to control and effectively propagandise, thus far had there been at least formal acceptance of the insanity/asylum correlation. Asylum doctors, in both the public and the private sectors, professionally buttressed what had begun as a socio-morally based administrative expedient, until the logic of their own position startled them into awareness. Economic and administrative realities handicapped the practical realisation of total asylumdom, but approximations were visibly proving medically disastrous and socially disturbing. By the 1860's, Gaskell, more conscious of the realities of the asylum than his colleagues, indicated the diffuse nature of lunacy, and argued that it was unwise to act as if all labelled insanity, 'whether ... the slightest aberration, or ... total loss of mental power and mental control,' was susceptible to the same kind of legally-formed institutional response:

> How marked a difference is here observable in respect of bodily complaints, for which we have both general and special hospitals, dispensaries for milder cases, as well as convalescent and seaside houses. And why ... have we not asylums adapted to the slightest as well as to the most severe forms of mental diseases. (128)

In some parts of the country, and in Scotland, a system of 'boarding out' chronic patients had spontaneously grown up. (129) which contradicted the ethos of asylumdom. Naturally, there were objections, but these, as one proponent of the system indicated, were 'largely theoretical' and could be obviated by commonsense organization and proper supervision. (130) Wide scale adoption of the system would relieve pressures on asylums, and hopefully destroy 'monster establishments', thereby restoring practicability to the curative function and providing individual, open treatment on a volunteer basis which, of itself, would preclude abuse. (131) Though attractive enough in theory, practical application was limited, most notably in areas where need was greatest. In industrial Yorkshire, the superintendents of the Wakefield and Wadsley Asylums decided that the character and density of the population in the district precluded wide-spread adoption of the tactic. (132) More immediately practicable was the sending of suitable cases from asylums to the home of friends, a form of boarding-out known as the'trial-out' system. In many cases, the kinds of patient most susceptible to this system - the senile, the idiotic and the epileptic - had been removed by family or friends in the first instance because they were either unwilling or unable to cope. Simplified medical out-relief was not the answer either, as Thompson pointed out:

> The epileptic who fifty years ago passed easily through life without giving his friends anxiety except as to his safety, is now driven wild and uncontrollable by being drenched with bromide of potassium, obtained chiefly at the out-patient departments of the hospitals ... (133)

The notion of any out-relief for positively-ascribed insanity was almost inevitably going against the law. Since the Commissioners in Lunacy demanded registry of all certified cases, and since local authorities were legally bound to notify all such cases, a family containing a certifiable lunatic could not secure professional attendance without risking removal of the insane member. The image of the madhouse and the stigma attaching to certification were common to all classes. There was, anyway, widespread popular fear of hospitals of any description, and a distrust of the medical profession, even when lives were at stake. (134) There was, then, unwillingness throughout the community to take that early action which psychiatrists deemed essential for cure. In one sense, the affluent faced a heightened cultural dilemma: as a writer in 1880 nicely put it, ' ... the general feeling of the community is strongly opposed to private asylums ... and the preference is given to them by the same community when the question of placing a lunatic under care arises ...' (135) The desired degree of secrecy, motivated by stigma-fear, could only be obtained at the risk of profiteering, and moreover, could only surely be obtained under circumstances within which the risk of wrongful incarceration was maximised.

The fate of pauper lunatics, however, involved no such conscientious problem. It rested not with the family, not with the professional specialist, but with the Poor Law authorities. Attitudes to pauper lunacy reflected a double standard, and even the psychiatric Establishment could at times identify with Poor Law policy. Thus Bucknill could argue that where the destitute were concerned, 'their welfare must be combined with considerations of public thrift and convenience.' (136) Referring to statements of this nature, it is difficult to assess Bucknill's motivation in making comments like the following:

> The old brutalities have become rare and exceptional under the regime of the Commissioners, and instead thereof another evil has been evolved, and the asylum system in its whole vast extent has encompassed an ever increasing multitude, numbers of whom might well be enjoying moderate freedom and comparative happiness in their own homes. (137)

Joshua Stallard argued in similar tones, and cited the experience of Scottish alienists and of the Scottish Commissioners in Lunacy. 'For many years,' he noted, 'there was an undue horror of the lunatic asylum. People ... shrunk from enforcing ... removal because harshness, confinement, and other forcible means of treatment were too often the rule ...' (138) But with the progress of milder treatments, exemplified by the non-restraint system, and with the improved quality and quantity of institution-accommodation, the reluctance was disappearing. Previously, parental care, or filial care, even to the extent of suffering deprivation in economic terms, had kept the pauper insane within the family. 'Increased accommodation,' insisted Stallard, 'only leads to the necessity for more,' and he suggested that the asylum system had been carried too far: 'were we right in seeking to separate the mother from the child?' There was much scope for home-centred treatments, and Stallard demanded whether

> the same care, interest and money which are now employed upon the inmates of our lunatic asylums, might not produce even more successful results if made to support the efforts of parents and relations in their humble dwellings ... (139)

From the practical point of view, unthinking addiction to the unique propriety of the asylum had drawbacks:

> To keep the large numbers of helpless, bedridden and harmless people in lunatic asylums simply because they are, or have been a little touched, ... is not only an injustice ... and cruelty to the patients themselves, but also to those around them. Such patients absorb all the attention of medical men and nurses, which ought in such establishments be devoted to the curable and dangerous classes. They interfere with the discipline and amusements of the rest and there is nothing in their state which requires the special arrangements of a lunatic asylum. (140)

Stallard here was on dangerous ground, and was conscious of it. (141) If medical opinion was divided, grass-roots officialdom had definite yardsticks: cost and convenience. And the central Poor Law authority shared these criteria. The destitute insane were properly located in the cheapest convenient receptacle: the workhouse for the tractable, the barrack-asylum for the unmanageable. Hence, many 'recent' cases had had a trial in the workhouse. (142) The notion of utilising special accommodation in workhouses was superficially attractive but transfers of asylum-tractable patients were all too seldom successful. (143) Convinced of the unique necessity of asylumdom, the Commissioners in Lunacy accepted, though unwillingly, the economic inevitability of large asylums. The Local Government Board was more sanguine. Allbutt, (144) who seldom minced words, whilst complaining that oversized asylums were 'creating another wilderness of lunatics which no man can know,' placed the blame squarely on the L.G.B. As a Commissioner in Lunacy, he had pressed for what amounted to Gheel-type farm colonies - a generation after the psychiatric Establishment had achieved consensus on the issue - but ' ... the L.G.B. had control of the purse strings (and) always destroyed the whole idea and plumped for barracks.' (145)

The medical hostility to Poor Law authorities was innate in their separate functions, (146) but there were also those who challenged the medical profession's monopoly of control, and suggested a causal connection between the alienists' prejudices and asylum growth. An anonymous religiophile, writing at the end of the century, was succinct:

> Granted that some reform was necessary, the refined and ridiculous treatment of the present day is harmful to the whole community, and it swells the numbers of the so-called insane with persons who are not otherwise deranged than that they require, it may be, the advice of a judicious clergyman, ... There are now asylums of all kinds ... possessing ... a sort of fascination like spiders' webs for flies ... (147)

It was not just the insane who were slotted into convenient receptacles, conceptual and concrete. The flux of social change was having increasingly visible effects as the century progressed, and there was the inevitable demand for the return of 'order'. And 'order' in a categorizing as well as in a police sense. The institutionalization of society's deviants and unfortunates, begun in the second quarter of the century, modish in mid-century, gained momentum after 1860. From the 'fifties and 'sixties date most of the mental hospitals, prisons and workhouse wards that later became hospitals. From the 'seventies, the 'organization' of charitable activities and the spread of segregated provision: for orphans and juvenile delinquents, ranging from Dr. Barnardo's 'family' to the training hulks on the Mersey; for the idiot and the physically handicapped. (148)

The extension of the surrogate community was far from a social expression of what Dicey naively saw as incipient collectivitism. (149) It was the addiction of public a authority to a tried and tested solution to problems of social disorder. By mid-century the experts had convinced the legislature of the propriety and suitability of asylumdom. A quarter of a century later, the principle had become widely acceptable to local officialdom. Given a sufficient time-lag, the solution gained grudging popular acceptance. But by this time, the experts were rethinking. The public's mentality, and, more importantly, the public's money, were over-committed to the institution form as consolidated between the mid-'forties and the mid-'sixties. In practice - as in popular mythology - differences between institutions tended to be simply spatial; if workhouses often performed hospital or asylum functions, the lunatic asylums offered the services of drying-out, geriatric homes, rest homes and remand centres. The physical dimensions of asylumdom changed in the second half of the century, as did aspects of the self-image of its curators. Yet essentially, the role of the institution-type remained constant; and the treatment of inmates changed, in practice, only in degree.

VII

The madhouse-image of the eighteenth and early nineteenth centuries lingered. Reaction to the brutalities of confinement as revealed in the investigations of 1814 and 1815 tended to elevate the importance of abandoning unhealthy accommodation and 'mechanical' restraint, (150) and of adopting environments and therapies modelled on the Tuke/Pinel ideal. The abolition of mechanical restraint was a fashionable topic in the 'thirties (151) and has been open to much misinterpretation by historians of psychiatry. (152) There was contemporary controversy over who should be credited with the introduction of non-restraint, (153) though the expression, like that of moral management, was a loosely-defined label, susceptible to varying interpretation. Mechanical restraint was abandoned early at Lincoln Lunatic Hospital, Hanwell and the Northampton Asylum. Elsewhere, it was seen as a last resort, for example at Lancaster Moor, under Gaskell, and at the Stafford Asylum, under Wilkes, (154) though neither of these was dogmatic on the issue. In the large, understaffed asylums, mechanical restraint was deplored but felt necessary.

(155) The Commissioners in Lunacy were against mechanical restraint completely, and considered that its abolition was 'a mere question of expense,' easily soluble through structural alteration in asylums and increased staff/patient ratios. (156) Here they were simply rehearsing Gardiner Hill's (157) axioms, with all the nonchalant enthusiasm of single-minded bureaucracy, divorced from actual contact with the situation. (158)

Moral treatment did not necessarily preclude mechanical restraint, but sought to obviate its use by physical or psychological repression. These alternatives coupled with sedative-based medical management, were the core of the non-restraint system: their practice could prove dangerous, even fatal. (159)

Despite the optimism of the 'thirties and 'forties, the very size of the barracks-asylums, with their shortage of attendants and overpopulation, precluded universal practice of non-restraint. From the beginning, there had been objections to the system, especially to one alternative, that of seclusive confinement, in which the Commissioners were quick to spot the potentiality of abuse. (160) By the end of the century, doctrinaire acceptance of non-restraint was being challenged, and Thomas Lawes Rogers, Superintendent of Rainhill Asylum and sometime Commissioner in Lunacy, was, in the 'seventies, avant garde in remarking on his colleagues' over sensitivity on the issue, and in hinting at the wrongheadedness of trying to remain true to the tradition of Conolly. (161) American and French psychiatrists have always shown a healthy scepticism, (162) based on eminently chauvinistic premises.

The Commissioners in Lunacy adhered to the spirit of the mid-'forties, when the Conolly method was at the height of its popularity. By law, any usage of restraint had to be recorded, in both public and private asylums, and the inspectorate's reports reflected their distaste when they noted restraint entries. (163) Within the physical realm of asylumdom, however, the use of gloves and straitjackets obstinately continued, together with intermittent resort to padded cells. From the 1860's onwards, the dictates of a custodial, as opposed to a curative milieu, reinstated restraint as a humane and obvious therapeutic aid.

From both public and private sectors, psychiatrists, voiced doubts on official policy. 'Whenever I see in the reports of the Commissioners,' wrote L.A. Weatherley, 'the statement, "We are glad to see that there is no record of mechanical restraint," I often wonder what substitute has been used.' (164) P. Maury Deas, medical officer of a registered hospital, and former Superintendent of Macclesfield County Asylum, pointed out that

> Restraint of some kind is the basis on which all treatment of the insane, whether legal or medical, is based; and the enlightened modern treatment of

> the insane does not lie so much in the abolition of restraint as in the carrying out of the various kinds of restraint under constant and humane supervision.
> 'Manual restraint,' 'the restraint of drugs' ... the restraint of discipline and restriction need as much care and discretion in their use, and are as liable to be abused as 'mechanical restraint.' A physician ... ought to be as free to employ 'mechanical restraint' ... as he is to use drugs or any other recognised mode of treatment ... (165)

By the 'eighties and 'nineties, asylum practice was producing environmentally-conditioned inmates who differed little from those described in Bethlem in 1815. Montague Lomax, for example, described the practice of 'behind the table' confinement for troublesome patients, who 'bestialized, apathetic, mutinous ... malevolent, ... sit all day in their miserable corner ... the most degrading example of our "humane and scientific" treatment of the pauper lunatic.' (166)

Colney Hatch offered a typical example of changing attitudes. From its opening in 1851, the asylum had been committed to non-restraint. (167) From the late 'sixties, despite the Lunacy Commissioners' opposition, mechanical restraints were re-introduced by Edgar Sheppard, medical superintendent of the male department from 1862 to 1881. Opponents of non-restraint took this as evidence of the inapplicability of the system to large pauper institutions, especially since it came from an institution singled out by Shaftesbury as an exemplar. (168) Conolly himself had feared a return to restraint: endless addition to existing buildings, he argued in his Presidential Address to the AMOAHI, would 'make efficient inspection impossible, and ... become the pretext for the revival of strait waistcoats, and straps ...' (169) An eminent German alienist visiting Colney Hatch pointed up the same moral, and the Commissioners in Lunacy, blackballing Sheppard at the Royal College of Physicians on the one hand, admitted that the magnitude of the institution was the source of the departure from acceptable seclusive and medical treatments. (170)

The weakness in the inspectorate's argument, indicated by Deas, originated in the assumption that insanity, as a disease entity, must be susceptible of medical cure, if treated in a proper environment. The Metropolitan Commissioners in 1844 had urged that all asylums have resident medical staff, complaining that asylums too often were 'constituted less with regard to the cure of the lunatics to health and society, than to their ... safe custody.' They were scathing about institutions where

> ... occasional doses of medicine are administered, when incidental deviation from bodily health, or any contingency call for their use, but the application of medicine and other restorative means, on any determined plan, with a view to promote recovery, and to restore

> the mental faculties to a sound state, appears in some Asylums never to have been contemplated... (171)

Their opinion, however, reflected the outmoded optimism of an earlier generation, and by mid-century, medical treatment to most institution psychiatrists consisted of strengthening bodies with tonics, and in quieting the violent with narcotics. Most treatments were stock-in-trade of general practice, with cold baths, Turkish baths and dietaries forming the biggest aids to moral treatment. (172)

Drugs were primarily instruments of restraint, seldom of cure: opium, morphine, and the like, and their usage was not even always medically supervised. (173) Little real medical work was performed in nineteenth-century asylums; as James Crichton-Browne showed, the amounts spent on medical and surgical supplies in public asylums - one penny per patient per week - precluded real medical activity. (174) David Cassidy of Lancaster Moor Asylum indicated the fundamental patterns of treatment as being non-medical.

> With regard to Medical or Therapeutical treatment, every year brings us such stores of new drugs, new preparations and improved methods, that there is some danger of suffering from an embarrassment of riches ... We have experimented with electricity, with Massage, and with new drugs such as Hydrobromate of Hyoscine, which in our experience, has no advantage over the older extract of Hyoscianine; and with Hyprone, which has been found useful in some maniacal cases ... with Urethan, which seems to have little to recommend it; with Paraldehyde, an advantageous sedative ... After all, the staple medicines now are, and always must be, plenty of good food, fresh air, and exercise, ... (175)

Since a high proportion of inmates of the large pauper asylums was suffering from physical and mental debility consequent on poverty, bad housing, harmful working conditions and malnutrition, the positive virtues of these staples were self-evident. (176)

VIII

More stress was laid by the medical Establishment on the environment of the asylum, and fundamentally on construction and staffing, in promoting recovery or facilitating humane care. And of the staff, the attendant was seen to be the key member. 'The happiness and welfare of the patients,' wrote Charles Mercier, 'depend far more on the character and conduct of the attendants than on those of the rest of the staff put together ...' (177) This was a reasonable comment. In the larger asylums especially, the superintendent was an administrator rather than a medical agent, and assistant medical officers could never hope to establish proper contact with the vast numbers of patients involved. (178)

Pinel had advocated the recruitment of attendants from

amongst convalescing patients, since these would have become 'habituated to obedience, and easy to be drilled into any tactics which the nature of the service might require.' The tactics included 'intimidation without severity ... oppression, without violence' - and the physician-superintendent was to enjoy a dominating, authoritarian position. (179) And ironically, it was his medical 'expertise' which legitimised that authority. (180) The attendant's role, ideally, was submissive obedience and mediation of the physician's will. (181) The emphasis on 'moral treatment' in English institutions during the first three-quarters of the nineteenth century elevated the importance of the attendant's role, but also assumed a willingness and ability to interpret the will of an administrator whose therapeutics represented humane idealism rather than practical routine treatment. (182)

Until the 1880's there were no formal attempts to train attendants and they were simply thrown on the wards to learn from experience. In general hospitals, by 1870, trained nurses had been recognised as an integral part of practical medicine; in asylums, however, attendants 'entered into it frequently after failing in some other means of livelihood,' and the majority of asylums, according to the Superintendent of Prestwich Asylum in 1873, were

> ... officered by persons who are learning to be attendants ... not that they may acquire a character and obtain a promotion in that particular Asylum ... but that after a few months, (may) transfer their newly acquired experience to some other institution or ... other branch of the public service. (183)

There was no career structure; numbers were few, conditions harsh and wages low - 'considerably below that which is required by ordinary servants in gentlemen's families.' (184) As with workhouse attendants, recruitment was largely from the Army, and some asylums determinedly sought ex-bandsmen for their musical ability. (185) Inter-asylum movement was the main guarantee of a trained workforce, but this inevitably led to a high rate of staff turnover: Mercier reckoned an average of 33% p.a. It could be even higher. Commissioners Cleaton and Greville Howard noted that two-thirds of the attendants at Rainhill Asylum, in 1873, had changed since the Commissioners' last visit. (186)

The situation in private asylums, though variable in time and space, was substantially different from that in the pauper establishments. (187) The transition from keeper to nurse was easier to achieve in the former, and the higher income of the private institutions enabled a better quality and a greater number of attendants to be recruited. (188) There seems to have been some mobility between private and public sectors, doubtless to the advantage of the latter (189) though one suspects that the transference was one way: the type of attendant expected by J.G. Davey for his asylum near Bristol would have precluded the employment of run-of-the-mill county asylum employees. (190) The latter worked in undeniably arduous conditions, which were aggravated by their numerical inadequacy in situations demanding high staff: patient ratios for effective nursing. Male attendants were hardest to recruit, and in asylums which would not admit mixed nursing this could prove dangerous, (191) since it placed added burdens on already overworked and overdisciplined staff. (192) The high incidence of bedridden, paralytic and epileptic patients in the larger county institutions increased the dangers; reflexive physical brutality was often the only alternative to saturating sedation. (193) Despite hysterical accounts of sadism given by ex-patients (usually from private asylums), attendants' offences against patients, or at least such as were reported and investigated, seem largely to be results of laxity, overwork, or literal interpretation of asylum rules. (194)

In terms of career and salary there were no particular advantages in working in an asylum rather than a workhouse. A nurse at Prestwich, for example, in 1860, received £12 to £18 p.a. (195) At Manchester Workhouse she would have received £15 for working in the lunatic wards. (196) Male attendants in the workhouse received upwards of £22 p.a.; in the Asylum, they would receive between £12 12s. and £50, mostly in the medium ranges.(197)

In America, penitentiary inmates were, as policy, transferred to asylums as attendants. (198) Barbarity akin to criminality had, according to Pinel in France and Mitford in England, characterized asylum keeper-attendants in the eighteenth and early nineteenth centuries. (199) By mid-century, the colours of English asylum attendants were not drawn quite so starkly, but their class status was seen as too near the residuum for comfort: many attendants, complained Conolly, came from 'the dangerous classes of society; their appearance announces it; their effect on the terrified or disgusted patients, declares it; and their manners, habits and conduct ... frequently prove it.' (200) An anonymous writer in 1850 referred to 'ignorant, idle and ferocious keepers, acting without conscience or control,' and the Select Committee of 1859 heard evidence of widespread abuses in both sectors, with frequent dismissal of low calibre attendants. (201) Use of mechanical restraints appears to have been a major cause of complaint. The Commissioners in Lunacy attempted to set up a registry of attendants, and obtained powers to be notified of all dismissals for misconduct. (202) However, asylum proprietors and asylum committees had ideas of punishable misconduct which had little bearing, most times, on the attendants' qualities as nurses, (203) and so figures of dismissals or reprimands reveal little of behaviour towards patients.

Further up the asylum establishment, there were glaring differentials in salary and status between the superintendent and his assistants, which aggravated staffing and supervisory problems, and encouraged a turnover rate in junior medical staff which must have militated against the interest of the patients. Between 1850 and 1890, salaries increased. There were variations throughout the country, but the gaps were constant (204) and it was the underpaid assistants who had most general supervisory tasks and whose special duty was care of the patients. (205) Discrepancies between the alleged function of attendants and junior staff and their practical capabilities was an important factor in the demise of the curative role of pauper asylums. When Mortimer-Granville entitled the Lancet report on lunatic asylums The Care and Cure of the Insane, in 1877, he was expressing an ideal. John Bucknill was more honest when, three years later, he published his collected articles as The Care of the Insane and their Legal Control. The image of the old Gothic madhouse as a depository for the unwanted of the middle- and upper- classes was distortedly mirrored in the barracks for the socially undesirable and economically inept. Between 1790 and 1890, only physical dimensions changed. The Rev. Henry Hawkins, chaplain to Colney Hatch, painted a charming canvas of asylum life for the Churchman's Magazine, which hinted at even 'a tendency ... towards overindulgence and ultra-refinement' in the treatment of the insane. (206) His descriptions of the 'entertainments' especially are at once condescending and redolent of the emptiness of the gestures involved:

> During the winter months frequent dances, known as 'balls' take place ... Numbers look on as spectators only. The mechanical manner in which some of the dancers take part ... is noticeable. They are interested, but it seems in the way of business rather than pleasure. (207)

Ordered pleasure could be little other than a facade. And in public asylums cost-cutting minimized even that: why hire a brass band to play Mozart, when a hack fiddler should be good enough for lunatic paupers? (208)

IX

The siting and architecture of asylums were key determinants of the nature and function of the institutionalization process. In both public and private sectors, structural criteria dictated organizational and therapeutic milieux, (209) and asylum buildings reflected the priorities of those responsible for their construction. Since few private asylums were purpose-built, most attention here will be given to subscription hospitals and county asylums. (210)

In London, both the New Bethlem (1812 - 15) (211) and St. Luke's were designed as exclusive special accommodation for lunatics. (212) In Liverpool and Manchester, the lunatic hospitals were seen, initially, as integral parts of the existing infirmaries. (213) According to Conolly, there was no specialist literature in English on the design of asylums prior to 1845, (214) and construction even later, when supervised by the Commissioners in Lunacy, (215) seldom reflected current medical opinion on the subject. (216) Siting and environment seem to have concerned asylum building committees more than structures, in the years before 1850, and the aspect of many early asylums reflects less the current medical optimism than the lay concern with custodial segregation: St. Luke's, for example, designed by George Dance, the architect of Newgate Gaol, bore similarities to the latter, and with its arrangement of large wards was, like the Gaol, outmoded. (217)

By the later eighteenth century, cellular confinement, in both prisons and asylums, was becoming theoretically more desirable, and New Bethlem's cells were seen as a revolutionary advance on the congested wards familiar through Hogarth's representation of Bedlam. (218) The factor of residential confinement, however, kept asylums close to prisons in both appearance and internal organisation. (219) The influence of Bentham's Panopticon, with its outlooking administrative/supervisory centre and facilitated segregatory and classificatory provisions, was visible in several early asylums, again reflecting the prison/asylum identity. (220) The later widely adopted H-plan asylums (221) were modifications on this basic design, stressing the custodial function of the institution and the 'watching over' role of the attendant nurses. This latter feature was retained in the trend towards the 'improved linear plan' which retained the central building, substituting extended wings on each side for the earlier H-uprights. (222) Systems of wards and corridors, and single or small-number sleeping rooms, were planned into many public asylums during the 1850's and 1860's, and even institutions dating from the first quarter of the century proved adaptable to the newer principles of classification. (223) However, though meeting the requirements of alienists and Commissioners as regards site, elevation and available grounds, (224) most establishments quickly became unfit for avowed purposes of cure. Even features praised in the original construction could rapidly become sources of unwelcome criticism. (225) Demands, from alienists and Commissioners alike, that a two-storey maximum was essential, led to vast straggling buildings, increasingly divorced from the central controlling block. (226) Additions to the original structure, where sanctioned, fragmented the designed authority structure, throwing more responsibility on attendants, and made the institution far larger and more unwieldy than any but the ratepayers would have wished. (227) During the second phase of asylum building, in the 1870's and 1880's, the more adaptable block system was widely used, (228) though this could encourage yet greater accumulations of buildings on the same large site, rendering impossible the degrees of paternalistic control and supervised inspection envisaged by Pinel, Tuke, Conolly or Kirkbride. (229) Exteriors were throughout the period acceptably 'plain and unpretending' (230) whilst internal arrangements tended to reflect poor law mentality rather than the cheerfulness and warmth achievable in private asylums and projected for the county institutions. (231)

Constant, too, was the desire to maintain the isolation of the surrogate community from normal social intercourse. The early asylums were sited as far from centres of population as the exigencies of communications and supplies allowed. When spreading urbanisation overtook them, they were often re-sited (232) whilst asylums located in residential areas were treated disapprovingly by the Commissioners. (233) Separation from towns made the custodial function easier to disguise: where there were too convenient railway lines, as at Colney Hatch, asylums had built-in sentry mechanisms. (234) Undoubtedly, the original motivation for rural seclusion lay in positive desires for the natural beauty of the surroundings, and availability of land for cultivation or expansion, (235) but the character of the institution was moulded inexorably by its location and form. The 'otherness' of the insane was emphasised by their geographical separation from 'normalcy'; the custodial nature of care was structurally reinforced; the vast predominance of 'chronic' and 'incurable' inmates in the asylums further stressed the reality that isolation and confinement had little to do with medical treatment in the hope of cure.

CHAPTER THREE

DIMENSIONS OF ASYLUMDOM 1800 - 90

There are no official records of numbers of private madhouses prior to 1774, and even where figures exist thereafter, they are not entirely reliable since there were unknown numbers of unlicensed houses. (1) Parliamentary returns from 1819 to 1844 provide more adequate information, from which it becomes apparent that the number of madhouses - both in London and in the provinces - rose steadily through the first half of the nineteenth century. (2) Numbers declined as a dramatic drop in the number of pauper establishments followed the county asylum legislation of 1845, though there was some compensatory increase in the numbers of houses catering for private patients only, so that by the end of the century, there were approximately as many private asylums as there had been at the beginning. (3)

TABLE 1

Number of provincial and metropolitan licensed houses 1774 - 1890 (4)

Date	Prov'l Houses	Receiving paupers	Metrop'n Houses	Receiving paupers
1774	unknown		16	unknown
1807	28	unknown	17	"
1815	38	"	34	"
1819	49	"	40	"
1831	68	"	38	"
1841	90	38	33	"
1844	100	45	39	3
1855	88	25	41	5
1870	64	4	44	5
1880	61	5	35	5
1890	58	3	33	5

As Parry-Jones has shown, the increase in the number of private madhouses was associated in the first half of the century with their more widespread geographical distribution, (5) though there was a relatively high concentration in certain areas: Lancashire, Durham, Gloucestershire, Hampshire, Warwickshire, Somerset and Yorkshire. Population density was one causal factor; availability of alternative asylum accommodation in the area was clearly a second. Local factors also played a part: thus the York Retreat influenced the establishment of several near namesakes in the locality. Somerset displayed a high number of licensed houses since, despite being the sixth largest county at mid-century, it lacked a public asylum or registered hospital. (6) Elsewhere, the concentration was occasionally quite remarkable: in 1825 all four Durham madhouses were in Gateshead, whilst three Warwickshire houses out of four were at Henley-in-Arden. (7) Somerset's several houses were operated as a family concern, as were those in Wiltshire belonging to the Finch family, whilst, as Parry-Jones points out, 'it seems likely that the presence of one or more madhouses in a single neighbourhood fostered the establishment of others in that area. (8) Another kind of offshoot of existing madhouses was the setting up of asylums by former attendants, not infrequently in the same locality. (9)

Private asylums flourished before 1845 partly because so few counties took advantage of Wynn's Act of 1808 (10) - only nine had built asylums by 1825: Bedford in 1812 (180 beds; cost £20,500); Nottingham, 1812 (170 beds; cost £36,800); Norfolk, 1814, (220 beds; cost £50,000); Lancaster, 1816 (593 beds; cost £100,695); Stafford, 1818 (120 beds; cost £36,500); Yorkshire, Wakefield, 1819 (420 beds; cost £46,620); Cornwall, 1820 (172 beds; £18,780 excl.land); Gloucester, 1823 (120 beds; cost £42,856). Chester Asylum was in process of construction at this date. (11) Sixteen years later, at the time of the national investigation by the Metropolitan Commissioners in Lunacy, only six further counties had built public asylums: Middlesex (1831), Suffolk (1829), Dorset (1832), Kent (1833), Leicester (1837) and Surrey (1841). (12)

The private sector had cashed in on this tardiness. Thus, of the 100 provincial madhouses extant in 1844, sixty-five had opened since 1808 and forty-four of the hundred received paupers only. (13) Where there was adequate alternative provision, or, at least, substantial provision for pauper lunatics, private establishments tended to restrict their clientele to private patients. Thus, in Lancashire, only one of the seven licensed houses in 1844 received paupers: Haydock Lodge, which had only opened that year. (14)

Institutional provision for private and pauper patients increased steadily until the compulsory legislation of 1845, and quite rapidly in the public sector thereafter. At the time of the appointment of Wynn's Committee in 1807, there were, in addition to the private asylums, six asylums and part of one hospital in the provinces given over to the care of the insane, and two in London. By 1844, there were fifteen county asylums, two asylums established under local acts, (15) two services' hospitals, (16) nine registered public asylums, Bethlem and St. Luke's, and a total of 139 private madhouses: a total of 166 institutions for the insane. (17) Ten years later there were 178 institutions, and a change in the balance of public and private sectors had occurred: there were now thirty-three county asylums, twelve registered hospitals and 129 licensed houses. (18) The decline in the numbers of the latter was matched during the next thirty years by an increase in county asylums: in 1864 there were 102 private establishments and forty-two county/borough asylums. By 1880, the respective figures were ninety-four and sixty-one. (19)

The multiplicity of institutions reflected the enormous increase in certified insanity from the beginning of the century, especially amongst the lower classes. The legal requirement of confinement following certification meant that any increase in vigilance by parish officers would necessitate a widening of provisions for the labelled insane. Conversely, once expensive asylums had been erected, vigilance would be enjoined on officials to ensure maximum use of institution-space. In this vicious circle, growing numbers of the lower orders became trapped within the asylum system. Initially, in the eighteenth century, it had been the upper and middling ranks of society which had been most susceptible to asylum confinement, and growth in the numbers of labelled insane tended to reflect awareness of madness within these groups. At times, madness became, in a sense, fashionable. In the glare of publicity following the illness of George III in 1788, the attention fixed on insanity prompted attempts to estimate its incidence in the nation. (20) Fears of insanity's rapid increase were sown which lasted for a century, despite the soothing assurances of physicians that increased totals of certified lunatics reflected not national deterioration, but more efficient public notice. As early as the first decade of the nineteenth century, the number of lunatics was seen to have risen dramatically over a generation. (21) In 1810, Dr. Richard Powell, secretary of the Commissioners of the Royal College of Physicians, published figures relating to private madhouses which indicated a rise in the number of insane in the country from 1800 (1775 - 79) to 2275 (1805 - 1809), (22) in an attempt to discover 'how far the relative numbers ... would support the popular opinion respecting the rapid increase of that most difficult, delicate and important disease.' Powell's less than critical use of his data was fuel for popular opinion, but ten years later, George Man Burrows indicated the operation of socio-political factors in the creation of the apparent increased incidence. Commenting on Powell's histogram, Burrows argued that

> Many important causes, physical and moral, have superadded since the origin of the register (of private asylums) ... and greatly influenced the number of entries in the different lustra ... Thus, the late King's first illness ... (1788 - 9) ... produced ... an unusual interest in the condition ... The result superadded an unprecedented number of entries to the fourth lustrum, which commenced in 1790 ... In 1807, Parliament appointed a Committee to investigate the state of pauper and criminal lunatics, and an Act, commonly called Mr. Wynne's passed in 1808, for the better care and maintenance of them. This inquiry and the report thereon ... incited fresh attention to the condition of the insane of all ranks; and hence a vast number, before dispersed, and of course unregistered, were sent into asylums and licensed houses, and greatly augmented the returns. The result was an increase of entries in 1809, which closes the seventh lustrum: it continued from the commencement of the eighth (1810), arrived at its maximum in 1813, and declined in 1814; before the Reports of the Parliamentary Investigation in 1815 - 16 were published. (23)

Parliamentary and private investigations between 1807 and 1828 attracted more attention to the insane of all classes. Official figures as to total numbers of insane in England and Wales were invariably underestimates, in no small part due to the non-co-operation of local authorities in making returns to Parliament. Even so, large increases were apparent. According to the Select Committee of 1807, returns showed 2,248 certified pauper lunatics throughout the country, a figure erring on the low side, as there had been no return from

> Southampton, ... and the counties of Hereford, Bedford, Cumberland, and Cambridge did not return a single lunatic. Essex returned only three, and Gloucestershire ten; while from Suffolk and Norfolk, where the returns have been corrected ... the numbers amount to 114 in the former and 112 in the latter. (24)

Returns for 1819 showed 1,282 insane paupers in public asylums and gaols. Private asylums and workhouses were excluded from the totals. Seven years later, official returns gave the total number of insane of all classes as 4,782, but amended figures, supplied by Sir Andrew Halliday, showed 8,070 certified - though not necessarily confined - lunatics for the year 1826. (25) A county by county breakdown, again the work of Halliday, for the year 1828 - 29, gave the number of recognised lunatics as 12,547. (26) By 1844, this total had risen to 20,893. (27)

Compulsory public asylum provision, improved basic care, and an invariably high proportion of incurables amongst admissions to asylums, produced vast accumulations of patients after 1845, which progressively increased simple aggregates of certified lunatics: 30,312 in 1854; 44,631 in 1864; 62,027 in 1874; 73,113 in 1881. (28) The numbers of insane of all classes increased beyond the growth of the population. In 1849, the ratio was 16.14 per 10,000 of the population; in 1875, 23.55 per 10,000. Both numerically and proportionately, the biggest jump was amongst pauper lunatics: the population increase from 1849 to 1875 ran out at about 22.7%; during the same period there was an increase in private patients of 48.39% and in pauper lunatics of 77.47%. (29)

Moreover, the increase in the numbers of certified pauper lunatics marches well ahead of the rate of increase in the total pauper population. There was an absolute increase in the numbers of paupers of all categories in the second half of the century, but the ratio of paupers to the total population fell significantly. In contrast, despite fluctuations, there was a big increase in the ratio of pauper lunatics to paupers, as shown in Table 2.

Once more, it has to be remembered that these figures represent accumulations, though regional variation between rural areas (where accumulations tended to be more significant than in manufacturing areas, where the towns pushed mortality rates up) and urban districts suggest that the incidence of insanity was higher in the latter, thus indicating that much of the growth of insanity amongst paupers was real and not a statistical illusion. Hack Tuke, for example, showed that for 1857, the proportion of pauper lunatics to the total population was higher in definably manufacturing districts (26.40 per 1000) than in agricultural areas (18.37 per 1000). (30) Moreover, simple accumulation cannot explain away the progressive and substantial annual increases in the numbers of admissions to asylums of patients of all classes, but particularly of paupers. After 1845, pauper lunatics began to be sent to county institutions as a matter of course whenever they became too troublesome, too old or too sick for the workhouse to handle.

TABLE 2

Increase in pauper lunacy 1859 - 89

Date	Total No. of Paupers of All Classes	Total No. of Pauper Lunatics and Idiots	Total Paupers to Population %	Total Pauper Lunatics to Paupers %
1859	862,078	31,782	4.37	3.68
1860	844,475	32,993	4.24	3.90
1861	891,868	34,381	4.43	3.85
1862	964,166	35,709	4.64	3.77
1863	1,142,624	37,611	5.53	3.29
1864	1,011,753	39,219	4.84	3.87
1865	974,772	40,160	4.60	4.11
1866	924,813	41,634	4.31	4.50
1867	963,200	43,031	4.44	4.46
1868	1,040,103	44,960	4.73	4.32
1869	1,046,569	47,002	4.70	4.49
1870	1,084,821	48,433	4.82	4.46
1871	1,085,661	50,301	4.76	4.63
1872	981,042	51,998	4.24	5.30
1873	890,372	53,273	3.80	5.98
1874	832,370	54,735	3.50	6.57
1875	817,822	56,403	3.40	6.89
1876	752,887	57,407	3.08	7.62
1877	732,523	59,039	2.96	8.05
1878	747,811	60,846	2.98	8.13
1879	805,080	62,107	3.17	7.71
1880	843,854	63,571	3.28	7.53
1881	809,341	65,372	3.10	8.07
1882	803,381	67,089	3.04	8.35
1883	803,719	68,842	3.00	8.56
1884	779,038	70,470	2.87	9.05
1885	788,902	71,215	2.87	9.03
1886	813,014	71,663	2.92	8.81
1887	822,215	72,443	2.91	8.81
1888	831,353	74,171	2.90	8.92
1889	817,190	75,632	2.82	9.25

Source: adapted from Commissioners in Lunacy, Forty-third Report (1889) pp. 18-19.

Workhouses continued to retain tractable lunatics and employable idiots, partly for economic reasons, partly because asylum provision everywhere failed to keep pace with increased certification of insanity. From mid-century, however, there was a pronounced trend towards asylum maintenance at the expense of workhouse confinement. Licensed houses continued to expand their intake in absolute terms, clearly reverting to exploitation of the middle and higher income groups as the pauper trade declined (see Table 4 and Table 5). (31) For all classes of lunatics, confinement in an institution became the norm.

TABLE 3

Certified lunatics of all classes admitted to asylums and single care 1869 - 88

	No.of certified lunatics			Ratio (per 10,000) of lunatics to pop'n.		
Date	Male	Female	Total	Male	Female	Average
1869	5,283	5,189	10,472	4.88	4.55	4.71
1870	5,045	5,174	10,219	4.60	4.48	4.54
1871	5,301	5,227	10,528	4.78	4.46	4.61
1872	5,255	5,349	10,604	4.67	4.51	4.59
1873	5,535	5,677	11,212	4.86	4.72	4.78
1874	5,963	5,949	11,912	5.16	4.88	5.02
1875	6,210	6,232	12,442	5.30	5.04	5.17
1876	6,366	6,491	12,857	5.36	5.18	5.27
1877	6,516	6,453	12,969	5.42	5.08	5.25
1878	6,657	6,686	13,343	5.46	5.20	5.33
1879	6,342	6,759	13,101	5.13	5.18	5.16
1880	6,364	6,876	13,240	5.08	5.20	5.15
1881	6,653	6,851	13,504	5.24	5.12	5.18
1882	6,665	6,956	13,621	5.19	5.12	5.15
1883	7,013	7,454	14,467	5.38	5.43	5.41
1884	7,044	7,268	14,312	5.33	5.21	5.27
1885	6,426	6,928	13,354	4.80	4.91	4.85
1886	6,651	6,912	13,563	4.90	4.83	4.87
1887	7,032	7,263	14,295	5.11	5.01	5.06
1888	7,157	7,617	14,774	5.14	5.18	5.16

Adapted from Commissioners in Lunacy, Forty-third Report p.17

Amongst certified private patients, males exceeded females throughout the period. Amongst paupers, females exceeded the males in absolute numbers, but were significantly fewer in proportion to the number of females in the pauper population. (32)

The reasons for the higher numbers of female admissions were early seen to have economic rather than pathological origins. Thus John Thurnham in 1845 noted that

> Women, indeed, are sooner rendered entirely dependent as a consequence of mental disorder, than men; and I should conclude that any greater indulgence to, and tolerance of, the eccentricities of the sex, when the subjects of insanity, is more than compensated by the frequently greater difficulty of effecting the removal to an asylum of their insane brother, father or husband.

The Metropolitan Commissioners' Report for 1844 indicated an excess of females of all classes over males of 4%; and of pauper females over males of 12%. But as Thurnham showed, incidence varied regionally and over time. In addition, the accumulation of patients could distort figures, and in breaking figures down so as to isolate admissions of persons attacked with insanity for the first time, Thurnham illustrated higher incidence amongst males in many areas, concluding that

> In nearly all points of view ... women have an advantage over men in reference to insanity; for not only do they appear to be less liable than men to mental derangement, but when the subjects of it, the probability if their recovery is on the whole greater ... On the other hand, the probability of a relapse or of a recurrence of the disorder, after recovery from a first attack, is somewhat greater in women than in men. (33)

In the upper and middle classes, there was a massive preponderance of males over females confined, if figures for occurring insanity rather than for existing insanity were computed, though Thurnham admitted that this could reflect the fact that women in these social groups were more likely to be kept at home than either men of the same class, or women of lower classes. (34) Notwithstanding this qualification, where information was available from public asylums as to admission for a first attack, there was an excess of females over males only at Hanwell, Bethlem, the York Retreat and one metropolitan licensed house. Over a period of twenty-six years, there was a 27% excess of males over females at Lancaster; a 29% excess at Nottingham (thirty-one years); 31% at Cornwall (twenty-two years); 26% at York Lunatic Asylum (twenty-five years); 19% at Lincoln Lunatic Asylum (twenty-one years); and 12% at Gloucester (twenty years). The excess of females at the Retreat simply reflected the higher proportion of females to males in the Society of Friends than in the population at large. (35) Women seemed to have a higher recovery rate than men - though criteria of 'cure' used were often dubious and varied from asylum to asylum, as well as from time to time, making real comparisons impossible. Bethlem, for example, would only take in potentially curable cases; St. Luke's, too, was selective. County institutions had no choice in their admissions, yet despite high proportions of chronics, tended for most of the century to display high cure-rates. It is not possible to discover how many of these 'cured' patients were subsequently readmitted for the same malady since there was little formalization of asylum records before the third quarter of the century. Even the Lunacy Commissioners' statistical tables were subject to periodic variation in style and subject until the 1870's, making it impossible to make real comparisons as to relative incidence of disease, cure etc., by sex, age, occupation, or other categories, over any long period.

TABLE 4

Distribution of certified lunatics 1828 - 81

Date	County Asylums	Registered Hospitals [a]	Licensed houses	Workhouses	Other [b]
1828	2,503 [c]		3,734	88	6,222
1844	4,489	879	5,273	9,339	1,013
1854	12,962	1,128	4,880	10,653	689 [d]
1864	21,551	1,647	4,455	16,251	727 [e]
1874	31,371	2,337	4,713	15,018	8,152 [f]
1881	41,355	2,948	4,626	16,811 [g]	7,373 [f]

a. Public asylums operated by subscription; insane wards in hospitals recognised by the Commissioners in Lunacy.
b. Bethlem, St. Luke's, the military and naval hospitals; single patients; unconfined.
c. This figure includes patients in public asylums other than county institutions and in hospital insane wards.
d. Total relates only to Bethlem, St. Luke's and the military and naval hospitals.
e. As (d) but patients in Broadmoor Criminal Lunatic Asylum added.
f. As (e) with addition of Royal India Asylum and private single patients, outdoor paupers and unconfined lunatics.
g. Including Metropolitan District Asylums.

Sources: Halliday, Letter to Lord Robert Seymour; Metropolitan Commissioners in Lunacy, Report to the Lord Chancellor, (1844); Commissioners in Lunacy, Reports, 1855, 1865, 1875, 1882.

Thurnham's tables for the years before 1844 show greater percentages of recovery on admissions amongst women in his selected institutions, and higher aggregate recovery rates in asylums receiving private and pauper patients or private patients only, than in pauper establishments. For the nine county asylums taking paupers only, the average proportion of recoveries to admissions was 36.95%. For county asylums with mixed populations, the figure rose to 46.87%. (36) By the last quarter of the century, patients discharged cured from county and borough asylums were averaging 40.32% on admissions. (37)

TABLE 5

Certified lunatics in licensed houses 1844 - 90

Date	Total lunatics in all asylums		Prov'l licensed houses		Metrop'n licensed houses		Total in licensed houses
	Private	Pauper	Private	Pauper	Private	Pauper	
1844	3,790	7,482	1,426	1,920	973	854	5,173
1847	4,065	9,767	1,530	2,332	1,103	1,664	6,629
1854	4,429	15,026	1,533	1,000	1,206	1,141	4,880
1860	4,927	18,790	1,606	750	1,342	602	4,300
1870	5,924	29,989	1,478	726	1,666	1,034	4,904
1880	7,152	41,127	1,554	533	1,854	608	4,549
1890	8,364	53,621	1,397	582	1,641	927	4,547

Sources: Metropolitan Commissioners in Lunacy, Report (1844); Commissioners in Lunacy, Further Report (1847); and Reports for 1855, 1865, 1871, 1881, 1891.

TABLE 6

Ratios of male and female lunatics to respective pauper populations, and of children under sixteen, 1859 - 89

Date	Male adult pauper lunatics to male adult paupers: %	Female adult pauper lunatics to female adult paupers: %	Child pauper lunatics to child paupers: %
1859	7.9	4.72	0.20
1864	7.98	5.06	0.20
1869	9.17	5.85	0.22
1874	13.09	8.07	0.36
1879	14.56	9.95	0.41
1884	16.65	11.61	0.54
1889	16.27	11.81	0.55

Source: Commissioners in Lunacy, Forty-third Report, p.19.

The progressive institutionalization of pauper lunatics was not uniform throughout the country. Especially in Wales, residence with relatives or friends remained of primary importance even in the last quarter of the century. Generally, however, the trend was away from care within the community to confinement in the asylum or, in heavily populated districts, the workhouse lunatic wards (Table 8 and Table 9).

The continued importance of the workhouse reflected economic considerations rather than social strategies, and significantly, definably agricultural counties, with lower population densities than the towns, and with fewer lunatics per head of population, relied less on the workhouse than did industrial areas, being more able to afford to keep asylum accommodation in step with their relatively lower rates of increase in pauper lunacy. Conversely, Middlesex, the West Riding of Yorkshire, Lancashire and other counties with marked urban industrial development fell back on workhouses constantly, maintaining a significant number of their insane paupers outside the asylum throughout the second half of the century.

TABLE 7

Distribution of pauper lunatics and idiots 1859 - 89

Date	Total No. of lunatics*	Asylums/ Hosps./ Lic.H.	Work-houses	Relatives and others	Prop'n % to total No. A/H/LH	Wrkhs.	Rel.&o.
1859	31,401	17,640	7,963	5,798	56.18	25.36	18.46
1864	38,758	22,507	9,710	6,541	58.07	25.05	16.88
1869	46,732	28,564	11,181	6,987	61.12	23.93	14.95
1874	54,334	32,477	15,018	6,839	59.77	27.64	12.59
1879	61,627	39,392	16,005	6,230	63.92	25.97	10.11
1884	69,959	46,504	17,377	6,078	66.47	24.84	8.69

* The totals of pauper lunatics differ slightly from those in Table 2. This is because the Commissioners used January figures for the statistics from which this table is extracted, and mid-year figures for the tables used to assemble the figures in Table 2.

Source: adapted from Commissioners in Lunacy, Forty-third Report p. 36.

TABLE 8

Distribution of pauper lunatics and idiots 1844.

County	Total pauper lunatics and idiots	In asylums	In licensed houses	In W/houses	With friends or elsewhere
Bedford	137	53	-	55	29
Berks	260	11	169	60	80
Bucks	147	10	48	43	46
Cambridge	143	36	14	28	65
Chester	287	117	1	55	114
Cornwall	335	116	-	132	87
Cumberland	173	15	43	67	48
Derby	173	4	36	51	82
Devon	547	25	102	145	275
Dorset	210	97	21	48	44
Durham	264	5	103	71	85

TABLE 8 (Cont.)

Distribution of pauper lunatics and idiots 1844

County	Total pauper lunatics and idiots	In asylums	In licensed houses	In W/houses	With friends or elsewhere
Essex	354	8	109	115	122
Gloucs.	392	142	24	115	111
Hereford	151	5	28	20	98
Herts.	225	57	24	53	91
Huntingdon	65	30	5	17	13
Kent	522	225	54	143	100
Lancaster	1,153	494	18	399	242
Leicester	249	73	1	102	73
Lincoln	304	68	40	98	98
Middlesex	970	451	245	241	93
Monmouth	117	19	25	24	49
Norfolk	457	173	7	106	171
Northants	291	95	18	81	97
Northumber'd	325	-	120	111	94
Nottingham	258	100	-	109	49
Oxford	201	5	66	62	68
Rutland	26	7	1	9	9
Salop	248	17	38	85	108
Somerset	584	12	160	153	259
Southants	452	3	199	135	115
Stafford	412	148	8	174	82
Suffolk	386	187	21	74	104
Surrey	537	302	49	146	40
Sussex	278	8	85	69	116
Warwick	248	19	63	76	90
Westm'land	57	-	14	24	19
Wilts	373	12	174	73	114
Worcester	307	31	79	99	98
York ER	183	33	52	55	43
York NR	152	13	47	35	57
York WR	662	263	6	215	178
Anglesey	65	-	-	-	65
Brecon	66	2	4	6	54
Cardigan	119	2	1	-	116
Carmarthen	162	-	8	12	142
Carnarvon	149	2	-	1	146
Denbigh	84	5	-	9	70
Flint	60	5	-	11	44
Glamorgan	155	-	26	14	115
Merioneth	83	1	-	7	75
Montgomery	107	4	2	11	90
Pembroke	105	15	-	18	72
Radnor	22	-	-	1	21

Source: Metropolitan Commissioners in Lunacy, Report (1844) Appendix F.

TABLE 9.

Relative distribution of pauper lunatics and idiots, 1871 and 1889

County	Total pauper lunatics and idiots		% in asylums & lic.houses		% in workhouses		% with friends and others	
	1871	1889	1871	1889	1871	1889	1871	1889
Anglesey	91	108	26.37	50.00	1.10	11.10	72.53	38.90
Bedford	377	486	61.27	79.20	15.39	9.90	23.34	10.90
Berks.	713	804	64.94	76.00	18.37	15.40	16.69	8.60
Brecon	147	179	48.30	78.80	13.61	5.60	38.09	15.60
Bucks.	441	490	72.79	75.30	14.29	15.50	12.92	9.20
Cambs.	446	601	60.31	73.40	17.94	10.30	21.75	16.30
Cardigan	158	318	39.24	46.20	0.63	12.30	60.13	41.50
Carmarthen	309	368	30.74	51.40	5.83	9.80	63.43	38.80
Carnarvon	261	329	34.87	44.10	10.34	14.00	54.79	41.90
Chester	959	1,495	56.00	72.90	30.45	18.60	13.55	8.50
Cornwall	567	801	70.72	77.50	15.17	13.70	14.11	8.80
Cumberland	463	569	60.47	73.70	23.76	20.00	15.77	6.30
Denbigh	147	287	51.02	54.70	21.77	25.80	27.21	19.50
Derby	597	767	67.67	69.70	20.94	23.50	11.39	6.80
Devon	1,438	1,849	55.77	67.20	21.70	18.80	22.53	14.00
Dorset	489	578	66.05	73.50	14.32	15.80	19.63	10.70
Durham	893	1,607	62.04	80.10	25.08	14.60	12.88	5.30
Essex	1,017	1,544	61.36	73.90	18.58	16.50	20.06	9.60
Flint	202	117	50.00	60.70	24.26	18.80	25.74	20.50
Glamorgan	685	1,205	60.58	74.90	10.66	9.20	28.76	15.90
Gloucs.	1,492	1,950	51.54	59.80	30.76	28.40	17.70	11.80
Hereford	414	525	54.11	67.60	12.56	13.30	33.33	19.10
Herts.	516	606	60.47	78.10	18.60	13.20	20.93	8.70
Hunts.	134	146	73.88	85.60	15.67	11.00	10.45	3.40
Kent	1,864	2,916	71.62	74.60	19.05	20.60	9.33	4.80
Lancs.	5,538	9,141	54.62	73.00	39.85	25.30	5.53	1.70
Leics.	805	979	62.48	74.20	23.85	16.90	13.67	8.90
Lincoln	867	969	65.40	68.30	15.69	16.40	18.91	15.30
Merioneth	108	142	26.85	49.30	13.89	26.10	29.26	24.61
Mid'sex	7,312	12,664	69.04	62.20	26.33	35.80	4.63	2.00
Monmouth	547	759	66.54	76.90	12.07	9.10	21.39	14.00
Montgomery	197	254	50.25	62.60	17.77	17.30	31.98	20.10
Norfolk	1,135	1,385	54.71	64.80	22.47	19.90	22.82	15.30
Northants	622	749	55.31	69.80	20.90	20.60	23.79	9.60
N'hmbrlnd.	773	1,103	62.09	77.20	22.77	14.60	15.14	8.20
Notts	786	1,240	54.07	58.00	30.79	19.80	15.14	22.20
Oxon	556	664	64.75	65.10	16.73	20.20	18.52	14.70
Pembroke	256	263	37.50	63.50	5.47	8.70	57.03	27.80
Radnor	45	66	51.11	62.10	4.45	21.20	44.44	16.70
Rutland	51	64	76.47	78.10	19.61	11.00	3.92	10.69
Salop	695	791	63.88	73.30	18.42	18.20	17.70	8.50
Somerset	1,272	1,464	52.52	63.50	22.09	22.80	25.39	13.70
S. Hants.	1,312	1,922	56.25	65.50	30.41	22.90	13.34	11.60
Staffs.	1,264	2,369	64.48	63.40	26.58	25.00	8.94	11.60

TABLE 9 (cont.)

Relative distribution of pauper lunatics and idiots 1871 and 1889

County	Total pauper Lunatics and idiots		% in asylums & lic.houses		% in workhouses		% with friends and others	
	1871	1889	1871	1889	1871	1889	1871	1889
Suffolk	853	969	59.32	68.20	15.24	14.70	25.44	17.10
Surrey	2,590	5,148	77.22	70.00	17.68	27.20	5.10	2.80
Sussex	1,060	1,441	60.66	63.80	22.36	26.00	16.98	10.20
Warwick	1,486	2,409	65.55	74.90	21.06	20.60	13.39	4.50
W'mrland	131	150	58.78	69.30	28.24	22.00	12.98	8.70
Wilts	806	914	59.06	69.40	16.87	17.70	24.07	12.90
Worcs.	1,088	1,006	65.07	76.70	18.38	15.60	16.55	7.70
Yorks ER	585	781	65.47	73.50	27.52	22.00	7.01	4.50
Yorks NR	436	694	68.12	79.50	16.74	11.10	15.14	9.40
Yorks WR	2,641	4,436	57.21	70.80	31.43	24.00	11.36	5.20

Sources: Commissioners in Lunacy, Reports 1871 and 1889

CHAPTER FOUR

THE MEDICAL CONTEXT OF ASYLUMDOM 1790 - 1890

Dr. Johnson once remarked that any attempt to define poetry served only to define the narrowness of the definer, and his dictum was eagerly adapted by nineteenth-century medical writers to justify their vagueness and imprecision when discussing the nature and causes of insanity. It was, however, necessary to erect systems of identification to locate the mad, and to organize modes of response. To this end functional definitions were offered, by legal and medical professionals, which facilitated professional communication but caused inter-professional conflict and mystified the layman. (1)

I

The medical position, developed in the later eighteenth century, rested on the overwhelming conviction that insanity was a disease. The Rev. Dr. Francis Willis' treatment of George III proved an impetus to determined experimentation and diffusion of ideas, and his claim to a high rate of curability focussed attention on treatments. (2) In England, France and America, psychiatry was given a 'leg up to respectability'; Pinel and Rush communicated with Willis, and English contemporaries hastened to back up his claim, delineating their own treatments which were largely physical. (3) Insanity was invariably referred to as a 'disorder' or 'distemper' or 'disease' - though one non-medical madhouse owner believed that 'there is scarcely a gentleman of the faculty but would gladly give up this part of his practice.' (4) The medical gentlemen, however, in England and America, displayed little of this temerity. John Haslam was dogmatically in agreement with Battie that madness was akin to other distempers, though, like most English psychiatrists, he disputed Rush's notion that insanity was related to fevers. (5) By the first decades of the nineteenth century, few practitioners doubted that insanity was a disease of the brain, viewed as the organ of the mind; mental disorders, then, were organic.

Until the mid-nineteenth century, Lockeian influences were strong amongst English alienists, at least in theory, (6) most notably amongst those who favoured moral management. (7) This led to an elevation of the importance of the will and a fervent belief in the therapeutic value of moral force. (8) In this climate, medical perspectives were heavily imbued with philosophical and religious currents. (9) Concurrent developments of individualism in economic and political theory stressed a subjectivity which alienists found attractive to adapt: the internalisation of mental disorder was an expression of early nineteenth-century Zeitgeist. With individualism went the notion of self-help, which had its impact on psychiatry. (10)

'Madmen,' argued Locke, 'do not appear to have lost the faculty of reasoning; but having joined together some ideas very wrongly, they mistake them for truths, and they err as men do that argue right from wrong principles.' (11) Madness here is located as a defect of the intellect, and by the early nineteenth century writers were accepting that insanity basically was identifiable with unreason. (12) However, medical men inevitably tried to locate an organic source responsible for this intellectual lesion. (13) Clinical investigation in England was not as prevalent as in America or Continental Europe; concern was less with the formulation of medico-psychological theories than with legislative reform and hospital organization. (14) Where there was clinical progress, it tended to follow the lines laid down by Willis and Haslam: study tended to concentrate on the brain and the blood vessels leading to it. (15) Insanity as a disease of the blood was postulated by Sheppard in a crypto-Cartesian treatise which, by dismissing brain lesion in favour of a 'morbid condition of the circulating fluid', maintained the moral force of the mind in controlling insanity. (16) By mid-century, however, this was an eccentric position. Isaac Ray, much respected in England, attested that

> No pathological fact is better established ... than that deviations from the healthy structure are generally present in the brains of insane subjects ... The progress of pathological anatomy during the present century has established this fact beyond reach of a reasonable doubt. (17)

Control of the intellect by the will could still be maintained as the arbiter of insanity, (18) but the operation of pathological factors became increasingly highlighted. The need for more fundamental investigation became obscured, from the third quarter of the century, by a preoccupation with classification which owed much to Continental borrowings, (19) and was intensified by the identification of psychiatry with the asylum. The student of insanity was offered this consoling certainty by Hack Tuke:

> Whatever definition of insanity is adopted by the student, it is all important that he should regard disease as an essential condition; in other words, that insanity is a condition in which the intellectual faculties, or the moral sentiments, or the animal propensities, any one or all of them have their free action destroyed by disease, whether congenital or acquired. He will not go far wrong if he regards insanity as a disease of the brain ... (20)

There was a conspicuous omission to bring out why insanity should be regarded as a disease and a tacit refusal to admit the alienists' secondary role in the labelling process. Medical Superintendents came into contact solely with the certified or institutionalized insane: thus their empirically-derived knowledge was shaped by its objects, cases already successfully labelled. The social nature of this labelling was reflected in the classes of inmates of asylums; it was essential that these classes, then, be made amenable to the proclaimed objectivity of medical classification. In the second half of the century, a changed medical perspective began to emerge in response to psychiatrists' prolonged exposure to the madness of the asylum.

In contrast to the optimistic writings of Tuke and Conolly, there was, as early as the 1830s, a pessimistic challenge to the individualist school. James Cowles Prichard (21) introduced the concept of 'moral insanity', consisting in 'a morbid perversion of the feelings, affections, habits, without any hallucination or erroneous conviction impressed upon the understanding; it sometimes co-exists with an apparently unimpaired state of the intellectual faculties.' (22) This ran counter to Locke, by introducing the element of a-social behaviour, rather than damaged understanding, but the role of the physician remained crucial: only he can discriminate objectively in the area of conduct. (23) This primitive formulation of a theory of psychopathy as an addition to, not a replacement of contemporary awareness of the nature of insanity, was crucial in relocating the alienist's attention. As developed by Maudsley, (24) the organic nature of madness became teamed with Prichard's concept, and the result was a view of the insane as a particular element within a wider residuum of physical and social degeneracy. The influence of Darwin and Spencer on Maudsley and Hack Tuke is glaring. Insanity is seen to consist of the loss of moral sense (25) and the physical constitution of the individual, or of his ancestors, is the cause of that loss:' ... of some criminals as of some insane persons, it may be truly said that they are born, not made...' (26) Confrontation with the ascribed and real madness of the lower orders had, by the 1870's, forced psychiatric opinion steadily away from the Conolly ideal. The collapse of mid-century optimism, reflected in the myth of the Great Depression, (27) extended to psychiatry, offering a further weapon with which to assault the inhabitants of Darkest England. (28) Hack Tuke confirmed the alienation of the alienist from his pauper patient:

> The constitution of the mind must be distinguished from an allied but different organization which is marked by native stupidity, and constitutes an infirm type of humanity largely met with in the lower classes and especially the population from which the great county asylums of England are fed. On admission 'No good' is plainly inscribed on their foreheads. (29)

Hack Tuke here seems to be offering a psychiatric equivalent to the contemporaneously evolving concept of a criminal class, (30) with a somewhat higher reliance on socio-economic factors. (31) In broader terms, this psychiatric Darwinism was redolent of a hardening attitude towards philanthropy: the moral context of mid-century charity stressed that recipients must be deserving, and that the charitable activity should inculcate a self-sufficiency attuned to the approved social ethic. (32) By the third quarter of the century, bureaucratic controls were being introduced to curtail 'indiscriminate' charity towards the residuum of the poor, whether 'deserving' or not. (33)

The mad, and especially the pauper insane, were patently not susceptible to the high degree of self-regulating improvement demanded by this ethic. Therefore, the location of insanity in the malleable area of 'Personality' - where approved educative/therapeutic assault mechanisms could work to restore reason (i.e. acceptable conduct) - gave way to an emphasis on the role of Character, inherited and unchangeable, in determining whether an individual successfully used his will to control his behaviour so as to fulfil an assigned social role. (34) The demise of an internalised structure of insanity led not to an acceptance of societal responsibility, but to a convenient faith in the 'tyranny of organization' through which 'moral degeneracy', at times indistinguishable from vice and crime, (35) is constitutionally communicated. (36)

Ethical, moral and even religious elements were retained, especially for discussion of the insanities of those outside the 'dangerous' or 'perishing' classes. And for the latter, too, indulgence in sexual vice and drink, though emanating from intrinsic psycho-moral degeneracy, were, as causes of insanity, still subjected to moralistic censure more than scientific investigation. (37)

Victorian psychiatry was both thorough and imaginative in locating the predisposing and exciting causes of madness. (38) The reports of county asylum superintendents and licensed house proprietors show a wide range of variables, within which heredity and intemperance figure highest amongst identified physical causes. (39) Most asylums, however, published their causation tables by taking information uncritically from admission orders: thus, the superintendents were simply giving a professional sanction to the 'diagnoses' of parish officials, magistrates and non-specialist medical officers. The determinism and pessimism of the 1870's and after evidenced the psychiatrists' inability to reconcile medical with moral and cultural identification of insanity. Organic defect was, of course, often found to exist in labelled madmen: but only after autopsy.

II

A modern authority has offered the dictum that mental health 'can only be achieved in an environment which provides opportunities for self-expression, social usefulness and the attainment of human satisfactions.' (40) Nineteenth-century social and economic structures precluded the existence of such an environment for the vast proportion of Englishmen and women. At a time when it was being noted with satisfaction how greatly the physical health of the population was improving, there was bewildered helplessness before the ever-increasing numbers of the insane. By the end of the century, there was sufficient public concern to prompt a special official investigation. (41) The reason for the increase, accepted as obvious by mid-century, was both simple and complex. Simple, because it merely reflected the combination of widened institutional provision with sophisticated administrative procedures, which broadened the bases for candidature for the madness label. Once the asylum had become the primary response strategy, and once it had been forced into a custodial function, the numbers of identified/confined lunatics inevitably grew, especially when custodial care prolonged the lifespan of the permanently institutionalized 'chronic' patients. Maudsley was fatalistic about the effects of tighter controls which guaranteed that the potentially certifiable were officially noticed; Bucknill saw in the tendency 'the nicer touch of a finikin civilization' which had 'shrunk from the contact of imperfect fellow creatures.' (42) Yet there was a more complicated question involved: why were alienists widening the scope of their identification?

One reason has been offered above: the need to give medical legitimacy to criteria of social control. A second was the attempt to erect a sociological context for psychiatric theorising by exploring the links between 'civilisation' and insanity. Causal links were posited by European and American alienists in the 1820's, (43) and developed throughout the century. Rothman insists on a qualitative and quantitative change in transplanted European ideas in this context, as developed by American alienists before the Civil War and maintained afterwards. His evidence fails to support his contentions, however, and the argument that the civilisation/insanity link remained in vogue in America after its disappearance in Britain is simply untrue. (44)

We may adopt a portion of Rothman's American model, however, namely the existence of a broadly-based awareness of political, economic and social change on an unprecedented scale, which extended to the medical profession and prompted reassessment of the relationships between society and illness. (45) So far as the alienists were concerned, it occasioned an attempt to provide widened contexts for explaining mental disease.

The dangers of Rothman's overall thesis here become apparent: the asylum-system was, in a sense, 'revolutionary', but it is scarcely valid to carry over what is revolutionary in one area of social organization to an entire theory of society. Simply because there was in America in the 1820's and 1830's a reverential attachment to what was felt to be Colonial social morality, does not permit the conclusion that there was a widespread wish to alter the structure of antebellum society. (46) The belief that insanity was a product of the contemporary social situation led to recognition of a responsibility, which took the form of the erection of surrogate communities. It did not lead society to the recognition of the need to transform <u>itself</u>. The English experience was similar. The loss of traditional values of social morality was lamented with varying degrees of conviction and intensity, and the awareness of loss was confirmed by increasingly visible aspects of change. Yet although there was a wide range of discontent with some of the results of change, there was exceedingly little evidence of desires to rescind the change and return to the past, (47) or to alter the fact of change in any way. Where there was concern it was to effect a finer balance in the incidence and distribution of the effects of change. (48)

When nineteenth-century physicians referred to 'civilization' they appear to have meant one of two things. Either the chain of processes which elevated man from the ranks of the beasts into controlled social intercourse; or, specifically that urban, industrialized society that had explosively emerged in the later eighteenth century. (49) The second seems to have predominated. What concerned those writers who, from the second decade of the nineteenth century to the last, emphasised the civilization-insanity link, was not so much the fact of economic change, but rather the gradually apparent effects of that change on social and cultural and moral life. The thesis was constantly reiterated with little change, save in emphasis. It formed a basic aspect of the alienist's dualistic approach to mental illness. Insistent upon a medical model, yet unable to offer medical treatments or anything but metaphorical medical diagnoses, alienists related the bulk of predisposing and exciting causes of insanity to the suppositious organic consequences of social and cultural variables. There was little attempt to explore the precise nature of the connections; instead, general assumptions were expounded regarding the influence of poverty, malnutrition, bad housing and so on. Most surprisingly in such a self-consciously numerate environment, there was little serious attempt at statistical analysis. In lieu of careful smallscale investigation Regency and Victorian psychiatrists turned to the grand assertion.

At times these assertions dealt with a specific social or political structure, though the function of such structures was always implicit. 'Civilization' came gradually to refer to the industrialized, urbanized social structures of western advanced economies, though traces of late eighteenth-century implications of a corrosive sophistication of manners and morals, as common to declining Rome as to expanding Britain, remained. There were, too, writers like T.B. Belgrave, who contrived to extrapolate purely political climates as direct causal forces, even operating on epidemic scales:

> It appears that the evident decadence of Danish power of late years has so afflicted the national sentiment as to induce a general gloom and melancholy ... A conviction pervades the Danish nation that it is doomed to absorption in Germany ... In social intercourse the destiny of the nation is constantly discussed and lamented. One result of this painful feeling is an increase in the proportion of lunatics to the general population. The predominating form of mental disease is melancholia, characterised in the majority of instances by a distressingly strong tendency to suicide. (50)

Belgrave was offering 'concrete' evidence of a hypothesis put forward half a century before by the influential Burrows, (51) who argued that insanity

> bears always a striking relation to political events. Great political or civil revolutions in states are always productive of great enthusiasms in the people, and correspondent vicissitudes in their moral condition; and as all extremes in society are exciting causes, it will occur, that in proportion as the feelings are acted upon, so will insanity be more or less frequent. (52)

Burrows was suggesting that insanity was rooted not so much in the individual - a somewhat dissentient note for his day - but in the social structure itself. Moreover, certain variations in that structure would inevitably produce insanity within the population. The stress was on moral/emotional identification, located 'within the people': implicit, then was the hypothesis that (extreme) change must beget insanity; that having experienced a change of this nature, society could not rescind or alter the new circumstances in any 'extreme' fashion without producing more frequent insanity. The logical, though unstated, outcome must be that there is a potential situation in which the 'people' become 'insane' in inevitably increasing numbers, until, conceivably, the insane will form a majority within the population. Since the only proffered yardstick by which insanity might be measured was that of relative normality, all meaningful identification collapsed. (53)

Burrows' only other departure from the accepted line was his dismissal of the lesser liability to insanity of primitive tribes. This Rousseauesque myth was widespread and tenacious. (54) Sir Andrew Halliday succinctly presented the total evidence for the belief: 'we seldom meet with insanity among the savage tribes of men; not one of our African travellers remark their having seen a single madman.' (55)

The appeal of the travestied 'noble savage' myth is clear, and its popularity outlived its existence as an acceptable truth. By the second decade of the nineteenth century, the immunity of savages to insanity was an accepted part of the alienist's canon. William Browne took the fact as read, and used it to support the idea of a causal link between 'mechanical civilization' and madness:

> With civilization ... come sudden and agitating changes and vicissitudes of fortune; vicious effeminacy of manners; complicated transactions; misdirected views of the objects of life; ambitions, hopes and fears, which man in his primitive state does not or cannot know. But these neither constitute nor are they necessarily connected with civilization. They are defects, obstacles, which retard the advancement of that amelioration of conditions, towards which, every discovery in arts, or ethics, must ultimately end. To these defects and not to the amount of improvement

> or refinement of a people is insanity to be traced. (56)

Browne was preaching a moral lesson: modern society was going downhill because it was losing sight of a traditional morality in the urgency of industrialization. Civilization was guilty of being unable to control the forces it spawned. (57)

'Tradition' was an important criterion. In 1816, a writer in the Quarterly Review pointed to the mental ill effects of social and cultural ambition: the new breed of capitalist farmers with their 'desire ... to soar into the Superior ranks of life' had laid themselves and their families open to the risk of nervous disorder (a 'shade of actual lunacy') or madness by altering their traditional lifestyles. The farmer's wife suffered 'ennui', since 'she gave herself up to all the indulgencies of the tea-table, and sent her **daughters** to the boarding school to be manufactured into misses.' In this climate, 'the apothecary is the only individual who has benefitted by the conversion of cultivators of land into cultivators of arts and sciences.' (58) The lower orders were seen as becoming 'nervous with the nervousness of the times' (59) and their lack of native wit exposed them to the mental ravages of a socially-disruptive Methodism which their social superiors could resist. (60)

Civilization, by mid-century, was generally seen to be a disposing factor in the causation of insanity. (61) The specific incidence of madness was seen to be mediated by class cultural factors, (62) though some forms of insanity, produced by vicious living, were felt to operate independently of class norms. (63) Propensity to such lifestyles, however, or opportunity to indulge in them, were seen as personal inadequacies (lack of 'will power') aggravated by the dynamics of changing civilization. (64) There were early research-based refutations of the theory, but these were largely ignored. P.L. Panum, for example, studied the population of the Faroe Islands with respect to the incidence of both measles and insanity, and concluded:

> Since it has been proved that the frequence of mental diseases is generally in direct proportion to civilization and its accompanying social collisions, it might be surmised that these diseases are extremely rare in the Faroes ... But ... there is hardly any other country, or indeed any metropolis, in which mental diseases are so frequent in proportion to the number of people as the Faroes ... (65)

Other writers began doubting the usefulness of existing language, though the prevailing orthodoxy was not discarded. Edgar Sheppard of Colney Hatch was one of the first to challenge the inexactness of the term 'civilization' and called for investigations into the differential prevalence of insanity, relative to sex, age, environment and so on. (66) Another plea came from W.R. MacDermott, who advocated the study of the frequency of mental diseases in specific temporal and spatial contexts, (67) but the medical profession as a whole remained concerned with broader views.

During the 1860's a more sanguine attitude emerged. The socio-political critique of Burrows and Belgrave (and of Rothman's assemblage of American critics) was transformed by English alienists into a strategically more insidious identification. Maudsley, the 'father of English psychiatry', was anxious to show insanity as essentially consisting in degrees of moral and organic degeneration. The insane were assessed as victims of the side-effects of rapidly industrializing civilization: overpopulation, overcrowding, stress, poverty. The insane were, essentially, those too weak to adapt to prevailing conditions. Just as bodily disease indicated organic maladaptation to the physical environment, so mental disease showed up inherent personality failure in people described as 'the waste thrown up by the strong but silent stream of progress.' Thus, the prevalence of mental disorder was not a symptom of national degeneration, but the opposite: the mad were 'examples of decaying reason thrown off by vigorous mental growth, the energy of which they testify.' (68) This was the language of hardened laissez faire tinged with Darwinian determinism which eventually produced elsewhere such outbursts as the following, from the economist Alfred Marshall:

> There are no feeble people in the prairies. Some feeble people go there, but they either get back quickly to a large town, or else they die. Charity and sanitary regulations are keeping alive, in our large towns, thousands of such persons, who would have died even fifty years ago. Meanwhile, economic forces are pressing heavily on them, for they can do nothing but easy monotonous work, most of which can be done as well or better by machinery or children. Public or private charity may palliate their misery, but the only remedy is to prevent such people from coming into existence ... (P)ersons in any rank of life who are not in good physical and mental health have no moral right to have children. (69)

Emphasis had moved completely away from the individual; but 'blame' no longer attached to the abstraction of 'civilization', which was seen to have a corrosive force only on those individuals naturally determined to be corroded. There could be, therefore, no reason to effect changes within the social structure so as to enable the weak to adjust to a social role.

The more simplified version of the civilization-insanity thesis retained a strong hold until the end of the century. In their classic textbook of 1858, Bucknill and Tuke declared that 'other things being equal, civilization does, on the whole, render men more liable to mental disease.' (70) Popularisers dropped all qualifications: for the ever-assertive L.S.F. Winslow, 'mental alienation' was essentially a by-product of 'modern European civilization.' (71) In

Lancashire, the high incidence of ascribed insanity amongst the immigrant Irish prompted the Superintendent of Prestwich Asylum to offer a localized variant:

> It would appear as if the general tendencies of civilization, in large cities and populous manufacturing districts, are such as to exhaust nervous vitality and predispose to structural nervous degeneration. The Irish peasant, in his native country, has a marked immunity from these ... forms of brain disorders, but when transplanted into centres of labour and activity like Lancashire or Middlesex, he is often apt to acquire a form of mental disease ... progressive in its nature, and little susceptible of cure. (72)

Hack Tuke even rehearsed the psychiatric version of the 'noble savage' - though his attitude was inconsistent. Elsewhere, his association with Spencer took him into Maudsley's camp, when he argued that the apparent absence of insanity amongst savages was the result of the non-survival of the unfittest. Tuke was representative of the psychiatric Establishment in his uneasy grasp of the social and cultural concepts with which the profession was attempting to deal. The lower orders of civilized communities were envisaged as differing in kind from primitive savages, yet in ways not always comprehended by their superior fellow countrymen. It was thus necessary for Tuke to explain an apparent departure from the 'immunity of savages' notion: 'A South Seas Islander might be much more ignorant than the Wiltshire labourer, and yet not be so circumstanced that he would likely to transgress the laws of mental health.' (73) In amplifying his point, Tuke leapt from a quasi-sociological stance into thinly disguised moral polemic: 'European civilization' was definitely 'a cause of insanity' - but

> ... when I say this, I do not mean that if we take one man and educate and refine him, and take another man and make him a labourer on a miserable pittance, with a large family to bring up, living in a crowded dwelling, half-fed, yet frequently half-drunk, the former will degenerate into insanity or imbecility more readily than the latter; but I say, that the labourer of a civilized community is often more exposed to unfavourable psychological influences than the members of a wholly uncivilized tribe ... (74)

The decisive factor was 'the mixed character and influence' of European civilization:

> ... its action on the one hand in evolving forms of mental life of exquisite delicacy and sensibility, easily injured or altogether crushed by the rough blasts from which they cannot escape; and on the other hand in producing a state confounded with ... savagery, but which differs from it ... Recklessness, drunkenness, poverty, misery,

> characterize the class; and no wonder that from such a source spring the hopelessly incurable lunatics who crowd out pauper asylums, to the horror of ratepayers and to the surprise of those who cannot understand why the natives of Madagascar ... do not require a single lunatic asylum. (75)

This substratum of society was in a condition worse than savagery, being 'squalid, and drunken and sensual.'

The reversion to Hobbesian language in the grandson of the founder of the Retreat was indicative of the degree of disillusion experienced by British alienists in the 1870's. The optimism of the early part of the century had rested on the belief that proper social values could be communicated to the labelled transgressor, who might then be restored ('cured') to society. But in the alienists' own eyes, the mass of lunatic paupers had never 'belonged' to society in the first place, so were not susceptible to moral, restorative treatments. The situation was aggravated by the addition to the residuum of large numbers of immigrants. When sane Irishmen were simianised by Victorian writers, cartoonists and politicians, the alienist had clearly small chance of acculturating the mad into an acceptable social role. (76)

Cultural alienation had a dual influence for first-generation Irish in England. (77) Their 'white negro' role subjected them to a wide range of deviance-labels, whilst their, generally, low economic status hindered stable transfer of any community-based welfare strategies they might have possessed in Ireland. (78) Differing in race, creed, language from their peers, they were initially still further removed from those who sanctioned official assessments of their behaviour. In areas of Lancashire where Irish settlement was heaviest, and employment more sensitive to the fluctations of overseas trade, admissions into the asylum rose. (79) Dietetic and housing disadvantages increased liability to physical collapse; the ascription of insanity, whether deriving from socially challenging refusal or inability to become 'assimilated', or from local poor law tactics, drove up the proportion of Irish to total confined lunatics to the outrage of Lancashire ratepayers. (80) The stresses inherent in the social structure, which alienists recognised from at least the 1850's, as militating against the mental health of the working class as a whole, exposed the immigrant to high pressures at a time he was least able to withstand them. (81)

Modern research has indicated that preliterate groups exhibiting low incidence of insanity tend to increase their proportionate share of mental disorder when translated to a more advanced cultural context. Forms of disorder which had been totally absent in the original environment assume an above average incidence. (82) Although the Irish asylums in fact predated the English (83) and admitted a similar range of patients, Irish pauper lunatics in the Lancashire and Middlesex asylums displayed a tendency towards syphilis of the brain (84) which was absent or not diagnosed in Ireland.

Behaviour patterns tolerated within the community in Ireland were subjected to official assessment, so that despite preserved familial structures, it is likely that persons were institutionalized in England who would have been communally protected and/or disciplined in rural Ireland. (85) At least half of the Irish in Lancashire settled in and around Liverpool, and hence were taken into Rainhill Asylum if the madness label were successfully applied. From the opening of the institution (1851) the Irish figured highly: rising from 29% of the asylum admissions in 1853 to 38% in 1871. A high proportion appears to have been incurables; at the latter date, Irish patients accounted for 45% of the total numbers resident. (86) At Lancaster Moor Asylum, for the year 1862 - 63, there was a 65% admission. (87)

The majority of Irish immigrants were suffering from what a Scottish Lunacy Commissioner perceptively described as 'want of civilization'. Sir James Coxe argued that urban industrial society had produced a situation in which the greater portion of its members were afflicted with a range of bodily and mental failures resulting from their position outside the beneficient operations of that society. Coxe urged a reassessment of existing relationships, but refrained from proposing social change. In what amounted to a restatement of the humanism of the Romantic psychiatry of the 1820's and 1830's, Coxe demanded that the deviant be changed and/or protected by benevolent use of the resources of society, from the ills incident to the accumulation of those resources. (88) Inevitably, the role of the asylum was bolstered: only there might the benefits of civilization be tasted without exposing the inadequate to the sideswipes of the Hobbesian free-for-all by which the momentum of civilized progress was maintained. But other total institutions were not so favoured by psychiatrists. Turning away from the lower orders, Hack Tuke warned of the susceptibility of the 'cultured mind' to attack: at school or college, over indulgence in study could lead to 'graduating in a lunatic asylum.' Even the bourgeois virtues of application and hard work could, if not moderated, lead to mental collapse. The key to moderating the pressures of civilization was Moderation itself - in all things. Significantly, Tuke lumped the upper and lower classes together in terms of immoderation: a self-indulgent lifestyle, whether afforded by luxury or as an escape from 'monotony ... misery and anxiety' was a common source of 'preventable lunacy.' For the middle classes, Tuke gave first mention to the machinations of the liberal economy: 'stress of business, excessive competition, failures ...' The moral gulf implicit was a wide one. (89)

III

The vast majority of lunatics under legal restraint during the nineteenth century were paupers. With contemporaneous increases in insanity and pauperism, the authorities looked to discover relationships, and, if possible, any element of common causality. The commonsense of Maudsley and others who pointed to the factors of increased institutional accumulation of cases, and to the tighter working of the lunacy laws, was untypical. The poverty of available statistics was recognized, but figures were popularly believed to underestimate. By the third quarter of the century, official opinion was sharing popular concern, especially as the proportion of pauper lunatics in the already high pauper population rose dramatically. (90) Administrative development, in this case the New Poor Law, was a key factor in the pauperisation of many who would, under flexible implementation of the Elizabethan Poor Law, have maintained themselves precariously in the ranks of 'the poor'. (91) The voices of authority here spoke in terms of an individualist ethic, set in a matrix of utilitarian Christianity and trapped out as science: their point of contact with the alienist was plain. Recognition that the poor seem always to be with us, led to a comfortable theory that unemployment and poverty were economically organic: an unfortunate necessity when viewed in the abstract; the result of improvidence and self-willed idleness when one came down to the individual. (92) The demoralizing and dehumanized role of pauper, firmly scripted by the Benthamite bureaucrats of 1832 - 34, entailed a moral as well as a socio-economic ascription of failure, whilst private charity tended to reflect the donor's spiritual ambition (personal or for the receiver) and claim to status. (93) Ideally, statutory and communal responses were to reinforce the moral censure, which could be retained even where seemingly acknowledged as inapplicable. An anonymous writer in 1836 admitted that

> When a large share of the poverty amongst us has been assigned either to causes of general operation, or to the direct influence of moral disorder, there still remains an extreme class of indigent sufferers, whose misfortunes arise from circumstances peculiar to individuals, or unconnected with personal culpability ... such are the incurably insane, idiotic or diseased; the deaf and dumb; and the irremediably blind.

However, he continued to indicate that these unfortunates were either morally corrupt, or suffering from the results of the corruption of others:

> In these cases, the primary causes of poverty have commonly been regarded as utterly beyond the reach of human control. Recent medical testimonies have, however, shown that an almost incredible proportion of the worst diseases, which prevail among the poor, are either the direct consequence of habitual drunkenness, or are entailed upon them by the intemperance of their parents. The most hopeless cases of insanity are those which proceed from the use of ardent spirits ... (94)

It had been one argument against out-relief that the poor would only spend subsistence cash on drink, or re-sell payments in kind for drink-money, (95) and the profusion of gin-shops and, after 1830, beer-houses, in the towns indicated the extent of the working classes' predilection for alcohol. Blinkered by their own confused morality, economists, alienists, sociologists and clergy mistook cause and effect with disastrous results. Maudsley and Coxe, for example, granted importance to the working and living conditions of the lower orders as decisive factors in physical and mental illness careers. (96) According to Coxe,

> ... it may be assumed, that it is not the overstraining of the powers of the mind that mainly tends to produce insanity, but those causes of physical disease to which the lower orders are chiefly exposed. Such are dissipation in its various forms, over-work of body, insufficient food, the respiration of a corrupted air, and the neglect of intellectual and moral culture. (97)

Friedrich Engels was at least physically nearer the lower orders for some time, and was more understanding of the relationship between poverty, drink and disease.

There was, he indicated, the basic detrimental factor of malnutrition, for which the individual was not responsible: 'Nearly all suffer from indigestion, and consequently from a more or less hypochondriac, melancholy, nervous condition. Their enfeebled constitutions are unable to resist disease...' Engels, too, understood the social and psychological function of alcohol: 'Liquor is almost their only source of pleasure, and all things conspire to make it accessible to them ...'

The blame was to be located in the environment, not in the individual's character:

> His unnerved, uncomfortable, hypochondriac state of mind and body arising from his unhealthy condition, and especially from indigestion, is aggravated by the general conditions of his life, the uncertainty of his existence, his dependence upon all possible accidents and chances, and his inability to do anything towards gaining an assured position ... his social need can be gratified only in the public house ... It is morally and physically inevitable that, under such circumstances, a very large number of working-men should fall into intemperance ... Drunkenness has ceased to be a vice ... (98)

This, Engels noted, was especially true of the Irish population - an impression borne out by the scale of admissions of Irishmen into the Lancashire asylums.

Few writers shared these views. The observable fact that the poor drank was sufficient, apparently, to justify the notion of a causal relationship which could only work in one direction. By the third quarter of the nineteenth century, the causal force of drink in begetting pauperism was part of the orthodox sociological canon. In 1883, Francis Peek could assert unhesitatingly that 'full three-fourths of England's pauperism is the direct or indirect effect of drunkenness.' (99) Inevitably, since there was such a significant incidence of labelled pauper insanity, drink must play some causal role: Shaftesbury placed his own estimate of insanity induced by drink at 60%, though medical specialists were more conservative. (100) Alienists had stressed the causal role of intemperance, as both predisposing and exciting factor, since the mid-eighteenth century. Battie had referred to

> The many bottle-companions whose pulses beat high and quick, whose faces are flushed with blood in the same manner as if they were strangled, who are first wild and then stupid, who drink till they see double, and then drink on till they cannot see at all, as well as the crowds of wretches that infest the streets and fill our hospitals evidently prove to the vulgar as well as to the Physician that vinous spirits instantaneously provoke an irregular action of the muscles succeeded by temporary delirium; and that, if the same noxious draughts are taken in too large doses or frequently repeated, they become a very common, tho' remoter cause for continual madness. (101)

Burrows categorically delineated 'habitual drunkenness' as 'a moral lesion, productive among the common people of the larger number of the insane,' whilst Moseley saw alcohol as producing 'a deteriorating effect on the brain, as the spur which stimulates the horse.' (102) Daniel Noble grouped alcohol with cannabis and opium as destructive of brain and nervous system. (103) From then the belief was ingrained, and by the 1870's, Maudsley could casually point to alcohol as a major factor in the differential prevalence of insanity between civilized and African nations. (104) In the supercharged atmosphere of the late 1890's, L.S.F. Winslow addressed himself to his public thus:

> The object I have in writing this book is to place before my readers ... (a) question which has come before the considerations, on more than one occasion, of the House of Commons, as to the alarming increase of insanity ... I have endeavoured to show that the increase ... is real and not apparent ... due to that terrible vice, indulgence in alcohol ... (105)

This was the culmination of a half-century's accumulation of statistical evidence. From the early 1850's, the medical officers of the big county asylums had reproduced tabular confirmation of local officialdom's assigned causes, in which intemperance was prominent. Hood at Colney Hatch coupled drink with debauchery as key causal factors of madness among pauper males; Eccleston at Rainhill linked alcohol with perverted religious feelings. (106) Clinical writings from outside the public sector confirmed the model. Right through until the turn of the century, the causal force of drunkenness was proclaimed: Rainhill's figures indicated a higher incidence in the 1890's than in the 1850's, despite the growing psychiatric insistence on hereditary organic defect and on neuroses. The other Lancashire asylums followed the pattern: whilst heredity began to match intemperance in frequency in causality tables, the latter maintained its pre-eminence in most years. (107) In 1879, for example, the Prestwich MO had noted a significant decline in admissions of drink-induced insanity, and pointed to the increase in the combination of hereditary with other factors; but attachment to orthodox psychiatric theory did not last: during the later 1880's and the 1890's, Prestwich was again showing over 20% of admissions as being drink-caused. (108) In the 1870's, attacks were launched on the simple correlation of alcohol and madness. John Bucknill criticised easy acceptance of shaky numerical date, and stressed the inadequacy of working from information on admission orders:

> If a lunatic of the lower classes has been drinking at all heavily, the relieving officer will be sure to know of it, and will be extremely likely to put down intemperance as the cause of insanity, whether it be so or not. (109)

At Prestwich Asylum, H.R. Ley executed a complete volte face. In 1875, he had asserted that

> The question of the increase or decrease of insanity resolves itself into one of the increase or decrease of causes, and it cannot be too widely known that Intemperance, directly or indirectly, wholly or in part, is incontrovertibly one of the chief causes of insanity in Lancashire.

Four years later, he was following the trend set by the Darwinian psychiatry:

> In all cases where any reliable history can be ascertained, the disease has been traced to a combination of causes, in which hereditary and other disturbing influences, both moral and physical, would seem to be the most important factors. A marked decrease is observable in the number of those to whom intemperance in drink exists as a complicating cause. (110)

During the 1870's Rainhill continued to feature intemperance highly - perhaps serving a seaport, this might be simply explained, - but a sophisticated approach was being exhibited elsewhere. In 1880, a meeting of the B.M.A. in Cambridge indicated the scope of changed attitudes. Dr. Bacon, the MO of Fulbourn Asylum, suggested that the relationship between alcohol and insanity was grossly exaggerated: of 75 cases of insanity assigned to drink in his own asylum, at least 40 could be attributed to other causes. (111) Dr. J. Seaton went further: he had never met a single case where the chief cause of insanity was drink. Other speakers were less sweeping, arguing that the indirect effects of alcohol were of greater importance (Dr. Ridge of Enfield), or that alcohol was a contributing cause, promoting insanity in men who, ordinarily temperate, resorted to drink in personal crises (Dr. Brushwood of Brookwood Asylum). (112) An article by William Huggard pointed out that when signers of certificates claimed that insanity was caused by drink, what they really meant was that it was preceded by it. (113)

During the 1850's and 1860's, asylum superintendents were prone to accept the admission order's glib reference to immediate antecedent causes as sufficient for their own statistics, (114) but the growth of interest in hereditary factors led to a desire for as much information on prepatient careers as possible - though this was rarely forthcoming from the local authorities, normally the workhouse or the police. (115) Thus asylum causation tables, and Lunacy Commissioners' compound figures, continued to reflect the post hoc, propter hoc diagnoses of relieving officers. Intemperance retained its position, though there were attempts to view it within a broader perspective: the Prestwich superintendent offered an amalgam of cultural, Maudsley-Darwinian and economic matrices:

> ... in Lancashire, there is a constant immigration going on from Ireland and the neighbouring counties of people attracted to the manufacturing districts in the hope of finding employment. Many of these are persons of originally defective mental organization, who are easily upset by the hardships and worries of their new life ... Intemperance in drink ... instead of acting alone, has efficiently aided some other agency, and so produced the disease. (116)

In the Lunacy Commissioners' reports after 1870, intemperance always figured highly, for recognizably industrial areas. In agricultural districts - Cumberland, Westmoreland, the south-west, the south-central and eastern counties - drink was an insignificant factor. (117)

Thus, in the Commissioners' Report for 1877, intemperance was indicated as the highest single known cause of disorder in all the Lancashire county asylums, and in the county or borough institutions of Chester, Macclesfield, Derby, Durham, Glamorgan, Colney Hatch, Hanwell, Monmouthshire, Nottingham, Stafford, Wandsworth, Brookwood, the North Riding, the West Riding, and Birmingham. (118) Of asylums catering to definably industrial areas, only Sheffield and Newcastle failed to follow this pattern, whilst none of the agricultural districts featured intemperance highly. Ten years later, despite the questioning of the 1870's, James Shaw was able to give the following causation table, computed from the Commissioners' reports for the years 1878 - 89: (119)

TABLE 10

Causes of Insanity

Moral Causes of Insanity	Percentage of Cases Male	Female	Total
Domestic (including bereavement)	4.2	9.7	7.0
Adverse Circumstances	8.2	3.7	5.9
Mental anxiety/Overwork	6.6	5.5	6.0
Religious Excitement	2.5	2.9	2.7
Love (including Seduction)	0.7	2.5	1.6
Fright or Nervous Shock	0.9	1.9	1.4
Physical Causes of Insanity			
Intemperance (Drink)	19.8	7.2	13.4
Intemperance (Sex)	1.0	0.6	0.8
Venereal Disease	0.8	0.6	0.7
Self-abuse	2.1	0.2	1.2
Over-exertion	0.7	0.4	0.5
Sunstroke	2.3	0.2	1.2
Accident/Injury	5.2	1.0	3.0
Pregnancy		1.0	0.5
Parturition		6.7	3.4
Lactation		2.2	1.1
Puberty		0.6	0.4
Change of Life	0.2	4.0	2.0
Fevers	0.7	0.5	0.6
Privation/Starvation	1.7	2.1	1.9
Old Age	3.8	4.6	4.2
Other Bodily Disease	11.1	10.5	10.8
Previous Attacks	14.3	18.9	16.6
Hereditary	19.0	22.1	20.5
Congenital Defect	5.1	3.5	4.3
Other Known Causes	2.3	1.0	1.7
Unknown	21.3	20.1	20.7

The table includes private as well as pauper patients, but is instructive as to the continuing trend. A breakdown of the Commissioners' own tables in a random year gives conclusive indications of the persistence of the idea: (120)

TABLE 11

Assigned Causes of Insanity, 1881

Cause	Male	Female	Total
	Percentage		
Drink	19.3	6.6	12.9
Hereditary	18.2	21.2	19.7
Previous Attack	14.5	18.8	16.7
Unknown	21.8	22.1	21.9

When arranged by class the figures resolve as in Table 12

TABLE 12

Cause	Male	Female	Total
Paupers			
Drink	19.3	6.3	12.7
Hereditary	18.8	20.5	19.7
Previous attack	14.8	19.2	17.1
Private			
Drink	19.1	8.3	14.0
Hereditary	14.9	25.1	19.7
Previous attack	12.9	16.4	14.5

Male paupers lent weight to the drink-insanity link, and the higher total incidence in private patients casts doubts on the sincerity of those alienists who had claimed relieving officers' incompetence as explanatory of high alcoholic insanity figures amongst paupers: no relieving officer signed papers for private patients, but a magistrate and two doctors. (121) A closer look at the figures shows that in county asylums and borough asylums, drink figured highly only in the institutions shown in Table 13.

TABLE 13

Asylum	Total Admissions	Drink	Hereditary	Unknown
Chester	176	34		
Parkside	117	20		
Durham	284	58	63	80
Lancaster	327	51	90	91
Rainhill	190	35		66
Prestwich	395	69		112

TABLE 13 (Cont.)

Asylum	Total Admissions	Drink	Hereditary	Unknown
Whittingham	266	43	62	72
Banstead	263	17		197
Colney Hatch	460	62		194
Hanwell	249	41	54	46
Nottingham (County)	106	24		32
Wandsworth	354	46		71
Brookwood	210	30	46	
Wakefield	457	90	152	
Wadsley	482	67	132	71
Birmingham	209	42		
Hull	66	12	17	15
Stone	64	20		
Newcastle	90	20		
Nottingham (Borough)	93	16		

If male paupers only are taken, drink induced insanity emerges as the highest accepted assigned cause in eleven out of the twenty institutions. (Table 14)

TABLE 14

Asylum	Male Admissions	Drink	Percentage
Chester	90	30	33
Parkside	61	16	23
Durham	150	52	35
Hanwell	121	28	23
Nottingham (County)	36	13	36
Wadsley	204	57	28
Birmingham	99	30	30
Hull	31	9	28
Stone	36	15	42
Newcastle	42	15	36
Nottingham (Borough)	53	11	21

In all other asylums, except Wandsworth, Brookwood and Wakefield, where hereditary causality was dominant, the highest proportion of admissions were marked down as unknown as to cause of disorder. At all except Prestwich and Whittingham, drink emerged as the highest known cause. All twenty asylums catered to populous industrial or manufacturing areas. (122)

The moral dimensions were not lost to the psychiatrists. David Yellowlees of the Glamorgan Asylum recorded that during a strike lasting nine months, male admissions to the asylum were down by 50%, whilst there was little change in the number of females admitted, and was confident that 'the decrease is doubtless mainly due to the fact that there is no money to spend in drink and debauchery.' (123) H.R. Ley was equally certain of the connection between economic well-being and madness:

> The greatest number of admissions in this asylum always occur during the month or six weeks following the Lancashire Carnival, Whitweek. In the month of June last year, no less than 17 males and 4 females were admitted suffering from mania induced by excessive and persistent drinking ... These instances of the direct effect of intemperance occurred with scarcely an exception among a class who were in receipt of good wages from regular employment, and who, therefore, had not the excuse of the half-starved and ill clad poor. There is no disguising the fact, that among the labouring classes insanity has of late years increased by a reckless course of inebriety, favoured in great measure by a plethora of money and an abundance of leisure... (124)

Classical economists had argued that for the economic health of the nation, the poor should be kept poor. Apparently, such a state would aid its mental health, too. That it would ease ratepayers' minds was also evident. Edmund Whitcombe, Assistant MO at the Birmingham Borough Asylum communicated the institution's experience of drink-induced insanity to the local press. Between 1851 and 1876, one pauper in seven had had his or her malady caused by drink, and their maintenance had cost £36,000. (125) The Lunacy Commissioners' report of that year showed 3,172 cases of alcoholic insanity out of a year's total admissions of 33,527. This gave the staggering general proportion of one in eleven, (inclusive of all categories of sex and status). Average county asylum costs in 1875 - 76 were 10s. per head per week, which entailed an annual expenditure of £26,108 on this class of disorder. (126)

Hack Tuke considered the public's sense of proportion needed changing, and suggested inhibiting the sale of alcohol:

> Although ratepayers grumble about the building of large lunatic asylums, it is amazing how meekly they bear with the great cause of their burden and how suicidally they resent any attempt to reduce by legislation the area of this widespread and costly mischief. (127)

In view of the political influence of the brewing and distilling interest, (128) Tuke was being unrealistic. But he was indicative of the medical profession's growing desire for government controls in the drink trade. (129) The doctors, like the rest of Victorian society, did not distinguish too carefully between drunkenness and alcoholism, nor were they always specific about the kinds of alcohol they had in mind, (130) Since Battie had spoken of 'vinous spirits' and asylums throughout the next century and a half used wine and porter as tonic treatments, one is left to assume that the psychiatrist, like the average temperance man, was anti-spirits rather than totally against alcohol. (131) By the 1860's and 1870's, the social and dietetic functions of alcoholic consumption had changed. From being a staple meal drink, beer had begun to acquire its present-day status, as alternative beverages became cheaper and entered the diet of the lower classes. At the same time consumption of beer and spirits increased.(132) Class differences in the venue of consumption led to a higher frequency of home drinking amongst the middle and upper classes, which relegated the public house and beershop to low-status group haunts. From the 1830's the beershops had been associated with civil disturbances; from the third quarter of the century, the clientele of drinking places encouraged middle-class identification of drink with public disorder, violence, vice and crime. (133) As early as the 1840's, Delinquency was added to square the Drink- Pauperism - Insanity triangle. Areas displaying high crime: drunkenness ratios, were seen also to show a high incidence of alcoholic insanity. Cultural criteria were invoked to indicate the high rural prevalence of both crime and insanity from the 1830's to the 1870's. (134) The dubious nature of the statistics - and of all statistical date in this area (135) - failed to alter conviction. Mr. Justice Wightman was adamant:

> According to my experience, at least three quarters of the criminal charges that are brought to trial at the assizes originate in habits of intemperance, and spending all leisure time in public houses, the parties being usually ignorant, unable to read or write, and as it would seem, incapable of appreciating any other mode of enjoyment or occupying their leisure. (136)

Mid-century reformers were appalled at the level of juvenile crime, and it seemed only natural to trace the acquisition of delinquent behaviour to fraternization with the (obviously criminal) clientele of the beershop. The Rev. H. Worsley placed the beershop top of his list of causes of rural crime and intemperance as the major cause of juvenile delinquency. (137) Looking back to his youth, Joseph Arch noted that 'lounging and boozing in the public house' was the only alternative recreation to bowling for the young of the village, (138) and Worsley's memoir of the lad who graduated to organised poaching in such an environment was cautionary: the 'ruin' brought about by the beershop could lead to not just breach of the game laws, but, by association, to 'sanguinary violence'. (139) The connection between drink and violent crime was real enough - and more so in the towns than in the countryside, (140) though the responsibility of alcohol in crimes against property, asserted anecdotally rather than statistically, was negligible. (141) Crimes against property were seen to increase at the same time that consumption of alcohol increased, and for similar reasons: an upswing in the trade cycle which brought more diffuse prosperity. Want and crime were not related; the lower orders drank more when they had money, but larcenies and thefts were commonly committed by members of definable subcultures. (142) Even begging was not easily entered upon by distressed workers. (143) Yet there were commentators who stressed the role of drink in turning workers into criminals. The Recorder of Birmingham, for example, in 1847:

> In the Manufacturing districts a flush of prosperity, which suddenly enhances the rate of wages, overwhelms the working classes to indulge in liquor - a cause of crime which is more potent for its increase than the diffusion of plenty is for its diminution. (144)

The acceptance of belief in rural prevalence, placed at mid-century at between 5% and 7% above the crime average for the nation as a whole, (145) encouraged the alienist to point a simple connection of deviance forms:

> It is evident that the same causes which conduce to the increase of pauperism and crime promote also the development of insanity ... The cause of crime and insanity prevailing more in the rural districts than in towns may, perhaps, be ascribed to the circumstances of the uneducated poor in the country not having the same stimulus to mental activity as the working classes in the towns. When the agricultural labourer has tilled the ground and the seed has been sown, he is comparatively idle. He may ... find other employment, but how, in adverse weather and during the long winter evenings does he pass his time? In towns the poorer classes find their way into mechanics' institutes, reading rooms, or, perhaps, places of public amusement ... but in the country no such resources exist. The village beer shop is the common place of resort ... (146)

Drink, and the public house, were however, an integral part of working class life in many areas - both rural and urban - until the early twentieth century. Drink played a part in the workday in northern workshops and southern farms that had an ancient ancestry. Despite the changes noted by Harrison, pubs in Salford at the turn of the century still functioned as wage-paying centres, and Suffolk ale-houses had strategic roles in preserving a lively popular culture, aspects of which the middleclasses were just beginning to approve. (147) The literate culture that Hood and others saw as some protection from vice and insanity was in towns confined to the labour aristocracy and its cultural hangers-on. And literacy was no proof against insanity, or the labelling processes which resulted in confinement. High illiteracy levels amongst convicted criminals were found; and criminality was seen by some as product of the lack of intellectual ability and attainment. Yet Eccleston in 1851 showed that of 297 admissions into Rainhill, 110 could read and write, and 84 were able to read. (148)

Hood was simply wrong. Drink-caused crime, like drink-induced insanity was markedly higher in manufacturing areas. (149) Thus a table of the relative incidence of apprehensions as 'Drunk and Disorderly' for 1868 provides the following extract:

TABLE 15

Town	Population	Apprehensions	Proportion to Population
Bolton	70,395	1,217	1:58
Birmingham	296,076	2,310	1:128
Huddersfield	22,163	817	1:69
Leeds	207,165	1,364	1:151
Liverpool	443,938	14,451	1:30
Manchester	338,722	9,540	1:35
Warrington	26,431	836	1:31
Exeter	33,738	43	1:803
Norwich	74,891	103	1:727
Oxford	27,560	11	1:2,469

(Source: Adapted from Graham's Temperance Almanack 1868-70)

By the 1870's some of the more simplistic couplings of drink and deviance were being reassessed - though the reassessments were not universally popular within the medical profession where they originated. The phenomenon of drunkenness was becoming separated from that of drinking. Moral opprobrium attached to both, but the former, when habitual, was, by some doctors, being viewed as a disease comparable to insanity, but not necessarily constituting insanity. (150) By 1879, a Commons' lobby, led by Donald Dalrymple, had succeeded in obtaining a Select Committee investigation (1872) and a permissive Habitual Drunkards Act. 'To speak of "liberty" in connection with drunkenness (whether insane or not), is in very serious earnest,a total abuse of the word,' wrote W.T. Gairdner. 'The irreclaimable drunkard... can only be restored to anything at all resembling liberty by putting him under some restraint.' (151)

Bucknill, addressing the Rugby Temperance Association, before the passing of Dalrymple's Act (which, significantly, was to be piloted through the Lords by Shaftesbury), (152) argued that the medical profession was tackling the wrong problem. It was a mistake to see drunkenness as a disease in itself. The kinds of asylum proposed by Christison (and existing on a voluntary basis as 'drying-out' centres on Skye and elsewhere in Scotland) were 'an unfortunate attempt to coddle drunkenness.' Intemperance, said Bucknill, was plain and simply a vice.(153) In practice, it mattered little whether the perspective was ethical or clinical: the detention of paupers was an available tactic under the Lunacy Laws. Relieving officers and policemen - often identical - sent habitual drunkards to asylums on the usual admission orders. Whilst doubting lay officials' diagnostic capabilities, medical officers were agreeable to a confinement which they were obliged to accept initially, but which they need not have continued beyond ascertainable relief of symptoms (i.e. 'cure'). In 1898, Cassidy at Lancaster indicated the willingness of superintendents to implement the spirit of the proposals of the 1870's. He urged that cases of assigned alcoholic insanity be detained in asylums after their particular form of insanity had worn off, in order to discourage an immediate lapse on leaving the institution. It was a confessedly coercive moral tactic: a widening of the asylum solution, enabling other behaviours to be separated from madness in conceptual terms, but confounded with responses to insanity in arbitrarily determined instances. (154)

Drunkenness was actually on the decline from eighteenth-century heights when public and professional attention began focussing on the phenomena involved as social and medical 'problems'. The most noticeable drops were occurring whilst theoretical links between pauperism, madness, crime and alcohol were being forged. After 1850, licensing regulations and the temperance ideology of substantial parts of the workingclass elite, had some effect in reducing the scale of drunkenness, though temperance gains were scarcely as pervasive as the Webbs suggested. (155) And inevitably, since consumption increased whilst drinking habits generally seemed to have been changed, immense quantities of alcohol were being consumed by a smaller proportion of the population. Tradition and socio-psychological factors meant that sections of the lowest economically-defined classes were the above average consumers, and for cultural and economic reasons, these were the same sections most likely to be stigmatized by pauperism and most likely to be subjected to police or other social controls. In primary groups, higher degrees of drink-induced behaviours might be tolerated, even expected, and even the agents of secondary identification - the police - on personal bases, at least until the 1880's, seem to have retained their class-acculturated attitude to alcohol. (156) But from the 1870's, more efficient policing brought more individuals within the scope of the flexible labelling process which had been developing from mid-century. As moral imperialism became more effective, stepped-up social controls produced increasing amounts of drink-induced assaults, thefts and insanities. The mid-1870's were the start of a rise in beer and spirit consumption that was maintained until the eve of the First World War. They were also the years in which public attention became fixed on the habitual drunkard and the psychiatric Establishment began becoming Darwinian. Unlike the temperance reformers of the mid-century who had related directly to the drinker, the psychiatrists and moralising evangelists tended to 'objectify' - i.e., depersonalize the drunkard. As imported medical theories on alcoholism and on the bio-chemical effects of alcohol became absorbed, the alienists' position was strengthened, and though public drunkenness began to wane, admissions of drink-induced insanity increased. (157) The estrangement of assessor and assessed was complete. Organic theories of economy, of society and of madness combined in the perception of intemperance. The existence of the asylum offered a surrogate community for maladapted social and economic units; the asylum predated the identification of those units, so it was the task of the asylum's spokesmen to discover unifying criteria for the types of deviance which public opinion was declaring intolerable. The flexible concept of civilization and the apparently objective assessment of the role of intemperance provided an efficient sociological and medical cover for applied morality. The asylum was the central feature: the activity of Dalrymple, Christison and the rest, was an attempt to apply the madness label to those who had escaped it. (158) A claimed medical pathology of drunkenness justified the drunkard's detention; (159) the economic concerns of local authorities ratified it; the public - if not the people - demanded it.

CHAPTER FIVE

LOVING MAD TOM AND JACK THE RIPPER: IMAGES OF MADNESS IN THE EIGHTEENTH AND NINETEENTH CENTURIES

Bishop Percy stated that the English had more songs and ballads on the subject of insanity than any of their neighbours:

> Whether there by any truth in the insinuation that we are more liable to this calamity than other nations, or that our native gloominess hath particularly recommended subjects of this class to our writers, we certainly do not find the same in the printed collections of French and Italian songs. (1)

At the beginning of the twentieth century, the pioneer folksong collector, Cecil Sharp, remarked the predilection of many English country singers for 'mad songs' and his view has been endorsed by a modern authority. (2) A vast number of such songs exists in manuscript, broadside and printed collections, and apparently survived in oral tradition. It would be a logical assumption to consider them as evidence of contemporary popular imagery, and an imagery which they reinforced as well as reflected. (3)

I

Amongst many individual songs and verses, two principal song-families stand out: 'Bedlamite' verses and 'mad songs.' The former, dating from the sixteenth century and much in vogue in the later seventeenth, use the theme of the beggar released from Bethlem, (4) bewitched and bizarre, with his memories of chainings and whippings. The image of Mad Tom is a sympathetic one, often stylised in the manner of other insalubriously picturesque heroes of eighteenth and early nineteenth-century street ballads, the 'jolly beggarman' and the 'rambling sailor'. (5)

In Percy's reprinted ballads, insanity is a theatrical device adding novelty to conventional tales of thwarted or unrequited love, or in one instance, adding bite to socio-religious satire. (6) All texts come from sophisticated pens. An exceptional piece is <u>The Lady Distracted with Love</u>, originally printed by D'Urfey, and represented as coming from a <u>Don Quixote</u> play of 1694 - 96. The writer presents his madwoman progressing through five stages of madness, from 'sullenly mad' to 'stark mad,' with a perfect eye for capturing stereotyped images of the madness state and encapsulating them all in graphic portrayals of the glaringly abnormal. (7) The highly conceited verses of the playwrights and poets utilised the frenzied imaginings of the lunatic as a vehicle for their own verbal fantasies, yet their imagery was fairly constant: the madman was perceived in an unreal environment, where 'brave bracelets strong' and 'sweet whips' were the hallmarks of his existence. (8) Mad Tom occurred in less conceited form in later broadsides. A song printed by

Harkness of Preston in the second quarter of the nineteenth century, To Find My Tom of Bedlam, makes a play of the fantasies within the head of Mad Maudlin, any yet Tom and the 'bonny mad boys' are represented as frightening only in so far as their imaginings are stocked with barbarous images. (9)

The second group of songs again relates to Bethlem, reflecting the fate of the unfortunate maiden awaiting release from confinement, usually to be effected by her lover. A typical pseudo-setting for the 'forsaken damsel' theme, the Bedlam location does, however, offer another instance of the archetypical perceived form of the madman and the mad environment. In some versions of the song, the girl is explicitly mad - driven so by the opposition of her parents to an intended love-match:

> O my cruel parents have been to me unkind
> They banished me and drove me and to (sic) raved my mind. (10)

In other versions, she is placed in the madhouse simply to prevent her having contact with her lover. Constant are the trappings of madhouse environments:

> As I was a-walking one morning in Spring,
> I heard a maid in Bedlam so sweet-i-ly she sing,
> Her chains she rattled with her hands and this she sigh and sing,
> I love my love because I know he first love me. (11)

Chains were an accepted convention,consonant with the confounded prison - asylum image. Mad Tom had 'come forth' from a 'sad and darksome cell,' and called upon Vulcan to 'knock off my troublesome shackles.' (12) The other stock appurtenance was straw, which clothed, bedded and decorated the lunatic - the Bedlam maid wove it into a garland in some versions of the song. (13) These images were mixed with what may be hints of hallucination, or perhaps simply apposite borrowings from earlier mystical or magical songs (14) to produce yet another sympathetic figure whose situation is macabre, but whose perceived persona is as human as the melodramatic format allows.

In addition to the two larger groups, there is a vast number of songs which follow no pattern. For example, there is The Middleton Overseer and the Madman, printed frequently by Swindells of Manchester and by Harkness. Here the madman is cast in the role of wily hero: the underdog who outwits the personification of authority, the parish overseer sent to take him to Lancaster Moor Asylum. (15) Other songs afford an excuse for bizarre narrative or jocular diversion, whilst there are countless songs and dance tunes with 'Mad' as part of the title which have no clearly definable relationship with madness or the mad. (16) The profusion is indicative of the appeal of the subject matter, even where implied rather than actual: broadside printers were businessmen with usually good market sense. (17)

The higher realms of literary creation offer an equally wide over-view of the perceived nature of the madman. Shakespeare's evocations of insanity were, especially in Lear and Hamlet, sufficiently powerful to promote a time-consuming passion amongst Victorian psychiatrists: the classificatory analysis of the symptoms of all plausible Shakespearian contenders for the madness-label. (18) The standardized imagery changed little from Dekker to Hogarth, from Hogarth to Reade. The reification of the insane was the commonplace response. Even before the Bedlam show became modish, Dekker had his asylum-controller admit a visitor thus

> ... But gentlemen, I must disarm you then,
> There are of madmen as there are of tame,
> All humour'd not alike. We have some,
> So apish and fantastic, play with a feather;
> And tho' 'twould grieve a soul to see God's image
> So blemished and defaced, yet do they act
> Such antic and such pretty lunacies,
> That spite of sorrow they will make you smile;
> Others,again, we have, like hungry lions,
> Fierce as wild bulls, untameable as flies:
> And these have often times from strangers' sides
> Snatch'd rapiers suddenly, and done much harm ... (19)

The madness-environment, whether in Bedlam or, later, in some Gothic madhouse, was invariably one of imprisonment: of cells, clanking chains and filthy straw. Even Dickens' non-institutionalized Barnaby Rudge had a penchant for straw. (20) Amidst the bizarre show of degredation, the madman lost his humanity and became a spectacle. A former patient told John Harriott, a Thames Police magistrate, that inmates in a madhouse were as 'golden fish' to be looked on. (21) The very setting of the forsaken maid in Bedlam emphasized the dramatic potential of the madness state: the girl is alienated from the 'real' world which observes her, and it is only the conventionalized trappings of madness which afford her communicated persona.

This image, though one of an attenuated humanity, goes further than the alternative popular view of the insane as brute animals. The figure of Mrs. Rochester in Jane Eyre is symptomatic of the response of refined normalcy to which the mad are alien:

> In the deep shade at the further end of the room a figure ran backwards and forwards. What it was, whether beast or human being, one could not, at first sight tell: it grovelled, seemingly on all fours; it snatched and growled like some strange animal: but it was covered with clothing and a quantity of dark grizzled hair, wild as a mane, hid its head and face. (22)

However drawn, the image of the madman was indissolubly linked with that of confinement. Confinement might be in the past: Loving Mad Tom; the present: the maid in Bedlam; or putatively in the future: the Middleton Madman. Confinement might be seen as legal, though unjust, as in Charles Reade's Hard Cash; or extra-legal, yet just as in Bronte; or simply as a fact, needing neither justification nor comment: Hogarth's Bedlam. Confinement was a reflexively acceptable response from the eighteenth century at least: Fielding in The Intriguing Chambermaid (1733) had a character express this correlation as a matter of course: 'Mr. Goodall, you are a poor, distracted wretch, and ought to have an apartment in a dark room, and clean straw.'

The two-dimensionality of the described madman reinforced popular conceptions of the incomplete humanity of the madman-as-observed. There was a dualism in these attitudes: the stock images invited either fear or pity. The second image was of a lightly-drawn, sketchily delineated individual, bewildered, incoherent, whose very gentleness is the hallmark of difference. Dickens introduces such a character in Pickwick Papers (1837) and Wilkie Collins does so in The Woman in White (1860). These characteristics are non-institutionalized, as are the quasi-oracular madmen, Mr. Dick (David Copperfield, 1850) and Mad Jack (George Gissing, The Nether World, 1889) and the mad prophet in Ainsworth's Old St. Pauls (1841), and all have strategic functions in the 'real' world which depend upon their not being fully of that world. The archetype of the first image was provided by Professor Bell:

> To represent the prevailing character and physiognomy of a madman, the body should be strong, and the muscles rigid and distinct, the skin bound, the features sharp, the eyes sunk, the colour of a dark brown yellow tinctured with sallowness, without one spot of enlivening carnation; the hair sooty black, stiff and bushy ... If you watch him in his paroxysm you may see the blood working to his head ... he becomes restless, then, rising from his couch, he paces his cell and rings his chains ... There is vacancy in their laugh and a want of meaning in their ferociousness. To learn the character of their countenance ... we must have recourse to the lower animals, and study their looks of timidity, of watchfulness, of excitement, and of ferocity. (23)

Bell, like Bronte, bore out the observations of Bethlem apothecary, John Haslam. Remarking disgustedly on visitors' predilections for gazing into the 'recesses of the furious and naked maniac,' he offered a valid critique of the public's consciousness:

> To impress ordinary persons with the existence of insanity, some prominent and strongly marked features are absolutely required; as the popular intelligence concerning madness is the result of those glaring exhibitions, those caricatures of disease which the stage represents or romances propagate. (24)

The qualities of the madness-state for writers and artists were those of individuals observed after being confined and treated as mad. They were rather the result of careful observation at Bedlam shows than attempts to come to grips with the realities of labelled insane behaviours. Significantly, they did not provide indications of what actually defines the madness-state: Hogarth's Bedlamites in The Rake's Progress are plainly mad because they inhabit a mad environment. And as Defoe complained of defective madhouses: that very environment would derange the sane.(25)

II

Nineteenth-century writers departed little from the stereotypes laid down in the previous century. The presented image of the madman was invariably unreal because it posited a diseased condition whose physical manifestations were obvious. One result was to intensify the opinion that it did not need a qualified medical expert to operate identification codes. A second was to relegate to the madness-type any physical behaviours which suggested similarity to stock images of madness: epilepsy, for example, or the after effects of overindulgence in alcohol.

Popular attitudes naturally tended to veer towards fear and hostility when physical contact with potentially violent, deranged behaviour was more likely. When press accounts of criminal lunatics, or of murderous doings by escaped lunatics occurred, there was inevitably hostile reaction, which carried over to the whole class of the insane. The tactic of equating violent crime with actual or assumed histories of mental derangement became fairly common from the second half of the nineteenth century. A most glaring example of journalistic misrepresentation appeared in The Referee in 1902:

> The question of the premature discharge of lunatics is a very serious one ... To ... premature discharge are due many of the daily tragedies which startle the newspaper reader ... sometimes a massacre. The homicidal maniac who shocked the world as Jack the Ripper had been once ... in a lunatic asylum. (26)

Earlier, the wide publicity given to the cases which marked milestones in the evolution of the plea of diminished responsibility in criminal cases, provoked panic-inspiring arguments against the lenient treatment of deranged offenders. (27) The reaction to the acquittal of M'Naghten, the murderer of Peel's secretary, in 1843, exhibited that traditional fear of the insane which insisted upon their addiction to atrocity. The well-known doggerel which appeared in the Weekly Despatch envisaged the insane as

> a privileged class, whom no statute controls and
> their murderous charter exists in their souls. (28)

Four years before, without the prompting of an assassination, a representative of the psychiatric Establishment had written of'the unfortunate incurable Toms o'Bedlam,' who were 'discharged upon the world to commit murder or arson.' (29) The public imagination grasped such images more avidly than alternatives, often to the prejudices of arraigned lunatics whose 'defence does not receive a proper hearing' especially if the case 'appears one of unusual brutality.' (30)

These provocative commentaries operated amongst vestiges of ancient superstition and widespread ignorance. Amongst the unlettered, especially in the Celtic fringe areas of Britain, these relics at times prompted concrete action, at times militated against the activity of the medical establishment. The Hebraic strands in Christian belief had often interacted with pagan traditions in forming cultural attitudes. Notions of the divine origins of disease and pestilence helped to confuse madness with supernatural possession - which was not always considered undesirable.(31) The'age of reason' did not destroy all the machinations of the mystical/ecstatic religious forms which reached their peak in the later middle ages. (32) Primitive beliefs lingered, especially in the shape of cures for madness. Victorian folklorists noted the survival of domestic medicines: peony and laurel in Scotland, for example. (33) More dramatic was the continuation of faith in the power of holywells, where immersion was ironically reflected in eighteenth and early nineteenth-century asylum practice with the 'bath of surprise'. As late as 1871 there were reports of people in Sutherland carrying out ritual immersion as a madness cure - a procedure, known as 'bowsening' which had been common in Celtic areas throughout the eighteenth century. (34) This practice could be confounded with processes of witchcraft identification.(35) Harland and Wilkinson recorded a case of 'swimming for a wizard' as late as 1863. (36) Even where no exotic practice occurred, the hold of ancient half-belief could hinder the course of contemporary medical practice. In 1815, Thomas Bakewell noted an instance of relatives refusing a physician access to a boy whose 'phrentic insanity' they saw as demoniacally produced, and he was convinced that this was far from rare. (37) Over a century later, Bedford Pierce lamented similar survivals:

> It seems to me that ... prejudices are independent of any reasoned explanation and are due to traditional beliefs. That our lives are greatly influenced by these is not open to doubt. Superstitious notions are implanted in our minds from our earliest years ... and many beliefs so acquired form a permanent part of our mental furniture... (P)rejudices about insanity are directly descended from medieval beliefs about spirits and demoniacal possession ... I know of no remedy for these erroneous and cruel views but the gradual enlightenment of the public ... (38)

Popular attitudes to asylums and to alienists operated from associated stereotypes. The 'public conscience' had been understandably shaken by the revelations of government and private enquiries from the third quarter of the eighteenth century. An unshakeable belief grew up that private madhouses were simply convenient depositories for unwanted spouses or for hindrances to inherited wealth. The fear of confinement was present from the early eighteenth century:

> In England the most innocent person on earth is liable to be immured for life under the pretext of lunacy, sequestered from his wife and children and friends, robbed of his fortune, deprived even of the necessaries and subjected to the most brutal treatment from a low-bred barbarian, who raises ample fortune on the misery of his fellow creatures ... (39)

Lurid tales of seclusion in Gothic dungeons had appeared in the Gentleman's Magazine and elsewhere in the 1760's. In 1863, Charles Reade's Hard Cash, unsuccessfully translated to the Drury Lane stage as Ladder of Gold, rehearsed the same melodramatic conventions as if they represented contemporary truth. (40) Concern, however, from Defoe in the 1720's, to Louisa Lowe in the 1880's, was not with the insane themselves, but with those to whom the madness-label had been wrongly applied. (41) Right identification reflexively meant confinement. Perceptions of the private sector were carried over to public asylums, so far as images were concerned, but until the present century, there was little interest in questioning the legitimacy of confinement of bureaucratically ordained cases. (42)

Brutality - even criminality - existed, but were not the norm of asylum or madhouse practice. The profit-concern of licensees of private asylums, however, made them an easy target. The stigmatization of 'madhouse' and 'mad doctor' clung to both public and private sectors throughout the nineteenth century. (43) Fear of madness and hostility to the madman were easily transferred to the institutions, the more so given the stark Gothicism in which asylums were clothed. (44) The legacy of eighteenth-century abuse was passed on to succeeding generations of asylum doctors. Significantly, it was the higher classes of society - those susceptible to private asylum confinement - who were most vociferously affected. Even the Commissioners in Lunacy displayed an irrational dislike of private asylums, and proprietors suffered as much from official discrimination as from public acrimony. (45) Within the medical profession itself, there were instances of personal vindictiveness damaging to the public image of the alienist. J.G. Millingen, for example, after enforced resignation from Hanwell, produced a strange mixture of textbook and polemic to chastise asylums in terms which revitalized the cliches of the scandal-sheets with nuances of expert criticism. (46) The private sector was further compromised by the selfconsciously upright stance of public asylum doctors. John Bucknill offered this highhanded censure:

> It is in their character of custodians, and in their association with capitalists and speculators in the business of confining and detaining the inmates of

> these institutions against their will, that physicians engaged in the treatment of the insane must expect to be criticised by their professional brethren and by the public, and controlled by the law and its officers, without much regard to that professional dignity of which they have not themselves been too careful. (47)

Forbes Winslow, in his presidential address to the AMOAHI, lamented the perpetuation of the mad-doctor image, and attributed it to the almost universal incomprehension of the essential nature of insanity as a disease. Doctors were despised, he argued, because the law put them on the same footing as that breed of profiteers whose activities had aroused public hostility a century before. The very legislation which formed the basis of lunacy reform had, in its operation, necessarily instituted a system of pains and penalties, which inevitably cast the private asylum physician in the role of potential felon. (48) Yet criticism of both sectors was not unfounded, as the Commons' investigation of 1859 and 1877 proved. The pamphleteering of the Alleged Lunatic's Friend Society and the Lunacy Law Reform Association was, however, easier of access than Blue Books: indictments of the asylum system and of its purveyors and guardians generally took the form of episodic accounts of inhumane treatment meted out to the sane, in which little sympathy was afforded the insane. (49) Non-medical writings tended to exhibit an understanding of a madness-insanity polarity with no marginality; the medical stance was thus unintelligible to the layman. Medical sophistication and medico-legal niceties were alien to public conceptions of the plain madness of the madman. Popular response, however, could often be more tolerant of the individual insane, (50) and here the differences between medical arrogance and community-responsibility were more pronounced: 'the people' were, in practice, more understanding than 'the public'.

It was in the notion of diminished responsibility for criminal acts that the alienists divorced themselves most dramatically from acceptable social regulations. 'Moral insanity' was a double-edged invention, as viewed by stable middleclass opinion:

> ... If experts choose to say that all very great criminals and scoundrels of extravagant wickedness are 'ipso facto' morally insane, because their vices ... exceed the ordinary dimensions of everyday sin, we have no particular objection ... All that comes of it is to deprive the word 'insanity' of any real meaning ... In the gabble of medical science, irresponsibility is proved by the mere fact of extraordinary immorality ... Henceforth, the greater the knave, the less his guilt. (51)

The complementary relationship of madness and confinement served to perpetuate a confusion of images: the unconscious equation of 'mad' with 'bad'. Smollett, in the passage quoted above, designated the unjustly confined as 'innocent'. The fact that asylums were in practice principally custodial, produced a natural tendency to lump them together with penal institutions. This equation was facilitated by the long history of housing the insane in gaols, and by the similarities between the asylum and the penitentiary: cells, shackles, attendant-guards. The notion of punishment was never very far away from nineteenth-century treatments. And the very concept of moral insanity implied that recipients of the label were immoral. Although asylums evolved, from the second half of the nineteenth century, in an intentionally less prison-like manner, the past remained a formative influence on public awareness. Boards of guardians often pointedly referred to workhouse cells for the insane, and in 1868, a Derby councillor argued that the only guaranteed cure for insanity was to beat the badness out of the insane. (52)

Much of the moral obloquy which attached to the mad derived from the belief that madness represented non-operation of the will-power which separated man from the beasts. (53) The intrusion of religious and moral overtones afforded further grounds for public censure of madman and mad doctor. The Rev. John Barlow thought he stated the obvious in arguing that

> the difference between sanity and insanity consists in the degree of self-control exercised ... (let) anyone ... note for a short time the thoughts that pass through his mind, and the feelings that agitate him: and he will find that, were they all expressed and indulged, they would be as wild, and perhaps as frightful in their consequences as those of any madman. But the man of strong mind represses them ... the man of weak mind yields ... and then he is insane. (54)

Weakness of mind evidenced weakness of will, and the clergy or upright laymen were seen as viable assessors of insanity and caretakers of the mad. Half a century after the appearance of Barlow's layman's handbook, there were still attempts to return to the realm of value judgements those kinds of behaviour which medical specialists were insisting were of a pathological nature: the public image of the asylum and of the alienist received a further reduction of status. (55)

CHAPTER SIX

CENTRAL CONTROL AND INSPECTION: THE COMMISSIONERS IN LUNACY 1828 - 90

The new conception of the role of the state, emergent from the second quarter of the nineteenth century, blurred older, traditional distinctions. Social legislation inevitably brought within the purview of the law activities not in themselves either immoral or reprehensible. The growth of central administration was among the most characteristic features of the period, arising from the diffuse awarenesses of the inadequacy of local authorities in the implementation of edicts that were unpopular. Benthamite influences on practical administrators like Chadwick illumined the expediency of conferring fuller powers on government-authorized central agencies. In the new machinery of administration, the inspector had a key role. As Herman Finer has written,

> The inspector may begin as a kind of disciplinary invigilator, merely to see that the law is complied with ... But in the course of time, he becomes considerably more, undergoes a transfiguration, as the potentialities of the human link between the human beings at the centre and in the localities are appreciated ... He becomes the repository of central knowledge, wisdom and tradition; he learns from the diverse experience of the different places and people he observes, and can offer comparative, sifted knowledge about the alternative ways of fulfilling the same task. He can become a skilled adviser; a beneficial mediator as well. (1)

I

The crucial importance of the inspector was realised in the 1830's. The government Factory Act of 1833, which supplanted Ashley's original proposal, not only made inroads on classical economic and social theory, by limiting hours of work in factories, it was also seen to 'contain the seeds of mighty changes in ... domestic policy.' (2) The magisterial authority of the factory inspectorate was initially large - frighteningly so to some, (3) and the espionage function enjoined on inspectors by Russell during the Chartist disturbances of 1837 seemed to justify fears. (4) However, by 1844, much power was transferred by the Home Office from the inspectorate to itself. (5) In Lunacy matters, the principle of supervision in specified areas had been voiced as an ideal in the eighteenth century, and given circumscribed expression in 1828. (6)

In his evidence before the Select Committee of 1815, Dr. Weir, proposed a board of three Parliamentary visitors, who should 'correspond with and control every insane institution throughout the kingdom.' (7) The Metropolitan Commissioners in Lunacy (1828) were designed to overcome the inadequacies of the inspectorate of the Royal College of Physicians, but were not greeted enthusiastically by every reformer. S.W. Nicoll, Recorder of York, and a leading figure in the attack on York Asylum, considered the new body simply as a mixture of existing forms of inspection by magistrates, asylum governors and the Royal College of Physicians. The Commission, he declared, 'comprised no new stimulus, no new intelligence.' Consisting of five magistrates, five private gentlemen, and five physicians, the inspectorate was markedly unprofessional, and was too extensive for individual responsibility. (8) Nicoll was astute enough to see the remedy:

> Nothing but a board established in London, and thence, from time to time, visiting all the institutions in England, could offer ... advantages ... They would visit with far more authority than any set of visitors from a neighbouring town and with far more independence. (9)

Full-time professional inspectors alone could provide the necessary degrees of duty, skill and experience. Ten years later, J.G. Millingen was even more demanding: the role of the inspector should extend to 'every stage of admission and discharge, as well as supervising the conduct of asylums.' The state power was to be preponderant in the asylum system:

> All lunatic asylums, whether public or private, should be placed under the immediate care of government ... under the control of inspectors, metropolitan and provincial ... No patient should be sent to a public or private institution until the case had been submitted to the inspectors, with proper medical certificates, and the confinement of the lunatic sanctioned by them as indispensable. The inspectors should have the power of discharging those persons whose further confinement they should think improper.

Millingen thought that nationwide circuits should be established, with four inspectors for each, of whom two should be medical men. (10)

The Metropolitan Commissioners were scarcely an answer to such requests. Their early reports indicate a self-satisfaction and optimistic faith in the bulk of licensees that ring discordantly with the disclosures of their wide survey a decade later. It is inconceivable that such retrogression could have occurred in so short a time, on so large a scale - especially within the Commissioners' own immediate jurisdiction. The discrepancy must repose in their initial inattentiveness and superficiality. Thus, in the first year of their operations, they licensed thirty-eight houses, in which they usually found 'a most ready attention on the part of proprietors to such suggestions as we have thought it right to make, so that we cannot but review our labours with some degree of pleasure ... (O)ur inspections have been with few exceptions, very satisfactory.' (11) Half a dozen pages, on average, sufficed to recount the Commission's annual activity and reproduce the statistics they considered relevant. Jones unaccountably finds these impressionistic reports 'very impressive.' (12) From 1830 to 1840, the reports suggest mainly self-deception.

Between 1832 and 1836, the Commissioners 'attended every reasonable request made by the patients,' even going so far as to make a point of 'frequently ... tasting the food in the pauper asylums.' (13) Where it had been necessary to 'animadvert' upon the condition of the pauper wards, the desired effects soon materialized. Cases of ill treatment by staff had been followed by discharge of the culprits, the Commissioners asserted, and they managed to obtain 'some remedy' for all evils, 'whenever a remedy has been practicable.' (14) In contrast to this bureaucratic jargon, their silence on occasions when the case precluded remedy enforces the suspicion that they were unwilling to face that eventuality, or at least, not prepared to admit it publicly. (15) Not until 1837 did the Commissioners record an instance of flagrant illegality, and even then they were unable to gain satisfaction. (16) This proved to be the year of disillusion - or of honesty. In cases outside their immediate jurisdiction, it was difficult to find 'that readiness of co-operation' expected in the light of earlier experience in the Metropolis. (17) So accustomed had the Commissioners become to compliance, at a superficial level, at least, they were quick to lament their circumscribed authority, and desirous of widening their 'advisory' capacity in line with the conception they held of the legislature's object of securing a 'complete and general registry in lunacy.' (18) In fact, the Board seems to have been concerned almost exclusively about the non-provision of figures by provincial officers. The following year saw a rehearsal of the same complaint, now broadened into an attack on the magistracy's neglect of licensing and visitation - their inadequacies contrasted starkly with the Commissioners' assiduous amassing of records, and diligent, intelligently-conceived routine of inspection. (19) The message was clear: in the provinces existed unknown expanses of neglect and evasion of the law's letter; in the Metropolis the Commissioners' vigilance ensured that 'offences against the letter, or the spirit of provisions, have become gradually less frequent ... causes of great abuse or wilful misconduct have latterly been almost unknown.' (20) The Commission was limited in its powers, but not in its vociferousness. There was communication with the Secretary of State on all major issues that came to the attention of the Board but were beyond its control. (21) By 1840, the business of the Commissioners had become increasingly concerned with provincial communications, and their early complacency received a sharp corrective. Reflected in the closer attention to their charges, the anxiety of the Board led to a time-consuming concern with special investigations and minute application to individual cases which was 'productive of very satisfactory results' - releasing many who would otherwise have been confined needlessly. (22)

In 1842, two of the Parliamentary Commissioners secured

extended inspectoral powers for the Board. (23) The resulting report illustrated the desperate inadequacies of the obtaining system. (24) As is often the case with the unique, this report has been elevated beyond its true worth: contemporaries and modern commentators alike ignore the more erroneous conclusions of the Commissioners, or find their unfortunate recommendations insignificant, compared with the valuable insights of the 'Doomsday Book' of the insane. (25) What was immediately confirmed was the Commissioners' suspicions regarding general conditions in the country at large. Not only were the formalities of licensing and visitation almost a dead letter, but the most flagrant inhumanity was found to exist, either undetected or ignored by the county magistrates. The appended 'Suggestions for the Amendment of the Law regarding Lunacy' bore the mark of overriding concern with the liberty of the subject, which was already compromised by the Commissioners' awareness of the conflicting necessity for early treatment. The two major impediments which were to haunt the Lunacy inspectorate throughout the century - detention of the curable in workhouses, and overcrowding in asylums replete with chronic and incurable cases - were noted helplessly. Even more alarming was the fact that twenty-one counties in England and Wales were unprovided with an asylum, public or private. Profiteering in the private sector was repeatedly evidenced, and though county institutions were free from this charge, many were unsatisfactory in terms of site, design or accommodation. The Commissioners were unrealistic in some of their responses. Aware that the expense of constructing asylums inhibited widespread adoption of the provisions of Wynn's Act, they expected to counteract the overcrowding of 'curative' establishments by additional provision for the incurable. Despite the lack of realism, the Board had justified its own existence, and presented a sufficiently good case for the extension of its powers, though Ashley was romanticizing when he assured the Commons:

> You can prevent, by the agency you shall appoint, as you have in many instances prevented, the recurrence of frightful cruelties; you can soothe the days of the incurables, and restore many sufferers to health and usefulness ... (26)

The 1845 Act gave Ashley and his Commissioners the opportunity they sought. To evaluate their subsequent operation, it will be useful to bear in mind John Harris's analysis of the factors which contribute to the success of central government inspection. These may be stylised as: (i) The number of inspectors; (ii) The skill and competency of the inspectors; (iii) The mode of organization; (iv) The frequency of inspection; (v) The freedom of the inspectorate to interpret central authority's definition of its task; (vi) The adequacy of legal means for securing information from local government; (vii) The effectiveness of other means of control and central supervision; (viii) The newness of the inspectoral system; (ix) The diversity of local government activity involved; (x) The independence of the authorities to be inspected. (27)

II

There are more points of dissimilarity than of likeness, in function, in constitution and in powers, between the Commissioners in Lunacy and, say, the Factory, Health or Poor Law inspectorates. The 1845 Board (28) grew immediately out of the experience of the Metropolitan Commissioners, itself very much a successor to the inspectorate of the Royal College of Physicians. (29) Both early inspectorates were merely toothless watchdogs for the Metropolis until 1842. It is instructive to contrast the Metropolitan Commissioners' position with that of Althorp's Factory inspectorate. An opponent of Factory reform complained that

> The powers of the inspectors are already greater than were ever before committed to any individual in this country, and greater than ought to be entrusted to <u>any</u> individual in <u>any</u> country. In all matters not especially provided for by the Act, the inspector's <u>will</u> is <u>law without appeal</u> ... (30)

Their powers curbed in 1844, the Factory inspectors yet developed a larger and more potent discretion than was available to the Lunacy Commissioners from the following year. (31) Nor did the Lunacy Commission ever exercise - even in its Metropolitan domain - that kind of autonomous autocracy so feared from that other contemporary board at Gwydr House. (32)

The Lunacy Commission was, however, at least free from the antagonism between professional and bureaucrat which marred much of the history of the Public Health department. (33) The Metropolitan Commissioners had a one-third professional composition, and the national inspectorate by law possessed an inspectorate of doctors and barristers in equal proportion, all of whom were members of the central policy-making board, which at no time exceeded eleven. (34) Thus, there was a difference between Lunacy and Factory inspectors once more: when the latter lost their quasi-judicial independence they became tools of a central board, whereas the Lunacy Commissioner always had a dual role: inspector and board-member. This identity precluded the need for individuality displayed in the early implementation of the Passenger Acts, (35) for, Shaftesbury proudly informed the Selct Committee of 1859, the Board had known only one division since its inception. (36)

Before 1845, inspection in the provinces was in the hands of local magistrates exclusively, and in London in the hands of the Commissioners. Both agencies were charged with the licensing of private asylums, and the visitation of public and private institutions. Licences could be withdrawn or refused where a house was legally defective; prosecution could be brought for criminal actions committed in public asylums. With regard to county institutions, visiting committees had little power - save in so far as the appointment of the asylum superintendent lay in the committee's gift. Moreover, since the visitors were usually laymen, there was **little** likelihood of criticism unless a superintendent was overspending. Prior to 1845, provincial inspection was largely negative. (37) It remained so in great part even afterwards, but there was at least regular supervision of the non-professional element, and scope for propaganda and persuasion.

The Commission operating on a national level had little discretion. It hands were often tied even in regard to the immediate objects of its responsibility, and the only remedy it possessed was the possibility of working through other agencies: Poor Law authorities or the Home Office. Hence the Commission operated as much as an adviser or stimulator as an executive agency in its own right. The efficient role of the Lunacy Commission was one of co-ordination, though its principal assigned role was superficially greater. Its purpose was dual: in the former role, Provision, in the latter, Protection. The latter, where the Board enjoyed its fullest measure of independence and power, was a role most often acted out in relation to private asylums and single patients. (38) The Commissioners were responsible for all lunatics, wherever housed, but the vast proportion were paupers, detained in workhouses or county asylums, where the fate of the individual lunatic rested far more with local and central Poor Law authorities. Although there was statutory control of pauper institutions, (39) actual enforcement of the law depended more on the goodwill and co-operation of other agencies than on the power of the Lunacy Commissioners to enforce the law. In some ways, there was more need for real power over the private sector: the danger of profiteering was ever-present. From a political point of view, it was more expedient to grant wider powers in this area: anti-centralist opinion and assertive local autonomy might reject too strong a government interest in the spending of local rates, but public opinion was suitably outraged by press revelations of madhouse brutality. Outdated before it matured, the 'public conscience' was a powerful force in shaping legislative response - more so than the lessons of the Commissioners' accumulated experience - and a conditioning factor on the implementation of the Board's duties. (40)

The most favourable function of the Commission, in the eyes of the medical profession, was evolved, rather than statutorily enjoined. The role of information bureau was more acceptable to supervisees than that of dictator, and in recognising that experiences gained in one sphere might be of use in another, the Commission laid the foundation for its real importance in the development of mental health services. Admittedly, the issues occupying the Board's attention were, for the most part, legal, and much freehanded advance on the part of asylums was short-circuited by insistence on the letter of the law. Yet there was a small degree of tacit approval for infringement of redtapism where the spirit of the statutes was served, and the influence of the Commissioners in encouraging progress, by the communication of successful curative programmes, by collecting and disseminating statistical information, and by generally bringing institutions into contact with their mutual problems and possible solutions, was counterbalancing to the harm incident to their brand of petty bureaucracy.

The inspection of mental institutions was still by and large in the hands of traditional agencies - the Metropolis excepted. Even after 1845, there was an unfortunate dualism: the Commissioners acted the role of JP in addition to their own, within the London area. Although professional, the inspectorate was divided in function and power. To have any lasting effect on the magistracy, it had to obtain Home Department support; to influence boards of guardians, it had to call on the central Poor Law authority. The granting of licences remained in the hands of the local magistrates. In effect, all the Commissioners often possessed was 'auctoritas': they had little 'potestas.' Because the former attribute could so readily prevail upon conscientious asylum staffs, visiting committees or other bureaucrats, there was reality in the Lunacy Commissioners' function. The Board was dogmatic, though perhaps, less so than, say, Factory or Poor Law authorities. And it was more humane, though no less theoretical, in its dogmatism. Larger theories, of economy, of society, were less obviously important on an administrative level, though they were formative factors in the shaping of the Board's conception of the nature of insanity and the purpose of institutional provision.

The 'authority' of the Board was established by its work-methods. Often greeted hostilely, as purveyors of red-tape and inhibitors of progress, as enemies of private enterprise and effort, the Commissioners succeeded in a short time in gaining respect for themselves and their function, including some of their ex-cathedra pronouncements. Antagonisms remained: the private sector rightly saw the Commissioners as a threat to their existence; county asylum superintendents were exasperated by incessant quibbling over trivia. But there was eventual acceptance, based on awareness of the necessity of supervision, and realization that the Board constituted an effective public relations officer for the asylum system, as well as potentially becoming a professional advisory body to the legislature.

III

The Lunacy Commission statutorily consisted of six professional inspectors: three doctors, three lawyers, and up to five honorary members. The salaried professionals received £1500 p.a. plus travelling expenses. Initially there was provision for superannuation payments, but as none of the original membership wished to take advantage of the scheme, Ashley prevailed on Trevelyan to have the Treasury refrain from making salary deductions. The salary was attractively high to compensate the right kind of potential candidate for loss of private practice, and compared very favourably with other government offices. (41) A tradition was established early on that Commissioners retiring from the active inspectorate whilst still of sound health and ability, were drafted onto the Board as part of the honorary complement. The honorary membership was rarely filled, and honorary members seldom attended routine meetings. Weekly meetings were held on either Monday or Wednesday, and normally consisted of two or three inspectors and the secretary. Office rules demanded the attendance of at least one physician and one barrister. There was further provision that at the first meeting each month, the reports of inspectors and visiting committees on public and private asylums should be considered. (42)

A full-time secretary was employed on a salary scale of £800 to £1000 p.a. Here again, a tradition was soon established: when a vacancy arose amongst the legal Commissioners, the secretary was promoted, provided his length of service had given him sufficient experience. Under the 1845 Act, a clerical staff of two was provided for, with authority to make a third appointment if necessary. Within six months, the Board had taken advantage of this provision, and the secretary's staff consisted of a senior clerk (£200 p.a.) and two clerks (£80 p.a.) (43) This number was made inadequate by the increased work-load entailed by the legislation of 1853. Looking back to that year, the Commissioners remarked that

> The admissions in county asylums and hospitals during that year had been nearly 8000, an increase of 1200 over the preceding year. The Discharges and Deaths had increased in like proportion. The quarterly returns from the unions, which give rise to much correspondence, had increased to 16000 annually, showing during the last four years an increase in each quarter of 1000. In various other matters, the labours of the clerks had been increased by the legislation of 1853, and the preparation of the Statistical Tables, such as those which accompany our recent annual Reports, had rendered necessary as amount of skilled labour not contemplated in our original arrangements, involving a very large amount of exact care, labour and correspondence in the collection and revision of such returns ... (44)

The Board negotiated with the Treasury and secured the appointment of two new clerks at a higher salary, to attract the right kind of candidate. In 1861, the Treasury acceded to the request for two further clerks, and raised office salaries: that of the chief clerk rose to £450 p.a. There were to be two clerks in the second class grade, and four in the third. New appointments were to be made at the bottom of the lowest grade, despite the Board's appeal for one higher appointment. (45) Higher qualifications for clerkships were considered essential in the light of the Board's expanded functions, and after consultation with the Secretary of the Civil Service Commission, it was decided to bring in an examination. The tests - introduced in 1862 - comprised:

1 Exercises to test writing and orthography.
2 Copying from manuscript and writing from dictation.

3 Correspondence.
4 Précis, involving preparation and digest of Tabular statements and of Returns with summaries.
5 Arithmetic, including vulgar and decimal fractions.
6 Calculations of Percentages and Averages.
7 Latin or any one Modern Language. (46)

The age limits for appointments were 18 to 30. By 1877, the office staff had grown to nine.

The Commissioners' first offices were in Abingdon Street, Westminster, but before long, they needed more spacious accommodation. Negotiations for the premises then used by the Ecclesiastical Commissioners broke down at the end of 1845, and the Board was forced into less favourable quarters in Spring Gardens. Larger premises were eventually found in Whitehall Place, and towards the end of the century, another move took the Board to Victoria Street. The Commissioners, however, were never really satisfied. In 1877, for example, the secretary complained to the Select Committee of Whitehall Place. It was, he claimed, totally unsuitable for the Commissioners' needs, and he told of one Commissioner, whose office in a former stable, caused him to be 'baked in summer and frozen during the winter.' When plans were made in the 1870's to rehouse them in the new government offices, the Commissioners found themselves once more overlooked after the needs of the Home Office and Colonial Office had been satisfied. (47)

Within the Metropolitan area, the Commissioners acted as licensing authority for private asylums, and fulfilled those duties performed in the provinces by local justices. Outside the Metropolis, they had the dual function of inspection and report, which they also had for their home area. The Board was responsible for all lunatics, save Chancery Lunatics; and thus all institutions and locations of single patients came within its purview. In addition, other duties were performed which had evolved from statutory duties, but were not prescribed by law. In his evidence to the Select Committee of 1877, secretary Charles Perceval outlined these extra duties:

> There is all the superintendence of the building and the alteration and construction of the lunatic asylums throughout the country; there are constant alterations and enlargements going on and there are new asylums constantly opening. All the plans ... have to be approved by the Secretary of State ... and that is done always on the report of the Commissioners ... Then in the same way, all the rules for county asylums submitted for the approval of the Home Secretary are referred to him by the Commissioners ... and they have to be examined very carefully. (49)

The Commissioners' business snowballed, and the inspectors were quick to point out that, despite their numerical weakness their vigilance was constant:

> Notwithstanding the great addition to the class of persons placed more or less directly under our charge, we have not limited our visitations to asylums according to the numbers appointed by statute. From time to time, we have made extra and special visits to Asylums, Registered Hospitals and Licensed Houses; also to single patients both the pauper and private; as well as to dwelling houses reported to have one or more uncertified insane inmates ... and we are constantly in the habit of responding to applications made to us on the part of individual patients or their relatives ... (49)

Though patently overworked, the Commissioners were unwilling to see any increase in their membership. Shaftesbury told Grey, in 1859, that the smallness of the Board was one of its strongest points: 'we could not carry out the business of the board when the numbers had been greatly increased. At present we work together with the utmost harmony.' This harmony had grown from the presence on the Commission of a nucleus of the original appointees named in the 1845 Act. These had, as Shaftesbury noted with satisfaction, continued a 'traditional policy' which later appointees had been encouraged to identify with. (50)

Other voices, however, protested at the inadequacy of the inspectorate. As Secretary, Perceval was inclined to support an increase. (51) From outside, the medical Establishment and the Alleged Lunatic's Friend Society were anxious for a more powerful and numerically stronger inspectorate. John Arlidge, (52) for example, wished to see a more rational system of inspection. The law placed Chancery Lunatics under the supervision of the Lord Chancellor's Visitors in Lunacy, which in practice created a dual control. There was, as Arlidge conceded, sense in dividing jurisdiction in terms of persons and property, but there was no apparent good in placing the persons of lunatics 'so found' under the same protection as their property. (53) The Commissioners, said Arlidge, were 'the pivot upon which any system of supervising and protecting all classes of lunatics must turn,' and hence it was essential that they have a direct interest in every lunatic in the kingdom. (54) This would necessitate an increased inspectorate, and a rethinking of the organization of the Board. Assistant Commissioners to replace Chancery Visitors, and a set of workhouse visitors on the model of asylum visiting committees, were proposed, to increase efficiency without adding to the workload of the existing Commissioners. (55)

The Commissioners themselves added point to such arguments, especially as regards workhouse visits. (56) By 1859, the inspectors had to make 354 statutory visits each year - discounting those to single patients and to workhouses. The latter were supposed to be visited annually, but the 1853 legislation left to the discretion of the Commissioners the frequency with which they fulfilled the duty. Shaftesbury explained that 'it was found to be so extremely onerous, that it was necessary that there should be limitation to it'.(57) Admiral Saumarez, chairman of the ALFS, was forthright in his evidence before the Select Committee of 1859. He stressed the difference between the 'bona fide' Commissioners and the Honorary Commissioners, dismissing the relevance of the latter to any discussion of the Board's actual work. He was especially annoyed at the specious argument that there was a strong personal link between the Lord Chancellor's Visitors and the Lunacy Commissioners, (58) and went on to argue that

> Honorary members are very different from the working members; the latter are worked to death ... when you reflect upon the number of individuals they have to look after, and the different asylums they have to superintend the building of, and the applications they have to attend to, it is utterly impossible that they should perform a fraction of their duties ...

Saumarez suggested the appointment of a second body of inspectors, supervised by the Lunacy Commissioners, and, with an eye to forestalling any government complaint about the higher costs of additional salaries, he pointed out that

> The (new) Commission ... might consist of men of middle age requiring but moderate incomes. You will find a number of medical men of the highest respectability who, for £500 a year, would undertake the work, and thus form a Board of Sub-Commissioners. (59)

In addition to increasing the numbers of the inspectorate, there were some proposals to promote greater efficiency of control by reducing the scope of the Board's function. John Perceval, secretary of the ALFS, wanted to see the Commissioners operate in the Metropolis as they did in the provinces, that is, simply as a supervising body of visitors. (60) The anomaly of the disparate Metropolitan and provincial operation of the Board revealed the inadequacy of the inspectorate to undertake the entire work of implementing the Lunacy Laws on a national scale. To Arlidge, a believer in centralization, this was clear reason to increase the size of the Board. He thought magisterial authorities prejudiced and parsimonious: only the Lunacy Commissioners could be relied on for impartial and efficient supervision. (61) John Conolly's barrister son shared this view, and suggested that JPs should be deprived of their licensing duties. More efficient controls could be provided if the Commissioners performed those tasks provincially, as they did in the Metropolis. The membership of the inspectorate would, of course, have to be increased. (62) Forbes Winslow thought that at least four or five additions ought to be made. (63) The ALFS were contrastingly distrustful of the central Board. Perceval wanted the inspectors to exercise their powers more widely, but as an adjunct of the magistracy. As an ex-patient, he had reason to be sceptical of professional competence, especially where the supervisor shared the basic ideology of the supervised. Whilst Arlidge expressed the professional's disapproval of the ignorance and inaction of the amateur, Perceval considered there was 'a frankness of character in the magistrate ...' whilst 'there is in the Board of Commissioners a duplicity ... I will call it an adherence to technicalities.' (64) The defender of the liberty of the subject was frightened by the implications of Shaftesbury's assertion that 'there is no case without plausible ground for, ... confinement,' a view which was rightly seen as protecting the pretensions of the alienist, rather than the personal freedom of the labelled madman. (65)

Shaftesbury, too, was anxious to draw attention to the positive function of the honorary Commissioner. After the tradition of appointing superannuated inspectors to the non-professional complement had been established, there was a valid point to be made, in so far as the honorary membership was experienced and served as an active advisory element as well as dynamically preserving traditions. Yet it is difficult to deny the claims of those demanding an enlarged professional body: the most urgent need was not for wise counsellors, but for more physically active inspectors, and the honorary membership failed to fulfil this requirement.(66)

1859, the year of Walpole's abortive Lunacy bills, and of the first sitting of the Select Committee on Lunatics, naturally brought the organization of the Lunacy Commission into the spotlight. The AMOAHI held a special meeting to discuss the proposed legislation at the Great Western Hotel, Paddington, in February, and the report of proceedings in their journal indicates their concern over the nature of the inspectorate. Amongst its provisions, Walpole's first bill proposed the appointment of a new group of officers to inspect asylums. Termed Medical Examiners, these officials were to be selected from men unacquainted with insanity professionally, and were to enjoy wider powers than the Commissioners, to whom, however, they would be responsible. (67) After throwing scorn on the non-specialism of the proposed inspectors, and indulging in righteous indignation at the threat of 'espionage', the meeting proceeded to make general comments on the supervisory system. Predictably, the private asylum contingent was the more vociferous, since both the Law and the inspectorate's opinion tended to be weighted against them. C.M. Burnett complained that the Lunacy Commission had the same origin as other public bodies, and that the mode of making appointments to the Board did not ensure any specialist membership. He admitted that two recent appointments had placed ex-county asylum superintendents on the Commission, but went on to rehearse the private asylum doctor's stock complaint about the system of recruitment: as a result of the appointment of two men from the public sector.

> We naturally get a great deal of information conveyed to the Commission, which was likely to be of general service in the treatment of the insane. Nobody can deny that fact; but I contend that if justice had been done, instead of electing two physicians or surgeons from the County Asylums, two ought to have

> been elected from the private asylum; because those who have charge of the insane in private asylums have placed upon them a very heavy weight of responsibility, such a responsibility as, perhaps, does not fall to the lot of any other section of our fellow subjects; for we not only have the medical charge of those who cannot speak for themselves, but we are in that apparently painful position, which implies that we really have care of them in a money sense ... (68)

More justice would be served, more reasonable and skilled supervision achieved if, instead of appointing 'medical examiners' the law provided for the augmentation of the Lunacy Commission by co-opting representatives of the private sector. Forbes Winslow, whose presidential address to the Association, eighteen months earlier, had focussed on this very issue, attacked the defective constitution of the Board and stressed the need for future appointments to be made after consideration of the competence of nominees. (69) The county asylum's spokesman was Bucknill. He chastised Winslow for 'uncivil' rejection of Walpole's proposals - but joined in the condemnation: the 'Examiners' would be useless. More beneficial would be the increased frequency of the Commissioners' visits to licensed houses, which could be achieved without addition to the inspectorate, if the law were changed so that on half of the statutory visits, inspection were by one Commissioner instead of two. Further reduction in the inspectorate's tasks, he argued, could be achieved by removing from their brief the inspection of workhouses, which should come under the supervision of the local magistracy, via specially appointed officers. The Commissioners' major province, insisted Bucknill, was the private asylum system, and their time should be taken up principally with its supervision. (70) After his appointment as a Chancery Visitor, in 1872, Bucknill began to elevate the relative importance and viability of the Royal Prerogative, upon which the Chancellor's authority over lunatics was based. He argued the futility of a dualistic system whereby an asylum may be visited at the same moment by the Lord Chancellor's Visitors. The Visiting Commissioners, and the Visiting Justices, and indicated the wastage of time and money, before comparing the relative position of Prerogative authority with that of Statute. Predictably, he concluded with the suggestion that the Prerogative absorb the statute-based Commission. (71) He was alone in this stance. The majority of public asylum men, and not a few private asylum physicians had, by the 1850's, come to recognize the value of the Lunacy Commission, and especially of its 'traditional policy.' The next section considers the making of that tradition in the first year of the Board's existence.

IV

The first Board was convened on 6 August, 1845, at 12, Abingdon Street, Westminster, with six of the statute-named Commissioners present. (72) On a motion from Gordon, Ashley was elected permanent chairman, after both had been sworn in. (73) It was Gordon again who took the lead in organizing the routine, moving that 'a board be held at least every Wednesday. That on the first Wednesday in every month, the reports and entries of the visiting Commissioners and Justices respectively as to County Asylums, Hospitals and Licensed Houses generally be read.' The barrister members were constituted a committee to draw up a scheme of regulations for the conduct of the office and the transaction of business. Office hours were fixed between 10 a.m. and 5 p.m. daily. (74) At the next weekly meeting, the secretary was instructed to keep a book for entering cases to be specially attended to by Commissioners on circuit, and to prepare a form of answer to questions of points of law and construction of the Lunacy Acts. A fortnight later, the board lost its first member.(75)

Provincial visitations commenced on 20th August, though the circuits were not mapped-out until the following February. (76) It was immediately discovered that 'questions of an important nature, requiring the assistance of the Medical and Legal Commissioners, were occurring continually at the office in London; and it was found necessary that meetings ... held once a week ...' should have in attendance one physician and one barrister. The monthly meetings 'deliberating the more important and difficult questions ... should be attended by all the medical and legal Commissioners' unless their presence was urgently required elsewhere. Proctor and Prichard were told off to collect and arrange materials for a general report to be presented the following year, based on the particulars of the 949 institutions subject to visitation and control.(77) The first public action of the new board was to place bi-weekly notices in appropriate journals, demanding notification of all single lunatics. (78) Their activities for the first twelve months of their existence thereafter, may be thus summarised:

A seven-point questionnaire was drawn up and distributed to ascertain the fitness and competence of applicants for licences and, surprisingly, revocation was found necessary in only one case. (79) In conformity with s. 43 of the Act, a Circular was sent to the medical superintendent of every hospital known to receive lunatics, requiring that they register. All responded, save the naval and military hospitals, and Guy's. (80) The excuse offered at the latter was that 'the patients were altogether incurable and therefore not under medical treatment,' and so there was no particular medical officer responsible, who might apply for registration. Despite constant appeals from the Commissioners' solicitors to the Treasurer of the Hospital, there was no satisfaction: the stock reply was that there was no regulation of the establishment relating specifically to lunatics, and that the wards did not come within the meaning of the Act. (81)

Although the duty of examining the validity of orders and certificates of confinement transmitted to the office was not statutorily prescribed, Commissioners checked carefully for any irregularities and omissions, and 'endeavoured to have them remedied.' In their first report, they noted that there were very few instances of defective certification in pauper cases, and that surprisingly little advantage had been taken of the permission to receive patients initially on the authority of a single certificate. (82) Asylums, the Board claimed, were diligent in forwarding notices of admission, death and discharge, but it was remarked with regret that 'the transmission of the copies of the visitors' entries had frequently been neglected.' Nor were all superintendents conscientious in keeping the prescribed Case Books, until a strongly-worded Circular of 9th January, 1846, effectively reminded them of their obligation. (83) Powers of night visitation and dietary control were used only once or twice respectively. (84) The plan adopted for implementing sections 76 and 77 of the Act, concerning the liberation of patients, was adapted from the practice of the Metropolitan Commissioners: it was first suggested to a friend of the patient, or to the parish officers, that the patient be removed, and only in the rare instances of their refusal would the Commissioners act on their own powers. In the provinces, attention to particular cases deemed suitable for release was directed by entries in the Patients Book: visiting magistrates invariably complied. Especially valuable, thought the Board, was the provision for temporary removal for reasons of health - 'a valuable amendment of the lately existing law.' (85)

Not every section of the Act was greeted with such enthusiasm by its guardians. The constitution of a private committee of a single patient, for example, proved 'in practice ... extremely inconvenient,' and the powers assigned to three of the Board in this regard, were as effectively performable by one, at least of the professional membership. (86) The whole question of single patients was, in fact, a constant source of doubt and difficulty, especially as to the forms of orders and certificates, and the frequency of medical visitation. (87) Nor were the Commissioners satisfied with their powers to protect the property of lunatics, which consisted in the duty of notifying the Chancellor in the hope that proceedings might be obtained before the Masters in Lunacy. The expense incurred rendered the procedure useless for parties of slender or moderate means. Powers to visit (under sections 112, 113) were equally meaningless in most instances, since the Commissioners possessed no penalizing discretion by which they might enforce obedience to the rulings. (88)

The statutory visits to gaols (twenty county and borough institutions were visited in the first year) revealed that the provisions of 3 & 4 Vic. c. 54 had been carried out: only two or three feebleminded persons were found, sentenced to short terms of imprisonment. Acting under the provisions of 8 & 9 Vic. c. 126 s. 28 the Commissioners received plans from various counties, and had consultations with experienced architects, before issuing a Circular making suggestions as to the site, structure and arrangements of asylums, together with instructions requiring specified preliminary plans to be forwarded to the Board for official approval. It was not sufficient for a county to be conscientious in wishing to erect suitable accommodation for its insane: Middlesex, for example, was refused permission on its initial application for additional asylum provision, because the proposed institution was too near the existing buildings at Hanwell. (89) The Board accordingly advised the Secretary of State to withold consent until the magistrates had been persuaded to transfer the site to the eastern part of the county, where the Commissioners felt the need to be greater. Surrey, too, was obliged to amend plans for a projected addition to Wandsworth. (90) No attempt to pressurize counties unprovided with asylum accommodation was made until August, 1848, after which the Commissioners acted through the Home Secretary, with indifferent success. (91) The Secretary himself prevailed upon the Board to implement section 40 of the Act more rigidly than the inspectorate would have liked, and the result was a 'Proposed General Rules for the Government of Lunatic Asylums' which was circulated to all county asylums. (92)

At the end of their first year, the Commissioners could detect 'a great improvement of receptacles for the insane ...' produced by their own and the county magistrates' supervision and suggestions. Co-operation was acknowledged at every level, and special praise was bestowed on the county institutions. (93) The members of the Board had been kept fully employed throughout: their report stated that the

> Legal and Medical Commissioners (were) absorbed by the business of the Commission; by visitations; by reports; by examination of plans, estimates and accounts; by long and frequent interviews with Magistrates, Architects and private individuals, and by attending the Boards held for the dispatch of business. Questions of considerable nicety have frequently occurred ... and these have involved the necessity of some of the Legal and Medical Commissioners being constantly present at ... weekly and other meetings. (94)

The amount of ordinary business at the office 'far exceeded our expectations' and additional office staff had to be employed. Special enquiries proved a positive hindrance to the already full routine. Within an eighteen month period, 107 regular Boards were held; 409 asylums were inspected, entailing travelling by the six professional inspectors totalling 10,776 miles, and the personal examination of 17,749 patients. (95)

The following four narratives act as illustration of the kinds of problems - routine and exceptional - faced by the Commissioners, which laid the pattern of the Board's style of operation and provided administrative expressions of the Commissioners' ideology.

(1) <u>A Conflict of Principles: Lincoln Asylum.</u>

Opened in 1820, the Lincoln Lunatic Hospital was a

registered hospital in terms of the 1845 Act. Accordingly, it was not subject to visitation by local magistrates, but by its own Board of Governors and by the Commissioners in Lunacy. In the 1830's, Lincoln had gradually abolished the use of mechanical restraints, innovating a system of moral management which inspired the entire psychiatric Establishment. (96) Its legal status, however, inspired the Lunacy Commissioners to embark on hostilities in 1846. In their report for 1847, the Commissioners indicated the status of the registered hospitals, and urged that they might be brought under the same visitation as county asylums. In illustration, they gave, in an Appendix, the unfavourable report of the two inspectors visiting Lincoln in 1846. (97) The Governors' statement for the same year set the tone of the divergence of view-points:

> It has been found in this Institution, that the sound system of improvement consists in the firm and continuous removal of abuse and inconvenience, whenever they may present themselves: without attempting to establish any system upon abstract general principles or a priori grounds ... The Board have in consequence found themselves in possession of some useful principles, based on practical and progressive experience and have, in these cases, not felt themselves restrained by undue deference to current opinions, which have passed from one writer to another without practical examination, or which have arisen under the peculiarities and difficulties of cases in more private practice. (98)

In eschewing general principles and concentrating on empirical observation, the Governors were placing themselves on a plane divorced from any the Lunacy Commissioners could afford to occupy. The Governors were asserting the benefits of tailoring systems to particular situations; the Commissioners were concerned to direct a regulated uniformity embracing all their charges. The basis of the Commissioners' function - the Lunacy Laws - was criticized by the Lincoln Governors because of its originating preconception:

> A fundamental error has pervaded the whole system of Asylum regulation, until a very late period, an error which has tainted legislation in so many instances ... the error of dwelling with intense exclusiveness upon extreme cases, and cases of rare occurrence and framing the provisions with an exclusive view to them. (99)

When these opinions were voiced, there had been no confrontation with the Lunacy Commissioners. Earlier reports show that the asylum had been managed on similar principles for more than a decade. Not all features were of a kind to receive external support from elsewhere in the asylum system: in marked contrast to most public asylums was Lincoln's rejection of the idea that institutions could be at least partially run and provisioned by inmates' labour. The non-restraint campaign, however, was Lincoln's pride, and the asylum's reports faithfully chronicled its progress until there was complete abolition of mechanical restraints. When Turner and Proctor visited the establishment in September, 1846, they remarked on the non-use of instrumental restraint, and stated they had 'no objection.' Even more than accompanying general censures, this offhandedness stung the Governors, who

> felt much hurt at this mode of treating the greatest improvement ever made in the management of the insane. Is the Board to consider that the abolition of instrumental restraint is only tolerated by the visiting Commissioners and that they have a latent dislike to it which is repressed by the overwhelming weight of public opinion?

The Commissioners' careless language provoked a published response, and not all remarks were as carefully discourteous as the one quoted. The whole system at Lincoln came in for sharp criticism and robust defence. The two visiting Commissioners had spent part of the two days making their inspection, and their minute and report recorded five principal objections concerning: classification, the almost indiscriminate admissions of strangers, the dietary, the powers and duties of the house surgeon, and the practice of turning all the patients over each month to a different physician.(100) In short, they were condemning a planned set of arrangements worked out from experience, because it failed to match their theories. In an earlier report, the asylum managers had emphasised the particularity of their system - though they indicated that this was due to defects in the staffing and construction of other establishments. (101) At Lincoln, the Commissioners claimed, 'there is essentially no classification whatever amongst the male or female patients ...' and they found this intolerable, since it mixed the dirty with the clean, the noisy with the tranquil, and exposed women to the obscenities of the male wards and courts, (the sexes were separated, but frequently within sight and sound). The Governors had earlier explained their methods: it would be 'mischievous' to treat certain patients as a 'class' (e.g. 'dirty' patients) since this would tend to intensify their particular characteristics and propensities, offering no benefit to patients and increasing the problems of the staff. Seclusive classification often entailed the assumption of a kind of hierarchy, with certain (acceptedly 'inferior') groups, for example, the 'disorderly', being packed off to the least inviting parts of the building. (102) More important still, there were positive benefits to be enjoyed: whilst seclusive classification 'only tends to increase and aggravate the inconveniences which have been made the ground of such seclusion,' admixture improved the material welfare of inmates. In June and July 1845, certain disorderly male patients were transferred to separate parts of the building and grounds, and it was found that they became sullen and morose. When restored to the society of other patients, they responded positively. (103) After repeating the experiment with female patients, ('with a material mitigation of the disorderly character of that department') the principle of classification was relaxed and modified. Outdoors, the idea of having a great number of small courts was dropped, and patients were seen to enjoy the benefits of less limited opportunities for exercise and variety of scene and company. (104) Small wonder that the management described the Commissioners' observations as representatives of theories that 'have been deduced from the economy of prisons.' The inspectors, indeed, pointedly referred to 'keepers' and 'cells' - at Lincoln the words were never used. (105)

At a special Board on 11th November, 1846, the Governors answered their attackers, rehearsing the justifications of their scheme of classification. They indicated, too, that the frequent visiting by persons unconnected with the asylum (which the Commissioners regarded as akin to the old Bedlam shows) was the only safeguard against abuse and malpractice. They refused to limit the facility of inspection as demanded by Turner and Proctor, and summarily dismissed the other heads of dissent outlined by the inspectors. (106) The inspectorate was powerless to force its opinions on the asylum management, but the tone of their future dogmatism had been set. In their report, which reiterates their basic grounds for disagreement, no notice was taken of Lincoln's apologia, but merely expressions of offended authority. The central Board, then, immediately began showing itself intolerant of what it called 'deviation' from standards approved by itself, but independently of practical demonstration on a scale sufficiently wide enough to make generalization innocuous, let alone valid. (107) The degree of conformity to general rules had to depend on the particular nature of given establishments, and the Commissioners were prepared to tolerate near misses. But the thought that one institution might be so structured as to benefit its inmates by completely different modes of operation was plainly too much to be appreciated. Whether, in fact, the Lincoln Governors were overstating their case is immaterial. What is significant is the unwillingness of the central authority to make objective criticism, and their ideological intolerance of self-determination in the organization of treatment.

(2) A Special Investigation: Haydock Lodge.

Haydock Lodge was a 'large, handsome mansion,' situated near Newton-le-Willows, just off the Manchester-Liverpool railway line. It had 'an extensive range of outbuildings and offices, and excellent walled gardens, and also a park and a farm containing together about 400 acres.' (108) Between 1831 and 1841, it had been used as a barracks, then remained untenanted until 1844, when it was leased to a George Coode, who, backed by his sister's capital, applied for and received a licence to accommodate 200 lunatics, of whom 160 were to be paupers. (109) The sister became licensed proprietor, and Charles Mott, ex-assistant Commissioner for the Poor Law, was appointed resident superintendent. At the time, there was heavy pressure for increased accommodation for paupers, especially in Lancashire, and in July, 1844, the licence was extended for a further 200 patients. Between August 1845, and February, 1846, Haydock Lodge was licensed for 450 lunatics, of whom 400 were to be paupers. The local justices had granted the various extensions on the understanding that all necessary additions and alterations would be made before the patients were admitted. But Mott failed to comply. The early reports of the Lunacy Commissioners were unfavourable (110) but their suggestions were ignored.

A surgeon named Porteus was appointed in August, 1844, but disagreement with Mott led to his resignation (July 1846). In February of 1846, a Welsh gentleman (111) contacted the Lunacy Board with complaints about general mismanagement, cruelty, neglect and an excessively high mortality rate. The Commissioners immediately referred the matter back to the licensing magistrates, whose enquiry acquitted the attendants charged with cruelty and neglect. (112) In July and October, the Board made its own investigations, which aroused some misapprehension in the Commons when the Commissioners refused to allow the evidence to be printed. (113) Some touchy correspondence ensued, between the Board, the Home Secretary, and the two MPs pursuing the case in the House, W.O. Stanley and Thomas Wakely, the latter demanding access to all relevant material. By the end of the year, pressures on the Commissioners to submit their report were intensified. In addition to the earlier complaints, Rochdale, Leicester and a number of Welsh unions were strongly criticising Haydock Lodge. Mott had been forced to resign, and had been replaced by a Mr. Whelan, ex-steward of Hanwell, who, if less idle and corrupt, still failed to live up to the Commissioners' standards. A series of special meetings of the Board resulted in Mylne's drafting a report for Home Secretary Grey (January 1847) and a personal interview of the principals involved prompted the Commissioners to recommend to Kirkdale Quarter Sessions that they grant the licence to Coode, and insist that he reside on the premises. (114)

The report contains appendices consisting of the two earlier reports made, and of immediate interest is the description of the instructions given to four visiting Commissioners on their special visit in October. (115) Their brief was to enquire into the 'state and management' of the asylum, with special reference to the high mortality rate. A twenty-nine point instruction was given, divided under four heads: Mortality; General State of the Asylum; Diet and Medicine; Duties of the Officers. The first two were the most detailed. With regard to Mortality, the Inspectors had to

(a) Obtain figures 'as far back as evidence can be obtained.'
(b) 'State the history of all the fatal cases from the date of admission' and 'inquire particularly as to the mental and bodily state of each patient at the time of admission.'
(c) Examine the three physicians who had acted as visiting medical officers to the asylum.

(d) Make detailed enquiries into all post-mortems.
(e) Enquire as to the medical and dietary treatment of those who died.
(f) Enquire into the mortality figures of the neighbouring districts as to the prevalence of any febrile disorder, typhoid etc.
(g) Assess the heating provision of the asylum during the period of highest mortality.
(h) Enquire into the conduct and results of all inquests.

The second set of instructions consisted of fifteen detailed enquiries to be made respecting the siting, construction and furnishing of the asylum, to 'be made with the aid of a well-informed and impartial surveyor'. There was to be an investigation of the past history of the buildings, and the inspectors were asked to note any 'unwholesome manufactures' that might obtain in the neighbourhood. Provision for, and distribution of the patients were to be carefully investigated, together with the frequency of medical attention. The other two heads were similarly specific: the inspectors were to enquire about the 'diet professed to be given' and by examination of provisions and interview of all staff and 'reliable patients' ascertain 'what is actually given.' Full details of the nature, amount and costs of all foods and medicines were to be found. Finally, the duties, salaries, characters and competence of all staff and servants, from superintendent downwards, were to be reported, with an especial notice given to the number of 'each sex ... capable of speaking Welsh.' (116)

The inspectors' report was faithful to its instructions. The asylum was found to be basically sound, but 'always in a state of transition' which brought discomfort to the patients. The defects noted in earlier reports still existed, arising in the main 'from want of a uniform system of supervision' and from 'the precipitation with which the licence was granted, and subsequently extended before the alterations required for the adaption (sic) of the buildings to their new purpose had been completed.' (117) This implied a criticism of the magistracy's activity, but was cancelled out by the Commissioners' praise for the 'exemplary diligence' of the visiting JPs, who inspected the asylum eleven times between its opening and May, 1846, and whose 'entries in the Visitors' Book exhibit a degree of care and anxious attention ... which had never been exceeded ... and which helped counteract evils produced by circumstances.' (118)

Despite urgings to demand the revocation of the licence coming from several MPs, (119) the Commissioners deemed such a step 'unwise', since it would be impossible to accommodate properly the 340 patients anywhere else. (120) 'Frequent' and 'vigilant' inspection ultimately effected improvements to the Board's satisfaction. (121) The asylum was closed in 1851, after the county institutions at Rainhill and Prestwich opened, but re-opened a year later, a licence being granted to one John Sutton, for the reception of private patients only. (122) Gradually, the pressures for pauper accommodation built up again, and in 1854 the asylum was again licensed for pauper patients. Under Sutton's management the asylum improved, and the later reports of the Commissioners display great satisfaction. (123)

During the course of this special investigation, four Commissioners were occupied at two different periods for eighteen days. A further ten days were devoted to the consequent reports, and, in addition, there were eight six-hour meetings of the Board to discuss the evidence on the case. (124)

(3) Revocation of a Licence: West Malling Retreat.

On 5th December, 1850, Peter Davies, late 'superintendent keeper' (125) of the West Malling Retreat, was interviewed by Lutwidge and Turner at the Lunacy Board's offices, concerning his allegations of 'abuse and neglect' by the asylum's proprietor, Alfred Beaumont Maddock. (126) The following day, he confirmed his statements before a full Board. (127) He alleged inadequate dietary provisions, and affirmed that he 'could get no medicine for the patients from Dr. Maddock, who very rarely visits ...' More importantly, in the Commissioners' eyes, Davies stated that 'the restraint practised is most abominable though professed to be dispensed with ...' (128)

Lutwidge, as Secretary, was instructed to contact material witnesses, Maddock himself, and a Maidstone solicitor to deliver a summons to Maddock. The latter, informed of Davies' intention, had tried to forestall criticism by writing to the Board on the day the attendant first met the Commissioners:

> In reading over yesterday the last report of the Commissioners, in which I observed their comments upon the Registry of Attendants, (129) and in conformity with the expressed wishes of the Commissioners, I have deemed it my duty to inform you that I have been compelled to discharge ... H. Peter Davies ... on account of the total neglect of his duties, swearing and ... want of control over his temper ... (130)

Witnesses, however, backed up Davies' story, so Turner and Proctor were told off to make a special investigation. They made a two-day visit to the asylum within a week of the commencement of the investigation, and made a thorough inspection. In addition to their legally-required notice in the Visitors' Book, they produced a nine-page report for the Board. (131) From this, Maddock appears to have panicked. Arriving to inspect the food, the inspectors were told that the patients had already dined. They asked to see the cook, and were told that she had been discharged that morning. Superficial cleanliness and order failed to impress the inspectors, who seem to have virtually taken the place apart. Suspect entries in the Case Book proved to be Maddock's undoing. Significantly, the general bad treatment and antitherapeutic set-up could not be penalized. Nor could the disingenuous falsification of general medical records. All the Board could bring charges against Maddock for was 'unlawful entries' concealing restraint. (132)

Maddock and his surgeon, Perfect, got up a petition in their defence, signed by forty respectable citizens of West Malling. The Board received it on 10th February, 1851. Between then and the 16th, they also received four 'confidential' letters from Maddock. His stance changed. Originally arguing the injustice of being the first to suffer under the 'highly penal' section of the 1845 Act, (133) he next pointed out that he had removed the abuse, and finally, blamed any faults on his staff. The Board remained unimpressed: 'the Commissioners see no grounds for staying the proceedings,' (134) Maddock pleaded that the case was being brought solely 'on technical grounds' but a note (135) from one of the Commissioners urged that a public airing was essential in such an important area as misuse of restraint. More complaints came in, and one from a William Bridgen, engaged the attention of all the professional inspectors for almost a full day when a personal examination took place.(136) The fresh evidence secured the Board's case. Maddock pleaded guilty on two indictments and was fined £50 on each. (137) The local magistrates needed little prompting to refuse renewal of the licence, which reverted to the former proprietor, a Mrs. Rix, and after twelve months transferred to Dr. F.H. Lewry. (138) Maddock maintained himself in private practice, and wrote several monographs, derived from his experience of the insane. (139)

(4) <u>Conflict with Local Authority: the Henry Case, Lancaster.</u>

The Board was not always so successful in getting the magistracy on its side. On 16th May, 1863, a patient named Thomas Henry died in a struggle with an attendant at Lancaster Moor Asylum. At the inquest, the jury brought in an open verdict, attaching no blame to the attendant, Salisbury, but attributing the cause of death to the struggle. Subsequently, the visiting committee instituted their own enquiry, and at their insistence, Salisbury was charged before the borough magistrates. (140) The facts, as they eventually emerged, were that Salisbury, who was charged with 'killing and slaying' Henry, was chief attendant in Henry's ward. Henry, an idiot pauper, had been acting violently and Salisbury, assisted by a second attendant, Lord, removed him to a bedroom. Lord backed down when Henry attacked him; Salisbury, also assaulted, threw the patient on the bed and fell on him, The post-mortem showed a fractured rib, and the coroner assigned the physical cause of death to sudden pressure on the heart, aggravated by Salisbury's falling on him. (141) The asylum superintendent, Broadhurst, contacted the Lunacy Commissioners immediately, and the Board was assaulted by frequent querulous letters from a local citizen, James Robertson, who, in the first instance, addressed his accusations of conspiracy and concealment to Shaftesbury. (142) Throughout June, Robertson was demanding evidence of the

Board's activity, which had, in fact, begun on receipt of Broadhurst's notification of the fatality. Gaskell and Forster made a special investigation on 2nd June, and their report demanded the dismissal of Lord for an obvious breach of discipline. They were equivocal about Salisbury, though keen to attach some blame. (143)

Robertson indefatigably pursued the case, 'for reasons which will be divulged afterwards,' and claimed the inspectors had not dug up 'the whole truth.' (144) A whitewash was alleged, (145) but the Board retained a dignified silence. A copy of the inspectors' report was sent to the visiting committee, (146) whose clerk acknowledged it a month later, stating that the magistrates did 'not think it desirable that the matter should be re-opened,' and that Lord had been dismissed. Salisbury, whose record was excellent, was retained as chief attendant. (147) At least one Commissioner wished to have Salisbury sacked, and urged that the matter be referred to the Home Secretary. (148) The Board thought that the visiting committee's simple reprimand had been inadequate, though in their published report they made no mention of their proposal for dismissal, but merely noted their suggestion that Salisbury be transferred first to outdoor work, and then to a different ward. (149) The visiting committee declined to do this, and the Home Secretary, Grey, refused to act when the Board requested his interference.

The above four episodes illustrate well not only the mode of the Lunacy Commissioners functioning, but also the limitations of their powers. Within those limitations, however, the inspectorate worked assiduously to reinforce the legal controls of asylumdom as mediated by their own perceptions of the nature of insanity and of the role of the institution. These perceptions, as the preceding narratives indicate, tended to be conditioned by preconceived general ideas which remained fairly constant attributes of Board members throughout the nineteenth century. The personnel involved were active forces in maintaining the traditions evolved early in the Commission's life. The next section offers a brief discussion of the individuals involved.

V

Between 1845 and 1900, twenty-eight men were appointed to the professional membership of the Lunacy Commission, twelve lawyers and sixteen physicians. In order of appointment, these were:

(a) Legal Commissioners:(150) John Hancock Hall (1845); (151) William George Campbell (1845 - 78); (152) Bryan Waller Proctor (1845 - 61); (153) James William Mylne (1845 - 1855); Robert Wilfred Skeffington Lutwidge (1855 - 73); (155) John Forster (1801 - 72); (156) Charles Palmer Phillips (1872 - 95); (157) Hon. Greville Theophilus Howard (1873 - 77); (158) Sir Charles Samuel Bagot (1877 - 1903); (159) William Frere (1878 - 1900); (160) George Harold Urmson (1895 - 1907); (161) Frank Hardinge Giffard (1900 - 1908). (162)

(b) Medical Commissioners: John Robert Hume (1845 - 57);(163) Henry Herbert Southey (1845); (164) Thomas Turner (1845-56); (165) James Cowles Prichard (1845 - 48); (166) Samuel Gaskell (1848 - 66); (167) Robert Nairne (1857 - 83); (168) John Davies Cleaton (1866 - 93); (169) William Rhys Williams (1878-89); (170) Reginald Southey (1883 - 89); (171) Sir T. Clifford Allbutt (1889 - 92); (172) Sir Frederick Needham (1892 - 1924); (173) Thomas Lawes Rogers (1893); (174) James Wilkes (1856 - 78); (175) John Michael Augustus Wallis (1894 - 97); (176) Sir Edward Marriott Cooke (1898 - 1921); (177) Sidney Coupland (1898 - 1921). (178)

It has not proved possible to locate the precise path of recruitment in more than a few cases, in each of which patronage was the key factor. Of the six statute-named appointments, all had been Metropolitan Commissioners, as had the Board's secretary. Of the nine subsequent appointments to the legal inspectorate, five had been secretary to the Board: Lutwidge (1845 - 55); Forster (1855 - 61); Phillips (1865 - 72) Urmson (1889 - 95); Giffard (1855 - 1900). Of seven secretaries only William Spring Rice (1861 - 65) and Charles Spencer Perceval (1872 - 89) were not appointed to the professional inspectorate. Phillips had earlier been chief secretary to Lord Chancellor Chelmsford, and prior to his appointment had published The Law Concerning Idiots. Giffard, too, had been secretary to a Lord Chancellor (1886 - 92) and the inference of direct patronage is inescapable. Bagot had had a distinguished early career as secretary to Lord Justice Selwyn and Lord Justice Hatherley. Forster was a close friend of Proctor, through whose influence with Shaftesbury he obtained his secretaryship. (179) Howard was the second son of the Earl of Suffolk and Berkshire. Apart from the promoted secretaries, none of the legal Commissioners appears to have been particularly experienced in the Lunacy Laws prior to his appointment. Mylne had been a prominent barrister, and Frere, revising barrister for Wiltshire. Despite his professional standing, the latter, according to L.S.F. Winslow, a relative by marriage, was

> ... the last person whom I thought would be selected for such a responsible post ... As soon as he received the appointment, he wrote me a letter as follows: 'Dear Winslow, - I have just been appointed a Commissioner in Lunacy. I know nothing about the subject. Send me your book.' (180)

Of the sixteen medical Commissioners on the Board during the period reviewed, seven had been county asylum superintendents, and one physician to Bethlem. Hume's appointment might have been due to his position as Wellington's private physician. Southey had familial connections with a statute-appointed Board member. The eminence of Prichard and Allbutt in the medical world was sufficient justification for appointment, and the former was an influential theoretician in the field of mental disorder. Turner was a noted surgeon and medical writer, with an indirect contact with insanity early in his career, and great experience of the organization of medical institutions. Nairne and Coupland had been physicians to Metropolitan hospitals. (181) The appointment of the former, in 1857, had angered the psychiatric Establishment. Bucknill, then editor of the Journal of Mental Science, claimed spokesmanship for the AMOAHI membership when he described the choice of Nairne as

> ... a heavy blow, and a great discouragement of all medical men practicing in Lunacy, and especially to the class of asylum superintendents ... placed under the authority of strange medical men, who have no claim for such preferment and who, practically, ignorant of the responsibilities entailed in the management of asylums and the treatment of the insane, must come for what instruction might suffice them for an apparently decent discharge of their duties to the very men whose rightful position they have usurped ... It is fair to say, that in Dr. Nairne's appointment, no false pretence was made to knowledge which he did not possess. We are informed that he takes great credit in himself for bringing to the Committee a freedom from prejudice derived from his primitive ignorance in all that relates to asylums and the insane. (182)

The AMOAHI was generous in its later treatment of Nairne, who was made an honorary member in 1861, (183) although his obituary notice reminded readers of his initial damning inexperience. (184)

The wrath of the asylum doctors was so great partly from disappointed expectation, since in 1848, one of their own number, Samuel Gaskell, had been made a Commissioner. (185) Gaskell, in fact, began what might be termed the 'Lancastrian succession.' After a difficult start to his career, he had become resident MO at Lancaster Moor (1840), where he had abolished mechanical restraint, and so conducted the institution as to impress Shaftesbury, upon whose intercession the Lord Chancellor appointed Gaskell to the Board to succeed Prichard. He in turn was succeeded by Cleaton, from the Lancashire Asylum at Rainhill, and Cleaton's successor, briefly, was Rogers, also from Rainhill. John Wallis, whose career in medical administration had concluded with the superintendency of the Lancashire Asylum at Whittingham, replaced Rogers. Thus, of the seven appointees with public asylum experience, four came from the vast barracks institutions of Lancashire. Needham's experience had been gained in the medium-sized registered hospital at York and at Barnwood Asylum, Gloucester. Cooke had had experience of the relatively small county institutions catering to Worcester and Wiltshire; Williams had come from the radically different background of Bethlem, where only curables were admitted. Rogers and Needham had had very long tenures before appointment: thirty years at Rainhill, and thirty-four years at York and Barnwood respectively. Gaskell had had nine years at Lancaster, preceded by six at Manchester Infirmary and Lunatic Hospital. Wallis had spent fifteen years at

Whittingham. Both Cooke and Cleaton had varied experience, and only Williams seems to have been a rapid riser in the psychiatric Establishment, owing firstly to the patronage of Sir W.C. Hood, and secondly to that of Shaftesbury, who secured his appointment to the Lunacy Commission. (186)

Of twenty-eight appointments, direct patronage by members of the Commission is evident in three cases; patronage by high officials may be inferred in six. The 'secretarial' and 'Lancastrian' successions produced seven Commissioners. The positions were remunerative, in both status and income, and the appointment of top ranking, successful Establishment figures was inevitable. In the event, on the medical side, the proportion of appointments made on proven specialist experience - nine out of sixteen - indicates an unexpected degree of objective selection. The 'secretarial succession' provided on the legal side a leaven of experience which could counterbalance any initially ignorant placements.

The inspectorate's efficiency, and its dogmatic traditionalism, were reinforced by an extremely high incidence of long-service, from which even the initially inexperienced could not help but become well-informed and expert eventually. Eighteen of the twenty-eight professional Commissioners holding office during this period did so for over ten years, eight for over twenty: Campbell (thirty-three years); Needham (thirty-two years, including period as member of the Board of Control); Cleaton (twenty-eight years); Nairne and Bagot (twenty-six years); Phillips (twenty-three years, in addition to seven as secretary); Gaskell and Lutwidge (eighteen years, in addition to thirteen as Metropolitan Commissioner and secretary in the case of the latter); Proctor (sixteen years, in addition to thirteen years as Metropolitan Commissioner); Wilkes and Frere (twenty-two years); Reginald Southey (fifteen years); Hume and Urmson (twelve years, in addition to nine years as Metropolitan Commissioner and six years as secretary respectively); Turner, Williams and Forster (eleven years, in addition to six years as secretary in Forster's case); Mylne (ten years, in addition to thirteen years as Metropolitan Commissioner). Giffard was secretary for five years and a Commissioner for eight. Perceval, who never became an Inspector, was secretary for seventeen years. Six of the professionals became Honorary Commissioners on retirement from the inspectorate: Campbell (three years); Cooke (nine years); Nairne (three years); Proctor (thirteen years); Wilkes (sixteen years); Cleaton (seven years). Southey and Gaskell retired through failing health following road accidents. Williams and Howard were forced out by mental collapse. Ten Commissioners were active professional members until their deaths: Frere, Giffard, Hume, Lutwidge, Mylne, Needham, Prichard, Phillips, Urmson and Wallis. Lutwidge was actually killed on duty: on a visit to Fisherton House, Salisbury, he was attacked by an inmate who drove a nail through his skull.

Inevitably, there was criticism of the Commissioners, in both abstract terms and on specific issues. Organized critics fell into two groups: the psychiatric profession, and the self-appointed guardians of the liberty of the subject.

In 1817, John Haslam had expressed the basic hostility of the medical profession to centralized control and supervision in lunacy matters. 'Of late,' he wrote,

> ... it has seriously been proposed, in a great degree to remove both the medical treatment and the moral treatment of insane persons from the care of Physicians, and to transfer them into the hands of magistrates and senators. For the welfare of those afflicted persons, and for the security of the public, it is to be hoped that such transfer may never be established; but that the medical and moral treatment of the insane may continue to be directed by the medical practitioners, under the sanctions and superintendency of the College of Physicians.(187)

By 1845, however, the transfer was completed. The compulsory medical complement of the professional Commissioners went a long way to allay the anxieties of the profession, though the private sector did not feel appeased. Intra-professional control had proved ineffective, and the public agitation of the early nineteenth century inevitably strengthened the movement towards public controls which were perceptible elsewhere in the social sector. Initially, the Commissioners in Lunacy were widely welcomed by both public and private asylum doctors. But within a short time there was friction. Especially with regard to private asylums, the Commissioners were arbiters of a system of pains and penalties, which palpably identified the licensed house proprietor as less of a doctor than a businessman, and the private asylum man stood little chance of joining the inspectorate, even in theory. (188) The public sector fared better in this respect, though it was just as subject to the inhibiting redtapism of the Commissioners, and equally liable to take offence at the inspectorate's work methods.

Movements towards administrative discretion on the part of the Board met hostile receptions. Even where such tactics might be in the long-term interest of asylum doctors and administrators, the medical profession, having become subject to legal formalism, determined to adhere to the form of the law. Thus, on their own initiative, the Commissioners assumed

> the right to determine whether the documentation, upon which patients are admitted into asylums, are formal and correct, or otherwise, and ... required many medical certificates to be amended in consequence of the facts upon which the opinion of insanity was founded having appeared to them vague and insufficient. The authority appears to be exercised in default of any sanction given by Act of Parliament ...

Admitting the importance of the matter, and the defect of the law in that respect, John Bucknill went on to urge that it was 'most desirable' that the Commissioners 'requisitions ... should be strictly limited to and in obedience to the forms of the statute.' (189)

In 1866, British and Foreign Medical-Chirurgical Review assaults transcended the guarded dissatisfaction of the asylum superintendents. Most of the latter were attuned to the ideal of state-provision and state control, by central and local authorities, provided the medical function was recognized and fostered by the responsible agencies. (190) The Review confirmed John Arlidge's observation that 'There appears to be in the English character such an aversion to centralization as to constitute a real impediment to systematic government.' (191) Sparked off partly by the legislative amendments of 1862, the assault attacked the basis of the entire system:

> The English Lunacy Commission sprang out of great abuses; it arose when men's feelings were strongly roused by the wicked and cruel treatment the insane suffered, and the public were glad to see such crying evils swept away, even though it were by a somewhat violent stretch of authority; but with those evils has passed away the necessity for continuing a central despotism. Instead of resting satisfied with what powers they had, the constant aim of the Commissioners has been to add to it, and all the recent acts passed have been devised to enable them to crush some opposition, or to extend their power, to give them the right to inquire into somebody's business, or to legalise some vexatious interference. There is nothing broad, comprehensive, or statesmanlike in the acts of late years - nothing to convey the idea of a wise measure originated to carry out a principle, or to secure endangered rights or liberties; on the contrary, the provisions are ludicrously frivolous, and are more a collection of devices to overcome some obstacles met with in the would-be triumphant career of those enterprising officials. To be mad now is to become a patient of the State, and the prescriptions should properly be dated from No.19, Whitehall Place. The tyranny of the power of the Lunacy Board is so oppressive as affecting the management of private asylums that it has effectively extinguished all opposition and proprietors, however conscientious and upright, are compelled in self-defence to defer to the powers that be.
>
> As regards the rules of public asylums the case is not very different; for though country gentlemen do not always find the yoke easy, they too often, conscious of their ignorance, accept the dictum of a body who are always ready to suggest, and if their advice is not taken, can embarrass a committee by persevering opposition, and threaten them with the terrors of the Secretary of State. (192)

The article was wrong-headed in so far as the legislation

of 1853 and 1862 had been secured by the action of independently-minded MPs, (193) and the pessimism was unfounded. The Lunacy Commissioners were in no sense responsible for the abortive legislation of the 1870's and 1880's. Yet the impassioned journalism was symptomatic of reflex reaction to finicking interference, especially by individuals with little or no experience of asylum life.(194) The Board had its medical defenders: Lockhart Robinson, then editor of the J.M.Sc., attacked the Review article, arguing that state control was desirable, that the Commissioners were fighting a battle against avarice, cruelty and ignorance, and that their zeal infected the 'upright guardians of the insane.' (195) And one finds it difficult to accept the implied kowtowing of the magistracy: in practice, visiting committees responded to the Board's suasion when it suited them.

The public sector gradually identified itself with the Commissioners' policy. Though at times, specific remarks of the inspectors, or generalized statements of the Board came in for criticism, a united front was presented when the whole system of asylumdom and its controllers came under attack.(196) The private asylum doctors had less in common with the Board, and the Commissioners attitude towards individual licensees, and towards the private sector in general, was calculated to perpetuate mutual distrust, and not infrequent hostility. Most upsetting were the niggling and pettiness in much of the inspectorate's attitudes. Leonard Weatherley, who had been involved in the private sector from the 1870's until the Great War, gave several illustrations of bureaucratic smallmindedness and impersonal contact. One recollection casts an unnamed Commissioner in a thoroughly unattractive light: Weatherley had received into his house at Bath a major on sick leave from India, at the request of the man's relatives. Feeling the man might be recovered in a short time, he kept him away from the rest of the patients and treated him as one of the family:

> He made rapid improvement, and I felt justified, as he was about to go before a Medical Board in London, to discharge him as recovered but he wished to remain on with me, he wrote me a letter to that effect, and I duly got a magistrate's order to receive him as a voluntary boarder. All the time ... he had no idea he was in an asylum ... The day before he was due to go before the Medical Board ... (in the mean-time he had been promoted Colonel) ... the Commissioners paid my asylum a visit. The medical Commissioner saw my soldier patient and the following conversation took place:
>
> 'I am a Commissioner in Lunacy and want to ask you a few questions. Do you know where you are and under what conditions you came here?'
>
> The Colonel answered, 'Yes, I was very run down. Dr. Weatherley kindly took me for rest and treatment into his house.'
>
> 'I beg to differ with you,' said the Commissioner 'Nothing of the sort. You have been a certified lunatic and in an asylum, and you are now a voluntary

boarder ...' (197)

Weatherley offered further instances of arrogant redtapism, indicative of the tensions between the private asylum doctors and the inspectorate. In 1885, for example, he had bought a decrepit private asylum 'with potential' and spent several thousand pounds renovating it. The Commissioners visited and one of them (198) instructed that the hall needed improvement. Weatherley spent a further £500 in compliance, but at the next visit, the sole comment was 'the house is in good order, but we think Weatherley should get a new sofa for the gentlemen's sitting-room.' Weatherley angrily taxed the medical Commissioner, who merely said it was the Commissioners' duty to complain, but as a general rule, they never called attention to improvements. (199) Others were more tolerant, and pointed out that the law, and the scope of the Commissioners' duties were responsible for any shortcomings. L.S.F. Winslow found the inspectorate 'eager and ready to do their duty, but ... confused by the obscurity of the Lunacy Acts.' (200)

The second group of critics were more personalized in their attacks. The earliest organization formed to protect the English subject from illicit confinement as a lunatic was Luke James Hansard's Alleged Lunatic's Friend Society of 1845. (281) Its principal targets had been the madhouse proprietors: the central inspectorate, coeval with the Society, had been acknowledged as the only existing potential check on abuse, hindered in practice by numerical inadequacy. During the 1880's, however, the Lunacy Law Reform Association, directed by the hysterical polemicism of its lady secretary, aimed its shafts not only at the mad-doctors, but at the Commissioners as guardians of the 'madness mongers' and the corrupt and inefficient ranks of public officialdom. Louisa Lowe had experienced asylum life and was convinced of the existence of concerted activities to undermine the liberty of the individual for financial gain, on the part of unprincipled individuals who enlisted the support of immoral doctors and were protected by an inspectorate susceptible to bribery. If much of her writing was fanciful, and her arguments from circumstantial evidence unsound, there remained sufficient factual accounts in her attacks to indicate that the Commission was not totally untarnished. Her accusations of graft and corruption cannot be supported, even by uncritical acceptance of her own selective accounts, but as secretary of the Association, she had considerable knowledge of many cases that at times reflected the inspectorate's moral guilt, and, in at least one instance, downright dishonesty by a Commissioner.

Certain Commissioners were attacked by name, and one by inference. (202) Even Shaftesbury did not escape censure. Lowe's outpourings can, at certain points, be related to more substantial evidence, and John Cleaton can be shown guilty of gross negligence and inaccuracy which, if intentional, was criminal. In The Bastilles of England, Miss Lowe rehearsed details of the Petschler case, on which partial attention had been devoted by the Select Committee of 1877. Supportive evidence from the asylum superintendent involved indicated that Cleaton had lied in a special report on the case. Local feeling around Manchester, where Mrs. Petschler lived, ran high, but no action was taken by the Home Secretary, despite continued appeals. An anonymous pamphlet, distributed throughout the Manchester area, reiterated charges levelled first by a local JP, Alfred Aspland, and showed the public danger inherent in the structure and organization of the Lunacy Board. The Visiting Commissioners, the pamphlet indicated,

> are, as a rule, unknown by name to the patients, nor are they individually responsible for their reports, on asylums which are signed vicariously by their chairman. In fact, these Lunacy Commissioners, while endowed with the prestige and practical irremovability of law judges, form such a secret and irresponsible tribunal as has in all ages been prone to corruption ...

That the visiting Commissioners directly involved in the Petschler case (Cleaton and Greville Howard) had been bribed, was intimated by the pamphlet. Louisa Lowe stated this as an undeniable fact. (203) Foreign journalists joined the hunt. In the New York Sunday Times, 22 August, 1875, there appeared an article by Mrs. Helen Burnard on The Lunacy System of England, in which it was baldly stated that

> There can be no doubt that the sane, and especially sane women, are constantly incarcerated. The fact seems to be, that the Commissioners in Lunacy drive a profitable trade with the superintendents and madness-mongers, by detaining patients after recovery. (204)

Amid the fuss and accusations, the Board kept silent. There appeared neither corporate nor individual denials of specific or general charges: a silence that Miss Lowe found tantamount to an admission of guilt. There were grounds for suspicion of laxity, if not of corruption. The idleness of the Board's secretary and the disingenuous superficiality of the Commissioners in the theatrically-dimensioned Quail incident (205) in 1846 was matched by a similar lack of contact with reality by the Secretary (Perceval) in 1880. A female had been confined in Northumberland House Asylum, Stoke Newington, by her brother. As co-heir with her in their aunt's will, his motives were suspect, and his actions confirmed that he was mainly concerned to obtain control over his sister's affairs. The woman was let out on three months' trial, after signing a document confirming the leaving of the conduct of her interests to the brother. She was, of course, still under the original certificates and admission order signed by the latter, when she wrote to the Commissioners, requesting discharge, and including letters from various acquaintances attesting her sanity. Having been informed of the precise circumstances of the case, Perceval wrote the following amazingly inappropriate reply:

Office of the Commissioners in Lunacy,
19, Whitehall Place, S.W.

June 21st 1880.

Madam,

I have to acknowledge the receipt of your letter of the 17th inst. I am directed by the Commissioners to point out to you that your absence from Northumberland House, to which they readily gave consent, was for the purpose of testing your powers of self-control out of the asylum, as you were not considered sufficiently well to be discharged absolutely. They trust that no necessity for replacing you in Northumberland House may arise.

Your discharge will follow as a matter of course, if at the end of the three months no such necessity has arisen, and meanwhile, if advised to do so, your brother can discharge you at any time.

I am, Madam, your obedient servant,
Charles Spencer Perceval. (206)

The concern to establish protective barriers to swift removal was clearly antithetical to the alienists' stress on rapid transmission of the insane to the asylum. The obligatory medical certificates were supposed to ensure that detention of the non-insane did not occur, but in practice they failed. In the case of Dodwell, for example, two eminent alienists, Winslow and Winn, had declared the man sane, yet he remained imprisoned as a criminal lunatic. (207) The admission order offered no safeguard, since the signatory needed no other qualification than to have seen the patient within seven days of signing. Louisa Lowe was especially worried that 'no kind of relationship or acquaintance or equality of social rank need exist between the patient and the signatory of the order that consigns him to an asylum,' and that 'to the commissioners' own knowledge, servants had thus disposed of their own employers ...' (208)

The matter of patients' letters was one of the Association's main concerns, (209) and figured prominently in several of the most publicized cases - that of Mrs.Petschler, for example. The inspectors were legally required to check every letter written by a private patient and not immediately forwarded to the addressee. Perceval could not recall one instance of taking action on a case of illegal suppression, though in their Thirtieth Report, the Commissioners acknowledged that 'a few instances have occurred where letters ... have been sent to the person who signed the order for reception, instead of being laid before us ...'. By law these instances should have provoked prosecution, entailing a penalty of up to £20 in each instance. In evidence before the Select Committee of 1877, Shaftesbury, whose manner suggested he was unfamiliar with the content of the Report, maintained that there was only a suspicion of illegal interference with mail. (210) The Board's chairman was, at the time, scarcely in a position to answer Dillwyn's questions adequately, (211) and his declining degree of direct involvement with the Board's routine made him a poor witness. Lowe could not resist dealing a blow to his role which did little to commend her cause, though she was justified in attacking his ministerial signature of a document he plainly had not read properly.

Here it might be instructive to note the discrepancy between Shaftesbury's evidence at the 1859 hearing, and that at the 1877 enquiry, since it is indicative of that self-satisfaction that comes from imperfect knowledge. In 1877, he made the following comment:

> I ventured in 1859 to give as full a statement as I could of the state of things that had come under my own observation. I am happy to say that since 1859, nothing has occurred that would lead me to make such observation, and to say that the state of things required revision and superintendence in the way it did before; on the contrary, since 1859, we have been in a state of constant progress and very great improvement.

But in 1859, Shaftesbury had attributed abuses in the system of asylumdom not to defective legislation or inept supervision, but to the inherent cupidity of human nature. (212) Presumably, then, human nature had changed after his withdrawal from personal visitation of asylums. In 1859, he had been distrustful of medical specialists per se, and of licensees of private asylums in particular, whom he saw as being 'anxious to get as many patients as they can, and to stint them in medicine and comfort.' Even the best must be prone to temptation. (213) The disquiet of 1859 had become laudatory secondhand evidence by 1877, rendering Shaftesbury's evidence less valid than its source might suggest. (214) Oversatisfaction, rather than outright malpractice, might be a juster charge to level at the Commissioners. James Wilkes, one of Lowe's prime targets, gave evidence to Dillwyn's Committee which indicates a tolerance damaging to the inspectorate's reputation as guardians of all the insane in the kingdom. It was, he asserted,

> ... extremely difficult to refuse the renewal of a licence because to say that no licence should be granted would have the effect of reducing many families to absolute beggary ... In many cases, you shrug your shoulders and say, 'What a sad place this is, and what a person is at the head of it', but you cannot say to that person, 'though you have committed no offence, I will reduce you to beggary' ... The truth must be told, and I must say that we Commissioners have erred upon the side of lenity. We have endeavoured year by year to do things by persuasion till I have lost all patience ... (215)

This testimony strongly suggested that the accusations levelled by the LLRA's secretary were at least valid in principle: the Commissioners were too careful of the susceptibilities of the licensees to be adequate protectors of asylum inmates, whether insane or wrongfully labelled insane.

The Board's silence, both in print and in their surviving papers, makes it impossible to make a judgement on specific issues detailed by its critics. The attribution of idleness fails to hold good if the records of miles travelled and visits made are acceptable evidence of at least formal implementation of their duties. But the absurd understaffing of the inspectorate rendered formal performance the most that could be hoped for. The spirit of the law was impossible to bear in mind when even to keep the letter proved overpowering in terms of time and expense. That mistakes were made need not necessarily involve corruption, though the inspectors, if doing their duty properly, could scarcely have been thorough enough at all times to permit the superficiality of their inspections to be exceptional. Thus, for example, they made a visitation to Prestwich Asylum on 5th March, 1875. Their next visit was nineteen months later on 29th September, 1876. The workhouse at Ashton-under-Lyne union (Lancashire/Cheshire) was visited in 1849, and not again until 1852; four more years elapsed before the next visit. (216) Even where visits were made, the size of an asylum might preclude the full and rigorous investigation that the law (and the inspectors) desired. Philips and Williams, visiting the Lancaster Moor Asylum in 1866, concluded their minute with self-justifying vagueness:

> The asylum is now a vast pile of buildings and the patients are so numerous, that it must be difficult for any medical superintendent to keep up any distinct recollections of every individual patient under his care ... The case books are, as far as we had time to examine them, some evidence that proper attention is given to individuals. (217)

In public asylums, the Commissioners' contact with individual patients was perforce minimal. In the larger asylums, especially those with attached farmland, labouring patients were seldom inspected. There was more scope for individual contact in licensed houses, and, theoretically, the Commissioners would grant private interviews with 'suitable' patients, and public interviews with the more querulous. As John Bucknill pointed out, however, the reserved convalescent, i.e. the one most likely to benefit by removal, was the least likely to solicit an interview, and individual inspection was impossible. (218)

Visitation was not always as unexpected as the statute and the critics of asylumdom hoped. In his evidence before the 1877 Select Committee, James Wilkes admitted that where there were several institutions in the same district, forewarnings of inspection were inevitable. He told of a licensed house in South Wales where the superintendent cheerfully admitted that one of his attendants had witnessed the inspectors' arrival at Neath station and had given the house time to put itself in readiness. (219) Provincial visitation was more difficult then Metropolitan, and eight months a year were given over to the circuits. The nine divisions of the circuits were split between the six Commissioners, who alternated in their visitations in half-yearly circuits. In the Metropolis, there were six circuits, and since each institution had to be visited four times by two Commissioners and twice by a single Commissioner, Wilkes reckoned that six to eight days each quarter were given over to each Metropolitan circuit, making a yearly total of some four months. (220)

Since inspectors were Board-members, the question of their competence to interpret for themselves the central authority's definition of their task did not arise. But the Commissioners were not sole agents of supervision and control. In provincial matters, the Board was quick to acknowledge the role of the visiting justices:

> These gentlemen are more immediately the visitors to whose inspection the provincial Asylums are entrusted ... Their visits, are, by law, more frequent than ours; and the legislature seems to have selected them as the persons who are primarily to perform certain duties, which we, in our turn and at far more distant intervals, are required to perform ...

The bulk of the Commissioners' duties would have made efficient administration of the Lunacy Laws impossible, 'unless we received this assistance.' (221) Should the local magistracy decline to co-operate, the central inspectorate was practically powerless. Thus, the Commissioners, in 1850, complained that for several years Belle Vue House, Devizes, had continually proved defective, and urged the local magistrates to refuse renewal of the licence, but the chairman of the Quarter Sessions did not even reply to the Commissioners' letter, and in that, and the following year, the house was re-licensed. (222)

In the case of pauper lunatics, the Board had to deal with central and local Poor Law authorities. Difficulties in communication with the latter are discussed below (Chapter seven). With the former, relations were amicable and co-operative, provided the wider theories of neither Board were touched upon. To the Poor Law Commissioners/Board/Local Government Board, pauper lunatics were first and foremost paupers. Until 1874, when a 4/- capitation grant was introduced, (223) the principle that the county rate and local subscription should maintain pauper lunatics inhibited the transmission to asylums which the Commissioners deemed essential for cure. The separation of 'pauper' and 'mentally ill' categories was never completed. Over-insistence on one or the other inevitably led to friction. Allbutt recalled, in a letter to Leonard Weatherley, his experience as a Commissioner (1889 - 92) and complained that

> Our greatest obstacle was the Local Government Board. I sadly fear in its great strength and ambition it is about to capture the Ministry of Health .., The Local Government Board is a crocodile and a python ...

Allbutt scorned to say that redtapism was the besetting sin: it was 'their domination and greed of power, and ... unimaginative incompetency, 'which provoked interdepartmental friction. (224)

To implement their report-function adequately, the Commissioners needed the co-operation of asylum administrators and Poor Law officials. The latter seldom met the Board's requirements, especially in the furnishing of reliable statistical data. In the 1860's, the Commissioners began publishing in their Annual Reports a wide range of valuable statistical tables. The scope varied, but was increased and refined in the later 1870's. In compiling these tables, the Commissioners were reliant on the voluntary labour of asylum medical staff. (225) The size and structure of the Annual Reports indicates the changing style and purpose of the Commissioners' conception of their function. Gradually there emerged an overwhelming conviction in the potential benefit to the battle for mental health, of assembling as much statistical information as possible on the distribution and assigned causality of various types of insanity, in spatial, temporal and socio-cultural terms. All this was to be in addition to descriptive and analytical reporting of the state of asylumdom each year. The Commissioners' earliest reports were short: 49 pages in 1850, 40 in 1856 - with Appendices giving the numbers and institutional distribution of the insane. (226) The size and content of reports increased only slowly (227) until the 1860's. Fluctuations followed, but from 1869, the vast compendium became normal. In 1850, the <u>Report</u> had consisted of: an Address; notes on changed licenses; notes on new asylums; general remarks on visitations, with particular remarks and recommendations; remarks on matters of Law, especially Nottidge v. Ripley; note on criminal lunatics; reference to proposed legislation; tables; showing the number and distribution of the insane in England and Wales; tables showing the incidence of cholera in asylums during the recent outbreak. In contrast, the 1879 <u>Report</u> consisted of 140 pages of descriptive and analytical reporting, and 303 pages of statistical appendices. It contained the kinds of information that had been appearing spasmodically since the early 1860's and always included after 1869: detailed descriptions and comments on all asylums, hospitals and workhouses visited; general statements of policy regarding the construction and management of asylums; tables of casualties, suicides etc.; comparative tables of maintenance costs; hospital statistics; general discussion of the position of the insane in workhouses; details of prosecutions; discussion of the 1877 Select Committee. The appendices contained information regarding the distribution, condition, maintenance costs etc. of private and pauper lunatics in the various institutions; reproductions of the inspectors' reports of institutions visited; special notices of the military, naval and criminal asylums, and of workhouses; lists of all asylums with their superintendents/ proprietors etc.

It is apparent that the Board was quick to become figure-conscious. The gathering and assembling of information was dangerously near becoming an end in itself in the Commissioners' urgency to maintain a complete registry of all the lunatics in the Kingdom, and of all persons having care and control over them. Bucknill lamented the disappearance of the old-style reports in the rush to become part of the modish numeracy infecting other government departments:

> in the early years of the Commission, wide and scientific views of medical hygiene and medical treatment were to be found in the Reports, worthy of such able and eminent physicians as Dr. Turner and Dr. Prichard; but of late the medical spirit has been drowned in the flood of official duty, and it is vain now that we look for any signs of the consideration of Lunacy questions from a medical point of view ... (228)

The Board, however was sure of its purpose; simply to assemble the statistics:

> The statistical information given in our Annual Reports has gradually increased in bulk and importance, and we have reason to believe that among those interested in the care and treatment of the insane, and the question of insanity in its various aspects, this portion of our Report is considered to possess much value. At no time however, have we considered it our duty to draw but the most plain and obvious deduction from the figures ... nor can we deem it advisable or justifiable to offer ... any speculations or theories of our own based on these statistics. At present we do not feel our recorded experience is sufficiently extensive to warrant many certain conclusions ... and ... conjectures ... would not ... be attended by any public advantage. (229)

The medical profession might attack the Board for its non-medical bias, and the Commissioners were conscious of their legalistic stance: Shaftesbury told the Select Committee of 1859 that 'the business transacted at the Board is entirely civil in ninety cases out of one hundred. A purely medical case does not come before us once in twenty boards.' (230) But the function of the Board was legal. Its objects were the institutions which legally deprived an individual of his liberty, and those persons whose rights had thus been violated. That those rights had been removed - ostensibly at least - on medical grounds, and that the institutions operated - again ostensibly - from medical principles, was recognized by the Board's statutory complement of physicians, but the function of the Commissioners was not thus made medical. As Wilkes told the 1877 Select Committee, the Commissioners were not capable of judging sanity or insanity, simply by conversing with patients, which was, however, their only possible contact. (231) Despite formalism and redtapism, the Commissioners were essential to the operation of the Lunacy Laws, and thus, to the maintenance of asylumdom. Mortimer-Granville summed up the considered response of the medical Establishment; he indicated

> ... the permanent and increasing value of the services rendered to the cause of humanity, and indirectly to the interests of medical science by the Commissioners in Lunacy. We do not recognise the wisdom of all their recommendations ... But in the main the ... body of public inspectors has been Lord Shaftesbury's great claim to public gratitude ... (232)

Acceptance of centralized control was the product of experience, and of need, in Lunacy matters as elsewhere. As an inspector from a different sector pointedly remarked, 'public opinion ... though loudly denouncing centralization, is apt to clamour almost in the same breath for grandmotherly interference.' (233)

CHAPTER SEVEN

COMMISSIONERS, WORKHOUSES AND PAUPER LUNATICS: 1845 - 90.

Throughout the second half of the nineteenth century, workhouses continued to be used for the confinement of pauper lunatics. Despite progressive public asylum provision, and in face of the combined opposition of psychiatrists and Lunacy Commissioners, the pressure of local excesses of lunatics over asylum beds, and the need of local poor law authorities to economise their spending, forced all counties in England and Wales, and especially the most heavily populated, to fall back on union houses. The conflict between local authorities and the central lunacy inspectorate which dragged on from the 1840's affords an opportunity to look further into both the ideology and the practical working of the Lunacy Commission, and offers, too, further insights into public opinion as regards insanity as a condition and the insane as individuals. The singlemindedness of the Commissioners, closely linked to their unshakable faith in the asylum, and circumscribed by the letter of the law, was nowhere more in evidence than in their campaign against workhouse detention of the insane. Their work-rate and perseverance was nowhere more apparent than in their time-consuming and difficult visitation of workhouses, and in their indefatigable communications with central and local poor law agencies.

This chapter analyses firstly the legal aspects of workhouse confinement and the forms of the Commissioners' inspection of workhouse lunatics. The second section discusses the effects of their failure to stamp out workhouse confinement on the Commissioners' official attitudes. The physical dimensions of confinement are next delineated, with special reference to Lancashire and the metropolis, and the concluding section explores the extent to which the workhouse lunatic ward became, or was seen to be a surrogate asylum.

I

The 1845 Lunatics Act stated that it should 'not be lawful for any person to receive two or more lunatics into any house other than an asylum, registered hospital or licensed house,' and the Commissioners were understandably dissatisfied that a subsequent provision rendered union houses subject to their inspection, thereby implying the legality of detention within certain limits. (1) Shaw's Union Officers' Manual for 1845 - 46 showed that there were initially 750 workhouses under the Commissioners' jurisdiction in this respect, all of which might contain one or more lunatics. With such a daunting number of institutions confronting their limited manpower, the Commissioners were 'compelled to avail themselves of the doubtful language of the 111th section, in which the words "shall and may" have been construed to leave discretion in this respect and resolved to distribute the visitation of workhouses over a longer period than a year.' The first task was to determine the class of inmates with whom the inspectors were to deal. From the hotch-potch classification of the institutions, a general principle was adopted, applying to

> all persons kept in workhouses, who, by reasons of deficiency, infirmity, derangement, or other unsoundness of mind (whatever form it might assume, and whether they were violent or harmless, curable or incurable), were not deemed competent to take care of themselves, or proper to be left entirely under their own guidance and control without supervision ... and of course including all who, in consequence of their mental condition, stood on a different footing, in respect to their personal liberty, from ordinary paupers in the workhouse, and were not allowed to quit the house at their own discretion, upon ordinary notice to the master. (2)

Of course, legally, workhouse masters could detain no-one: normal inmates discharged themselves at will. With regard to insane paupers, the case was, technically, no different. But, as the Commissioners were aware, in practice the issue was complicated by the need for social control of mental disorder. Their Further Report (1847) indicated their awareness of illicit detention by poor law officials:

> How far a system of this kind, which virtually places in the hands of the masters, many of whom are ignorant, and some of whom are capricious and tyrannical, an almost complete control over the personal liberty of so many of their fellow men, is either warranted by law, or can be wholesome in itself, are questions which seem open to considerable doubt. Probably if the legality of the detention came to be contested before a judicial tribunal in any individual case, the same considerations of necessity and expediency which originally led to the practice, might be held to justify the particular act, provided it were shown that the party complaining of illegal detention could not be safely trusted at large, and that his detention ... was really for his benefit as well as for that of the community. (3)

The law gave no positive guidance, though it indicated provisions to be made for pauper lunatics not in asylums or licensed houses, and distinguished those 'fit' to be detained in asylums from those who might with propriety be detained elsewhere. (4) Those concerned with the custodial care of the insane were incensed by the harmful vagueness of the law, which failed to provide even minimum guarantee of pauper lunatics' rights by appointment of a responsible supervising agency. The danger did not lie solely in the fact that the insane would be untreated. John Arlidge, for example, warned that

> It certainly appears to be a great anomaly, that while the law, in its anxiety to guard the liberty of the subject, insists that no persons who are

> insane - not even dangerous pauper lunatics - shall be placed or kept in confinement in a lunatic asylum without orders and medical certificates in a certain form, it should be at the same time permitted to the master of a workhouse forcibly to detain in the house ... any inmate whom, in his sole judgement and responsibility, he may pronounce to be a person of unsound mind, and therefore, unfit to be at large. (5)

The power granted to masters was complemented by the discretionary powers allowed to overseers and relieving officers, who were obliged to report cases of pauper lunacy to a magistrate, but who could decide, on their own initiative, whether a person was suitable for workhouse confinement or not. There was little counterbalance from the union medical officers: as paid employees, subordinate to workhouse masters and subject to pressure from guardians, their attitude to the propriety of detention outside an asylum was scarcely likely to be disinterested, even if they were experienced enough and competent to make a valid judgement. (6) The situation was not improved greatly by the amending lunacy law of 1853. One section of the Act attempted to make the union medical officer the medium of communication with the central Board. But, although he was obliged to notify the Commissioners of all pauper lunatics within his area, he was not empowered either to enquire after such cases, or, where he had knowledge of their existence, to visit and assess their condition. (7) It was left open to the medical officer to act upon a report that an insane pauper was at large and 'deemed to be a lunatic and a proper person to be sent to an asylum', without actually seeing the individual concerned. The first link in the chain of decision making remained the relieving officer. Should he decide to transmit an insane pauper to the workhouse, the final choice had effectively been made, for although the medical officer would have to make a subsequent examination, it would, politically, 'be hazardous' for him to try to rescind a decision backed by the local authorities. (8) Furthermore, if the details of an alleged lunatic's existence were first made known to a relieving officer, or if a lunatic were already maintained in the union house, a medical officer possessed no legal obligation to make official notification to the Commissioners. Even where the obligation existed, however, it was not always observed. (9)

The central poor law authorities were obviously aware of the problems involved in workhouse detention of the mentally disordered, but official interpretation of the 1834 Poor Law Amendment Act circumscribed their actions. Section 45 prohibited the confinement in a workhouse of any person deemed a 'dangerous Lunatic, Insane Person or Idiot.' The Law Officers of the Crown had directed that the word 'dangerous' ought to be understood as applying to the second and third identifications as well as the first. (10) The Poor Law Commissioners disapproved of the directive:

> From the express prohibition of the detention of dangerous persons of unsound mind in a workhouse, contained in the clause ... coupled with the prevalent practice of keeping insane persons in workhouses before the passing of the Poor Law Amendment Act, it may be inferred that persons of unsound mind, not being dangerous, may be legally kept in a workhouse.

However, urged the Commissioners, ' ... with Lunatics, the first object ought to be their cure, by means of proper medical treatment ...' Since this was available only in asylums, ' ... the detention of any curable lunatic in a workhouse is highly objectionable on the score of both humanity and economy.' (11)

Convenience had been the principal reason for the law's toleration of workhouse detention: accommodation there was seen as temporary for lunatics in transit to asylums. The lunacy laws ordered that

> No pauper, who shall have lately become a lunatic, shall be received, lodged or detained in any house or place other than a County or Borough Lunatic Asylum, or a Public Hospital, or a Licensed House, for a longer period than shall be requisite for obtaining an order for his removal to such Asylum.(12)

Taken by itself, s. 48 of the same Act seemed to preclude the keeping of any insane person in a workhouse, and many magistrates and boards of guardians had so interpreted the law by transmitting to asylums, immediately after the passing of the Act, large numbers of inveterate and incurable cases from workhouse confinement or the care of friends. The supposed stringency of the Act caused many to be transferred at a time when physical disability rendered them unequal to the fatiguing excitement involved. (13) In the following year an intentionally clarifying piece of legislation was introduced which allowed for more flexibility. (14)

The official belief was that the majority of workhouse detainees were harmless idiots and incurables, whose confinement, though not illegal, nor even defective on medical grounds, was simply inconvenient. Parliamentary returns for 1845 showed a total of 4,860 pauper insane confined (August 1844), of whom 509 were in workhouses operated under local acts; and the Commissioners estimated a further 105 in non-union areas. (15) In some houses, up to fifty lunatics and idiots were maintained. An average of five to fifteen were assumed for England and Wales. The figures probably underestimated the total: by January 1847, there were 8,986 lunatics known to be confined in workhouses, and a further 173 in non-union parishes. (16)

The Commissioners organized visitation by starting with all houses known to contain ten or more lunatics, and any other workhouse which happened to be nearby, whilst in the course of visiting asylums and licensed houses. (17) Between August 1845 and August 1846, the Commissioners inspected 340 workhouses, and added a further 152 during the next six months. In a few instances a house was inspected twice. The adopted procedure was as thorough as time allowed, but the dynamics of workhouse confinement prevented even literal observance of the law's requirements. The master of the house was requested by the inspectors to indicate every person he considered insane or idiotic, and the inspector duly noted the information. The named inmates were then spoken to: and that was the nearest the Commissioners could come to any diagnostic interview. Enquiries were made as to diet and general treatment, especially as to seclusion and restraint. Rooms were inspected and a short minute entered in the visiting book. The limits of interference were the Commissioners' directions to guardians to effect the removal of any suitable pauper, and charges to masters to bring unfavourable criticisms to the attention of guardians. (18)

A thoroughly co-ordinated and systematic visitation of workhouses could not be undertaken until 1857. Between January of that year and July of the next, all 655 workhouses in England and Wales were visited, some more than once. The Poor Law Board gave an average of 7,500 lunatics confined in union houses during this period, though, once again, the total is probably an underestimation. The Commissioners were authorized to 'visit all such parish and union workhouses in which there shall be, or alleged to be any lunatic, as by Resolution of their Board may be directed,' and to enquire 'whether the provisions of the law as to Lunatics in such a Parish or Union have been carried out; also as to the dietary, accommodation, and treatment of the Lunatics in such workhouses; and they are to report in writing thereon to the Poor Law Board.' Strictly speaking, the Commissioners' brief ended there, but they attempted to go further:

> We have frequently thought it necessary, for the welfare of the insane inmates, to make various suggestions for their better care and treatment, and to recommend, amongst other things, removals to asylums from time to time, but the law invests us with no power to enforce the recommendations we may offer, no matter how important or essential they may be.

This situation might have been improved had such power rested with the central poor law authority, who were, on the surface, only too anxious to co-operate with the Commissioners. But despite a show of willingness on their part, 'it has not infrequently happened that, after prolonged correspondence between the Board and the Guardians, in cases where we have suggested amendments, its interference has failed to effect the desired object, and our suggestions have remained neglected.' (19) Their numerical inadequacies made the Commissioners view the workhouses as a peripheral element in their responsibilities. Yet their appointed concern was all certified lunatics in the kingdom. This made them anxious to retain direct interest and aim at more frequent visitation, though their inability to fulfil their aim led to suggestions for the introduction of a new class of district medical visitors to relieve the Commissioners, and even of the appointment of sets of visitors similar to asylum visiting committees. (20)

The Poor Law Commissioners had directed masters of workhouses to adopt a ninefold classification of paupers, in which 'class 4' was to comprise 'Insane, Idiots and Lunatics.' In practice, the ruling was imperfectly and negligently observed, making complete registration impossible. Inspecting Commissioners in Lunacy would only rarely be able to fulfil their duties of personal contact with all allegedly insane paupers, and even where attempts at classification were not entirely lacking, lunatics and idiots were likely to be seen as eligible for class 1: the aged, disabled and infirm; or class 7: the sick or injured. According to the Commissioners, it was 'not infrequently' that masters would yield to boards of guardians (who were, predictably, apprehensive of asylum charges) and simply ignore separate classification, resorting to their memories of simple 'ad libbing' to indicate class 4 eligibles to visiting inspectors. In houses managed under local acts or in Gilbert unions, the Commissioners claimed that this was 'invariably' the case. (21)

The Commissioners themselves adopted the following classification system: pauper insane were divided into congenital defectives (the most numerous); the demented or fatuous; the positively deranged. Epileptic and paralytic patients were found in all groups. The first subdivision, within which imbecility and weakmindedness were considered to account for two-thirds of the total, contained paupers usually placed amongst the able-bodied of their own age and sex if their bodily health was average. Their general treatment and diet were the same as for the rest of their assigned class. In some of the smaller houses, where there were few other able-bodied inmates, the Commissioners found that most of the gardening and outdoor labour was done by the males from this group, whilst the females performed the household chores. Direct supervision was minimal, though in the case of idiotic inmates the feeblest sort, whose habits tended towards the dirty or the violent, some measure of control was usual. Yet only in rare instances were even these separated from the generality of inmates. Victims of Time and the bottle were usually placed with the aged or infirm of their own sex and removed to the hospital ward when their general health failed. There were, according to the Commissioners, surprisingly few cases of genuine derangement that were not transferred to asylums - though the suspicion was that this was due to the fact of original concealment giving way to speedy removal when the symptoms of insanity became unmanageable, (or 'inconvenient' as the Poor Law Commissioners phrased it). (22)

The combination of epilepsy with mental illness was calculated by the Commissioners to account for one-fifth or more of the total workhouse lunatic population. The physical manifestations of the illness prompted more thorough separation and control than was customarily afforded to the workhouse lunatic or idiot. Epileptic paupers were usually accommodated in segregated wards with the sick, or in the workhouse hospital. This was the practice in the large houses at Manchester, Liverpool, Nottingham, Brighton, Plymouth, Marylebone and St. Pancras. Elsewhere, where there was high incidence of epileptic insanity, special wards were used: Birmingham, Clifton (York), Bath, and Stapleton (Bristol) workhouses followed this pattern, and regular visits by the medical officer were usual. The Commissioners were uncertain as to the propriety of detaining epileptics in the workhouse, adopting the flexible view that individual cases should be judged on their merits, though voicing wishes that Chronic Hospitals should be established. (23)

The legal distinction which annoyed the Poor Law Commissioners was equally disturbing to the Lunacy Commissioners. In their eyes, the sole criterion for determining the suitability of workhouse detention was not that of 'danger' but that of curability. All potentially curable cases should go to the asylum, they argued; but the prognosis rested not with a physician, but with workhouse masters. Often, a classifiably insane person would be excluded from a master's lists because, though incapable of earning a living outside the house, he proved useful and capable of some labour inside. (24) By an order of the Poor Law Board ('3 Off. Circ. 40'), it became illegal for guardians to detain persons of weak intellect unless there were reasonable grounds for supposing them incapable of taking care of themselves. This judgement,again, was to be made by laymen. A clear danger became apparent in cases of women who were allowed to discharge themselves, only to return pregnant. At Newark, for example, the Commissioners found two weakminded females who were constantly allowed to discharge themselves, each with three illegitimate children in the house. The guardians saw no reason to curb their liberty. Other houses provided instances of similar cases, illustrating the universality of circumstances which provided unions with more pauper mouths to feed whilst boosting the incidence of hereditary congenital idiocy. At Walsall, the inspectors found an idiotic female with four bastards; at Monmouth workhouse in 1846, there were two imbecile paupers each with three illegitimate offspring, one of whom was again pregnant. Calne workhouse offered an example of mental defect transmitted in this way over three generations. (25)

Magistrates and local poor law officials tended to take as their criterion an individual lunatic's propensity to violence. The general attitude was that 'harmless' patients were suitable for workhouse confinement, a view endorsed by the Commissioners in 1857. (26) The medical Establishment, however, disagreed. John Arlidge attacked the Commissioners' standard of curability, arguing that two-thirds of workhouse insane fell into the Commissioners' first subdivision, and thus could presumably be advantageously detained. These were, he urged, the last type of persons to expose to the society of the normal inmates of workhouses. (27) John Bucknill was more insistent:

> The term 'harmless patients', or in the words of the statute, 'not dangerous to themselves or others', I believe to be inapplicable to any insane person who is not helpless from bodily infirmity or total loss of mind; it can only with propriety be used as a relative term, meaning that the patient is not so dangerous as others are, or that he is not known to be refractory or suicidal ... The great majority of homicides and suicides committed by insane persons, have been committed by those who had previously been considered harmless. (28)

Asylum-standard vigilance was essential, therefore, and that was available only in asylums.

In practice, it appears that workhouse masters adopted a narrower definition of 'dangerous' than the law intended. Thus, in 1866, when the Commissioners were investigating a charge of cruelty at Salford workhouse, brought by one attendant against another, it was discovered that the system adopted in the lunatic wards for dealing with 'refractory' patients was 'throwing down all such ... as were troublesome, and forcibly keeping them there until they should have become quiet.' The alleged cruelty had occurred during one such attempted restraint, and the Commissioners found themselves unable in justice to prosecute an attendant for doing his job by the rules. However, they persuaded the Poor Law Board to interfere, and the guardians gave an assurance that the risk would be avoided in future: 'they had determined to send to a Lunatic Asylum, and not to retain in the workhouse, any pauper inmate of unsound mind who is of insolent or disorderly habits.' In so far as this was an advance, the inspectors were satisfied, until it became apparent that the workhouse would still receive the quiet 'melancholic' paupers, who very often exhibited propensities to suicide. (29) At the nearby Manchester Old Workhouse, in the same year, there was a suicide, of which the coroner's jury had acquitted all involved of blame. The Commissioners were less tolerant, and complained in their minute of visitation that 'it was impossible to avoid remarking that blame could not but exist where patients of suicidal tendencies were received in a place not only unfurnished with everything necessary to treatment, but accompanied by everything that must tend to exaggerate the malady.' Elsewhere, even when conscientious medical officers tried to intervene, they were often blocked by guardians in their attempts to arrange removals to asylums, not infrequently with fatal consequences. (30)

II

The Commissioners' attitudes were understandably hostile to the principle, as well as the realities of workhouse confinement. The stringent conditions of workhouse entry, designed to check abuse, were totally unsuitable when applied to the insane pauper. 'Where they do not tend to increase the mortality of patients,' complained the inspectorate, 'they serve to insure the prolongation of the disease.' The construction of workhouses could not easily or cheaply be adapted to the needs of the insane, and the small, prison-like yards which were the norm offered scant means of outdoor exercise. Even more harmful was the system of administration. Workhouses were managed by boards elected by the ratepayers, and by certain ex-officio guardians. Naturally, the electors were vigilant in their attention to expenditure, and the incentive of most boards was to curtail expensive comforts and to provide minimal responses to the needs of inmates. Rules designed to curb disorderly conduct amongst the ordinary pauper inmates were hardly suitable for the insane. The Commissioners noted despairingly that

> Any increase of excitement, or outbreak of violence, occurring in the case of such patients, instead of being regarded as a manifestation of diseased action requiring medical, soothing treatment, has subjected the individual to punishment, and in several instances, to his imprisonment in a gaol. (31)

Distinguished from other inmates in only one respect, the pauper lunatic became 'a prisoner ... for life, incapable of asserting his rights, often of signifying his wants, yet amenable to as much punishment as if he were perfectly sane, and a willing offender against the laws and regulations of the place.' (32)

The association of lunatics with the generality of the inmates, often the worst elements, was, according to the Commissioners, most pronounced in London, though this lack of classification was widespread throughout the provinces. Only one-tenth of the houses visited in 1857 - 58 had separate wards. The intermixing of inmates meant that there was 'no mode of complying with suggestions, made by the inspectors for the benefit of the insane, 'without disturbing the general economy of the house.' The Commissioners, however, were in principle hostile to the establishment of segregated lunatic wards. Where separated from the non-insane, pauper lunatics were judged to be insufficiently classified amongst themselves. Patients, said the Commissioners, resorting to generalization, 'were indiscriminately mixed together and there is no opportunity for classification' in houses which had segregated wards. In addition, there was 'no separation where the association is injurious and no association where such would be beneficial.' (33) Special wards were condemned as tending to be poorly constructed and exhibiting 'some portion of that disregard for humanity and decency which was at one time a prevailing characteristic in the treatment of insanity.' (34) Wards of recent construction were admitted to provide reasonable accommodation, but the Commissioners saw this vitiated by deficient superintendence, dietary and medical arrangements. What was disturbing the central inspectorate was clearly a fear that if lunatic wards were widely erected as adjuncts to union houses, patients who ought to go to asylums would be siphoned off into the cheaper establishments:

> In places where such wards have been opened, there is an obvious determination on the part of the guardians to consider them as constituting Lunatic Asylums. All or nearly all the patients belonging to the Union, whatever the forms of their disease, are in the first instance most improperly sent to the workhouse, and are then generally detained there. (35)

Dissatisfaction led the Commissioners into inconsistency. Commenting on the houses of Oldham, Blackburn and Nottingham, the Commissioners objected to the appointment of (respectively) independent matron, nurse and attendant, responsible directly to the guardians, to wards catering for segregated lunatics. The type of persons appointed was judged inferior and the inspectors recommended treatment of the insane as part of the general body of the workhouse, subject to the overall control of the master. (36)

The Commissioners' attitudes reflected their inability to impose on workhouses the standardisation of record-keeping and the minimum humane medically-orientated custody which they guaranteed in asylums and licensed houses. They had no authority over the persons of workhouse inmates, and their inspectoral function was, in their own eyes, reducible to a chance 'to detect the evil that exists at the time of our visit, and which, after all, we have not the power to remove.' (37) There was nothing they could do, for example, to prevent lunatics from union houses being punished as criminals. In 1857, several incidents occurred to show up the Board's impotence. An insane inmate of the East Grinstead workhouse was sent to Lewes gaol for six months for threatening the master; at Downham, a pauper of unsound mind was repeatedly allowed to discharge himself, and on his final quitting the house, he landed in Swaffham Gaol for indecent assault, even though both the master of the workhouse and the gaol governor confirmed his not being responsible for his actions, and unfit for gaol. The case caused some public stir, and the Commissioners brought the matter to the attention of the Home Secretary. Since the gaol's medical officer refused to certify the man insane, however, there were no grounds for interference. (38)

By 1867, a further ambivalence was apparent in the Commissioners' stance. In the same report they remarked that 'workhouse arrangements exist always on sufferance,' whilst the previous page outlined the response of certain types of patient to workhouse confinement, and concluded with the following statement with regard to 'chronic inmates' whose habits were 'not such ... as to render necessary a treatment not commonly extended to all.' They were

> employed with the rest indoors or in the gardens and fields, frequently enjoying some indulgence of diet

> ... and having none of the infirmities incident to the more helpless forms of mental disease, are even less sensible than the ordinary pauper of the structural deficiencies of the house, and are not depressed by the ... comfortlessness of the day rooms, and on the whole perhaps pass a less complaining life than many other class of inmates. (39)

These patients constituted the very class which the Commissioners had once believed should be specially treated elsewhere - preferably in an asylum, and their comments must be judged as expressive of disillusion rather than changed heart. (40) When it came down to particulars, the inspectorate's disapproval of the workhouse, though total, was graded. Very small and very large houses tended to elicit grudgingly favourable reports. (41) Those in between, effectively those belonging to town unions, came in for most specific condemnation. In their 1867 Report, the Commissioners generalized on town workhouses as places where lunatics who ought to have been in asylums were 'detained without anything of asylum comfort, where there are cheerless rooms, insufficient and incompetent attendance, a low diet, no records of the simplest kind and no provision at all of healthful exercise for the mind or the body.' (42) There was further retraction of dogmatic opposition to workhouse confinement after 1867, when, faced with the swamping of the new District Asylums in London with inveterate and incurable cases, they averred that chronic and harmless patients could be catered for adequately in the lunatic wards of liberally-conducted workhouses. (43) Yet the generality of workhouses remained obstinately illiberal. As examplars of liberal workhouses, West Derby (Liverpool) and Crumpsall (Manchester) stood almost alone. A list of houses in the other populous Lancashire unions was used to illustrate the inspectorate's unrewarded efforts: 'in the provincial unions ... the guardians continue to resist all suggestions for improvement involving any additional expense, even though it be of such primary importance as a good and efficient dietary.' The intractability of boards of guardians in Ashton-under-Lyne, Bolton, Bury and Wigan was cited in evidence. (44) There was, however, a certain disingenuousness in the Commissioners' presentation of their findings: no specific remarks were made as to the general condition of the houses, or of the patients, and the reader is left to infer that everything was as unsatisfactory as the dietaries, for the inspectors immediately proceeded to offer details of a contrasting 'good' workhouse (West Derby).

In 1862, the Commissioners had allowed themselves the optimism of seeing the lunacy legislation of that year as presaging a new era, in which poor law officers would transmit acute and curable cases immediately to asylums. (45) But the mood was short lived. The 1862 Act directed relieving officers to bring all alleged lunatics before a magistrate and to facilitate removal to an asylum. The inspectorate had even been successful in having omitted from the new law the discretionary power granted by earlier legislation to relieving officers. (46) Under the new law, the officer must report to a justice within three days any pauper known to be a lunatic. But in practice, and to the disappointment of the Commissioners, little was altered. Relieving officers disregarded the Act, and often reverted to simply removing the insane pauper to the workhouse, even though this made them liable to a fine. The Commissioners found themselves compromised by the Act. They were empowered to proceed against recalcitrant relieving officers, and claimed that in cases of wilful neglect of duty, they would invariably bring an action. But the technical difficulties of obtaining a conviction led them to justify a record of infrequent prosecution:

> ... if in certain cases we have hesitated and ultimately decided not to sue for penalties, it has been from the feeling that our object would be but little advanced by the conviction of a person whose obstructive action was not so much due to personal antagonism to the law as to the pressure put on him by the Board of Guardians to whom he is subordinated for all, or almost all purposes other than those of the Lunacy Acts. (47)

Relieving officers thus remained unprosecuted for the most flagrant breach of the law. Two contrasting cases will illustrate the Board's inconsistencies: In July, 1875, one Stephen Oxberrow was admitted to the Marland (Rochdale) workhouse. Five days after admission he cut his throat with a razor. He had been sent to the house by the relieving officer, who had written 'of unsound mind' on the order; and the master had added further comments on the back: 'attempted suicide; brother cut his throat; cousin hanged himself.' Despite his knowledge of these unusual and pertinent facts, the relieving officer failed to notify a magistrate and the workhouse medical officer noticed no indication of insanity. The relieving officer was not prosecuted, and though they deplored the case in their annual report, the Commissioners had no thought of prosecuting - no contemplated action is to be found in their minute books. (48) A Whitehaven relieving officer had been less fortunate six years earlier. In September, 1869, one Isabella Johnstone had attempted to drown herself in Whitehaven harbour. Her friends asked the relieving officer to arrange her admission into an asylum, but he merely arranged for her examination by the medical officer. Twenty-four hours elapsed before the examination could be made, whereon the doctor promptly declared the woman dangerous. Instead of notifying a justice within three days, the officer waited for five, and it was not until seven days after the attempted suicide that the asylum admission papers were signed. When the officer went to pick up the woman, he found her with her throat cut, and a few days later, she killed herself by jumping from a window in the infirmary to which she had been temporarily removed. The officer was prosecuted and fined 40/-. (49) In the former case, the Board knew it was helpless to prosecute all three culpable parties, since only the relieving officer was chargeable under the 1862 Act, so allowed the subordinate official to go unpunished, whilst in the Whitehaven affair, the relieving officer plainly had unique responsibility and could confidently be sued.

The inspectorate demanded fresh legislation 'to restrict, as a general rule, the admission of cases into the workhouse, unless they have passed through the asylum, and are certified by the medical superintendent as being harmless and chronic and suitable for removal.' The Poor Law Board co-operated in the design, issuing a circular stressing the duty of reporting to a magistrate 'every case of an insane pauper deemed a lunatic.' (50) The pleas and exhortation were vain, yet the very arguments of the Commissioners were once more indicative of their unease, and of their forced departure from psychiatric orthodoxy in an attempt to compromise with poor law officialdom in the interests of the curable lunatic. In 1844, the Metropolitan Commissioners had come under fire for adopting an over-simple division of lunatics into incurable/chronic cases and curable/recent cases, and for suggesting that 'the necessary expenses of a lunatic hospital are unnecessary for incurable patients; the medical staff, the number of attendants, the minute classification, and other requisites of a hospital for the cure of the disease, are not required to the same extent.' (51) John Conolly had pointed out the practical impossibility of such a simple division, and had lamented the cruelty of consigning the labelled incurables to a detention in which cheapness was the key feature. (52) The Commissioners accepted the censure, but their successors on the national inspectorate found themselves, twenty-six years later, forced back into the expedient of condoning the transmission of what were arguably the most sensitive patients to the kind of environment they most often condemned as depressing. (53)

This was a recognition of the fact that, despite the Board's efforts, local poor law authorities were determined to detain some classes of insane paupers in the workhouse. All the Commissioners could hope was to be able to determine which class. (54) Moreover, the inspectorate was not only facing the non-co-operation of local authorities, but was increasingly forced to abandon its ideals in view of the congested state of public asylums. Charles Spencer Perceval, secretary to the Board, in giving evidence to the Select Committee of 1877, outlined the one alternative to discharging patients back to workhouses or of maintaining chronics there from the first. He asserted that more paupers were sent to asylums in some counties than was strictly necessary, and that the practice of discharging certain classes of patients to the care of friends or relatives should be extended. The superintendent at Sussex Asylum reported beneficial results from this tactic, though it was not widely used elsewhere.(55) No payment was made to friends or relatives who received discharged uncured lunatics, though they were eligible for out-relief for their charges. The Board in this instance seem to have been trying to maintain their ideological opposition to the workhouse whilst providing relief for congested county institutions by reverting to personal care. As a workable tactic, however, the solution was suspect: pressure on asylums and reliance on the workhouse were heaviest in London and the industrial north and midlands. In these areas, Perceval was, in effect, recommending the transfer of asylum 'harmless' and 'incurable' lunatics to poor or pauper dwellings in towns not noted for their healthy environment. The tactic presumed also that kin or friends would accept discharged patients with no remuneration, yet it was probable that the patients concerned would never have been sent to an asylum in the first place if the kinship group had been able to support them, or the local authority been able to find boarding accommodation cheaper than the asylum. (56)

III

A broad distinction can be made between the insane inmates of workhouses: those lunatics confined whilst in transit to asylums, and those intentionally detained for an unspecified period. Samuel Gaskell urged that no lunatic ought to be taken directly to a workhouse unless a magistrate had declared his insanity doubtful. The Commissioners shared asylum superintendents' dissatisfaction with prolonged workhouse detention which aggravated a pauper's disorder before his commital to an asylum: in some cases, paupers were kept 'in transit' for one or two months. (57) Delays were sometimes unavoidable, as Andrew Doyle, poor law inspector for the midlands, told the Select Committee of 1859, but the generality of relieving officers did their job conscientiously: in Doyle's area. (58)

> The mode varies ... in the different unions ... (L)unatic inmates are ... admitted ... not because they are lunatics, but because they are destitute as paupers; when the relieving officer receives an application from A.B. that so and so is a lunatic, he visits the house and calls in the medical officer; if he finds that it is a proper case for the asylum, and that there are no means of attending to the patient in the house, he would ... very properly, give an order for admission to the workhouse; but generally, when the relieving officer finds that the case is one of that kind, it is removed directly to the asylum without the intervention of the workhouse. (59)

Doyle showed that during the Commissioners' eighteen-month tour of workhouse inspection, they had found only 3% of workhouse lunatics in his area 'improperly' detained, and added that there had been no charges of cruelty levelled at any of the sixty-three institutions in the area, casting doubt on Lord Shaftesbury's dramatic assertion that 'we are now returning to the system of things that prevailed in 1828, there being no means of classifying (lunatics) ... a large proportion of them were chained down and kept in the most horrible state of filth and suffering' in union houses.(60) The chairman of the Lunacy Commission was also brought to task for claiming that poor law institutions were 'overcrowded with lunatics to a frightful extent,' when scarcely 7% of workhouse inmates were lunatics or idiots, in the country as a whole. (61)

Notwithstanding this reassessment of the relative position of workhouse lunatics, the Commissioners were justifiably concerned about the fate of the individuals in the absolute number confined. Throughout the second half of the century, around one quarter of all pauper lunatics and idiots were detained in union houses. (62) In poor law establishments, general furnishings, bedding and washing facilities fell short of the Commissioners' minimum standards of cleanliness and decency. Defective arrangements in attendance and accommodation led inevitably to use of coercion and seclusion in 'dark cells, constructed for the solitary confinement of refractory paupers' which were often used 'for the punishment of the insane merely to prevent trouble.' (63)

The Poor Law Board, in 'General Consolidated Order 27', had instructed masters to report to union medical officers and to guardians all cases in which restraint was used, in an attempt to approximate asylum practice. But the instruction was, according to the Commissioners in Lunacy, hardly ever acted upon. Thus, when the inspectors visited Bury workhouse in 1856, they found three men confined to their beds; two strapped down and the third restrained by muffs. (64) Equally disturbing was the total lack of exercise facilities in most houses. At Bolton, for example, the exercise yard for lunatics was 'scarcely larger than a good-sized room' and at Clerkenwell, the lunatic wards were situated at the very top of the building making it impracticable for insane paupers to have access to the small yard below. Blackburn, Manchester, Whitehaven, and Wolverhampton workhouses were singled out as being particularly bad in this respect. (65)

Experienced - even capable - attendants were generally lacking. Usually, the lunatics were given into the care of a pauper inmate, with a wide range of unhappy results. In 1857, at the Bath workhouse, patients were found semi-starved: frauds and thefts by attendants had deprived them of half their normal food allowance, and the only complaint, wrote the disgusted Commissioners, 'was the wan and wasted looks of the inmates.' (66) At St. Albans, the inspector found that 'the Nurse having care of the insane females was herself decidedly of unsound mind,' and was rewarded with half a pint of beer daily. A terrible reminder of real danger was provided in the same year at St. Martin's workhouse in London, where a violent lunatic had been entrusted to the supervision of a seventy year old pauper. In the end, 'the Patient appears to have been placed in a room, in which were a poker and other dangerous articles; and on being relieved from some restraint which had been imposed on him, he struck the feeble old pauper on the head until he died.' (67)

Medical treatment was, in general, non-existent, complained the Commissioners. In the Leicester union, the medical officer visited only quarterly. At the Winchcombe workhouse in Gloucestershire, 'the Master could not speak with certainty as to the regularity of the Medical Officer's visit to the Infirmary.' It was not even laid down that the medical officer's ordinary workhouse visit should extend to the lunatic wards. (68)

The Commissioners found most cause for complaint in the industrial north and midlands. Visiting Blackburn workhouse in 1857, an inspector found that

> Several of the patients are stated at times to be excited and unmanageable and required to be restrained. The beds are generally clean but are all of straw, and only one blanket is allowed to each patient in the coldest weather. There is no system of bathing ... and the means of washing their persons are ... defective. The male patients especially were dirty and untidy, and their clothes torn and much worn. Their occupation and amusement are neglected ...

Twelve months later, the visiting Commissioner pronounced the room still 'in the greatest degree deficient in comfort.' (69) At Bury, the female insane were generally distributed in the ordinary wards, and although a small ward was reserved for the male idiotic patients, it was 'objectionable on account of the high windows and the remarkably small airing court.' In the same year, the Commissioners described the Huddersfield workhouse as 'shamefully defective' in its accommodation, and at a subsequent visit found no attempt at improvement had been made. Imbecile inmates were

> crowded together in rooms of insufficient size, poorly furnished, and badly ventilated. There is still no proper classification ... the insane and weakminded women being compelled to associate with low prostitutes. Wet and dirty patients are still placed to sleep together in the same bed. The bedding is scanty, and the dormitory floors are still saturated with urine. The means of washing and drying are still lamentably defective ...

The deadhouse was made to serve as a seclusion room for refractory patients. (70)

At Liverpool, there was no brutal neglect, but patients were kitted-out in uniform blue coarse-cut outfits with the word 'ASYLUM' stamped on them, giving them 'more the appearance of felons than of persons under treatment for a disease.' (71) Even good intentions were sadly unfulfilled. At Ribchester workhouse, the Commissioners had prevailed upon the guardians to make alterations to the poorly-arranged buildings. In 1862, when the new arrangements were to have been completed, the visiting Commissioners reported that

> ... from the position selected for the fresh rooms ... and from the character of the building itself, it seems

> as though it was designed that the new ward should be as little as possible an improvement on the old. This proposed additional building tumbled down three weeks ago, when within a few days of its (supposed) completion, and it is a pity that it should not then have been abandoned altogether, and a site selected ... where something like cheerful accommodation and opportunities for recreation and exercise would have been afforded. (72)

Patients were thus to be confined in a narrow, cheerless 'backyard' without even decent washing facilities, and although the master had, since his appointment, banned all restraint and insisted on a high standard of cleanliness, beneficial results were precluded by design of the buildings and understaffing in the ward. (73)

The Blackburn authorities lacked even good intentions, and despite continued harassment by the Commissioners, the pauper lunatics, especially the men, fared badly, as the visiting inspector noted in April, 1862:

> In a wretched little dismal front court, where the smell from the privies was almost intolerable, I found a number of the men crowded together, some lying on the stones, their dresses shabby and dirty and in disorder, and all of them wearing the dangerous heavy clogs, which the last visiting Commissioner reported to have been disused. No comfortable or moveable seats, as often recommended, have been placed in the dayrooms ... I was told that the <u>Leisure Hour</u> and <u>Illustrated Times</u> are now supplied, but I saw nothing in the hands of the patients. The washing troughs and basins are unfit to be used.

Even more disquieting was the attitude of the guardians to the purpose of separate lunatic wards. In addition to providing segregated accommodation for the insane, they doubled as a punishment block for sane inmates: on the visit made in 1862, the inspector found a woman confined amongst the weakminded by special order of the guardians, for alleged refractory conduct, and a second who had been transferred on account of her dirty habits. (74)

The Commissioners were seldom able to effect the change they desired, and boards of guardians tended to go their own ways. At Wigan, a long correspondence failed to achieve the simple task of having needless bars removed from workhouse windows. In Liverpool and Manchester, the poor law authorities were able to get away with policies that went against the intentions of the lunacy laws. (75) London presented similar problems until the late 1860's. The number of insane paupers confined to metropolitan union houses increased steadily from the late 1850's; in 1858, there had been 1,152 lunatics in workhouses; by 1865, there were 1,800. The increase was not uniform throughout the metropolitan area: for example, between 1858 and 1863, the workhouse of St.George the Martyr trebled its intake, whilst Newington and Lambeth reduced the proportional numbers of their insane to their total populations. (76) F.E. Anstie outlined defects of organization similar to those apparent in Lancashire. Thus, the St. Luke's workhouse, where annual admissions of pauper lunatics averaged seventy a year, was reminiscent of Ribchester. The guardians had responded to the Commissioners' criticisms but failed to produce the right kind of improvement. Dayrooms were 'disgracefully small' whilst a couple of padded rooms ('pillboxes') and a 'cupboardlike' room 'only fit for keeping linen in' were provided for refractory patients. At Chelsea, there was no attempt at segregation: the average population of twenty to thirty insane mixed with the ordinary paupers, except for 'two noisy old male lunatics' who were 'secluded in a miserable hole ... ill lighted, atrociously ill-ventilated, dirty and with the most wretched furniture and bedding.' Clerkenwell was described in similar terms. (77)

After 1867, the Metropolis began to differ from the pattern it had shared with the north and midlands. The Metropolitan Poor Act of that year placed the cost of maintenance of lunatics in asylums on the Common Poor Fund of the Metropolis, instead of on individual parishes and unions. (78) Removals from workhouses soared, despite the fact that there was no accommodation available in asylums nearer than Staffordshire, Somerset, the North Riding and Northumberland. Although charges ranged between 14/- to 17/6 per patient per week, boards of guardians transferred patients hurriedly, in an attempt to shift the financial burden on to the common purse. The immediate result was a repetition of the consequences of the 1845 Acts: chronic patients were shovelled into institutions intended for the curable. Since there was no discrimination between transfers, recent cases were often detained too long and deprived of chances of cure. Patients' needs were not considered: removal over long distances deprived them of visits by friends and relatives. By the end of 1869, London paupers in provincial country asylums were distributed thus: Salisbury: 57; Somerset: 39; Sussex: 60; Buckinghamshire: 17; North Riding: 33; and Lichfield: 44. An indeterminate number was confined at Fisherton House (Wilts.) and Haydock Lodge. (79) The parish of St. George the Martyr, Southwark, provided a typical example of indecent haste to cash in on the redistribution of financial liability. The parish maintained a house in Mitcham (Eagle House) which was situated in the country and provided a suitable accommodation for eighty tranquil patients. Reports by the Commissioners had always been favourable, but early in 1869, all the patients were removed to the Staffordshire county asylum at Burntwood, and the establishment was closed. (80) The volume of response to the 1867 Act quickly negated any therapeutic advantages to be derived from making transfers to asylums, and economic advantages were reduced as transport costs to distant asylums added to costs. As early as 1869, some unions were abandoning the attempt to find asylum accommodation. In the parish of St. Margaret's and St. John's, Westminster, 'the asylum being full, no steps to absolutely necessary removals have been taken for a long time,' and the medical officer of Whitechapel workhouse spent three fruitless months in constant correspondence with county asylums and licensed houses throughout the country, in an effort to find suitable accommodation for a single dangerous lunatic. (81) For chronic and incurable cases, there was even less chance of removal: the medical officer of Poplar described how 'it has become a perfectly hopeless matter to obtain admission for a single pauper paralytic patient into any lunatic asylum in Middlesex, and many provincial asylums have also declined to take such patients.' (82) The Commissioners' proffered solution was increased public asylum provision: a thousand bed institution to complement Hanwell and Colney Hatch. (83)

The Poor Law authorities, however, invoked the 1867 Poor Act in an attempt to provide the desired beds at less cost. The Poor Law Board was empowered by the Act to combine parishes and unions into districts to provide 'asylums for the reception and relief of the sick poor.' In 1867, an order of the PLB established the Metropolitan Asylum District to bear collective responsibility for organising 'the reception and relief of poor persons infected with or suffering from fever, or the disease of smallpox or who may be insane.' A Metropolitan Asylums Board was set up to represent the thirty unions and parishes in London (forty-five out of sixty members elected by the unions; the remainder appointed by the PLB), and it recommended the construction of two asylums, each housing 1,500 patients. (84) Sites were secured at Leavesden (Herts) and Caterham (Surrey), and the asylums were designed to meet the needs of quiet and harmless cases: the categories deemed suitable for workhouse detention by the Commissioners. In February, 1868, the Mile End guardians informed the new Board that they were keeping a dangerous lunatic in their workhouse and were unable to secure his admission into an asylum; they were anxious to know when the new asylums would be ready. The Board's reply was not encouraging: 'the Board is proceeding with the proposed asylum for imbecile patients with all possible despatch, ... but (has) no power to provide for the class of lunatics referred to.' The asylums were opened in 1870, but an Order from the Board stresses their inapplicability as even temporary relief for the Home Counties' asylums:

> The insane paupers to be taken in the asylums shall be such harmless persons of the chronic or imbecile class as could lawfully be detained in a workhouse. No dangerous lunatic or curable person such as would under the statutes in that behalf require to be sent to a lunatic asylum shall be admitted. (85)

Thus, Caterham and Leavesden were not asylums at all, but 'workhouses within the meaning of the Act' of 1845. Gathorne Hardy, President of the PLB told the Commons in February, 1867, that the Board's object was 'to classify the different inmates of workhouses ... in the first instance by building such an establishment as will be necessary for 2,000 lunatics and imbeciles.' (86)

The objective was not simply achieved, however. Decision as to eligibility for removal to the workhouse-asylums still lay with union house masters and their medical officers. The vexed question of classification still remained, and by the 1870's was being complicated by the success of specialised idiot establishments which were training many who had previously been consigned to the scrap-heap. (87) Moreover, local poor law authorities continued to see segregated lunatic provision as a possible dumping-ground for sane paupers and the district asylums offered wider scope for this activity:

> There is widespread feeling that workhouses are not suitable places of residence for the imbecile, the idiotic and the incurably insane ... The care and discipline required for these cases call for special appliances and methods of supervision, training and treatment, which cannot be provided in a general workhouse. Nor is it desirable - in an economic and prudential sense - that an abode for able-bodied paupers should be made the focus of such sympathy and solicitude as must needs be expended upon a refuge for the hapless victims of mental defect, decay or disease. It would be advantageous, if it were practicable, to eliminate even the sick poor and the infirm from the ordinary class of paupers ... Nevertheless, if asylums for the incurably insane are to be made depositories for the troublesome old people who throng the 'infirm wards' of poorhouses, we fear there will be reason to regret their existence. (88)

Seven years of experience with the workhouse-asylum taught guardians how to weed workhouses of troublesome inmates and cases that required expensive nursing:

> By calling the aged and peevish paupers of both sexes insane, and removing them to an institution where the requisite caretaking can be done in the lump, they save expense, and, if the transfer can be done cleverly, they may also take some credit for humanity. Moreover, by dragging idiots to an asylum for imbeciles, the cost of their education at suitable training establishments may be avoided.

Arrangements in the district asylum were unobjectionable to psychiatrists, and Mortimer-Granville thought them an admirable return for the ratepayers' money: all unnecessary outlay was scrupulously avoided. Indeed, he noted ironically, the domestic business of the institutions 'might be carried on with less paid assistance were it not desirable to make a show of strength and vigilance,' in an attempt to preserve the illusion of the asylums' being populated solely by the insane. (89)

IV

The Metropolitan Asylums uniquely expressed the dilemma confronting the asylum system and its guardians. Intermediate institutions between workhouses and lunatic asylums, they 'combined the evils and defects of both.' Their primary purpose of relieving curative institutions of incurables and mental defectives without risking the undesirable consequences of confinement in a general workhouse, was often lost on the unions. A grant-in-aid of 1874 made it marginally cheaper to send a metropolitan pauper to the county asylum than to the district establishment, but to secure admission to the former it was necessary to have the pauper certified; for admission to Caterham and Leavesden no certificates were necessary, making it easier to rid workhouses of the troublesome. (90) At the same time, the continued overcrowding of many public asylums forced workhouses, under the critical supervision of the Commissioners in Lunacy, to adopt more and more the aspect of asylums in their lunatic wards.

The origins of the Metropolitan Asylums, moreover, offer evidence of the unbridgeable gulf which separated the central poor law authority from the Lunacy Commissioners. In 1838, the Select Committee on the Poor Law recommended that the Poor Law Commission or the Home Secretary be empowered to unite several unions for the maintenance of a common lunatic asylum, adjoining the workhouse and distinct from the county institution, and in the following year, the Poor Law Commissioners suggested that control of county asylums should be transferred to themselves and the boards of guardians of unions, so that asylums for paupers might become an economic proposition. (91) Physicians understandably opposed the idea, and it was dropped after 1842, when the Lunacy Commissioners' powers were widened. The degree of control was eventually exercised, albeit on a local scale, after 1870, by the Metropolitan Asylums Board, and there were, predictably, demands from the central authority - by then the Local Government Board - to extend the metropolitan system both geographically and to cater for wider ranges of patients. (92)

By the 1870's, however, the function of the workhouse had changed dramatically from that intended in 1834, and the asylum: workhouse polarity was no longer as clear as it had been when poor law authorities were determining their policies. In 1834, the Poor Law Commission had assured the Cabinet that they intended to assign 'distinct, quiet and comfortable abodes for the impotent,' though they lacked the powers to enforce their intention on guardians. The general environment of union houses bore witness to the 'less eligibility' principle, and the sick and disabled, who were unable to find beds in the voluntary hospitals, tended to be mixed with able-bodied inmates. At the time of the Lancet and PLB investigations in 1866, London workhouses receiving large numbers of sick paupers were found to be generally unsuited for the task: thirteen out of the forty were beyond hope of improvement, according to the Poor Law Board's inspector. The situation was no better in the provinces, especially in rural areas. (93) Attendance and medical treatment were significantly lacking in most institutions, though there were notable exceptions. (94) But workhouses were, however inadequately, acting as hospitals, and providing for many better care than they might expect outside. (95)

Separation of the insane became increasingly more common as provisions for the sick generally were improved, and the Commissioners complained that, by 1857, 'in places where such wards have been opened, there is an obvious determination on the part of the guardians to consider them as constituting Lunatic Asylums ...' (96) The Commissioners had, in fact, twelve months earlier faced the unhappy fact that workhouse confinement would not be prevented and might as well be supervised. In a communication with the Select Vestry at Liverpool, where the workhouse had to cope with overspill from the county asylums, they formulated a set of regulations designed to make lunatic wards asylums 'in parvo' - with, perhaps, the unstated hope that this would show up workhouse detention as being no more economical than the asylum: (a) sufficient staffs of responsible paid nurses and attendants were to be employed; (b) a fixed liberal dietary was to be arranged by the medical superintendent of the local asylum; (c) a supply of good warm clothing and bedding was to be guaranteed; (d) the provision of flagged courtyards and planted gardens was to be arranged; (e) regular daily medical visitation was to be made; (f) books and registers were to be kept as in asylums. (97) The visiting committee of Surrey's county asylum bore out the Commissioners' insistence on segregated asylum-style provision for workhouse patients:

> The Committee adverted at considerable length in their last Annual Report to the circumstances of the Asylum being frequently unequal to the needs of the county, and of their intention to attempt to remedy the defect by discharging all those patients who, being harmless or inoffensive, it was considered might properly be taken care of in their respective union houses.
>
> The plan has been tried and has not been successful. Patients who, under the liberal and gentle treatment they experience in the asylum are quiet and tractable, are not necessarily so under the stricter regulations of a workhouse, indeed ... the reverse has been found to be the case; most of the patients so discharged having been shortly afterwards returned to the asylum ... in consequence of their having become with the other inmates of the workhouse 'a mutual annoyance to each other.' Any arrangements, short of an entire separation from the other inmates ... will be found to be inefficient. (98)

By this date, counties had become cautious of embarking on expensive asylum construction, as John Arlidge pointed out: 'it is with asylums as with railways, the present directors are reaping the instruction from the extravagance and errors its (sic) predecessors fell into.' (99) The chief error was seen to be costliness, and it was argued by psychiatrists that less elaborate, 'homely' buildings might provide extra space at reduced costs. Bucknill's experiments with detached blocks at the Devon Asylum proved the practicability of the idea of approximating asylum conditions to external living standards, but such additions were impracticable for the vast Home Counties, Lancashire or Yorkshire asylums, where needs were greatest, and where the Commissioners had already disapproved further building on or near existing sites. (100) In this climate, the workhouse became an essential part of the strategy of confinement. In London, the St. Pancras workhouse, by the mid-1860's, was able to show limited success in catering for its insane: a suite of wards on the ground floor, completely cut off from the rest of the establishment, had been provided, and airing courts with locked gates added. Female patients even had a small garden, and conditions generally were unexceptionable. However, the psychiatric Establishment was displeased:

> It is no small praise ... that they have raised the standard of the insane department so high; but it is impossible ... to bring it up to asylum level. The experiment tried at St. Pancras appears to be a crucial one, and its results ... prove that the present workhouse system will not bear the additional burden of the treatment of insanity on a large scale, including the management of acute cases. (101)

Local guardians, however, made sure that the burden was placed on the houses, and as hospitals and asylums the workhouse developed in the 1860's and 70's, with union medical officers contesting the authority of masters and guardians in order to secure minimum facilities for the sick and insane. (102) In Lancashire, the medical officer of the Ashton district resigned because his board refused to acknowledge the workhouse as a hospital; in Westminster Joseph Rogers fought continually with guardians and magistrates to obtain recognition of the right of insane paupers to medical as well as custodial treatment. (103)

By 1865, 104 of the 688 workhouses in England and Wales had separate lunatic wards, and despite the continual complaint of the Commissioners in Lunacy that 'the establishment of lunatic wards in workhouses leads to a direct violation of the lunacy laws,' the mode of inspection arranged by the Board for houses with separate wards tacitly recognised their changed status by putting them on the same frequency of visitation as county asylums. (104) The medical profession split on the issue: Rhys Williams of Bethlem (later to become a Commissioner) and Maury Deas of Macclesfield Asylum told the Select Committee of 1877 that workhouse confinement of pauper lunatics was improper; (105) ten years earlier, Charles Lockhart Robertson, in his Presidential Address to the Medico-Psychological Association, declared that his experience showed that the aged, the imbecile and the demented preferred workhouse detention to the asylum, since there was less discipline and an opportunity to associate with the sane. There was, he argued, a double benefit in selective use of workhouse wards: 'generally, 25% of pauper lunatics and idiots chargeable, may, with great relief to the wards of the county asylum, and with satisfaction to themselves and their friends, be kept under proper restrictions in the workhouse.' (106)

The reality of the asylum status of workhouse wards was confirmed in the public's mind, if not in the Commissioners. William White Parkinson, master of Bermondsey workhouse, and an ex-asylum attendant with wide experience, recounted for the Select Committee of 1877 the numerous instances in which workhouses were used as asylums by non-paupers too poor to afford private asylum prices, who sent relatives to the union house and paid for their accommodation when local public institutions were full. (107) There was even specialisation: the 'Lowers' (detention wards) in Mill Road Workhouse, Liverpool, accommodated eighty male and female patients, usually immigrants - particularly Canadians - with mental disorders. (108)

The fine idealism of the Lunacy Commissioners was doomed to failure in the matrix of economic, political, and demographic pressures besetting local poor law boards. It was not simply different conceptions of the nature of insanity or of its ideal treatment which separated the Commissioners and psychiatrists generally from lay administrators. There was a more concrete reason for continued workhouse detention, especially of many mentally defective and geriatric patients. The most virulent opponents of the workhouse invariably assumed the existence of alternatives, yet there were none where they were most needed. The argument that union houses failed to provide therapeutic and educative systems, especially for the feebleminded, was valid, but there was not sufficient accommodation either in asylums like Lancaster, where Gaskell had originated training schemes for idiots that were continued by his successors, (109) or in the handful of idiot asylums which existed before 1890. The alternative to the workhouse was residence with friends or relatives, but amongst the labouring classes, insanity in the head of a family reduced the rest to destitution, which effectively made that tactic inoperable for a substantial proportion of cases. (110) It is surprising that Ruth Hodgkinson, in her able summary of the dimensions of pauper lunacy in the nineteenth century, argues that a great proportion of workhouse patients should never have been detained, but should have been trained in asylums to do useful work. At the date she refers to (1871) only five institutions catered to the idiot specifically, and only three of these made arrangements for education of children. Only two admitted paupers, and then only in small numbers. (111) Later attempts by the Metropolitan Asylums Board to increase educational and training programmes were only marginally successful as the familiar pattern of overcrowding and proportionate increases in unimprovable cases shortcircuited educational asylums as it had curative lunatic asylums. (112) The workhouse, therefore, remained an integral part of asylumdom, and functioned, like the asylum proper, as a means of social control which subordinated medical to custodial concerns. Institutions for the mentally defective, which psychiatrists and Lunacy Commissioners had demanded as positive alternatives, were, on their eventual appearance, pressed into service as detention centres for 'moral defectives' until at least the 1920's, indicating once again that, no matter how lines were drawn theoretically between mad and sane, and between different classes of insane, in practice institutionalization was a generalized process as far as many lay administrators were concerned. (113) Specialised institutions simply made it easier to increase the number of categories into which candidates for institutionalization could be placed, and the admixture of disparate classes remained common to asylums and workhouses throughout the nineteenth century.

CHAPTER EIGHT

CONCLUSION.

The history of lunacy reform in Britain is the history of the idealization of an expedient. The precise contours of reform were local variants of a phenomenon common to western Europe and the United States, shaped and coloured by Britain's particular economic, social and political features. The expedient of confining the socially disruptive and undesirable became, during the nineteenth century, the first-resort solution to problems created by certain kinds of deviants, and the solution helped to identify the deviant. The perceived nature of the madman changed during the later eighteenth century, and the asylum was an integral part in that change. Roger Bastide has outlined the development of the ideological contexts of the transformation:

> ... with the Renaissance began what the Americans term 'secularization': madmen were then regarded simply as dangerous people on the same level as criminals, debauchees and beggars. They were, therefore, excluded from societies and 'confined' along with the other categories of the asocial, often in the same institutions ... philanthropy remained within the framework of the institutions; it did not try to break it ... Ey tried to discover the ideology underlying this 'alienation' of the insane. The madman, he wrote, plays the part of a stranger in our midst; 'he is the man from another world.' Consequently, as long as the ideology of our society was a religious one, the madman, because he no longer belonged to society, was considered part of the supernatural realm. The new ideology that emerged with the Reformation and the Age of Enlightenment, and finally triumphed with the French Revolution, was an ideology of individual freedom. The madman became the man who had lost his freedom. It thus becomes clear that the community and the doctor were led into 'alienating' him, banishing him, in fact, from a society where everything rested on individual freedom and responsibility. The reforms instituted ... by Pinel (and) Tuke ... have been described as a genuine revolution in the care of the mentally ill. It is true that their chains were removed but this was no more than a philanthropic gesture. Meanwhile, the first genuinely scientific conception of insanity was developing in quite the opposite direction: it aimed to show that the insane were radically different from other men. Far from disappearing, the alienating process was reinforced by this new development. However, the justification given for confining the insane was changed. It was now, in Esquirol's words, 'to break all the habits of the lunatic by taking him away from home, separating him from his family, his friends, and his servants, surrounding him with strangers and changing his whole way of life.' (1)

The psychiatrist occupied a key role in this transformation, though it was an equivocal one as Yves Pélicier indicates:

> ... madness has always been embarrassing to society. This embarrassment explains the continual swing of collective attitudes from tolerance to condemnation, from incarceration to liberal policies. Often the psychiatrist's attitude has gone in the opposite direction to that of the collective ... (T)here is a dialectical relationship between the ideas of the community and those of the psychiatrist ... Although he may be opposed to the ideas of his time, the psychiatrist is very much open to their influence. (2)

The relationship between psychiatric opinion and the collective awareness of insanity as expressed in nineteenth-century lunacy legislation in Britain, raises an important point of departure from orthodox medical history. Referring to the relationship of law and medical science in the treatment of mental illness, Henry Sigerist writes that

> the trouble was that medical science was at all times at least half a century ahead of the law. This is perfectly normal because the law does not lead but follows. A medical discovery must first be accepted by the medical profession; then it must win general acceptance by society, and finally it may be embodied in a country's law. Legal reform is thus a very slow process ... From the time of Pinel on, the law was increasingly bewildered by and resentful towards physicians, whom it frequently accused of endeavouring to prevent criminals from meeting with justly deserved punishment ... (3)

Whilst not disputing the last part of this generalized assertion, it is necessary to question the validity of the whole. In Britain, psychiatric expertise, whether in terms of classification, diagnosis or therapeutics, was developed within the confines of the asylum. The asylum itself was an outgrowth of earlier institution-forms, and those forms, together with the initial justification for secular interference with the insane, rested on three sources of state political power: the police power (i.e. the right of the state to protect the peace and public welfare), the role of 'parens patriae' derived from medieval kingship, and the powers of the state over the persons of the destitute, which had been developed from the sixteenth century. Internment of misfits had occurred in Britain, as elsewhere in western Europe, from the twelfth century, when disused leprosaria had been used for common paupers and vagabonds and 'deranged minds.' (4) Special provision for the insane in Britain preceded the development of British psychiatry, as the asylum was born out of the workhouse, bridewell, public hospital and private madhouse, in the late eighteenth century. The new institution-model had its ideological roots in the seventeenth century, marking a 'decisive event' in 'the history of unreason,' when 'madness was perceived on the social horizon of poverty, of incapacity for work, of inability to integrate with the group, the moment when madness began to rank among the problems of the city.' (5) This new institution-type, especially from the early nineteenth century, and especially in the form of the county asylum, was compulsory, and, like imprisonment, represented a total social exclusion. At the time of its inception, therapeutic science and skills were undeveloped: confinement was a tactic of preventive detention for the benefit of society, not a patient-orientated treatment service. The law regulated the institution, and legally-appointed officers engineered the formalities of confinement. The medical empiricism which constituted eighteenth and nineteenth-century psychiatry operated within legally-controlled institutions, and had as its subjects legally-defined mental patients, whose confinement had been socially ordained. It was as true for the eighteenth and nineteenth century alienist as it is for the twentieth-century psychiatrist, whose 'function ... is to search for the "causes" ... of the illness,' whilst 'society decides who his patients will be.' (6) Social and legal determinants were, therefore, crucial in the formation of psychiatric opinion: medical science was, therefore, in this respect, not 'half a century ahead of the law,' but was itself the product of legal initiatives which established the milieu for medical experimentation.

The links thus forged between the institution and psychiatry have lasted until the second half of the twentieth century, and the formulations of psychiatrists, originating in the asylum-environment, have, over two centuries helped to create lay attitudes to mental illness which have been marked by the centrality of the institution. Contemporary conservative critics of involuntary hospitalization tend to point to its misuse by state authorities, where the incarceration of the sane is 'a variation on the gas chamber and even more cruel.' (7) Like the members of the Alleged Lunatic's Friend Society and the Lunacy Law Reform Association in Victorian Britain, these writers imply that the confinement and treatment meted out in such institutions to those 'genuinely' afflicted with 'mental illness' is not inhumane: as Szasz points out in criticism of Medvedev and Solzhenitsyn, '(i)f involuntary mental "hospitalization" and "treatment" are moral obscenities on a par with the medical crimes of the Nazis, then it is not clear how such methods could be acceptably applied to <u>any human being</u>, well or sick, friend or foe.' (8) Medvedev, indeed, like John Perceval, William O'Connor or the anonymous author of <u>A Man's wrong Confinement in Haydock Lodge</u>, exhibits a propensity to special pleading: institutionalization of the insane is not questioned as a tactic of social control, and involuntary psychiatric treatment is seen as legitimate for those correctly identified as mad: that is, for those who are not the wrongfully-confined apologist involved, or, in modern instances, his friends and political sympathisers. (9)

It is temptingly easy to point to flagrant breaches of human liberty by the purveyors of the asylum-system in different countries at different times. Szasz himself singles out Earl Long, Ernest Hemingway and Ezra Pound as examples of American political and cultural oppression by means of madness-stigmatization and asylum confinement, and uses these and similar cases to bolster what becomes essentially a conservative attack on the roots of welfare state collectivism. (10) Szasz's chosen opponents, in fact, can be seen to share with him a common disavowel of the role of the psychiatrist, at least in formulating and operating identification codes. Szasz wishes to demythologize psychiatry, and to undermine the psychiatrist's prescriptive role in treatment of the deviant labelled mentally ill; Medvedev, once more like Victorian spokesmen for the 'alleged lunatic,' can <u>know</u> who is insane and who sane, and thus denies the expertise of the psychiatrist in deciding who should be institutionalized. Yet it is the psychiatrist's scientific sanctioning of a socially-determined diagnosis and commital which has, for two hundred years, aided by the power of the media, presented the lay public with materials for forming an opinion. The psychiatric back-ups to expedients of social control have, during this same period, emphasized the principle of confinement for the mad as a therapeutic as well as a social necessity. But there have always been cases of individuals whose disorder has been recognised, but whose confinement has been lamented. The most important of English lunacy reformers, Lord Shaftesbury, had moments of confused purpose, and indicated the difficulties inherent in the asylum system, which was operated under laws which prohibited exemptions for individual cases:

> Have been reading ... 'Life of Cowper'. What a wonderful story! He was, when he attempted his life, thoroughly mad; he was never so at any other time. Yet his symptoms were such as would have been sufficient for any 'mad doctor' to shut him up, and far too serious to allow any Commissioner to let him out, and, doubtless, both would be justifiable. The experiment proved that Cowper might safely be trusted but an experiment it was, the responsibility of which not one man in three generations would consent, or ought, to incur. We should, however, take warning by his example, and not let people be in such a hurry to set down all delusions (especially religious delusions) as involving danger either to a man's self or to the public. There are, I suspect, not a few persons confined whom it would be just as perplexing, and yet just as safe, to release as the poet Cowper. (11)

'Mutatis mutandis', there rests the essence of Szasz's special pleading for Pound, Hemingway and Long, stripped of its rhetoric. There, too, is the reason why the Medvedevs in Russia or the Pounds in America are institutionalized: they are seen by the authorities as dangerous to the public, or, more accurately, to the public interest as interpreted by the authorities in their own interest.

The asylum solution and institutional psychiatry, as

evolved in Britain, America and Europe from the late eighteenth century, provided a workable response to some social problems without offering independent means of identifying individuals who contributed to the problems. Because identification codes were systematised after the creation of response procedures geared to the institution, the institution itself became a factor in the identification of the deviant. Lay attitudes, which were the initiators of actions towards the mentally ill in the nineteenth century, as they remain in the twentieth, reflected then as they do now, the ambiguities of the asylum system in its relationship with the diagnosis of madness. As the survey undertaken by the Cummings showed, 'clinical experience supports the impression that many people define mental illness as "that condition for which a person is treated in a mental hospital" ... Mental illness, it seems, is a condition which afflicts people who must go to a mental institution, but until they go, almost anything they do is normal.' (12) Thus, the illness is defined by its cure; the problem defined in terms of its solution. Since the solution was conceived and developed in administrative, rather than scientific terms, it was, and is, naturally subject to the political, social economic and cultural beliefs of the administrators. Over two hundred years, and in different countries, the administrators and their beliefs have evidenced wide variations. The perception of madness as a condition, and the identification of the mad individual are thus subjective actions afforded a subsequent scientific legitimacy. The institution-response is the only constant, and it is necessary that it be judged, not in universal terms, but in terms of its nature and dimensions in a particular time and place.

In Britain during the period reviewed, the mental treatment laws, reflecting a complex interaction of social, economic and intellectual forces, provided the basic dimensions for an asylumdom whose contours were already in existence. The institutional care and control of the insane was often a function of group values only tenuously related to scientific or medical considerations. Especially, it was intricately bound up with series of economic and social factors, partly because county asylums and other institutions, such as idiot asylums and the metropolitan district asylums, were financed publicly; partly because the majority of patients came from low class backgrounds, and the cost of their protracted institutionalization had to be met out of local rates. The lunatic asylum had emerged as a differentiated institution in the eighteenth century, but its public form had always performed functions not always directly related to insanity. From its roots in the eighteenth century, the English asylum, like its American contemporary and the seventeenth-century French general hospital, was concerned with the custody of the aged and indigent and the socially disruptive, a crucial point which Rothman's Discovery of the Asylum ignores. Even in the formative period of asylumdom, from the 1790's to the 1840's, the English Lunatic Asylum had a dual purpose: the protection of the community against individuals who apparently constituted a threat to its security, and the provision of a therapeutic milieu, or at least humane custodial care, for the labelled insane. This meant that from the beginning, the institution had an ambivalent character, with potentially **conflicting responsibilities**:to the community and to the patient. Within the community, the pressures of demographic changes operating in new urban industrial settings produced more sophisticated awarenesses of deviance, and the asylum was closely tied to the growth of this new society. Its success led to its adoption in non-urban, non-industrial areas as a workable tactic combining social control with social welfare. Inevitably, the characteristics of an undifferentiated institution were reimposed on the public asylums. In the private sector, the therapeutic atmosphere was preserved so long as small establishments with choice of patients were maintained. (13)

Kathleen Jones has argued that the humanitarian reform movement which stressed care of the individual patient in small, medically-orientated communities, was betrayed after 1845, and that 'legalism' became the dominant element in the progress of reform, at the expense of social/humanitarian and purely medical channels of development. (14) Yet the lines of development possible were more limited than she implies. The desirability of blurring the distinctions between physical and mental disorders was not so obvious a social good as she implies: 'pure' medical science cannot be value-free, and physical, chemical or biological medical technologies which have since developed have quickly become recognised as tools of social control, whilst their underlying reductionist philosophies are inherently socially repressive. (15) Jones' favoured alternatives to the procedures of 'legalism', therefore, had only a dubiously humanitarian role aborted. Moreover, both in practical and ideological terms, the law was a more apt medium for delineating the asylum. Since there existed the dilemma of conflicting individual and community responsibilities in the asylum, legal forms were a convenient bridge: as formalized expressions of dominant community norms, they were inevitably used to protect the wider interests of the ruling classes; but within those classes, the law had been developed already as the safeguard of individual liberties. The lunacy reform 'movement' had from the first, in its attention to private madhouses, been concerned with individual liberty, whilst subsequent concern for the pauper lunatic had always been heavily geared to the need for social control. The optimistic psychiatry of the early nineteenth century was based upon faith in the potential cure/redemption of all madmen through cultural, normative treatment. The law, in determining the recipients of treatment, provided 'pure' psychiatric medicine with normative standards. Many of the early psychiatrists, like the legal reformers, were conscious of an evangelical vocation, and their religious convictions, whether Quaker or Protestant, often coincided with current perceptions of the functions of laws. Even before the emergence of a Psychiatric Darwinism compatible with the Social Darwinism of the later nineteenth century, there had been a psychiatry which saw mankind as being governed by certain immutable natural laws which provided a guide to proper living. Departure from these laws constituted a threat to physical and psychological wellbeing, and the laws reflected the normative values of the psychiatrists' culture (which were 'protestant' more often than 'secular', differentiating them from the psychiatry of the 1880's and 1890's). (16)

Even apart from this legal basis, the moral therapeutics of nineteenth-century asylums were not always designed in the patient's interests. 'Cure' was essentially behaviour modification, and was inevitably seen in culturally one-sided terms: for the pauper or the immigrant, Jones' 'pure' medicine could not but be a tool of cultural repression, however well-meaning its purveyors might be. (17) The course of lunacy reform and the growth of government control of asylumdom emphasised the close relationships between psychiatric medicine and social controls. The perception of abuses within the madhouse system, and the subsequent investigation and remedying of those abuses, were expressions of an essentially middleclass radical protestanism, in tune with other movements: for prison reform or the abolition of slavery. The first campaigners for asylum provision for paupers, however, were, albeit humanitarians, acting initially as statutory agents, whose principal concerns were with the preservation of public order. The asylum was thus, in practice, at the junction of the 'welfare state' with Kittrie's 'therapeutic state.' (18) Whilst much of the optimistic idealism of asylum superintendents and Lunacy Commissioners extolled its virtues as a function of the former, the operation of identification codes at grass roots level meant that it was more often a function of the latter.

After the compulsory legislation of 1845, the differences between public and private asylums became more marked, as clinical progress stagnated in the large barracks asylums. The consequent changed perceptions of the nature of insanity allowed a revaluation of the success of the institution system, with custodial provision outweighing curative achievement in the ranking of criteria. Thus viewed, the asylum was a success, and was imitated in provision for the feebleminded. (19) Cure rates remained virtually the same from the 1840's until the First World War. (20) That they were not higher was attributed by asylum psychiatrists to legal barriers to early treatment: Sir Frederick Needham, senior member of the Board of Control (as the Lunacy Commissioners were restyled in 1913) in 1918, singled out this factor as his predecessors had done sixty years ealier. (21) But the legalism which could hamper confinement in some cases, could also secure it in others: the private asylum patient was more subject to delay in admission than the pauper, whose institutionalization was legally ordained, and in 'urgent' cases might be effected even prior to the observance of legal forms. (22)

The principle of confinement remained central to treatment of the insane in England, though in Scotland the law permitted extra-institutional care without formal certification. (23) Until 1930, all inmates of public asylums were certified, and the stigma attaching to insanity was intensified by the trappings of the procedures of confinement. The asylum itself contributed to both the stigmatization and to the public's distrust of the asylum system's operators:

> The actual physical isolation of our mental hospitals (and we must remember they were far more isolated when they were first built than they are now in the age of the motor car), the legal barriers that separate them from the outside world ... the isolation from discussion and criticism that they have enjoyed almost up until recent months, have created of them a sub-culture within our own social structure - in which a different set of values prevails than in the general community. These are values of an authoritarian nature, and depite improvement of recent times, this authoritarian ethos has descended to the present day. (24)

Written by the MP for Carlisle in 1958, these words indicate that the 'otherness' of insanity was as physically and conceptually apparent in the mid-twentieth century as in the late eighteenth. Medical prerogatives helped to maintain the isolation of the madman from 'the world' so long as they could themselves be maintained, and the law was looked to as the guardian of individual rights which would be forfeited in that isolation. From the 1760's, through Alleged Lunatic's Friend Society in the 1850's and the Lunacy Law Reform Association in the 1870's and 1880's, to the hostility to the asylum system in the 1920's, England experienced public animosity to psychiatry and psychiatric institutions as virulent as that in contemporary America. As late as 1922, the Mental Hospitals Association felt impelled to issue a pamphlet affirming that 'no oligarchy exists in the administration of the Lunacy Laws,' and indicating that 'the old barracks-like buildings in which the insane poor were herded together have all been improved.' (25)

One can accept that the mental hospitals of the 1920's and 1930's were improvements on the lunatic asylums of the 1880's and 1890's, and that they in turn, despite their many defects, were improved versions of the 1840's model. But, as the various elements of this dissertation have shown, the asylum itself was designed, as an ideal, to emphasise the 'otherness' of the insane, and as a practical tactic of social control, forcing heterogeneity on to an intentionally differentiated institution type, tended to stress the social undesirability of its inmates. The attitudes of administrators, whether lay or medical, inevitably reflected confused moral, economic, scientific and religious judgements. The aims of moral treatment, which characterized the early institutions, were based on the manipulation of a specific environment in the interests of individuals and groups, to be precisely determined as particular needs arose. As Chapter Four indicated, these programmes were not necessarily patient-orientated, and often evidenced a kind of cultural imperialism. Yet at least in physical terms, they catered to inmates' needs as perceived by medical and ancillary staff. The almost total involvement of psychiatrists in administrative problems of the county and borough institutions after the 1840's, meant that even this circumscribed humanity was severely curtailed.

The role of the state was seen, again ideally, as confirming the minimum human rights of the insane, and the statutory composition of the central inspectorate indicated an attempt to come to some kind of balance of legal and medical opinion as to how that humanity might best be guaranteed. Yet the very nature of the asylum contradicted the humanity of the madman: if not perceived as a threat which had to be removed by his isolation in a prison-like environment, the lunatic was easily reduced to the absurd 'hero' of music hall joke or after-dinner anecdote. (26) As the terminologies of law and medicine passed into common parlance, they lost whatever precision they had possessed, becoming first euphemism, then insult. (27) In trying to erect new vocabularies, psychiatrists retreated into newer jargons; retreated, too, behind the walls of their asylums, again making verbal mysteries to cloak a mythology of mental illness which was already supported by the bricks and mortar and railings of the mental institution.

Public opinion equated insanity with asylum confinement; the lunacy laws were developed from the premise that confinement should follow correct labelling of insanity. The administrators of both the lunacy laws and the poor laws were in agreement as to the necessity of confinement, differing only as to its precise location. Psychiatry developed in the confined space of the asylum, and the Lunacy Commissioners attempted to supervise the certified lunatic, wherever confined, in his own interest and that of the state. In their assiduous registration of lunacy, the Commissioners unhappily further reduced the humanity of the madman, translating him from an individual to a statistic. Their role, and that of asylum superintendents throughout the century reviewed, was essentially altruistic, if only hopefully objective. They key failing of the asylum system and its safeguards was an inflexibility which allowed the insane to be indelibly marked as different from the rest of mankind once they had been admitted into the realm of asylumdom, the difference only being acknowledged after confinement, but legitimizing retrospectively the initial deprivation of liberty. The blurred distinctions between sanity and insanity which the nineteenth-century asylum perpetuated, equipped the controllers of the system, albeit unintentionally, with an effective means of social control and cultural repression. If not taken up in Victorian Britain so eagerly as in other countries, at other times, these tools were nonetheless available; if not used cynically, they were used at times misguidedly - not by a centralized dictatorship, but by far from disinterested local authorities. The ease with which an Orangeman-controlled Manchester constabulary secured the certification and confinement of a political opponent, the Rev. William O'Connor, is an indication of the potential use of the lunacy laws which, so far as has been determined, was happily unique. (28) Yet overanxious relieving officers and careless magistrates could effect infringements of civil rights which were just as serious for the individuals concerned, if not as damning to the ethics of the authorities. Shaftesbury, as early as 1844, summed up the reformers' dilemma, and provided a fitting epitome of Victorian asylumdom:

> Visited Peckham Asylum on Saturday last. Long affair - six hours. What a lesson! How small the interval - a hair's breadth - between reason and madness. A sight, too, to stir apprehension in one's own mind. I am visiting in authority today. I may be visited in authority tomorrow. God be praised that there are any visitations at all; time was when such care was unknown. What an awful condition that of a lunatic! His words are generally disbelieved, and his most innocent peculiarities perverted; it is natural it should be so; we know him to be insane; at least, we are told that he is so; and we place ourselves on our guard - that is, we give to every word, look, gesture a value and meaning which often-times it cannot bear, and which it never would bear in ordinary life. Thus we too readily get him in, and too sluggishly get him out, and yet what a destiny! (29)

APPENDIX 1 : PUBLIC EXPENDITURE ON LUNACY, 1840 - 1890

Expenditure of Counties on Lunacy

Year	Expenditure (in £000)
1840	9
1841	10
1842	11
1843	20
1844	22
1845	23
1846	11
1847	12
1848	15
1849	29
1850*	185
1851	165
1852	80
1853	94
1854	100
1855	103
1856	128
1857	191
1858	181
1859	190
1860	175
1861	165
1862	144
1863	160
1864	196
1865	192
1866	209
1867	216
1868	246
1869	310
1870	287
1871	385

* Until 1850, the figures cover the cost of maintenance of pauper lunatics. After 1850, the costs of lunatic asylums are added.

Source: Mitchell and Deane, Abstract of British Historical Statistics, pp. 412 - 13

Expenditure of Local Authorities on Lunacy

Year	Expenditure (in £000)
1875	1400
1876	...
1877	...
1878	...
1879	...
1880	1400
1881	1400
1882	1500
1883*	1300
1884	1400
1885	1500
1886	1500
1887	1400
1888	1500
1889	1500
1890	1500

* Until 1883, figures include expenditure out of loans. All figures include cost of maintenance of pauper lunatics.

Source: Mitchell and Deane, p. 417.

APPENDIX 2 : ASSIGNED CAUSES OF INSANITY IN PATIENTS ADMITTED TO LANCASHIRE COUNTY ASYLUMS, 1853 - 90; AND ADMISSIONS OF IRISH PATIENTS INTO RAINHILL, 1853 - 81.

The Tables on the following page are compiled from the Annual Reports of the Medical Superintendents of the four asylums in operation during the years covered. Data were not standardized amongst the institutions at this time, and individual asylums changed their style as they changed superintendents.

The first date used in each instance is the first date for which a particular superintendent provided the statistical information needed. It will be noted that, even where a superintendent began to assemble statistics, there was no guarantee that he would provide the same kinds of information in subsequent reports. The heads chosen are, clearly, not exhaustive, but comprise the most heavily-used categories of assigned causation during these years. Significant differences can be noted between institutions, especially as regards assigning cases to 'cause unknown' and in emphasizing the role of hereditary factors.

Only Rainhill Asylum - which catered to Merseyside - provided any run of figures on numbers of Irish admitted annually, though the Prestwich superintendent occasionally noted accumulations of Irish in his total resident population.

Gaps in the Tables indicate an absence of figures in the asylum reports. All assigned causes, other than Drink (Dr), Hereditary factors (Her), Previous attack (P) and Unknown (U) are omitted.

The big increases in admissions at Lancaster (1883) and Prestwich (1886) simply reflect the opening of new wings, which were immediately filled.

Year	Lancaster						Whittingham					
	Adm.	Dr.	Her.	P.	U.	Irish	Adm.	Dr.	Her.	P.	U.	Irish
1876	203	33	44		51							
1877	327	31	58									
1878	282	26	80		25							
1879	355	50	77		53							
1880	407	72	89		60							
1881	335	47	93	66	45							
1882	241	41	53	41	44							
1883	862	95	120	35	417		467	66	86	98	122	
1884	327	35	78	43	41		283	38	38	46	118	
1885	459	73	76	52	185		158	33	28	39	38	
1886	375	61	85	58	105			40	52	66	31	
1887	296	59	68	54	95		174	24	39	28	33	
1888	314	72	91	69			169	25	36	48	42	
1889	338	34	51	32	93		266	42	62	69	45	
1890	207	20	65	44	43		388	70	99	67	75	

Year	Rainhill						Prestwich					
	Adm.	Dr.	Her.	P.	U.	Irish	Adm.	Dr.	Her.	P.	U.	Irish
1853	145	34	9		47	42						
1854	122	33	7		29	33						
1855		27	8		30	26						
1856		30	7		32	33						
1857	78	10			32	22						
1858	97	15			48	39						
1859	70	2	1		39	22						
1860	285	11	6		162	88						
1861	246	33	3		153	59						
1862	172	17	4		100	44						
1863	134	6			103	44						
1864	158	17	6		104	45						
1865	176	27			118	50						
1866	132	14	1		94	57						
1867	160	14	4		110	57						
1868	140	6	1		116	53						
1869	108	8	1		86	44						
1870	147	6	2		115	49						
1871	151	18	1		116	59						
1872	151	10	1		122	49						
1873	320	17	5		265							
1874	202	17	1		158							
1875	138	11	1		107	44						

Year	Rainhill						Prestwich					
	Adm.	Dr.	Her.	P.	U.	Irish	Adm.	Dr.	Her.	P.	U.	Irish
1876	180	10	2		151	44						
1877	166	4	3		148	34						
1878	151	33	4		20	32						
1879	171	52	3		36	40						
1880	196	41	1	19	55	43						
1881	193	32	4	39	47	47						
1882	181	40	13	29	36							
1883	159	29	13	25	36							
1884	188	38	16	27	47							
1885	238	45	27	13	33		674	169	222	171	185	
1886		21	21	17	14		1003	195	273	199		
1887	345	70	22	31	89			226	256	180		
1888	539	65	51	45	254		648	222	195	153		
1889	515	138	133	109	189		608	163	191	135		
1890	508	128	93	115	171		659	163	186	140		

NOTES.

Introduction.

(1) 'Britain' denotes England and Wales. Ireland and Scotland, though evidencing similar conceptions of insanity, and following a similar line of psychiatric development, had their own styles of legal and administrative development and lie outside the scope of this study.
(2) W. Ll. Parry-Jones, The Trade in Lunacy, A Study of Private Madhouses in England in the Eighteenth and Nineteenth Centuries (London 1972)
(3) See below, Chapter Six, Section V.
(4) For example, Kathleen Jones, Lunacy, Law and Conscience 1744 - 1845 (London 1955)
(5) Michel Foucault, Madness and Civilization, A History of Insanity in the Age of Reason (English translation, Richard Howard, London 1967).

Chapter One

(1) The United States has recently been better served. Replacing the blinkered glibness of Albert Deutsch's The Mentally Ill in America: A History of their Care and Treatment from Colonial Times (New York, 1937), there have appeared two exceptionally good studies by Gerald N. Grob: The State and the Mentally Ill: A History of Worcester State Hospital in Massachussetts, 1830-1920 (University of North Carolina, 1966) and Mental Institutions in America: Social Policy to 1875 (New York 1973). Stimulating, though at times unreliable, and covering a broader area is David J. Rothman, The Discovery of the Asylum: Social Order and Disorder in the New Republic (Boston 1971). Searching for Freudians before Freud, and kindred pastimes, is common to both sides of the Atlantic, (see Rothman pp. xiv-xvi).
(2) For examples see, Gregory Zilboorg and Gregory Henry, History of Psychological Medicine (New York 1941); Franz G. Alexander and Sheldon Selesnick, The History of Psychiatry (London 1967); Henry Yellowlees, To Define True Madness (London 1953); David Stafford-Clark, Psychiatry Today (London 1952); Peter Hays, New Horizons in Psychiatry (London 1964) pp. 128 - 135.
(3) A one volume synthesis, with some amendment and post-1959 continuation is published as History of the Mental Health Services (London 1972).
(4) Daniel Hack Tuke, Chapters in the History of the Insane in the British Isles (London 1882). Tuke was a grandson of the founder of the York Retreat and there is much of the evangelist in his style and purpose.
(5) Cp. J. Hoenig and Marian W. Hamilton, The De-segregation of the Mentally Ill (London 1969) pp. 1 - 3
(6) Richard Hunter and Ida Macalpine. Three Hundred Years of Psychiatry 1535 - 1860 (London 1963), and George III and the Mad Business (London 1969).
(7) William Ll.Parry-Jones, The Trade in Lunacy (London 1972)

(8) Denis Leigh, The Historical Development of British Psychiatry (Oxford 1961).

(9) R. Hunter and I. Macalpine, eds, A Treatise on Madness by William Battie MD and Remarks on Dr. Battie's Treatise on Madness by John Monro MD. A Psychiatric Controversy of the Eighteenth Century (London 1962); An Enquiry concerning the Indications of Insanity with suggestions for the Better Protection and Care of the Insane. By John Conolly MD (London 1964); The Treatment of the Insane without Mechanical Restraints. By John Conolly MD (London 1973); Gregory Bateson, ed, Perceval's Narrative: A Patient's Account of his Psychosis 1830 - 1832. By John Perceval (London 1962)

(10) The best introduction is Roger Bastide, Sociologie des Maladies Mentales (Paris 1965). S. Spitzer and N. Denzin, The Mental Patient: Studies in the Sociology of Deviance (New York 1968) offers extracts of the most important works.

(11) E.M. Lemert, Social Pathology (New York 1951)

(12) Howard S. Becker, Outsiders: Studies in the Sociology of Deviance (New York 1963) p. 9. Cp Morton Schatzman, Soul Murder, Persecution in the Family (London 1973)Chapter 1.

(13) Erving Goffman, Asylums (New York 1961); Stigma (New Jersey 1963); Nicholas N. Kittrie, The Right to be Different: Deviance and Enforced Therapy (London 1971)

(14) Valerie A. Cowie, 'The Inheritance of Personality Disorders' in A.T. Welford, M. Argyle, D.V. Glass and J.N. Morris, eds, Society: Psychological Problems and Methods of Study (London 1968) pp. 113 - 131.

(15) Thomas J. Scheff, 'The Role of the Mentally Ill and the Dynamics of Mental Disorder: A Research Framework' in Sociometry (1963) 26. pp. 436 - 453; Being Mentally Ill (London 1966). See especially the diagram at p. 100.

(16) Thomas S. Szasz, The Myth of Mental Illness (London 1962; paperback ed 1972); Law, Liberty and Psychiatry (New York 1963); The Manufacture of Madness (London 1972).

(17) For a discussion of the secondary nature of the medical role see David Mechanic 'Some Factors in Identifying and Defining Mental Illness' in Mental Hygiene (1962) 46. pp. 66 - 74.

(18) Cp. Eric Berne, Games People Play: The Psychology of Human Relationships (London 1964). Scheff emphasises the involuntary nature of role-playing in mental illness careers; Szasz argues that whilst role-playing is not necessarily mostly voluntary, it is yet a strategy chosen by the individual as a way of obtaining help from others. In both cases, however, role-playing is seen as part of the social system. Szasz draws an analogy between the mental illness role and that of the typecast actor.

(19) ' ... bodily disease stands in the same relation to mental illness as a defective television set stands to a bad programme.' 'Sick' is used metaphorically to describe jokes or economies, but 'only when we call minds sick do we systematically mistake metaphor for fact. And send for a doctor to "cure" the "illness".

It's as if a television viewer were to send for a TV repairman because he disapproves of what the BBC puts on the air.' (New Society, 16 Dec 1971, pp.1213-14).

(20) Szasz, The Manufacture of Madness passim.

(21) R.D. Laing, The Divided Self (London 1959); The Politics of Experience (London 1967); R.D. Laing and Aaron Esterson, Sanity, Madness and the Family (London 1964).

(22) David Cooper, Psychiatry and Anti-Psychiatry (London 1967); R.D. Laing and David Cooper, Reason and Violence (London 1964).

(23) Aaron Esterson, The Leaves of Spring (London 1970)

(24) David Cooper, The Death of the Family (London 1972). Cp Schatzman, op.cit.

(25) Laing and Esterson, op.cit.; Joseph Berke in Mary Barnes and Joseph Berke, Mary Barnes (London 1971). For a fuller discussion see Michael Glenn and Richard Kunnes, Repression or Revolution? Therapy in the United States Today. (New York 1973).

(26) Grob, Mental Hospitals in America, pp. 132 - 73;Mechanic, 'Some Factors in Identifying and Defining Mental Illness' pp. 66 - 74.

(27) Thomas S. Szasz, Ideology and Insanity: Essays in the Psychiatric Dehumanization of Man (London 1973).

(28) See below, Chapter Four.

(29) A.H. Leighton and A.D. Leighton in A. Freedman, ed., Comprehensive Textbook of Psychiatry (New York 1967) p. 1528.

(30) Ibid.

(31) A.H. Leighton quoted in Hugh Freeman, ed., Progress in Mental Health (London 1969) p. 71. Cp. Norman Zinberg, 'The Mirage of Mental Health' in B.J.S. (1970) xxi p.264.

(32) Harold Perkin, The Origins of Modern English Society 1780 - 1880. (London 1969) p.1.

(33) Mechanic, 'Some Factors,' p.68.

(34) W.W. Rostow, The Stages of Economic Growth (Cambridge 1960) pp. 38 ff.

(35) W.H.B. Court, A Concise Economic History of Britain from 1750 to Recent Times (Cambridge 1954) p.16

(36) Perkin, op. cit. Chapters I to VI offers cogent analysis of principal themes.

(37) For a theoretical context for the disruptive impact of technological and allied changes on cultural forms see Marshall McLuhan, Understanding Media (London 1964) pp. 11 - 86; Edmund Carpenter, Oh, What a Blow that Phantom Gave Me! (London 1976) pp. 24-26, 43-44, 53, 63, offers a variety of instances from disparate cultures.

(38) For the 'professionalization' of medicine, see W.L.Burn, The Age of Equipoise (London 1964) pp. 202 - 211.

(39) For example in the gradual extension of suffrage rights the 'democratization' of local government, and the growth of centralized administration and inspection in social policy.

(40) R.S. Neale, Class and Ideology in the Nineteenth Century (London 1971) Chapter One.

(41) For twentieth century similarities see A.B.Hollingshead and F.C. Redlich, 'Social Stratification and Psychiatric

Disorders' in Am.Soc.R. (1953) 18. pp. 163 - 169, and Mechanic op. cit. Economic, sexual and ethnic factors were key determinants. For American parallels see Grob, op. cit. pp. 221 - 256.

(42) Charles Mercier (1852 - 1919) MD FRCP FRCS. Educated Merchant Taylors. Went to sea as cabin boy on father's death, when family's fortunes collapsed. Studied medicine at London Hospital after period of work in woollen warehouse in the City. Two junior appointments after studying under Hughlings Jackson, followed by period as licensee of a private asylum in London. Senior MO to City of London Asylum.

(43) 'Conduct' in D.H. Tuke, ed, A Dictionary of Psychological Medicine (London 1892) Vol I p. 242.

(44) Ibid. p. 245.

(45) J.M.Sc. (1858) iv p. 314.

(46) Sir John Charles Bucknill (1817-1897) MD (London) FRS FRCP, Educated Rugby and UCL. Medical Superintendent, Devon County Asylum (1844 - 62); Lord Chancellor's Visitor in Lunacy (1862 - 76); President British Medico-Psychological Association (1860); Lumleian Lecturer on the Law of Insanity (1878); Founder of Asylum Journal; sometime editor Brain and J.M.Sc. Knighted 1894.

(47) Daniel Hack Tuke (1827 - 1895) Grandson of founder of York Retreat. MD (Heidelberg). Distinguished career at St. Bartholomews; consulting physician; prolific writer on insanity and kindred topics; correspondent of Spencer; sometime editor of J.M.Sc.

(48) 'Eccentricity' in A Dictionary of Psychological Medicine p. 418.

(49) Ibid. p. 419.

(50) Ibid.

(51) John Stuart Mill, On Liberty (London 1859, Everyman edn. 1964) p. 126.

(52) Henry E. Sigerist, Civilization and Disease (Cornell UP 1943) p. 87.

(53) Most glaringly effective examples can be found in the Indian caste system, or in South Africa's 'apartheid'.

(54) Colin Blakemore, 'Mechanics of the Mind: Madness and Morals' (Fourth Reith Lecture, BBC Radio 3, 19 Dec 1976) Printed in the Listener (16 Dec 1976)

(55) Thomas S. Szasz, The Age of Madness. The History of Involuntary Mental Hospitalization presented in Selected Texts. (London 1975)

(56) Zhores A. Medvedev and Roy A. Medvedev, A Question of Madness (London 1971); Michael Glenn, Voices from the Asylum (New York 1974) pp. vii - xvii.

(57) Szasz, 'Undermind' in New Society (16 December 1971) p. 1214.

(58) Ibid. pp. 1214 - 15.

(59) Leonard Shelford, A Practical Treatise on the Law concerning Lunatics, Idiots, and Persons of Unsound Mind (London 1833) Vol. II p.7; Tuke, Chapters in the History of the Insane, pp. 287 - 88; Kittrie, The Right to be Different, pp. 8 - 10.

(60) Sigerist, Civilization and Disease. p. 91.

(61) Charles Reich, 'Individual Rights and Social Welfare:

the Emerging Legal Issues' in Yale Law Journal (1965) 74 p. 1245..

(62) Kittrie, op. cit. pp. 11, 39 - 44 and passim.

(63) Kittrie, p. 41.

(64) Ibid. p. 6.

(65) Ibid. pp. 11, 40 - 42.

(66) 'Asylumdom' as a description of the detention of the insane in lunatic asylums and other special institutions, was used in the last quarter of the nineteenth century. So far as can be ascertained, its first appearance in print was in an article, 'The Prerogative of **Asylumdom**' in B.M.J. (1879) i. p. 94.

Chapter Two.

(1) Edward G. O'Donoghue, The Story of Bethlem Hospital from its Foundation in 1247 (London 1914) passim; Daniel Hack Tuke, Chapters in the History of the Insane (London 1882) pp. 45 ff.

(2) Isolated houses have been traced to earlier periods: Parry-Jones The Trade in Lunacy p. 8. Boarding-out in private dwellings, a tactic used by parishes for their insane charges from the seventeenth century, seems to have been the origin of the private madhouse; A. Fessler 'The Management of Lunacy in Seventeenth Century England. An Investigation of Quarter Session Records', in Proc. R. S. Med. (1956) 49 pp. 901 - 7.

(3) F. Bateman and W. Rye, The History of Bethel Hospital at Norwich (Norwich 1906); Kathleen Jones. Lunacy, Law and Conscience, pp. 49 ff. for St. Luke's in London; Anon., An Account of the Rise and Present Establishment of the Lunatic Hospital in Manchester (Manchester 1771); Jonathan Gray, A History of York Asylum (York 1815); Charles Vaillant, Historical Sketch of the Emergence of Liverpool Psychiatry (Typescript, Brown Library, Liverpool 1962).

(4) David Owen, Philanthropy in England, 1660 - 1960 (Cambridge, Mass. 1965) pp. 36 - 61; Brian Abel-Smith, The Hospitals, 1800 - 1948 (London 1964) passim; George Rosen, The Hospital: Historical Sociology of a Community Institution, in Eliot Friedson, ed., The Hospital in Modern Society (New York 1963) pp. 19 - 23.

(5) Gerald N. Grob, Mental Institutions in America, pp. 13 - 15; Carl Brindenbaugh, Cities in Revolt: Urban Life in America, 1743 - 1776 (New York 1955) pp. 125 - 26; David J. Rothman, The Discovery of the Asylum, pp. 39 - 42.

(6) Grob, ibid. p. 15.

(7) Nina Ridenour, Mental Health in the United States: A Fifty Year History (Harvard UP 1961) p. 77. The Pennsylvania State Hospital, Philadelphia, was the first institution to receive mental patients (1752). The Williamsburg Asylum, Virginia, was the first establishment opened exclusively for the insane in 1773. See Grob, ibid. pp. 19-20, 26-29.

(8) In London, the Westminster Hospital (1719), Guy's (1721) and the London Hospital (1740) received lunatics. Guy's had separate insane wards in 1728. Manchester's Lunatic

Hospital was originally an outgrowth of the Infirmary, as was Liverpool's, see W. Moss, The Liverpool Guide (Liverpool 1796) p. 79.

(9) Confinement of the insane began as part of a wider movement to control deviance by removing the affected outside the normal community. The Parisian Hospital General (1656) was to become a model for French, German and English Institutions: Michel Foucault, Madness and Civilization (Paris 1961; London 1967) pp. 39 - 41; Thomas S. Szasz, The Manufacture of Madness (London 1971) pp. 41 - 43; Emil Kraeplin, One Hundred Years of Psychiatry (Trans. Wade Baskin, New York 1962) p. 152.

(10) George Rosen 'Social Attitudes to Irrationality and Madness in Seventeenth and Eighteenth Century Europe' in J. Hist.Med. & All.Sc. (1963) vol. 18 p. 237.

(11) Ibid. p. 233.

(12) David Roberts, Victorian Origins of the British Welfare State (New Haven 1960) p. 27.

(13) Parry-Jones, The Trade in Lunacy, p. 11.n.

(14) Anon., An Account of the Rise and Present Establishment of the Lunatic Hospital in Manchester, p. 10; William Brockbank, Portrait of a Hospital, 1752 - 1948 (London 1952) pp. 21 - 24. The Lunatic Hospital was originally attached to the Infirmary, but continued enlargements made this arrangement impracticable, and in 1844 the buildings were returned to the Infirmary's use and the insane patients removed to a new quarters in the re-sited hospital, henceforth called the Manchester Royal Hospital for the Insane, or more simply, Cheadle Royal.

(15) Jones, Lunacy, Law and Conscience, p. 31; Edward Mansfield Brockbank, A Short History of Cheadle Royal Hospital from its Foundation in 1752 for the Humane Treatment of Mental Disease (Manchester 1934) pp. 11-15.

(16) The Gentleman's Magazine article appeared in January 1763, and it was in August that the infirmary trustees set up a committee to discuss separate provision for the insane. The Trustees' pamphlet of 1771 is hostile to madhouses but makes no overt reference to the press reports: Brockbank, loc. cit. The appeal launched in the local press (Manchester Mercury, September 13th, 1763) was anonymous, though one modern writer has suggested it was a 'plant' by the Trustees: Nesta Roberts, Cheadle Royal Hospital. A Bicentenary History (Altrincham 1967) p.4. Miss Roberts fails to note the role of the Newcastle campaign.

(17) E.M. Brockbank, op. cit. p.3.

(18) William Wentworth Fitzwilliam (1748 - 1833). Second earl; nephew and heir of Charles Wentworth, Marquis of Rockingham. Educated: Eton and Cambridge. Joined Pitt as one of the 'Old Whigs' and became President of the Council (1794); Lord Lieutenant of Ireland (1795), but recalled because of unauthorized expression of sympathy with Catholic emancipation; Lord Lieutenant of West Riding (1798); President of the Council (1806 - 7); dismissed from Lord Lieutenancy in 1819 for censure of Peterloo massacre.

(19) Charles G. Milnes Gaskell, Passages in the History of

York Lunatic Asylum (Wakefield 1902) p. 16.

(20) Mason, quoted by Gaskell, loc. cit.

(21) Jonathan Gray, A History of York Asylum (York 1815)p.26.

(22) Godfrey Higgins (1773 - 1833). Educated Trinity Hall, Cambridge, Writer on history of religion, notably Anacalypsis ... An Inquiry into the Origin of Languages, Nations and Religions (posthumously published in 1836). Described in an obituary notice in the Annual Register as 'levelling and destructive' in his politics and religion, and regarded as 'dangerous' by many contemporaries. Jones, Lunacy, Law and Conscience, p.84, unaccountably finds him 'a quiet country gentleman' which hardly squares with Higgins' desires to reduce the royal establishment, abolish the Irish Church and the Corn Laws, and to reform Parliament: see Gentleman's Magazine (1833) vol. ii. p. 371. Cp. Gaskell, op. cit. p. 43.

(23) William Tuke (1732 - 1822). Quaker tea and coffee merchant.

(24) D.H. Tuke, Chapters in the History of the Insane, p.113.

(25) D.H. Tuke, Chapters in the History of the Insane, pp. 113 - 151. The interest was not just insular: see, for example, Isaac Ray's comments in Am.J.Insanity (1847) iv p. 112. French commentators coupled Tuke with Pinel: see remarks by Ferrus, ex-physician to Napoleon, cited by D.H. Tuke, ibid. p. 132 and cp. Parchappe, Les Principes à suivre dans le Fondation et la Construction des Asiles d'Aliénés (Paris 1853) p. 226.

(26) See entry in D.N.B.

(27) D.H. Tuke, op. cit. p. 116.

(28) Samuel Tuke, A Description of the Retreat, an Institution near York, for Insane Persons of the Society of Friends (York 1813).

(29) D.H. Tuke, op. cit. p. 115.

(30) Jones, Lunacy, Law and Conscience, p.59.

(31) Jones, ibid. pp. 92 - 96 outlines the public image of Bethlem in the first quarter of the nineteenth century.

(32) D.H. Tuke, op. cit. p. 122; Edinburgh Review (1817)xxvii p. 433.

(33) Sydney Smith, Essays Reprinted from the 'Edinburgh Review' (London n.d.) pp. 235 - 241.

(34) H.C. Hunt, A Retired Habitation. A History of the Retreat, York (London 1932) pp. 49 - 50.

(35) Cp. The Pennsylvania Quakers and the Pennsylvania Hospital: Grob, Mental Institutions in America, p.17.

(36) George Rosen, 'The Philosophy of Ideology and the Emergence of Modern Medicine in France' in Bull.Hist.Med. (1946) xx. pp. 328 - 331.

(37) Cited by Eric T. Carlson and Norman Dain, 'The Psychotherapy that was Moral Treatment' in Am.J.Psych. (1960) cxvii. p. 519.

(38) Michel Foucault, Madness and Civilization (London 1967) pp. 255 - 78.

(39) The same holds true for America, See Grob, Mental Institutions in America, Chapter II.

(40) Szasz, The Manufacture of Madness, pp.77 - 78.

(41) David J.Rothman, The Discovery of the Asylum, p.xviii

(42) Ibid. p.xiv.

(43) For discussions of further aspects of Rothman's ideas, see below, Chapter Four, Section II.

(44) Transatlantic Quaker links were very strong. American Quakers, following the lead of the Retreat, were heavily involved in founding both sectarian institutions (as groups) and, as individuals, in helping set up non-sectarian hospitals, see Grob, op. cit. p.48. In America, the following hospitals were founded in direct imitation of the Retreat: Bloomingdale Asylum (N.Y.); The Hartford Retreat (Conn.); Frankford Asylum (Penn.); and the McLean Hospital (Boston); Goshen, Documentary History. p. 475.

(45) Jones offers a most uncritical acceptance: Lunacy, Law and Conscience, pp. 31 - 39, 102 - 106, 135 - 144.

(46) Parry-Jones, Trade in Lunacy Chapters 8 and 9, offers a balanced assessment of the evidence for abuse within the private sector throughout the period covered.

(47) Esther Moir, 'Sir George Onesiphorous Paul', in H.P.R. Finberg (ed) Gloucestershire Studies (Gloucester 1957) pp. 195 - 225.

(48) Jones, Lunacy, Law and Conscience, pp. 70 - 78

(49) Suggestions of Sir George Onesiphorous Paul, Bart., to Earl Spencer, printed as an Appendix to the Report of the Select Committee on the State of Criminal and Pauper Lunatics in England and Wales (4 to London 1807)

(50) Paul was a friend of John Howard, the prison reformer, and Howard and Elizabeth Fry had been visitors at the Retreat: W.L. Clay, Memoir of the Rev. John Clay, BD (London 1861) p.63.

(51) Jones, Lunacy, Law and Conscience, p.68.

(52) John Haslam (1764 - 1844). MD Aberdeen. LRCP. Apothecary to Bethlem Hospital (1795 - 1816).

(53) John Conolly (1794 - 1866). MD Edinburgh. FRCP. Hon DCL (Oxon). Professor of the Practice of Medicine, London University (1827 - 31). Resident Physician, Middlesex County Lunatic Asylum, Hanwell (1839 - 44), Consulting Physician (1845 - 48) and Visiting Physician (1849-52). Chairman of AMOAHI (1843, 1851). President of Medico-Psychological Association (1858).

(54) Henry Maudsley (1835 - 1918). MD London. Medical Superintendent of Cheadle Royal (1859 - 62). Editor of J.M.Sc. (1862 - 78). Physician of West London Hospital (1864 - 74) Professor of Medical Jurisprudence, University College, London (1869 - 79).

(55) See Grob, Mental Institutions in America, pp. 20 ff. 146, 167, and passim.

(56) Quoted in Kraeplin, One Hundred Years of Psychiatry, p.152

(57) Szasz, Manufacture of Madness, p. 43

(58) Foucault, Madness and Civilization, Chapter IX.

(59) William Battie, Treatise on Madness (London 1757) p.68.

(60) E.M. Brockbank, Short History of Cheadle Royal, p.11.

(61) W. Moss, The Liverpool Guide, p.80

(62) Pinel, Treatise on Insanity. pp. 63, 91,and passim.

(63) George Man Burrows (1771 - 1846). MRCS. LSA. MD St. Andrews. FRCP. Owner of a private asylum in Chelsea

(1814 - 23) and of the Retreat, Clapham (1823 - 43).

(64) George Man Burrows, Commentaries on Insanity (London 1828) pp. 696 - 97).

(65) John Haslam, Considerations on the Moral Management of Insane Persons (London 1817) pp. 14 - 15.

(66) Leigh, Historical Development of British Psychiatry, p.96 Cp.obituary notice in Lancet, July 27th 1844.

(67) Vieda Skultans, Madness and Morals, Ideas on Insanity in the Nineteenth Century (London 1975) p. 3.

(68) Foucault, Madness and Civilization, p. 274.

(69) Cited in Tuke, Chapters in the History of the Insane, p. 117.

(70) Roberts, Victorian Origins of the British Welfare State, p. 27.

(71) Tuke, Description, p. 50.

(72) The Retreat was not opposed in principle to mechanical restraints, at least in its early days, Tuke's Description, p. 113

(73) Though 'medical treatment was by no means despised.' Ibid.

(74) Ibid. p. 141.

(75) Ibid. p. 110 - 112.

(76) Cp. Foucault, Madness and Civilization, Chapter V.

(77) The title of one chapter in Pinel's influential Treatise was 'The Importance of an Enlightened System of Police for the Internal Management of Lunatic Asylums.'

(78) Sir Andrew Halliday (1781 - 1839) MD (Edinburgh), LRCP (London), FRCP (Edinburgh) FRS (Edinburgh), Physician to Duke of Clarence, later William IV. Writer on insanity.

(79) Sir Andrew Halliday, A General View of the Present State of Lunatics and Lunatic Asylums (London 1828) p.17.

(80) Sir William Charles Ellis (1780 - 1839) MD (St.Andrews), MRCS. First medical superintendent at West Riding County Asylum (Wakefield, 1818 - 30) and Middlesex County Asylum (Hanwell, 1831 - 38). Proprietor of Southall Park Asylum (1838 - 39).

(81) Halliday, op. cit. p.19.

(82) Cited in Halliday, General View, Appendix III, p.94. See also pp. 41 - 44 for a discussion of the role of employment in Irish asylums.

(83) 'Constant employment' was a feature of the Retreat, though strikingly different in nature and purpose from that in public asylums: Edinburgh Review (April 1814) pp. 190-198. Cp. Pinel, who punished refusal to work: Foucault, op. cit. p. 268.

(84) The positive rationale of Benthamite 'less eligibility' encouraged a return to normal work at the first opportunity. The 'Outdoor Labour Test Order' of 1842 was an extra-institutional extension of this principle, produced by economic depression. For discussion of the seventeenth-century European evolution of the work-ethic, and its role in legitimizing institutionalization. See Foucault, op. cit. Chapter II.

(85) Thomas Eccleston, Report of the Superintendent of the Lancashire County Asylum, Rainhill, 1851 (Newton 1852) p. 14.

(86) John Conolly, On the Construction and Government of

Lunatic Asylums and Hospitals for the Insane (London 1847) p. 78.

(87) Bryan Crowther, Practical Remarks on Insanity (London 1811) pp. 86, 102 - 6; Burrows, op. cit. passim. Cp. Hunter at York Asylum with his secret nostrum, Gray, History of York Lunatic Asylum, p.24.

(88) Conolly, Construction and Government of Lunatic Asylums, p.1.

(89) Ibid, p. 131; Samuel Gaskell in B.M.J. (May 1861) p.268.

(90) Conolly, ibid. p. 7; J. Mortimer-Granville, The Care and Cure of the Insane (London 1877) Vol. 1. p. 75.

(91) Derbyshire's attempt to be forward-looking was baulked by the Commissioners in Lunacy: Conolly, Construction and Government at Lunatic Asylums, p.11.

(92) Tuke, Chapters in the History of the Insane, p.209 The asylum, sited at Springfield, was built in mock-Tudor style and initially cost £85,367 including land. It was originally designed for 350 patients. Mortimer-Granville, op. cit. pp. 215 - 16.

(93) Special Return to the Epiphany Quarter Sessions by the Visiting Justices appointed to Superintend the Erection and Management of the County Lunatic Asylum (1843)p.1.

(94) Their criterion of curability, like that of current psychiatric opinion, was duration of attack. After twelve months the disease was diagnosed as chronic, and inferentially, incurable. Shaftesbury rehearsed this accepted medical tenet to a public meeting in 1861: Hodder, Shaftesbury, p.526.

(95) Report of the Metropolitan Commissioners in Lunacy (London 1844): Mortimer-Granville, Care and Cure of the Insane, pp. 218 - 19.

(96) Ibid.

(97) Metropolitan Commissioners, Report, (1844). p.90.

(98) Mortimer-Granville, The Care and Cure of the Insane, p. 229.

(99) Ibid. p. 5. 'It is much to be regretted,' wrote Mortimer-Granville, 'that, being provided with all the most approved appliances, Brookwood was not jealously kept to its true purpose as a hospital for the cure of recent cases, instead of being at once crowded with chronic cases removed from other asylums and licensed houses ... This economic blunder is now (1877) visited on the county by an urgent demand for a third asylum ...'

(100) Cp. remarks of visiting committee in their first report, quoted ibid pp. 7 - 8.

(101) Ibid.

(102) Ibid p. 9. By 1877 the construction and extension costs at Springfield had mounted to almost £200,000 and at Brookwood to nearly £180,000. Adding on the annual repairs, to both (c. £86,000) this meant that provision for the county's 2140 institutionalized pauper insane had cost £214 7s. 2d. per bed.

(103) Ibid.

(104) J.C. Bucknill and D.H.Tuke, Manual of Psychological Medicine (London 1858) quoted in Mortimer-Granville, Care and Cure of the Insane p.9.

(105) Commissioners in Lunacy, Eleventh Annual Report (1857) p. 10.
(106) Mortimer-Granville, op. cit. p. 125.
(107) Ibid.
(108) J.M.Sc. (1865) xi. p. 483; Mortimer-Granville, op. cit. p. 147.
(109) Robertson loc. cit. J.C. Bucknill, J.M.Sc. (1858) iv loc. cit.
(110) B.M.J. (Jan 1879) p.94.
(111) See Jones, Lunacy, Law and Conscience, pp. 221 - 23
(112) Sir Charles Alexander Lockhart-Robinson, (1825 - 97). BM Oxon. MD Cantab and St. Andrews. FRCP (London and Edinburgh) . Superintendent Sussex County Lunatic Asylum (1859 - 70); Lord Chancellor's Visitor in Lunacy (1870 - 96); President, Medico-Psychological Association (1867).
(113) S.C. (1877) q. 1091.
(114) Cited in J.M.Sc. (1866) xii. p.21
(115) J. Thurnham, Observations on the Statistics of Insanity (London 1845) passim; Conolly, Construction and Government, p.3 See Rothman, Discovery of the Asylum, for American parallels.
(116) Samuel Gaskell (1807 - 86). Educated local schools, Warrington and Liverpool. Seven years apprenticed to Liverpool publisher/bookseller; turned to medicine despite discouragement, and went through necessary curriculum at Manchester and Edinburgh. Resident MO Stockport Cholera Hospital (1834); Apothecary, Manchester Royal Infirmary and Lunatic Hospital (1834-40); Superintendent, Lancaster County Asylum (1840-49) Commissioner in Lunacy (1849 - 66). Street accident (1865) forced retirement.
(117) 'On the Want of Better Provision for the Labouring and Middle Classes when Attacked or Threatened with Insanity' in J.M.Sc. (1860) vi. p. 321.
(118) Robert Boyd (1808-83). MD Edinburgh. FRCP. Resident physician, Marylebone Workhouse (1848). Superintendent, Somerset Lunatic Asylum. Owner of private asylum, Southall Park. President Medico-Psychological Association (1870). Killed,with his second son,trying to save patients from fire in asylum. Wrote extensively on the pathology of psychological medicine.
(119) 'The Care and Treatment of the Insane Poor' in J.M.Sc. (1870) xvi.pp 315 - 20.
(120) Jones, Mental Health and Social Policy, pp. 33 - 40
(121) Sir George Savage in T.C. Allbutt and H.D. Rolleston, eds., A System of Medicine By Many Writers (London 1899) Vol. viii. p. 429.
(122) 'On Some Common Misapprehensions as to the Curability of the Admissions of County Asylums' in J.M.Sc. (1877) xxiii p. 187.
(123) L.A.B. (1880) Report of the Superintendent of Lancaster Asylum, p.18.
(124) Ibid., p. 19.
(125) J.B. Tuke, 'Lunatics as Patients, Not Prisoners' in Nineteenth Century (1889) xxv.
(126) George Thompson, in the Lancet (11th May 1889).

(127) L.A.B. (1879) Report of the Superintendent of Prestwich Asylum, p. 69.
(128) B.M.J. (May 1861) p. 268.
(129) Cp the famous Gheel colony in Belgium. American superintendents during the 1860's and 70's were similarly beginning to question automatic institutionalization, see J. Parigot, 'The Gheel Question: From an American Point of View' in Am.J. Insanity (1863) pp. 332 - 54, which also offers an interesting interpretation of divergent psychiatric opinion in Britain and the Continent.
(130) Lauder W. Lindsay, 'The Family System as Applied to the Treatment of the Chronic Insane' in J.M.Sc. (1870) xvi. pp. 516 - 22.
(131) Ibid., pp. 516 - 17.
(132) D.H. Tuke, The Past and Present Provision for the Insane Poor in Yorkshire with Suggestions for the Future Provision for this Class (London 1889) p.22.
(133) Lancet, 11 May, 1889.
(134) Eric Midwinter, 'The Cholera and Dr. Duncan' in Old Liverpool (Newton Abbott 1971) pp. 92 - 93. For popular preference for dying at home, see Thurnham, Observations pp. 43 - 44; George Sturt, Journal 1890 - 1927 London 1967, ed., E.D. Mackerness p. 602.
(135) J.M.Sc. (1880) xxvi. p. 69.
(136) J.C. Bucknill, The Care of the Insane and their Legal Control, p.54.
(137) Ibid., p. 5.
(138) Joshua Harrison Stallard, Pauper Lunatics and Their Treatment (London 1870) p. 7.
(139) Ibid, pp. 8 - 9. Costs were significantly cheaper in boarding-out schemes: in Scotland, the daily cost of keeping a lunatic in an asylum was 1/4d., in the poorhouse, 11d; in private dwellings, only 6½d. (p.10) Stallard calculated that, if an equal number of paupers were boarded out in England as in Scotland, the annual saving to the Metropolis alone would be £20,000, and £60,000 for the rest of the country, and this without including the savings on extra buildings. Stallard was seemingly oblivious to the possibility of attempts at profiteering from out-relief, which would work against the interest of the pauper lunatics, In England, unions in the north west eagerly adopted the expedient for children: Lindsay, 'Family System'. In America, the linked questions of separate provision for curables and incurables, and the use of boarding-out as an alternative to asylum provision seems to have occasioned not only a predictable split between the medical profession and lay welfare administrators, but also a deep division within the psychiatric Establishment, Grob, Mental Institutions in America, Chapter VIII.
(140) Stallard, p. 14. Home-Relief was, of course, antithetical to poor law policy as laid down in 1834.
(141) He offered the instance of a 54-year old Scotswoman whose dipsomania had brought her to Colney Hatch. Deprived of drink, she exhibited 'perfect' behaviour, therefore, argued Stallard, since she required neither

supervision nor treatment, she ought not to be confined ... Ibid., p. 13.

(142) L.A.B. (1872) Report of the Superintendent of Prestwich Asylum, p. 62.

(143) The overcrowded Lancashire, Yorkshire and Middlesex asylums periodically attempted this tactic, with reluctance and very mixed results: Mortimer-Granville, passim; D.H. Tuke, Past and Present Provision for the Insane Poor in Yorkshire, pp. 22 ff.; LAB (1861) Report of the Superintendent of Lancaster Asylum, p. 17.

(144) Sir T. Clifford Allbutt (1836 - 1925). Educated St. Peters School, York, and Caius, Cambridge, and St. George's Hospital. Consulting physician in Leeds (1861 - 69); FRS. KCB. PC. Commissioner in Lunacy (1889 - 92). Regius Professor of Physic, Cambridge, (1892). Physician to Addenbrooks Hospital (1900).

(145) Quoted in L.A. Weatherley, A Plea for the Insane, (London 1918) p. 74.

(146) Weatherley cites a pleasant anecdote from Theodore Hyslop, Superintendent of Bethlem, indicative of latent hostility: 'I had the pleasure of taking the Right Hon. John Burns, when he was President of the LGB, round the hospital. When passing through a male ward one of the patients remarked: "Why, there goes Honest John." John Burns heard the remark with evident satisfaction and said to me, "That man appears to be quite sane." "Alas, no," I replied, "he is suffering from chronic delusional insanity, and is, I fear, incurable."' Loc. cit.

(147) Anon., Lunatick Asylums (London 1898) pp. 2 - 3.

(148) Kathleen Heasman, Evangelicals in Action. An Appraisal of their Social Work (London 1962) Chapters VI, VII, XII; William Edmondson, Making Rough Places Plain: A History of the Manchester and Salford Homes (Manchester 1921); J.J. Tobias, Crime and Industrial Society in the Nineteenth Century (London 1967) Chapter 11; S. Lane-Poole, 'Workhouse Infirmaries' in MacMillan's Magazine (July 1881) pp. 223 ff.; Abel-Smith, The Hospitals, passim; Records of the Catholic Social Services Bureau, Liverpool (Brown Library, Liverpool) passim; A. & C. Reed, Memoirs of the Life and Philanthropic Labours of A.C. Reed (London 1863) passim; Tuke, Chapters in the History of the Insane, pp. 300 ff; S. Keir, The Royal Albert Institution, Lancaster (Lancaster 1937); G.E. Shuttleworth, 'The Education of Children of Abnormally Weak Mental Capacity' in J.M.Sc. (1888) pp. 80 ff.; D.G. Pritchard, Education and the Handicapped (London 1963) passim.

(149) A.V. Dicey, Lectures on the Relationship Between Law and Public Opinion in England during the Nineteenth Century (London 1905) Lecture VII.

(150) Tuke, Chapters in the History of the Insane, pp. 96-100; 148-162; Jones, Lunacy, Law and Conscience, pp. 92-98; 102-107; 114; S. Gordon and T.G.B. Cocks, A People's Conscience (London 1952) pp. 101-51.

(151) Robert Gardiner Hill, A Concise History of the Entire Abolition of Mechanical Restraint (London 1857); Conolly, op. cit. pp. 122 ff; and The Treatment of the

Insane without Mechanical Restraints (London 1856); cf E.P. Charlesworth, Remarks on the Treatment of the Insane and the Management of Lunatic Asylums (London 1828) pp. 16-18; Alexander Walk 'Some Aspects of the Moral Management of the Insane up to 1854' in J.M.Sc. (1951) c. pp. 807-837; Hamilton Labbatt, An Essay on the Use and Abuse of Restraint in the Treatment of the Insane (Dublin 1847).

(152) Jones, Lunacy, Law and Conscience, pp. 149- 56.

(153) Robert Gardiner Hill, Lunacy, its Past and Present (London 1870). There was an undignified dispute between Hill and Charlesworth. Stafford Clark, Psychiatry Today p. 52, attributes the initiative to Conolly, who undoubtedly had greater success, Tuke, Chapters in the History of the Insane, p. 205; Leigh, Historical Developments of British Psychiatry, pp. 220 ff.

(154) James Wilkes (1811 - 94). LSA. MRCS. FRCS. Superintendent, Stone Asylum, Staffs. (1845 - 55). Commissioner in Lunacy (1855 - 78). Honorary Commissioner in Lunacy (1878 - 94).

(155) Metropolitan Commissioners in Lunacy, Report (1844) pp. 143-46; Commissioners in Lunacy Eighth Annual Report (1854) Appendix G.

(156) Restraint was defined by the Commissioners as the use of 'dresses, gloves, belts or other similar contrivances.' (Metropolitan Commissioners, Report, 1844, p. 139); Tuke, Chapters in the History of the Insane, p. 214

(157) Robert Gardiner Hill, (1811 - 78) MRCS. LSA. LRCP (Edinburgh). Resident MO, Lincoln Lunatic Hospital (1835 - 40); Joint Owner, Eastgate House Asylum,Lincoln (1840-63) and of three private asylums in London and Middlesex (1863 - 78).

(158) Robert Gardiner Hill, Total Abolition of Personal Restraint in the Treatment of the Insane (London 1839) pp. 21, 37 - 42; Tuke, op. cit. pp. 228 ff.

(159) Commissioners in Lunacy Eighteenth Report (1864)pp.97-99

(160) 'Seclusion' was the logical conclusion of separation from the community, and in the early part of the century, 'seclusion' and 'separation' had been used as interchangeable terms (Burrows, Commentaries, p. 696). By the 1840s the isolation of violent maniacs and epileptics was commonplace, and seen as beneficial (Tuke, Chapters, p. 229), though the practice had inherent dangers (ibid., p. 215); Commissioners in Lunacy, Eighth Report, loc. cit; J.A. Campbell, 'Remarks on the Use and Abuse of Seclusion' in J.M.Sc. (1887).

(161) J.M.Sc. (1875) xx p. 328.

(162) American psychiatrists were very hostile to Conolly. Non-restraint was seen as self-deception, seclusion and isolation as even more detrimental to patients than mechanical restraint, Grob, op. cit. p. 207. English alienists were equally critical of American institutions' reliance on restraint: Lancet (Nov 13th 1875); J.C. Bucknill, Notes on Asylums for the Insane in America (London 1876) pp. 65 ff. Pinel in Paris had early noted the inapplicability of 'moral treatment' in identical forms to disparate races, and approved the use

of restraints and coercions to instil 'repentance' or 'as punishment for the improper demeanour of maniacs' as a last resort'. Goshen, Documentary History, p.265; cp. Foucault, pp. 260 ff; Pinel, Treatise, pp. 205 ff.

(163) J.M.Sc. (1867) xiii. p. 289 Cp. J. Crawford, Observations on the Expediency of Abolishing Mechanical Restraint in the Treatment of the Insane in Lunatic Asylums (London 1842).

(164) Weatherley, A Plea for the Insane, p.33.

(165) Report of the Medical Superintendent of Wonford House (1891), cited ibid, p.34.

(166) Montague Lomax, The Experiences of an Asylum Doctor, (London 1921) pp. 48 - 49.

(167) Commissioners in Lunacy, Eighth Report (1854), Appendix G; J.G. Davey, first superintendent of the female department, had been Conolly's assistant at Hanwell, as he prominently proclaimed in an advertisement for his private asylum two years later, Lancet (26th March 1853); Richard Hunter and Ida Macalpine, Psychiatry for the Poor (London 1974) pp. 71 - 76.

(168) Commissioners in Lunacy, Twentyfourth Annual Report (1870) p. 180 Twenty-eighth Annual Report (1874) p.162; E.E. Wilson, 'A Brief History of Friern Hospital, 1850-1950' in Friern Hospital Magazine (1950) i p. 10; Hunter and Macalpine, Psychiatry for the Poor. p.86.

(169) J.M.Sc. (1859) v. p. 71.

(170) C.F.O. Westphal in J.M.Sc. (1868) xiii. p. 516; Commissioners in Lunacy, Twentyeighth Annual Report, p. 162.

(171) Metropolitan Commissioners in Lunacy, Report, (1844) pp. 113 - 14.

(172) Andrew Wynter, The Borderland of Insanity (London 1875) pp. 156 - 59; Joseph Williams, An Essay on the Use of Narcotics and other Remedial Agents calculated to produce Sleep in the Treatment of Insanity (London 1847). Hydrotherapy was standard asylum practice, see entry under 'Baths' in D.H. Tuke, Dictionary of Psychological Medicine (London 1892); Parry-Jones, op. cit. pp. 192-98, for medical treatments in private asylums. American parallels once more existed: Samuel Woodward, 'Observations on the Medical Treatment of Insanity' in Am.J.Insanity (1850) vii pp. 1 - 34. Cp. Foucault, pp. 166 - 72.

(173) LAB (1857) Report of the Committee of Visitors of Lancaster Asylum, p.9.

(174) Cited in Weatherley, A Plea for the Insane, p.114. Weatherley disputed this claim for the private sector, but expressed a desire for the attaching of general physicians to asylums, indicating the need by reference to an 'able medical superintendent' who, whilst competent in administrative and psychological terms, admitted to being unable to recognize pneumonia, and to be at a loss as to how to treat it anyway. Ibid. p.116.

(175) LAB (1887) Report of the Medical Superintendent of Lancaster Asylum, p. 23. Cp. the regimen at Gheel: J. Webster, Notes on Belgian Lunatic Asylums, including the Insane Colony at Gheel (London 1857)

(176) LAB (1861) Report of the Superintendent of Lancaster Asylum, p. 17; James G. Davey, 'On the Insane Poor in Middlesex' in J.M.Sc. (1867) xiii p.317

(177) Charles Mercier, Lunatic Asylums, Their Organisation and Management (London 1894) p. 284.

(178) B.M.J. (1st July, 1871) p. 13.

(179) Pinel, Treatise, pp. 59 - 63, 91, 99, 190.

(180) Foucault, Madness and Civilization, pp. 269 - 278; cp. the role of the physician, as an authority figure, in confinement procedures at the York Retreat, Tuke, Description, pp. 89 - 90.

(181) 'The physician who justly understands the non-restraint system well knows that the attendants are his most essential instruments ... They may often be considered, indeed, his best medicines; and they should be well chosen and well preserved ...' John Conolly, The Treatment of the Insane without Mechanical Restraints (London 1856) pp. 98-99.

(182) The physician 'entrusts them with the happiness, by day and night, of all the patients under their special care. To control the violent, without anger; to soothe the irritable, without weak and foolish concessions; to cheer and comfort the depressed to guard the imbecile and the impulsive, and to direct all - these are great duties to be demanded from such instruments; and no security is to be found for their proper performance except in the character of the attendants themselves ...' Ibid. p. 100.

(183) L.A.B. (1873) Report of the Superintendent of Prestwich Asylum, pp. 70-71. This criterion led the Rainhill MO to prefer inexperienced attendants who would be less likely to leave soon: L.A.B. (1887) Report of the Superintendent of Rainhill Asylum, p. 70. Thomas Clouston established an in-service training scheme with examinations, under the aegis of the Medico-Psychological Association: Mercier, pp. 291 - 92.

(184) Commissioners in Lunacy, Thirteenth Report (1859) p.63; R. Hunter, 'The Rise and Fall of Mental Nursing' in Lancet (1956) i. pp. 98-99.

(185) Mercier, p. 290. As in workhouses, inmates could be involved: at Prestwich in the 1880's, patients were used as night attendants' assistants, L.A.B. (1886) Report of the Superintendent of Prestwich Asylum, p.62.

(186) Mercier, p. 294; L.A.B. (1873) reproduction of the visiting Commissioners' minute, in Report of the Superintendent of Rainhill Asylum, p.14. Often staff left because their own health, mental or physical, had cracked: L.A.B. (1890) Report of the Superintendent of Lancaster Asylum, p. 26.

(187) Parry-Jones, Trade in Lunacy pp. 184 - 192, and passim; Alexander Walk, 'The History of Mental Nursing' in J.M.Sc. (1961) cvii. pp.4 ff.

(188) Parry-Jones, op. cit. pp. 186 - 87.

(189) Ibid. p. 185.

(190) 'Attendants themselves should not appear cloe than respectable domestics, nor should they be allowed to address themselves to patients otherwise than in the

accents of respect and consideration ...' Quoted in Commissioners in Lunacy, Eighth Report (1854) p. 181. In other private asylums, attendants were seen as body servants or valets; Parry-Jones, The Trade in Lunacy, p. 189.

(191) For example, Colney Hatch: Hunter and Macalpine, Psychiatry for the Poor, pp. 101 - 102.

(192) Staff discipline was harsh in both public and private sectors, for typical examples see Parry-Jones, op.cit. pp. 189 - 192; Hunter and Macalpine, ibid. pp. 97-100.

(193) The Commissioners' Reports from 1845 - 90 show remarkably little reliance on sedatives in the county institutions, and usage was generally at night. In asylums where non-restraint was attempted, physical coercion inevitably increased, with an inevitable increase in accidents, cp. the Henry Case at Lancaster, below Chapter **Six**, section IV.

(194) For former, see Manchester Central Library, MS/923/8/REL. Account of a Man's Wrong Confinement in Haydock Lodge Asylum, 1826 - 30; Montague Lomax and R. Grant-Richards, The Experiences of an Asylum Patient (London 1922) pp. 77 - 92; the attendant of the post-1845 period was easily confused with the keeper of earlier periods, a case of the sins of the fathers ... (Parry-Jones, pp. 244 - 249).

(195) L.A.B. (1860) Report of the Medical Superintendent of Prestwich Asylum, p. 38.

(196) Manchester Central Library, M4/2/7. Manchester Union, Weekly Returns, (5th Feb. 1859).

(197) Board and lodging included in both cases. Asylums tried to compete by raising salaries: L.A.B. (1873) Report of the Superintendent of Prestwich Asylum . pp. 70 - 71.

(198) Grob, Mental Institutions in America, pp. 212-213.

(199) Pinel, Treatise p.66; John Mitford (?), A Description of the Crimes and Horrors in the Interior of Warburton's Private Mad-house at Hoxton, commonly called Whitmore House (n.d. 1825 - 30?, in Hume Tracts, UCL Library) Part One, p. 31.

(200) J.M.Sc. (1855) i.p. 182.

(201) pp. 1859 Sess 1 (75) 111. Report from the Select Committee on Lunatics ...,pp. 34 - 36, 56; Anon, Familiar Views of Lunacy (London 1850) p. 122.

(202) Commissioners in Lunacy, Fifth Report (1850) p. 10; 16 & 17 Vic. c. 96 s. 7 (1853); Commissioners in Lunacy, Ninth Report (1855) p. 40 - 41.

(203) Cp. regulations for nurses and attendants at Colney Hatch, cited in Hunter and Macalpine, Psychiatry for the Poor, p. 102. At Duddleston Hall Lunatic Asylum, attendants were fined for not attending morning and evening prayers and could be dismissed for communicating with patients' relatives, or for going into the room of staff of the opposite sex. Parry-Jones, Trade in Lunacy, p. 191.

(204) E.g., in 1852, the Prestwich Superintendent received £350 p.a. and the house surgeon £100. By 1886, the superintendent's salary was £1200 p.a., and those of the 'assistant medical officers' £250 and £200 and £150

(two), L.A.B. (1852) Report of the Superintendent of Prestwich Asylum, p.70; L.A.B. (1886) Report of the Superintendent ... p. 85. In smaller asylums, salaries were lower all round, but the wide differentials remained; in 1888, at the N. Riding Asylum, the superintendent received £800 p.a. plus £287 in allowances (house, food, servants); the assistant MO received £170 plus rations and apartment, D.H. Tuke, Past and Present Provision for the Insane Poor in Yorkshire, pp. 46-47. Junior staff could also be subjected to petty restrictions of personal freedom: Hunter and Macalpine, ibid. p.79.

(205) Mercier, Lunatic Asylums, p. 246.

(206) Glimpses of Asylum Life, reprinted in J.M.Sc. (1869) xv. pp. 321 - 322.

(207) Ibid. p. 322. Cp. Dickens' interior of St. Luke's at Christmas: 'A Curious Dance round a Curious Tree', in Household Words (17th Jan. 1852).

(208) Cp. B.M.J. (Feb. 1871) p. 199.

(209) For discussion of the private sector see Parry-Jones, Trade in Lunacy, passim.

(210) The first purpose-built private asylum was Brislington House, near Bristol, in 1804: Hunter and Macalpine, George III and the Mad Business, p. 327. Even at later dates, conversion of property was more normal; Haydock Lodge, near Newton-le-Willows, Lancs, was used as a barracks before its conversion in 1844: Commissioners in Lunacy, Sixteenth Report, p. 25.

(211) Bethlem had been moved to Moorfields (1675) but the buildings proved too small and inconvenient, and was replaced by the buildings in St. George's Fields: O'Donoghue, Story of Bethlem, pp. 302 ff.

(212) C.N. French, The Story of St. Luke's Hospital, (London 1951) p. 40.

(213) Hunter and Macalpine, George III p. 331; E.M.Brockbank, History of Cheadle Royal, pp. 10-11. The Liverpool Asylum was the product of the work and ideas of James Currie. More influential was Alexander Hunter, whose York Asylum exemplified his dictum that 'An Asylum for Lunatics should always be a separate and independent charity; a union with an Infirmary is unnatural.' (Cited in Hunter and Macalpine, loc. cit.).

(214) John Conolly, The Construction and Government of Lunatic Asylums and Hospitals for the Insane (London 1847) p. 5.

(215) Commissioners in Lunacy, First Report (1846 - 47) p. 32. Submission of plans to the Commissioners was made compulsory in 1853; 16 & 17 Vic. c. 97. s. 45.

(216) John Conolly, A Letter to Benjamin Rotch Esq ... on the Plan and Government of the Additional Lunatic Asylum for the County of Middlesex about to be erected at Colney Hatch (London 1847) pp. 1 - 10 and passim; cp. Mortimer-Granville, op.cit. pp. 7 - 8.

(217) E.P. Charlesworth, Remarks on the Treatment of the Insane and the Management of Lunatic Asylums (London 1828) pp. 5 - 11; Helen Rosenau, Social Purpose in Architecture: Paris and London Compared, 1760-1800 (London 1970) pp.67, 87. Cp. Halliday, General View p.18.

(218) Rosenau, ibid. p. 69. Cells permitted a higher degree of classification to be practiced, and this concern motivated asylum doctors' espousal of the system, cp. Conolly, The Construction and Government of Lunatic Asylums, p. 11.

(219) O'Donoghue, p. 306 for groundplan of Bethlem which gives good indication of this. William Stark's Glasgow Asylum was modelled on Ipswich Prison. Stark was influential in England through his work Remarks on the Construction of Public Hospitals for the Cure of Mental Derangement (Edinburgh 1807) (Rosenau gives date of publishing wrongly as 1810 and place as Glasgow, ibid. p.73) which pleased the Select Committee of 1815. Stark admired the York Retreat, but believed in the value of necessity of restraint, and custody was his principal concern: D.H. Tuke, Chapters in the History of the Insane, p. 122. Glasgow Asylum was based on a cross, with radiating wings for segregation by sex and rank, attached to a central administrative block: Rosenau, p. 71, and p.84 for plan of Ipswich Gaol.

(220) Jeremy Bentham, Panopticon; or the Inspection House (London 1791), and Panopticon versus New South Wales (London 1812); Samuel Tuke favoured the inspection principle: Practical Hints on the Construction ... of Lunatic Asylums (1815).

(221) A good example is Wakefield Asylum (1818), designed by Watson and Pritchett with advice from Samuel Tuke: J. Watson and J.P. Pritchett, Plans, Elevations, Sections and Descriptions of the Pauper Lunatic Asylum lately erected at Wakefield (York 1819). Conolly followed Tuke in recommending the H-form of construction: Construction and Government p. 11.

(222) This style was developed in America by Thomas Kirkbride: On the Construction, Organization and General Arrangements of Hospitals for the Insane (Philadelphia 1954) as the ideal of asylum structure. It was in use in England earlier: Colney Hatch, designed by a pupil of Pritchett, is the best example: Hunter and Macalpine, Psychiatry for the Poor, pp. 21 - 29. On both sides of the Atlantic, Kirkbride's plans appealed because they were formulated by an experienced asylum alienist: Grob. Mental Institutions, pp. 143 - 44; Goshen, Documentary History, pp. 505 ff. Kirkbride's plan was available to Daukes, the architect of Colney Hatch, for although not taken up in practice in America until after his book appeared, it had appeared in print in 1847: 'Remarks on the Construction and Arrangements of Hospitals for the Insane' in Am.J.Med.Sc. (1847) xiii. pp. 40 - 56, see Grob, ibid. p. 143 n.

(223) For example, Lancaster Moor; see Metropolitan Commissioners in Lunacy, Report to the Lord Chancellor (1844) p. 126. The Commissioners' criteria for classification were, and remained, somewhat different from much asylum opinion, but the broad principle was a common feature of their policy from 1845 to 1890. Asylum design had an obvious formative effect on the scale and type of classification. Except at Lancaster, 'mixed

classification' was rarely used.

(224) Cp. Commissioners in Lunacy, Suggestions and Instructions in reference to (1) Sites (2) Construction and Arrangement of Buildings (3) Plans of Lunatic Asylums (1887); 1894); see Commissioners Reports, 1845 - 90, passim, for specific comments on siting of particular institutions, e.g. Ninth Report (1854 - 55) p. 4. for Buckinghamshire County Asylum; Conolly, Construction and Government of Lunatic Asylums, p. 8.

(225) W.J. Seward, 'Notes on the History of Colney Hatch Asylum' in J.M.Sc. (1908) liv. p. 606; Hunter and Macalpine, Psychiatry for the Poor, pp. 30 - 32.

(226) Kirkbride, in Goshen, Documentary History, p. 506; Hunter and Macalpine, Psychiatry for the Poor, p. 26; Conolly, Letter to Benjamin Rotch, p. 12.

(227) Mortimer-Granville, The Care and Cure of the Insane, pp. 153 ff.

(228) This was seen as permitting a more complete classification of patients: D.H. Tuke, Past and Present Provision for the Insane Poor in Yorkshire, p. 12.

(229) Combinations of enlargements, additions and detached blocks produced nothing but vast impersonal colonies of lunatics: Rainhill and Colney Hatch being the biggest in Europe, cp. Bucknill in B.M.J. (25th Feb. 1871) p. 199.

(230) Tuke, ibid., makes a virtue of plainness for the poor, criticizing Menston Asylum (1888) for being over-embellished and more suitable for the middle classes. Cp Commissioners in Lunacy, Ninth Report, p. 4.

(231) Conolly, The Construction and Government of Lunatic Asylums, p.8.

(232) James Gerard and Others, An Address to the Magistrates of the County of Lancaster on the Situation Proposed for the intended County Asylum (Liverpool 1810); William Brockbank, Portrait of a Hospital, p.79.

(233) For example, Bodmin Asylum and St. Peter's Bristol: Metropolitan Commissioners, (1844) p. 15; Liverpool Lunatic Hospital: Commissioners in Lunacy, Thirtyfifth Report (1881) p. 370.

(234) Hunter and Macalpine, Psychiatry for the Poor, pp.26-27.

(235) Gerard, ibid; Conolly, The Construction and Government of Lunatic Asylums, p. 8; cp. American ideas synthesised by Kirkbride: Goshen, Documentary History of Psychiatry, p. 518; Halliday, General View, p. 19, implied a rural setting was essential for setting patients to work.

Chapter Three.

(1) Report from the Select Committee on the better Regulation of Madhouses in England together with Minutes of Evidence taken before the Committee (1815) p.169.

(2) Parry-Jones, The Trade in Lunacy, p. 32.

(3) Ibid. pp. 34 - 35.

(4) Sources: Select Committee Reports, 1807, 1815; Parliamentary Returns, 1819, 1831; Metropolitan Commissioners in Lunacy, Reports, 1841, 1844; Commissioners in Lunacy, Reports, 1856, 1871, 1881, 1891.

(5) Parry-Jones, Trade in Lunacy, p. 32. The number of counties containing private madhouses rose from sixteen to thirty-two. Many houses were short-lived. Often, proprietors moved from one house to another within the same area, transferring both licence and inmates.

(6) Ibid. p. 36.

(7) R. Paternoster, The Madhouse System (London 1841)pp. 78, 80; Parry-Jones loc.cit.

(8) Ibid. p. 36.

(9) John Conolly, 'Fourth Notice of the Eighth Report of the Commissioners in Lunacy' in J.M.Sc. (1855) i. p. 183.

(10) Jones, Lunacy, Law and Conscience, pp. 74 - 77.

(11) Tuke, Chapters in the History of the Insane, p.163.

(12) Ibid. pp. 208 - 209.

(13) Ibid. p. 212; Parry-Jones, Trade in Lunacy, p. 31.

(14) Parry-Jones, Trade in Lunacy, p. 34.

(15) St. Peter's Hospital, Bristol, and Haverfordwest Asylum, Pembroke.

(16) Fort Clarence, Chatham (1819) was a military hospital; Haslar Hospital,Gosport (1818) served the navy.

(17) Tuke, Chapters in the History of the Insane, p. 211; Metropolitan Commissioners in Lunacy, Report to the Lord Chancellor (1844) pp. 9, 10.

(18) Tuke, ibid. p. 230.

(19) Ibid. p. 533.

(20) Hunter and Macalpine, George III and the Mad Business, pp. 291 - 93.

(21) Thomas Bakewell, A Letter addressed to the Chairman of the Select Committee of the House of Commons (London 1815) p. 4.

(22) Hunter and Macalpine, op. cit. p. 293.

(23) George Man Burrows, An Inquiry into certain Errors relative to Insanity (London 1820) pp. 58 - 64.

(24) Sir Andrew Halliday, General View, p. 90.

(25) Ibid. pp. 90, 91.

(26) Sir Andrew Halliday, A Letter to Lord Robert Seymour, with a Report of the Number of Lunatics and Idiots in England and Wales (London 1829) p. 54.

(27) Tuke, Chapters in the History of the Insane, p. 211.

(28) Ibid. pp. 230, 240, 252, 259.

(29) Ibid. p. 250.

(30) Tuke, Manual of Psychological Medicine, pp. 53 - 54.

(31) By 1859, only fourteen provincial licensed houses received paupers, and these, for the most part, exhibited a marked geographical concentration: four in Yorkshire; three in Co. Durham; two in Wiltshire; and one each in Glamorgan, Gloucester, Norfolk, Hereford and Lancashire. In the metropolitan area, five licensed houses received paupers, all of them large (300 and above patients) establishments with a pauper intake ranging from a half to two thirds of the total confined. Four of the provincial houses catered for over 100 patients, and only six for fewer than fifty. The pauper intake ranged between one-sixth (for the Hereford house which received only nineteen patients) and six-sevenths of the total received: Commissioners in Lunacy, Fourteenth Report (1860) pp.108 - 17. Thereafter, the

metropolitan figure remained static until the end of the century; whilst in the provinces, houses receiving paupers fell dramatically to three by 1890 (see Table 1)

(32) See Table 6. The preponderance of female patients was evident in earlier returns. Halliday's figures for 1828-29 show more females of all classes confined than males, and more certified females than males at large or confined with friends: A Letter to Lord Robert Seymour, p. 54.

(33) John Thurnham, Observations and Essays on the Statistics of Insanity (London 1845) pp. 145 - 54.

(34) Ibid. p. 148.

(35) Ibid. pp. 150, 153.

(36) Thurnham, op. cit. pp. 29, 137.

(37) Tuke, Chapters in the History of the Insane, pp. 262-63. The average was worked out for the period 1871 - 80.

Chapter Four

(1) Legal terminologies - lunacy, unsoundness of mind, imbecility, etc. - were freely mixed with medical - mania, melancholia etc. - and with indefinite terms like insanity. One specialist's neologism became another's bogey: in the first quarter of the nineteenth century, for example, the introduction of the legal concept of 'unsoundness of mind' confused the medical profession's elite, see John Haslam, Medical Jurisprudence as it relates to Insanity according to the Laws of England (London 1817); A Letter to the Rt.Hon. Lord Chancellor on the Nature and Interpretation of Unsoundness of Mind and Imbecility of Intellect,(London 1823). The Law demanded a higher degree of precision than medicine: where case histories or clinical methods were discussed, the terminological framework was of secondary importance to describable behaviours and treatments.

(2) Hunter and Macalpine, George III and the Mad Business, pp. 269 ff.

(3) Pinel, Treatise, pp. 49, 108-109, 254. Pinel spoke of insanity as a disease; Rush linked 'madness' with several other diseases': Benjamin Rush, Medical Inquiries and Observations upon the Diseases of the Mind (Philadelphia 1812) pp. 195 - 96; Grob, Mental Institutions in America, pp. 20, 43, 47; Hunter and Macalpine, George III and the Mad Business, p. 276; William Battie, Treatise on Madness pp. 93 - 94; George Nesse Hill, An Essay on the Prevention and Cure of Insanity (London 1814) pp. 203-204; George Man Burrows, An Enquiry into Certain Errors relative to Insanity (London 1820) passim. Blisterings, vomits and purgings figured prominently in treatments, though Pinel claimed to have lost 'faith in pharmaceutic preparation.' Willis himself published no details of his own therapeutics.

(4) Thomas Bakewell, The Domestic Guide in Cases of Insanity (London 1805). One of the earliest popularizations, aimed at 'Private Families and the ... Clergy.' For Bakewell, see Parry-Jones, Trade in Lunacy, pp. 12,14,

82 - 83, and Hunter and Macalpine, George III and the Mad Business, p. 271.

(5) John Haslam, Considerations on the Moral Management of Insane Persons (London 1817) p. 3; L.H. Butterfield, ed. Letters of Benjamin Rush (Princeton 1951) p. 774; D. Uwins, A Treatise on those Disorders of the Brain and Nervous System, which are usually called Mental (London 1833) pp. 51, 198 - 99.

(6) Practical application of empiricism was lacking in eighteenth and early nineteenth century psychiatry, as in other branches of medicine: G.S. Rousseau, 'Sowing the Wind and Reaping the Whirlwind : Aspects of Change in Eighteenth Century Medicine', in Studies in Change and Revolution, ed., Paul J. Korshin, (London 1972) pp. 129 - 160.

(7) Skultans, Madness and Morals, p. 6.

(8) Samuel Tuke, Description, p.163; Skultans, p. 11. misinterprets Tuke's attitude to domination as a tool in restoring willpower. Daniel Noble, Elements of Psychological Medicine (London 1853) p. 11.

(9) Willis was archetypal in the eighteenth century: Hunter and Macalpine, George III, p. 269; Bakewell thought the clergy professionally more suited than doctors to the care of the insane, ibid, p. 271.

(10) John Barlow, Man's Power over Himself to Prevent or Control Insanity (London 1843) pp. 10 - 11, 26 - 36 and passim.

(11) John Locke, An Essay Concerning Human Understanding (London 1690; 1959 edn.) p. 209.

(12) John Haslam, Observations on Madness and Melancholy (London 1810) pp. 15 - 16, 209.

(13) Hunter and Macalpine, Three Hundred Years of Psychiatry, passim; J.M. Cox, Practical Observations on Insanity (London 1806); Bryan Crowther, Practical Remarks on Insanity (London 1811).

(14) Zilboorg and Henry, History of Psychological Medicine, p. 409.

(15) Paul Slade Knight, Observations on the Causes, Symptoms and Treatment of Derangement of the Mind, founded on an extensive Moral and Medical Practice in the Treatment of Lunatics (London 1827); William Ellis, Treatise on the Causes, Symptoms and Treatment of Insanity (London 1835)

(16) James Sheppard, Observations on the Proximate Causes of Insanity (London 1844).

(17) Isaac Ray, A Treatise on the Medical Jurisprudence of Insanity (Boston 1853) pp. 69, 129. The failure of specific autopsies to reveal organic lesion was taken to imply simply that current skills were too crude to produce accurate results.

(18) John Charles Bucknill, Unsoundness of Mind in Relation to Criminal Insanity (London 1954) pp. 27-28. The 1830's and 1840's had seen the high point in the emphasis on will (though Skultans, p. 14, with no evidence, states that the 1850's were the peak years): typically see W. Cooke, Mind and Emotions in relation to Health and Disease (London 1839).

(19) J.C. Bucknill and D.H. Tuke, A Manual of Psychological Medicine (London 1858) pp. 89, 154; Zilboorg and Henry History of Medical Psychology pp. 417 ff; G.F.Blandford, Insanity and its Treatment (Edinburgh 1871).

(20) Bucknill and Tuke, ibid, p. 88.This was in tune with Continental thought; Wilhelm Griesinger, Pathology and Therapy of Psychiatric Illness (Berlin 1845); Jean Etienne Esquirol, Mental Maladies, a Treatise on Insanity (tran. E.K. Hunt, Philadelphia 1845); Goshen, Documentary History of Psychiatry, pp. 314 - 369, 384 - 416.

(21) James Cowles Prichard (1786 - 1848) MD (Edinburgh). Private practice, Bristol. Commissioner in Lunacy (1845 - 48). Polymath, special interests in anthropology and insanity. Brief biography in Leigh, Historical Development of British Psychiatry, pp. 148 ff.

(22) James Cowles Prichard, A Treatise on Insanity (London 1833) p. 14.

(23) James Cowles Prichard, On the Different Forms of Insanity in Relation to Jurisprudence (London 1847)p.31.

(24) Henry Maudsley (1835 - 1913) M.D. (UCL). Medical Superintendent, Cheadle Royal (1859 - 62). Editor J.M.Sc. (1862 - 78). Physician to West London Hospital (1864 - 74). Professor of Medical Jurisprudence, UCL (1869-79).

(25) Henry Maudsley, Body and Mind (London 1873) p. 136; Mental Diseases (London 1874) p. 170.

(26) Body and Mind, p. 127.

(27) Traditionally 1873 - 96, a contemporary appellation conveying the malaise of staple industrial, commercial and agricultural sectors, and the first period of self-examination for laissez faire capitalism. See Donald N. McCloskey, ed., Essays on a Mature Economy: Britain after 1840 (London 1971) for recent reassessments of the period.

(28) William Booth, In Darkest England and the Way Out (London 1890) pp. 204 - 5.

(29) Daniel Hack Tuke, Insanity in Ancient and Modern Life with Chapters on its Prevention (London 1878) p. 152.

(30) Cp. Mary Carpenter, Reformatory Schools for the Children of the Perishing and Dangerous Classes, and for Juvenile Offenders (London 1851) p. 2. W.D. Morison, Crime and its Causes (London 1891) pp. 141-142; J.J. Tobias, Crime and Industrial Society in the Nineteenth Century (London 1967) pp. 59 - 87 and passim; and for a French parallel, see L. Chevalier, Classes Laborieuses et Classes Dangereuses a Paris pendant le premiere Moitie du 19eme Siecle (Paris 1958).

(31) Morison loc. cit.

(32) David Owen, Philanthropy in England, pp. 4, 98, and passim.

(33) Charles Stewart Loch, A Great Ideal and its Champion (London 1923) offers a partisan view of the Charity Organization Society (1869). Cp. Gareth Stedman Jones, Outcast London (Oxford UP 1971) passim. 'The marvel of Christ's Life in his repression of his powers of benevolence.' (Brooke Lambert, quoted ibid, p.243, from East London Pauperism: a Sermon to the University of

Oxford, (1868).

(34) Andrew Wynter, The Borderlands of Insanity (London 1875); Blandford, Insanity and its Treatment, passim; Maudsley, Mental Diseases, p. 289; Samuel Smiles, Character (London 1971); Skultans, Madness and Morals, pp. 18 - 19. Cp. Ralph Linton, The Cultural Background of Personality (London 1947); and Yehudi A. Cohen, ed., Social Structure and Personality, A Casebook (New York 1961) pp. 457 - 515.

(35) Maudsley, Mental Diseases, pp. 170 - 171.

(36) Maudsley, Body and Mind, p. 76.

(37) The causal role of masturbation, suggested in the eighteenth century by Rush and others, gained prominence in the mid-nineteenth century in Europe and America, retaining a strong hold in the latter and in England long after its demise in Continental Europe. This posited relationship offers one of the best examples of how psychiatric values were inextricably bound up with moral values: Robert H. MacDonald, 'The Frightful Consequences of Onanism: Notes on the History of a Delusion' in J.Hist.Ideas (1967) 28. pp. 423 - 431; E.H. Hare, 'Masturbatory Insanity: The History of an Idea' in J.M.Sc. (1962) cviii. pp. 1 - 25; Szasz, The Manufacture of Madness, pp. 210 - 236; Alex Comfort, The Anxiety Makers (London 1967) pp. 69 - 113; Benjamin Rush, Medical Inquiries, p. 33; Maudsley, Body and Mind, pp. 86 - 87. For attitudes towards drink, see below, Section III.

(38) For an unfortunately flippant, though interesting, discussion of some of the wilder flights of imagination, see R. Partridge, Broadmoor: A History of Criminal Lunacy and its Problems (London 1953).

(39) There was subtle, class-based differences between the usual candidates for admission to the two types of institution: D.H. Tuke, Insanity in Ancient and Modern Life, p. 124. For an early example of the range predisposing and exciting causes, see William Willis Mosely, Eleven Chapters on Nervous and Mental Complaints (London 1839) pp. 123 - 140. Moderation of all things is seen by Mosely, as by Hack Tuke forty years later, as the best safeguard of sanity.

(40) T.A.C. Rennie and L.E. Woodward, Mental Health in Modern Society (New York 1948) p. 35.

(41) Commissioners in Lunacy, Special Report on the Alleged Increase of Insanity (1897)

(42) Henry Maudsley, The Psysiology and Pathology of the Mind (London 1867) p. 200; John Charles Bucknill, The Care of the Insane and their Legal Control (London 1880) p. 4. Fears about the increasing incidence of insanity dated from the initial impetus to provide for its sufferers. Public discussion tended to be followed by a jump in the numbers of assigned nervous or mental illnesses: Hunter and Macalpine, George III and the Mad Business, pp.287-294. The French experience was similar, Pinel and Esquirol (Jones, Lunacy, Law and Conscience, p. 224) were echoed in England by Sir Andrew Halliday: General View, pp. 13 ff.

(43) Awarenesses of dynamic social change deepened in the years after Waterloo, when the impact of the first stage of industrialization and urbanization began exerting more visible signs on social and economic structures throughout Britian, at the very moment when heightened awareness of the incidence and prevalence of insanity startled the nation.

(44) Rothman, Discovery of the Asylum, pp. xiv, 113 ff. The European origin of the idea is granted, 'but to a surprising degree the Americans made it their own, grasping it with unrivalled intellectual enthusiasm and employing it in a very special way.' In fact it became the basis for Rothman's alleged critique: 'A specific and original analysis of the dangers of the existing social system.' Yet his cited texts show no apparent difference from British awareness and articulation of the relationship, nor does a survey of articles in the American Journal of Insanity. Before the Civil War, argues Rothman, no American physician doubted this causal link, One shudders instinctively at the generalization, but accepting it as conveying a prevalent as opposed to a universal belief, it can be shown to be common to a sufficiently meaningful proportion of British medical men to contradict Rothman's overstatement.

Yet one wonders whether he really believes his own case. European thought, he argues, early tended to depart from the simple analysis that derived the growth of insanity from the rate of the advance of civilization. But the Americans retained the diagnosis as central to their social critique. The second statement may have some justification; the first is simply untrue. Hack Tuke, writing in 1882, was as convinced of the relationship as any contemporary American physician. Perhaps Rothman is unaware of the British understanding of the terms involved: he certainly leaves the American meaning impressionistic. What happened in Britain was that the simplistic explanations of the causal nature of 'civilization' became more sophisticated over half a century, the principal shift being in the implications of the word 'civilization' itself. Belief in a simple connection was maintained. In denying this, Rothman resorts to verbal conjuring. As voices indicative of the European trend he cites Maudsley and Samuel Tuke. The only quotations produced show their joint scepticism on the issue of the immunity of savages to insanity. Had he read further in the Maudsley work he quotes, (written incidentally in 1867, the text implies it was produced earlier), he would have found, listed under the general predisposing causes of insanity, 'the state of civilization in a country ...' (Physiology and Pathology of the Mind, p. 200).

(45) Cp. M.C. Buer, Health, Wealth and Population in the Early Days of the Industrial Revolution (London 1926) passim.

(46) Indeed, had such issues existed, they would have been more properly retrogressive than revolutionary.

(47) For outlines of general European thinking on this, and on related issues, see Sidney Pollard, the Idea of Progress: History and Society (London 1968) pp. 31 ff; cp. R.W. Harris, Romanticism and the Social Order (1780 - 1830), (London 1969) passim. For America, see Alexis de Tocqueville, Democracy in America (1835; Fontana ed. 1966) Vol II. pp. 549 ff, 580-583, 725-788.

(48) P. Ford, Social Theory and Social Practice (Shannon 1968) pp. 5 - 40.

(49) If their critique was of the past, 'civilization' was used to delineate advanced economic cultures and their socio-moral structures, e.g. Imperial Rome or Renaissance Italy. Discussion on this level has proved perennially popular with psychiatrists: cp. Sigmund Freud, Civilization and its Discontents (Trans. J. Riviere, London 1953); Erich Fromm, The Sane Society (New York 1955).

(50) T.B. Belgrave, 'The Asylums for the Insane in St. Petersburg and Copenhagen' in J.M.Sc. (1867) xiii. p.17

(51) George Man Burrows (1771 - 1846). MRCS. LSA. MD (St. Andrews). FRCP. Proprietor of a Chelsea private asylum (1814 - 23) and of the Clapham Retreat (1823 - 43).

(52) George Man Burrows, Commentaries on the Causes of Insanity (London 1828) p. 70.

(53) Public opinion was quite soon round to this fact of life: 'In strictness, we are all mad when we give way to passion, to prejudice, to vice, to vanity; but if all the passionate, prejudiced, vicious and vain people in the world are to be locked up as lunatics, who is to keep the key of the asylum?' (Times 22 July, 1853).

(54) It even survives into the present era: 'The view has been put forward ... that incidence of psychiatric disorders in tribal Africa is one-tenth of that usually found in Western Europe and North America.' (World Health Organization, Technical Report Series, 1953, 73, p. 3); Burrows, Commentaries, pp. 21 - 23.

(55) Halliday, General View of the Present State of Lunatics, p. 79.

(56) William Browne, What Asylums were, Are and Ought to be (Edinburgh 1837) pp. 52 - 53; cp. Alexander Morrison, Outlines of Mental Diseases (Edinburgh 1824) pp. 74 - 75

(57) Alfred Beaumont Maddock, Practical Observations on Mental and Nervous Disorders (London 1854) pp. 12 - 13.

(58) Quarterly Review (1816) xv. pp. 398 - 99.

(59) Ibid.

(60) George Man Burrows, Commentaries, pp. 29-33. Opponents of Methodism were more keen to point up its inevitable links with insanity: '... the increase of religious madness is occasioned by and commensurate with the increase of Methodism ... a fact which many have verified at Bedlam.' From a Barrister, 'On the Evangelical Sects' in Quarterly Review (1810) xi. p. 500 One Methodist preacher retaliated: 'I should much rather send five thousand to Bedlam, than that one should be sent to Hell': Life of James Lackington (London 1791; 13th edn, 1810) p. 169.

(61) Esquirol in France shared the belief: Goshen, Documentary History, p. 316; Germany's most influential alienist was more circumspect: Griesinger, Pathology and Therapy, pp. 138, 157. For broader discussion, see Mark D. Altschule, Roots of Modern Psychiatry: Essays in The History of Psychiatry (New York 1957) Chapter 7.

(62) D.H. Tuke, Insanity in Ancient and Modern Life, p. 124; Henry Maudsley, The Pathology of Mind (London 1879) pp. 131 - 133, 168 - 70.

(63) Burrows, pp. 9 - 20; John Millar, Hints on Insanity (London 1861) passim.

(64) Browne, What Asylum Were, p. 51, The dynamics might include ideas: one German student argued the causal force of democracy in creating epidemic insanity, and had his thesis accepted by the Senate of Berlin University: Am.J.Insanity (1851) viii. p. 195; Bucknill, Unsoundness of Mind in Relation to Criminal Insanity, pp.27, 58 - 60; D.H. Tuke, The Influence of the Mind on the Body (London 1872) pp. 384 - 387.

(65) P.L. Panum, Observations made during an Epidemic of Measles on the Faroe Islands (New York 1846; Reprint New York 1940) p. 13.

(66) Edgar Sheppard, Lectures on Madness in its Medical, Legal and Social Aspects (London 1873) p. 13; George Rosen, Madness in Society: Chapters in the Historical Sociology of Mental Illness (London 1968) pp.185 ff.

(67) Ibid. p. 189.

(68) Maudsley, Physiology and Pathology of the Mind, p. 204; Pathology of Mind pp. 127 - 129.

(69) Quoted in Stedman Jones, Outcast London, p. 287, from the proceedings of the Industrial Remuneration Conference, presided over by Sir Charles Dilke, 1885. Victorian society lived in horror of the pauper, as the Tudors had lived in fear of the tramp: Owen, Philanthropy in England, p. 4.; Tawney, Religion and the Rise of Capitalism. p. 260.

(70) Bucknill and Tuke, Manual of Psychological Medicine, p.2.

(71) L.S.F. Winslow, Mad Humanity: its Forms Apparent and Obscure (London 1898) p. 27.

(72) L.A.B. (1888) Report of the Medical Superintendent of Prestwich Asylum, p. 70; for American similarities, see Gerald N. Grob, 'Mental Illness, Indigency and Welfare' in Tamara K. Hareven, ed., Anonymous Americans (New Jersey 1971) p. 262.

(73) D.H. Tuke, Insanity in Ancient and Modern Life, p. 92.

(74) Ibid. pp. 8 - 9. Tuke did not write 'civilized labourer' - implicitly, the labourer had an inherent 'otherness' which predisposed him to the deleterious effects of a civilization to which he did not belong.

(75) Ibid. p. 93.

(76) For Hobbes's view of madness: Thomas Hobbes, Leviathan (1651; ed. Michael Oakeshott, 1962) pp. 62 - 68. Skultans, pp. 5 ff., has argued that nineteenth-century psychiatry evinced polarity between Hobbes-influenced alienists (Prichard and Maudsley and their school) and Lockeians (Conolly et al). However, a much more pragmatic approach seems to have been taken: Bucknill

and Hack Tuke, the Establishment psychiatrists par excellence, straddled both camps with acceptably sublime inconsistency. For the Irish image, see Lewis P. Curtis Jr., Apes and Angels: The Irishman in Victorian Caricature (Newton Abbott 1971) pp. 29 - 58 and passim.

(77) Immigrants tend to end up in the poorest (and by inference most disreputable) parts of towns, attempting to prolong their existing cultural identity (and hence presenting a ghetto-image). Where there is acculturation, it is to the mores of the neighbourhood. Liability to a deviance-label increases where the neighbourhood is seen as deviance-producing by the authorities; children are likely to be more susceptible, especially where employment demands on parents produces 'latch key kids': J.A. Jackson, The Irish in Britain (London 1963) pp. 66-69, 160; Tobias, Crime and Industrial Society, pp. 200 - 201, and sources cited there, for Irish immigrants and crime; cp. Hermann Mannheim, Comparative Criminology (London 1965) pp. 536 - 44, for a general theoretical framework.

(78) The 'white negro' tag was economist Gustave de Molinari's (1880) in a comment on Anglo-Irish relations: Curtis, op. cit. p. 1. Negroes in America were seen to have an above average liability to lunacy and idiotism, sometimes in frighteningly high proportions: Am.J. Insanity (1851) viii. pp. 153 - 155; for Maine, the proportion was given as 1:14. Irish immigrants brought wage rates tumbling down, even before the Famine - e.g. in handloom weaving around Manchester in the first three decades of the century, though not elsewhere: Duncan Bythell, The Handloom Weavers (Cambridge UP 1969) pp.10, 62 - 64, - and exerted an influence fatal to 'the happiness of the labouring classes in England' (Malthus, 1826): Brian Inglis, Poverty and the Industrial Revolution (London 1972) pp. 155, 276 - 277.

(79) A. Redford, Labour Migration in England 1800 - 1850 Manchester 2nd edn. 1964) Chapters 8 and 9. The state of trade was seen to have an effect on asylum admissions: '... industrial crises and trade depressions ... are peculiarly productive of mental alienation,' L.A.B. (1879) Report of the Superintendent of Prestwich Asylum p. 133.

(80) Repatriation was inevitably demanded: Thomas Mackreth, Chairman of the Committee of Visitors, Lancaster Moor, in L.A.B. (1863) Report of the Committee of Visitors of Lancaster Asylum, p. 10.

(81) J. Hawkes, 'On the Increase of Insanity' in J.Psych.Med. & Ment.Path. (1857) x. pp. 519 - 20.

(82) B.M. Wedge, 'Occurrence of Psychosis among Okinawans in Hawaii' in Psych. Quarterly (1954) 28. p. 255. Intrusion of an alien culture on a static preliterate one has similar effects: Meyer Fortes and Doris Y. Mayer, 'Psychosis and Social Change among the Tallensi of Northern Ghana' in S.H. Foulkes and G. Stewart Prince eds., Psychiatry in a Changing Society (London 1969) pp. 33 - 72.

(83) As W.L. Burn points out, Ireland was a 'social laboratory' for English administrative experimentation. Irish institutions and bureaucratic controls were similar to English: Irish public asylums and Lunacy Commissioners predated English: W.L. Burn, 'Free Trade in Land: An Aspect of the Irish Question' in T.R.H.S. (1949) p. 68; Halliday, General View, pp. 39 - 44.

(84) Termed 'general paralysis of the insane' by nineteenth century alienists. An organic decay that was incurable, it figured prominently in asylums catering to industrial areas: L.A.B. (1888) Report of the Superintendent of Prestwich Asylum, pp. 70, 77.

(85) Lacking written records, it is clearly impossible to know whether admissions resulted from declining communal tolerance or from over-assiduous enforcement of the Lunacy Laws. As will be shown later, the latter were subject to pragmatic interpretation, and were a not uncommon means of 'shelving' problem individuals.

(86) Redford, Labour Migration, p. 155. Figures computed from L.A.B. (1854 through 1872) Report of the Superintendent of Rainhill Asylum, statistical tables, and are rounded up to nearest integer. The lowest proportion was 25% in 1861. The other Lancashire Asylums did not include information as to nationality regularly until tabular data were regularized for all four establishments in 1886.

(87) L.A.B. (1863) Report of the Committee of Visitors of Lancaster Asylum, p.10. There is no regularity in published tables, so no overall picture can be assembled prior to the late 1880s. Rainhill Asylum presented the most frequent and most detailed tables, but though admissions are broken down as to age, sex, occupation, nature of assigned disorder, and occasionally, religion, literacy, and other cultural variables, there is no correlation amongst the figures, so that one is left to surmise from group totals and psychiatric comment. From the Rainhill data, one can surmise that Irish patients figured highly amongst long-stay patients, and that it was likely that they shared characteristics of long-stay patients in other English asylums: ie. they were suffering from functional disturbance that was unremitting, or were geriatric or senile, or feebleminded. The first possibility is consonant with remarks by H.R. Ley, Superintendent of Prestwich: L.A.B. (1888) loc.cit. The others would be a natural reflection of communal inability to cope with the old or feebleminded when family economies suffered during trade recessions, or of the isolation of older family members in the port of entry, after those of working age/ability had moved inland to manufacturing and industrial centres. There is no reason to doubt that the Irish, in common with rural English immigrants, maintained their extended family structures - and hence kinship aid patterns - as long as was economically possible, or until there was interference from local authorities. For family structure in Lancashire, see Anderson, Family Structure in Nineteenth Century Lancashire (Cambridge 1971)passim.

Unfortunately, the study offers theoretical perspectives and quantitative data to the exclusion of the kinds of personalised information that permits the reconstruction of actual family experiences. So far as the present study is concerned this desirable objective cannot be realised: it may be possible to trace an occasional patient career, via asylum case-books, but prepatient careers were not often described by asylum medical officers - even if they knew of them. Pauper lunatics figure more often by initials than by a name, and for the Manchester and Salford areas even this is lacking for lunatics admitted via the workhouse (i.e. the majority) since the local authority, after the Second World War, destroyed all existing personal records of poor law lunatics, as a gesture towards the sensitivity of possible descendants. As aliens, and given the racial and political violence in Liverpool, Manchester and the S.E. Lancashire cotton towns from the 1860s to the end of the century, it is likely that the Irish were closely supervised by local authorities, and thus that certifiable insanity came more often than usual to the notice of primary official assessors: policemen, relieving officers etc. Cp. L.A.B. (1862) Report of the Superintendent of Rainhill Asylum, p. 109.

(88) Sir James Coxe, 'On the Causes of Insanity and the Means of Checking its Growth' in J.M.Sc. (1872) xviii. p.32.

(89) Tuke, Insanity in Ancient and Modern Life, pp. 91,104 - 105, 113, 121, 124. For the concept of the total institution, see Goffman, Asylums pp. 13 ff. Battie, Treatise p. 58, had in 1757, indicated the dangers of voluntary abstraction from society, singling out 'lazy Monks ... sedentary and chlorotic Nuns, and ... the senior Recluses ... at Oxford and Cambridge.' Tuke rehearsed this in a warning against 'unbridled asceticism,' (Ibid. p. 219).

(90) Maudsley, The Pathology of Mind, pp. 131-133; W.C. Hood, Suggestions for the Future Provision for Criminal Lunatics (London 1854) p. 63.

(91) Demographic change, and changes within industrial and agricultural employment structures were crucial in determining the antecedent states of poverty and immiseration. There were great differences, of course, over time and space, in the incidence of pauperism and the effects of Poor Law policy, whether Old or New. There had been concern with the problems raised by pauperism, and especially with the Elizabethan regulations, from the first quarter of the eighteenth century, and the groundswell of economic change forced reassessment of both theory and practice. For the period under review, see J.D. Marshall, The Old Poor Law 1795 - 1834 (London 1968) pp. 26-27, 40-41, and passim; Dorothy Marshall, The English Poor in the Eighteenth Century (London 1926) passim; S.G. and E.A. O. Checkland, The Poor Law Report of 1834 (Pelican edn. 1974) pp. 11-20, and text. For the effects of internal mobility: Redford Labour and Migration, passim, and for the population factor generally, E.A. Wrigley, An

Introduction to English Historical Demography (Cambridge UP 1966).

(92) T.R. Malthus, An Essay on the Principle of Population (1798; Pelican edn. 1970) pp. 93 ff; Patrick Colquhoun, A Treatise on Indigence (London 1806) passim; Sir George Nicholls, A History of the English Poor Law Volume II 1714 - 1853 (London 1854; Revised by T.Mackay, 1898. Reprint 1967) p. 247; J.R. Poynter, Society and Pauperism: English Ideas on Poor Relief 1795 - 1834 (London 1969) passim; Maurice Bruce, The Coming of the Welfare State (London 1961) pp. 89 - 153; S. Leon Levy, Nassau Senior 1790 - 1864 (London 1970) pp. 80 - 91; S.E. Finer, The Life and Times of Sir Edwin Chadwick (London 1952) pp. 93 ff.

(93) J.L. and Barbara Hammond, The Bleak Age (London 1937; Guild Books edn. 1947) pp. 91 ff. Stedman Jones, Outcast London, pp. 243 ff. which uses a theoretical framework derived from Marcel Mauss, The Gift (Transl. Ian Cunnison, London 1966). The upper classes maintained their paternalistic largesse throughout the century - receiving a declining return of deference, even in some rural areas: W.L. Burn, The Age of Equipoise (London 1964) pp. 238 - 46; the Charity Organization Society uniquely presented the circumspect ethos of 'bourgeoisie oblige' - Loch, A Great Ideal, passim, and cp. Henry Solly A Few Thoughts on how to Deal with the Unemployed Poor of London and with the 'Rough' and Criminal Classes (London 1868) pp. 9, 19 and passim.

(94) Anon., Essays on Charitable Institutions (London 1836) pp. 119 - 120.

(95) Nassau Senior, Three Lectures on the Rate of Wages (London 1830) pp. 16 - 17, 52, and passim; A.W. Coats, 'Changing Attitudes to Labour in the mid-18th Century' in EC.H.R. (1958) xi. pp. 35 - 51, and 'The Classical Economists and the Labourer' in Coats, ed., The Classical Economists and Economic Policy (London 1971) pp. 144 - 179; Bruce, Coming of the Welfare State, p.67.

(96) Maudsley, The Physiology and Pathology of the Mind, p. 204; Coxe 'Causes' p. 320.

(97) Ibid. Until the 1850s and 1860s, there had been little interest displayed in the 'intellectual culture' of the lower orders, in the sense of provision of opportunities for formal education. After 1870, the ruling classes became ever-conscious of the ways in which they were to 'educate their masters' into habits of intelligent obedience and articulate acceptance of the social and economic status quo.

(98) Friedrich Engels, The Condition of the Working Class in England in 1844 (Leipzig 1845; London 1892) pp. 135-36, 131. For discussion of the social role of drink in the nineteenth century see Brian Harrison, Drink and the Victorians: The Temperance Question in England 1815 - 1872 (London 1971) pp. 37-63, 297-318, and passim.

(99) Francis Peek, Social Wreckage, (London 1883) p. 78. Charles Booth was less alarmist about the impact of alcohol, stressing the relativity of drinking habits and differentiating between a numerically vast group of

drinkers, and a small proportion of drunkards: Albert Fried and Richard Elman, eds., Charles Booth's London (London 1969) p. 305.

(100) Peek, Social Wreckage, p. 78.n.

(101) Battie, Treatise, quoted in Goshen, Documentary History p. 243.

(102) Burrows, Commentaries on Insanity, p. 23; Moseley, Eleven Chapters, pp. 123 - 40. According to Moseley, drink was bringing the nation to imminent doom: ' ... these liquids are the destructive agents which have caused mutinies in our navy, disobedience to orders in our army, have filled our prisons with all kinds of victims; our hospitals and mad-houses with every description of mental and bodily disease; our domestic circles with strife; our cellars with want and misery; and our streets with blasphemy and obscenity.'

(103) Noble, Elements, p. 238.

(104) Maudsley, Pathology of Mind, pp. 127 - 128.

(105) Winslow, Mad Humanity, Preface. By this date the histrionics were passés though many psychiatrists shared Winslow's conviction. So too did lay administrators: the medically-based theories of the 1860s and 1870s had, by the last decade of the century, gained acceptance outside the profession. It was to the 'intelligent layman' that Winslow addressed himself - twelve months after the Commissioners in Lunacy presented their official report on the alleged increase of insanity.

(106) Hunter and Macalpine, Psychiatry for the Poor, pp.195, 197; L.A.B. (1852) Report of the Superintendent of Rainhill Asylum p. 19.

(107) A. Blake, A Practical Treatise on Delirium Tremens (London 1840); C. Wilson, The Pathology of Drunkenness (Edinburgh 1857); R. Macnish, The Anatomy of Drunkenness (London 1859); Forbes Winslow, On Uncontrollable Drunkenness, considered as a Mental Disorder, with Suggestions for its Treatment and the Organization of Sanatoria for Dipsomaniacs (London 1867); J.C. Bucknill, Habitual Drunkenness and Insane Drunkards (London 1878); Norman S. Kerr, Inebriety: Its Etiology, Pathology Treatment and Jurisprudence (London 1888). For the Lancashire asylums, see tables in Appendix Two. L.A.B. (1894) Minute of Commissioners in Lunacy, Prestwich Asylum.

(108) L.A.B. (1879) Report of the Superintendent of Prestwich Asylum, p. 133. The stress on 'hereditary taint' - indicative of the appeal of Maudsley's ideas - was heavy: L.A.B. (1800) Report of the Superintendent of Prestwich Asylum, p. 78, but from the early 1880s,drink was still heading the causality tables: L.A.B. (1882) Report of The Superintendent of Prestwich Asylum, p. 78. Males had a higher incidence than females at all times. Cp. Reports from the superintendents of all four Lancashire Asylums in the last fifteen years of the century: in 1891, for example, 39% of male admissions into Rainhill were assigned to drink, 20% in Lancaster, 19% in Prestwich and 25% in Whittingham.

(109) J.C. Bucknill, 'The Relations of Drink and Insanity' in J.M.Sc. (1876) xxii. p. 281.
(110) L.A.B. (1875) Report of the Superintendent of Prestwich Asylum, p. 71; L.A.B. (1879) loc. cit.
(111) J.M.Sc. (1881) xxvi. p. 461.
(112) Ibid. pp. 465 - 466.
(113) W.R. Huggard, 'The Means of Determining Causation in Insanity' in J.M.Sc. (1882) xxvii. p. 157.
(114) Hunter and Macalpine, Psychiatry for the Poor, pp.194-96.
(115) L.A.B. (1872) Report of the Superintendent of Prestwich Asylum, p. 62. Often the legally-required minimum information as to duration of disease and perceived causation were not entered on admission orders. Such information as was offered was usually 'purest conjecture' - officers were 'often apt to infer the cause of the disease from the character of the delusions ...' L.A.B. (1875) Report of Superintendent, Prestwich p. 70; cp. Hunter and Macalpine, Psychiatry for the Poor p. 195. n. 7% of Prestwich's admissions came directly through the police; two thirds from workhouses, L.A.B. (1886) Report of the Superintendent of Prestwich Asylum p. 65.
(116) L.A.B. (1884) Report of the Superintendent of Prestwich Asylum, p. 65.
(117) Comparisons are difficult. Higher incidence of lunacy were ascribed to agricultural areas, but calculations were based on accumulations - and many of the inmates of rural asylums were congenital idiots. Causality figures are not reliable though psychiatrists sometimes used them uncritically: Tuke, Insanity in Ancient and Modern Life, p. 96.
(118) Commissioners in Lunacy, Thirty-first Report (1877) pp. 55 - 56.
(119) James Shaw, Epitome of Mental Diseases (London and Bristol 1892) p. 86.
(120) Commissioners in Lunacy, Thirty-sixth Report (1881) pp. 52 - 55.
(121) 'Previous Attack' could disguise initial ascription to alcoholic causation as well as anything else, but there is no means of determining the issue. As an exclusive categorization it is therefore omitted from the following table.
(122) It is worth noting that where the ratio of the insane to the total county population was computed, agricultural counties displayed an above average incidence of ascribed insanity and assigned drink-induced insanity, manufacturing districts an average incidence. Where the ratio was worked out on pauper lunatics to the total pauper population, the situation was reversed, and rural areas dropped below average: T.S. Clouston, 'The Local Distribution of Insanity' in J.M.Sc. (1873) xix, pp.1-3; Robert Boyd, 'Statistics of Pauper Insanity' in J.M.Sc.(1871) xvii. p. 222. Figures fluctuate, of course, between 1850 and 1890, but an average of 12% to 15% was maintained in public asylums for drink-induced insanity in males and females combined; Clouston to Bucknill, 20 April, 1876, quoted by Bucknill, Relations of Drink

and Insanity, p. 268.

(123) Quoted in Tuke, Insanity in Ancient and Modern Life, p. 100; cp. David Yellowlees, Lunacy and Pauperism (Glasgow 1884).

(124) L.A.B. (1874) Report of the Superintendent of Prestwich Asylum, p. 71.

(125) An appositely seasonal communication: Birmingham Daily Post (26 Dec. 1876).

(126) J.M.Sc. (1877) xxiii. p. 97.

(127) Tuke, Insanity in Ancient and Modern Life, p. 99.

(128) Harrison, Drink and the Victorians, pp. 59-62, 249,269-71, 279-85, 343; and for a local discussion (Rochdale) John Vincent, The Formation of the British Liberal Party 1857 - 68 (London 1966) pp. 131 - 37, 141, 146-47.

(129) T. Needham, Remarks on the Necessity of Legislation in reference to Habitual Drunkards (London 1871) passim.

(130) W.F. Bynum, 'Chronic Alcoholism in the First Half of the Nineteenth Century' in Bull.Hist.Med. (1968) 42 pp.71 ff and see Harrison, Drink and the Victorians, pp. 21-22.

(131) Beer was used as standard beverage for males in most asylums until the end of the century. L.A.B. (1860) Report of the Superintendent of Prestwich Asylum, p. 12; Hunter and Macalpine, pp. 115 - 121, Psychiatry for the Poor; Commissioners in Lunacy, Forty-eighth Report (1894) p. 237. Sir Victor Horsley and Mary D. Sturge, Alcohol and the Human Body (London 1909) pp. 5 - 7 on the disuse of alcohol in hospitals; T.M. Dolan, 'Pauperism and Drink with some Remarks on the Medicinal Value of Alcoholic Beverages and the Mortality from Alcohol in Workhouses' in Med.Press & Circ. (1879) 28.pp 411 ff; Parry-Jones, Trade in Lunacy, p. 197; Gloucestershire County Lunatic Asylum, Report of the Medical Superintendent on the Supply of Beer to Patients and Attendants (1888)

(132) Harrison, op. cit. pp. 297 ff; Mitchell and Deane, pp. 355-58; Beer consumption rose from c. 20 galls. per head in 1820 to 39 galls in 1890; G.B. Wilson, Alcohol and the Nation (London 1940) pp. 331 - 32 for wine and spirit consumption.

(133) Harrison, op. cit. pp. 319, 81 - 86; cp. M.B.Smith 'Victorian Entertainment in Lancashire Cotton Towns' in Peter S. Bell ed., Victorian Lancashire (Newton Abbott 1974) p. 175.

(134) Prichard, Treatise on Insanity, pp. 334 - 37; Hood, Suggestions, pp. 65 ff; Tuke, Insanity in Ancient and Modern Life, p. 99.

(135) Tobias, Crime and Industrial Society, pp. 296-308; V.A.C. Gatrell, and T.B. Hadden, 'Criminal Statistics and their Interpretation' in E.A. Wrigley ed., Nineteenth Century Society: Essays in the Use of Quantitative Methods for the Study of Social Data. (Cambridge 1972) pp.337-96.

(136) Minutes of Evidence of the Royal Commission on ... the Execution of the Criminal Law (1847) p. 11.

(137) H. Worsley, Juvenile Depravity (London 1849) p. 63.

(138) Joseph Arch, Joseph Arch: The Story of his Life (London 1898) p. 34. For a cameo of rural drinking habits, see Richard Jeffries, Hodge and his Masters (London 1880;

Reprint 1966) Vol. II. pp. 80 - 94, which also relates styles of countryside crime.

(139) Worsley, Juvenile Depravity, pp. 63 - 72. The relatively higher incidence of crime in the countryside was a myth, partially deriving from rumoured migration of criminals from London and other towns after the setting up of police forces, after 1829: J.M. Hart, 'Reform of the Borough Police, 1835 - 1856' in E.H.R. (1955) ixx. p.411. The towns displayed more easily perceived relationship between drink and crime: the 'rookeries' of the criminal or semi-criminal residuum in London, Manchester and elsewhere, associated drinking places and criminal activity: Mary MacIntosh, 'Changes in the Organization of Thieving' in Stanley Cohen ed., Images of Deviance (London 1971) p. 111.

(140) W.C. Sullivan; Alcoholism (London 1900) pp. 162 - 164; Gatrell and Hadden, Criminal Statistics, pp. 365,369-371.

(141) J.W. Horsley, Prisons and Prisoners (London 1898) pp. 86 - 91.

(142) J.W. Horsley, Jottings from Jail: Notes and Papers on Prison Matters (London 1887) p. 57; Tobias reasserts this belief: Crime and Industrial Society, pp. 181 ff, though later analysis of available statistics indicates that property crimes in fact fell in times of prosperity and increased during economic troughs: Gatrell and Hadden, pp. 367-69. The latter, however, provide no analysis of the social distribution of convicted thieves, who might have been 'honest poor' driven to theft, or members of the 'criminal class' - the former could, through adverse circumstances, and, of course, corrupted by drink, turn to crime: J.M. Rhodes, Pauperism Past and Present (Manchester 1891) p. 64.

(143) See, for example, the account in Edwin Waugh, Lancashire Sketches (London 1869) pp. 275 - 285. Drink and begging were often seen as going together: William Chadwick, Reminiscences of a Chief Constable (Longdendale Amenity Society Reprint 1974) pp. 131 - 32.

(144) Matthew Davenport Hill, Suggestions for the Repression of Crime contained in Charges to Grand Juries of Birmingham (London 1857) p. 109.

(145) F.G.P. Neison, 'Statistics of Crime in England and Wales,' in Statistical Journal (1848) ci. p. 55.

(146) Hood, Suggestions, pp. 76, 78.

(147) Harrison, pp. 297 ff. Robert Roberts, The Classic Slum: Salford Life in the First Quarter of the Century (Manchester 1971; Pelican edn. 1973) pp. 121-123; Bob Copper, A Song for Every Season (London 1971) passim; M.B. Smith, 'Victorian Entertainment' pp. 172-174; cp. David Harker, 'Cecil Sharp in Somerset: Some conclusions' in F.M.J. (1972) 2 pp. 220 - 40, for a provocative analysis of the middleclass discovery of 'folk music.' 'Places of public amusement' in towns tended to sell alcohol, and customers could always bring in their own, as they did at the theatres in Lancashire: John Dunlop, The Philosophy of Artificial and Compulsory Drinking Usages in Great Britain and Ireland (London 1839) p.243. There was immense regional variation in drinking habits:

Ralph Wightman instances his own Nonconformist village in Sussex as differing in this respect from neighbouring villages: Copper, op. cit. Foreword, p. xii.

(148) Gatrell and Hadden, p. 380; M.D. Hill, Suggestions, pp. 48 - 51; Report of the Superintendent of the Lancaster Asylum, Rainhill (Newton 1852) p. 11. A literate culture reduces participation in the total cultural tradition; the psychiatrist was once more offering generalised observation in terms of his own cultural ethic which he hoped to impose on the unlettered poor, ignoring their own valid cultural forms. Cp. J. Goody and I. Watt, 'Literate Culture: Some General Considerations' in P.W. Musgrave, Sociology, History and Education (London 1970) pp. 74 - 86. The alienist was trying to extrapolate sociological data from a moral setting: the assumption was that not to wish an approximation to his own culture was abnormal.

(149) J.P. William-Freeman, Effects of Town Life on General Health (London 1890) p. 11 and see Harrison, p. 315.

(150) Robert Christison, On Some of the Medico-Legal Relations of the Habit of Intemperance (Edinburgh 1861) seems to have set the ball rolling. Originally a lecture (July 1858) to the Scottish College of Surgeons, its main point was that 'ungovernable avidity for strong drink' should be treated as insanity: B.M.J. (1861) ii. p. 12. Legal provision for involuntary detention was essential for 'restraining insensate drunkards.' For Christison's influence see R. Christison ed., The Life of Sir Robert Christison, Bart., edited by his Sons (Edinburgh 1885).

(151) Harrison, p. 274; Donald Dalrymple, 'Asylums for Drunkards' in Macmillan's Magazine (1872) xx; W.T. Gairdner, Drunkenness and Dipsomania (London 1886) p.15

(152) Gairdner, Ibid.

(153) J.C. Bucknill, 'The Relation of Drink and Insanity' in J.M.Sc. (1876) xxii. p. 265.

(154) L.A.B. (1898) Report of the Medical Superintendent of Lancaster County Asylum, p. 14. Cp. J.H. Tuke 'Habitual Drunkards' in Nineteenth Century (1893) xxxiii; J.C. Bucknill, Habitual Drunkenness in Contemporary Review (1886) xxix; Horsley and Sturge, Alcohol and the Human Body, pp. 144 - 146; W.H. Kesteven, Proposals for the Amendment of the Laws relating to Lunatics and Habitual Drunkards (London 1885); W.T. Gairdner, Medical and Legal Preventives and Remedies for Drunkenness and Dipsomania, Two Addresses (London 1890).

(155) Tobias, op. cit. pp. 212 - 13, 299 - 300, 308; L.O. Pike, A History of Crime in England (London 1876) Vol. II. pp. 431 ff; S. and B . Webb, History of Liquor Licensing in England (London 1903; Reprint 1963) p. 144; Harrison, Drink and the Victorians, pp. 318 ff.

(156) Geoffrey Best, Mid-Victorian Britain 1851 - 1875 (London 1971) pp.218 - 222; A.S. Jasper, A Hoxton Childhood (London 1969) passim, for familial tolerance in the years before 1914; W.R. Cockroft, 'The Liverpool Police Force 1836 - 1902' in Bell, Victorian Lancashire, pp.156, 167. Pressure from Temperance Liberals, 1875 - 1881, forced the Liverpool police to saturate pubs with plain

clothes men so as to increase convictions for drunkenness. Public drunkenness decreased in the port as a result, though the chief constable ascribed this as much to the depression of trade and the demolition of the rookeries, ibid. p. 157.

(157) David C. Marsh, The Changing Social Structure of England and Wales 1871 - 1961 (London 1965) p. 252; Horsley and Sturge, Alcohol and the Human Body, pp. 60 - 71, 78 - 81, 120 - 138, 219 ff; T.N. Kelynack, The Drink Problem in its Medico-Sociological Aspects, by Fourteen Medical Authorities (London 1907) passim.

(158) For legal distinction, in context of pleas of diminished responsibility, see Nigel Walker, Crime and Insanity in England: Vol. One, The Historical Perspective (Edinburgh UP 1968) pp. 178 - 180.

(159) The conceptualization of drunkenness as a disease would not by itself have permitted restraint and confinement on an involuntary basis; it had to be made either a mad or a criminal behaviour to achieve that end. Cp. Szasz, The Manufacture of Madness, p. 151; Kittrie, Right to be Different, pp. 261 - 78. Cf. Commissioners in Lunacy, 1894, quoted in Hunter and Macalpine, Psychiatry for the Poor, p. 121. For public safety, clearly there was need for confinement in many cases, though in such cases the madness label would be superfluous as a rationalisation of restraint - e.g. murder. For cultural differentials in this respect see Walter Bromberg, Crime and the Mind (New York 1965) pp. 156 - 158.

Chapter Five.

(1) Thomas Percy, Reliques of Ancient English Poetry (London 1765; Everyman edn. n.d.) Vol. II. p. 148. Eighteenth century physicians lent weight to the 'insinuation': George Cheyne, The English Malady or a Treatise on Nervous Diseases of all Kinds (London 1734); Thomas Arnold, Observations on the Nature, Kinds, Causes and Prevention of Insanity (London 1782; 2nd edn. 1806) pp. 14 - 25. This weird medical chauvinism was persistent: Alfred Beaumont Maddock, Practical Observations on Mental and Nervous Disorders (London 1854) p. 13.

(2) Ewan MacColl, Liner note to Through Moorfields (Topic 12T 147, 1966).

(3) Stereotyped imagery of mental disorder is learned in early childhood and is continually reaffirmed in ordinary social interaction through ordinary conversation, jokes, conventional phrases; and amplified by the media: J.C. Nunally, Popular Conceptions of Mental Health (New York 1961) passim; Thomas J. Scheff, Being Mentally Ill: A Sociological Theory (London 1968) pp. 64 ff.

(4) Tudor anti-vagrancy laws prohibited begging. 'Toms o' Bedlam' were discharged patients licensed to beg. They wore a distinctive badge and costume, and were common until the mid-seventeenth century: John Aubrey, The Natural History of Wiltshire (1691; London 1847; Reprint

1969) p. 93; Isaac D'Israeli, Curiosities of Literature (London, New edn. 1859) p. 292; cp. Shakespeare, King Lear, Act II Scene 3. Professional vagabonds masqueraded as Bedlam Toms, and were known by the cant name of Abram men: John Awdeley, The Fraternity of Vagabonds (1561, 1575) in Gamini Salgado, ed., Cony-Catchers and Bawdy Baskets (London 1972) p. 62.

(5) Jack Lindsay, Loving Mad Tom: Bedlamite Verses of the XVI and XVII Centuries (London 1927) offers a rigidly exclusive definition of this song-family which is somewhat misleading in its brevity.

(6) Percy, Reliques, pp. 148 - 157. Six songs are reprinted: Old Tom of Bedlam, claimed by Izaak Walton to have been written by his friend Basse (Compleat Angler Chapter 3); The Distracted Puritan (Bishop Corbet); The Lunatic Lover (Blackletter broadside, taken from Pepys Collection); The Lady Distracted with Love; The Distracted Lover;(Henry Carey); The Frantic Lady (D'Urfey).

(7) Thomas D'Urfey, Pills to Purge Melancholy (London 1719) Vol. 1. Other mad songs from the stage of that era can be found scattered throughout Hive: A Collection of Songs (London 1723) 4 vols.

(8) The prototype song was From the Hagg and Hungry Goblin (Giles Earle his Book in BM.Add.Mss. 24. 665), which Jones, Lunacy, Law and Conscience, p. 12, wrongly refers to as Loving Mad Tom. Cp. D'Israeli, Curiosities p.293.

(9) The Madden Collection of Broadsides, 18 Vol. III, (The University Library, Cambridge). Other mad songs can be found in this unique collection: See Madden, 15. Vol.IX. The Original of To Find My Tom of Bedlam seems first to have been printed in D'Urfey's Wit and Mirth (London 1699). Variants can be found in Joseph Ritson, Ancient Songs (London 1790) and W. Chappel, A Collection of English National Airs (London 1840). Cp. chapbooks in the Roxburghe Collection, especially Vol. 1. 26 - 28, 206 - 207; Le Price d'Amour (London 1660), which have versions of the songs reprinted by Lindsay.

(10) Lucy E. Broadwood and J.A. Fuller Maitland, English County Songs (London 1893) p. 71. Elsewhere, grief for a destroyed lover provoked madness and confinement. Widespread is Young Edwin in the Lowlands Low, collected from Mrs. Hopkins of Axford in Hampshire (1907) by Vaughan Williams and Charles Gamblin: F.S.J. (1909) iii. pp. 266 - 67. Cp. versions collected in Sussex, (1901) i. p. 124, and again in Hampshire, G.B. Gardiner, Folk Songs from Hampshire (London 1909) p. 38.

(11) 'Bedlam,' collected by Cecil Sharp from Jack Barnard at Bridgewater in 1906: in Mss. Folk Words. Vol. 6 p.1004 (Clare College Library, Cambridge).

(12) Old Tom of Bedlam in Percy, op. cit. p. 148.

(13) Variously titled Bedlam City, The Loyal Lover, Through Moorfields, this song-family is vast and widespread: Love's Magazine (1740); R. Vaughan-Williams, Folk Songs from the Eastern Counties (London 1908); S.Baring-Gould, Songs of the West (London 1905); Lucy E. Broadwood, English Traditional Songs and Carols (London 1908).

Often found in oral tradition: F.S.J. (1902) i. pp. 146 - 47; (1909) iii. p. 290.

(14) As in the fantasy/desire/metamorphosis verse in which the maiden wishes to become, or sees herself as a swallow or a fish: Broadwood and Fuller Maitland, op. cit. p. 71.

(15) J. Harland and T.T. Wilkinson, Ballads and Songs of Lancashire (London 1875) p. 196. The theme is perennial: for a darker humour see Ken Kesey, One Flew Over the Cuckoo's Nest (London 1962).

(16) H.E. Woolridge, ed., Chappell's Old English Popular Music (London 1893) pp. 56, 74. Sifting through broadside collections yields many such titles as Mad Robin, Mad Moll, and even the Madman's Morrice. The second tune might be related to a calender custom: Mayday ceremonies at Hitchin, Herts., included the man-woman figure common to rituals nationwide, generally termed the Betsy, but there known as Mad Moll: William Hone, The Every Day Book (London 1864) Vol. I. p.287 records the ceremony as performed in 1823.

(17) Leslie Shepard, The History of Street Literature (Newton Abbott 1973) pp. 51 - 78 offers a brief account of broadside printers' activities from the sixteenth century, though emphasis is on London firms.

(18) For example, J.C. Bucknill, The Mad Folk of Shakespeare (London and Cambridge n.d.).

(19) Thomas Dekker, The Honest Whore (1604) Act. One.

(20) The prison-madhouse confusion is evident in the Bedlam City song-family where the scene is occasionally transferred to Newgate Prison without substantial textual alteration: F.S.J. (1907) iii. pp. 111 - 112. Charles Dickens, Barnaby Rudge (London 1841).

(21) John Harriott, Struggles through Life Exemplified (London 1815) Vol. III p. 373.

(22) Charlotte Bronte, Jane Eyre (London 1847) Chapter 26. The image accords well with the novel's Gothicism. Modern Gothic shows the same tendency especially in film: for a bestial delineation of the madman comparable to that of Bronte see the image of Renfield in Dracula (Tod Browning, 1930), and the varieties of ultra-Hogarthian madness in Bedlam (Val Lewton, 1946) which caused English censors to refuse the film a certificate.

(23) Sir Charles Bell, Essays on the Anatomy of Expression in Painting (London 1806) p. 153. Again, twentieth-century Gothic reproduces the gamut of these visual images: see, for example, The Cabinet of Dr. Caligari (Robert Wiene, 1919), especially the concluding garden-scene anticlimax.

(24) John Haslam, Medical Jurisprudence as it relates to Insanity according to the Laws of England (London 1817) p. 11. Cp. Scheff, Being Mentally Ill, p. 68.

(25) Daniel Defoe, Augusta Triumphans (London 1728) p. 31.

(26) From a clipping in Folder 1871 - 99 in the offices of the Mental After Care Association, Jermyn St., London. The tactic remains common, cp. Scheff pp. 71-74, and can be successfully applied to other deviant categories - e.g. Homosexuals, drug-addicts - to back up legal

suppressions, or offer a societally-based alternative to such tools of the 'therapeutic state': Szasz, The Manufacture of Madness, pp. 272 - 288;Kittrie, Right to be Different, pp. 210 - 60. Cp. Stanley Cohen, Folk Devils and Moral Panics (London 1973) for media manipulation and public opinion with respect to two other deviant groups, the Mods and Rockers of the mid-1960's.

(27) For discussion of the evolution of the diminished responsibility pleas, see Nigel Walker, Crime and Insanity, pp. 74 - 124 and passim.

(28) Weekly Despatch, March 12, 1843.

(29) J.G. Millingen, Aphorisms on the Treatment of Insanity and Management of the Insane (London 1840) p. vii.

(30) L.S.F. Winslow, Recollections of Forty Years (London 1910) p. 89. Cp. Szasz, Ideology and Insanity, pp.98 - 112, and for modern journalistic imagery, John Rowland, Unfit to Plead? Four Studies in Criminal Responsibility (London 1965).

(31) Mircea Eliade, Myths, Dreams and Mysteries (London 1960, paperback 1968) pp. 95 - 98: Schatzman, Madness and Morals, p. 5. Keith Thomas, Religion and the Decline of Magic (London 1971, paperback 1973) p. 575; George Rosen, Madness and Society, passim.

(32) J. Huizinga, The Waning of the Middle Ages (1924, Pelican 1965) pp. 184 ff; cp. Norman Cohn, The Pursuit of the Millenium (London 1957) and Vittorio Lanternari, The Religions of the Oppressed(London 1963) for cultural and political backgrounds to ecstatic/mystical religious movements in medieval Europe and the modern third world. Rosen,Madness and Society pp. 217 ff; W.C. Cadbury, ed., W.C. Braithewaite, The Beginnings of Quakerism (Cambridge 1955) p. 108; William Chadwick, Reminiscences, pp. 95 - 111; Zilboorg and Henry, pp.140-142. For Victorian attempts at cross-cultural studies of madness-possession, see M.D. Conway, Demonology and Devil Lore (London n.d.) Vol. I. pp. 261 - 62; E.B. Tylor, Primitive Culture (London 1871) Vol. I. p. 267.

(33) W.G. Black, Folk Medicine (London 1883) pp. 45,195,202.

(34) Tuke, Chapters in the History of the Insane, pp. 12 ff; J. Heron, Journey through part of Scotland (1793) and Carew's Survey of Cornwall (1769) p. 123 offer detailed accounts. See account of community ritual in Inverness Courier, August 31, 1871, quoted in Tuke, Chapters,p.20 n. Cp. Foucault, pp. 168 - 172; Sir Alexander Morison, Cases of Mental Disease, with Practical Remarks on their Medical Treatment (London 1828) pp. 44 - 45, 163 - 64; Parry-Jones, Trade in Lunacy, p. 196. Glen na Galt, Co. Kerry, owes its name ('valley of lunatics') to this tradition of water-cure. Holy Water was also used in cure **rituals**, adding to the demonaic possession connection: Tuke, p. 23.

(35) Nineteenth (and twentieth) century historians and physicians, on the whole, tended to see witchcraft within a psychopathological theory. Esquirol thought that witches were mentally ill, as did Pinel, and modern psychiatrists have tended to see the victims of witch-

trials, from the days of Sprenger and Kramer to Salem, as mentally disordered individuals suffering at the hands of a non-understanding society: Pinel, Treatise, p. 238; Esquirol quoted in Zilboorg and Henry, History, pp. 391 - 92; Deutsch, pp. 33 ff; Zilboorg and Henry, pp. 29, 140; Alexander and Selesnick, History of Psychiatry, pp. 68, 86. This facile identification has been questioned: Szasz, Manufacture of Madness, p. 109 and Grob, Mental Institutions in America, p. 12. n. There is no inherent reason for treating witchcraft as part of the history of mental illness. Identification codes and social strategies for dealing with both forms of deviance approximated at times, and the maintenance of belief in possession as a factor in causing mental disorder intensified some similarities. Professional assessors operated in both areas, legitimising societal repression: the fifteenth century Dominican Inquisitor was a counterpart of the nineteenth-century alienist: Heinrich Kramer and James Sprenger, Malleus Maleficarum (Transl. Montague Summers, London 1928); Thomas, Religion and the Decline of Magic; pp. 517 - 558, 638 - 698; C.L 'Estrange Ewen, Witch Hunting and Witch Trials (London 1929); H.R. Trevor-Roper, The European Witch Craze of the 16th and 17th Centuries (London 1969). Folkloric analysis offers a different perspective: Christina Hole, Witchcraft in England (London 1947). Indiscriminate usage of folklore-material has produced confused accounts confounding belief and actuality, which, by arguing the existence of practising witches, are diametrically opposed to the orthodoxy of psychiatric historians: Margaret Murray, The Witch Cult in Western Europe (Oxford 1921); G.L. Kitteredge, Witchcraft in Old and New England (Harvard 1928). More realistically, the witch and the madman have been shown to occupy similar socially-assigned roles: Szasz, Manufacture, pp.140-163. For a broader socio-political analysis see Joyce Bednarski, 'The Salem Witch-Scare, viewed Sociologically' in Max Marwick, ed., Witchcraft and Sorcery (London 1970) pp. 151 - 163, and A. Rebecca Cardozo 'A Modern American Witch-Craze', ibid, pp. 369 - 376.

(36) John Harland and T.T. Wilkinson, Lancashire Folklore (London 1882) p. 87.

(37) Quarterly Review (1816) xv. p. 389. Cp. Sigmund Freud, A Seventeenth Century Demonological Neurosis quoted in Szasz, Manufacture, p. 102; Charles Williams, Demoniacal Obsession and Possession as Causes of Insanity (London 1911).

(38) Bedford Pierce, ed., Addresses to Mental Nurses (London 1924) p. i.

(39) Tobias Smollett, Roderick Random (London 1748) and see also: Jones, Lunacy, Law and Conscience, pp. 31-40, 92-98, 102 - 107; cf. Parry-Jones, Trade in Lunacy, pp.221-280.

(40) R. Renton, John Forster and his Friendships (London 1912) p. 186.

(41) Louisa Lowe, The Bastilles of England (London 1883) passim; cp. Report of the Alleged Lunatic's Friend Society (1851)

p. 6 and passim.

(42) Accepted legitimacy of confinement did not, however, change the madhouse image; Perceval's Narrative, pp. 82-87, 92-108, 119-123; D. Davidson, Remembrances of a Religo-Maniac (Stratford-on-Avon 1912) pp. 81-113, 177-203; Lomax and Grant-Richards, Experiences of an Asylum Patient, pp. 73 - 84. There was a symbiotic relationship between the reported actual and the literary images of the madhouse, which served to perpetuate a remarkably consistent stereotype: H. Cockton, The Life and Adventures of Valentine Vox, the Ventriloquist (London 1840); Edgar Allan Poe, The System of Dr. Tarr and Prof. Fether, reprinted in Michael Glenn, ed., Voices from the Asylum (New York 1974) pp. 2 - 20; Thomas S. Szasz, The Age of Madness: The History of Involuntary Mental Hospitalization presented in Selected Texts (London 1975) passim; Parry-Jones, Trade in Lunacy, 227 - 233.

(43) J.C. Bucknill, 'The Newspaper Attack on Lunatic Asylums' in J.M.Sc. (1859) v. pp. 146 - 53.

(44) The basic imagery remains: Szasz, Ideology and Insanity pp. 113 - 139, and sources cited at p. 117. Filmic portrayals harden the stereotype: Shock Corridor (Samuel Fuller 1963); and most sensationally, The Snake Pit (Anatole Litvak 1948) where the treatment of the asylum-theme provoked heavy cutting by British censors.

(45) Weatherley, A Plea for the Insane, pp. 55 - 61.

(46) Millingen, Aphorisms, Introduction.

(47) J.C. Bucknill, The Care of the Insane and their Legal Control, p. vii. Association with the agencies of social control clearly did not impair the'professional dignity' of alienists, for only in this respect did Bucknill and his colleagues differ from the licensed house owner.

(48) J.M.Sc. (1858) iv. p. 312.

(49) John Tempest, Narrative of the Treatment experienced by John Tempest Esq ... during Fourteen Months Solitary Confinement under a False Imputation of Lunacy (London 1830); Anon., Account of A Man's Wrong Confinement in Haydock Lodge Asylum 1826/30 (Manchester Public Library, MS/923/8/REL - partial Ms.); Louisa Lowe, Gagging in Madhouses by Government Servants (London n.d.); Perceval's Narrative, pp. 122, 130.

(50) Flora Thompson, Lark Rise to Candleford (Oxford 1939-43) Penguin edn. 1973) pp. 426-28; Richard Hillyer, Country Boy (London 1966) pp. 11-12; cf. Weatherley, Plea for the Insane p. 2.; W.T. Gardner, Insanity: Modern Views as to its Nature and Treatment (Glasgow 1885) pp.18-20.

(51) Saturday Review, 25 Feb. 1865. The remarks were occasioned by the Townley case and its consequences: J.M.Sc. (1865) ix. pp. 591 ff and (1869) xv. pp. 99 ff.

(52) J.M.Sc. (1868) xiv. pp. 387 - 88.

(53) Cp. Foucault, Madness and Civilization, pp. 72 ff.

(54) John Barlow, On Man's Power, pp. 70-71; cp. 'Sepharial', On the Treatment of Criminals and Lunatics (Theosophical Publications Society, London 1891) which suggests the 'mad' - 'bad' equation in the glibbest terms.

(55) Anon. Lunatick Asylums, pp. 1 - 4.

Chapter Six.

(1) Herman Finer, in J.S. Harris, British Government Inspection (London 1955) pp. viii - ix.
(2) Times, 21 Sept. 1833. The relationship between classical economists and factory legislation has caused some debate: Arthur J. Taylor, Laissez-faire and State Intervention in Nineteenth Century Britain (London 1972) pp. 42 - 43. Cp. M.W. Thomas The Early Factory Legislation (Leigh-on-Sea 1948) passim.
(3) Robert Greg, The Factory Question (London 1837).
(4) M.W. Thomas, 'The Origins of Administrative Centralization' in Current Legal Problems (1950) p. 229
(5) 7 & 8 Vic. c. 15.
(6) Jones, Lunacy, Law and Conscience, pp. 141 - 44.
(7) J. Sharpe, ed. Report of S.C. (1815), p. 189.
(8) S.W. Nicoll, An Enquiry into the present State of Visitation in Asylums for the Reception of the Insane and into the Modes by which such Visitation might be Improved (London 1828) pp. 84, 88-89.
(9) Ibid. p. 79.
(10) J.G. Millingen, Aphorisms, pp. 179 - 80.
(11) PP (1830) XXX. p. 3.
(12) Jones, Lunacy, Law and Conscience, p. 170. Some awareness of real problems is evident in the later reports, and there are occasional sidetracks into psycho-administrative theory: PP (1841) Sess. 2 VI. p. 4, Report for 1836 - 37, but little indication of dynamic inspection.
(13) Ibid. p. 2.
(14) Ibid. The Commissioners were convinced that their 'Interference ... materially tended to insure humane treatment to the patient.'
(15) In view of later experience, it is not credible that the London asylums were guiltless. If the Board after 1845 could take issue over insufficiently-stuffed armchairs, surely there was something worthy of note in earlier years?
(16) Ibid. pp. 4 - 5. One William Mosely, advertising under the unoriginal name of Willis, was convicted of keeping an unlicensed asylum, but liberated after three months when his appeal to the Secretary of State had been seconded by the chairman of the Sessions trying him. The Commissioners were aware that he promptly began advertising again, still without licence, but realised that a prosecution would only waste time and money.
(17) Ibid. p. 5.
(18) Apparently the Board only became suspicious as to provincial conditions when requests for statistics were ignored, though one imagines that their correspondents in the country had earlier proffered ex parte evidence of abuse.
(19) Ibid. pp. 5 - 6, Report for 1837 - 38.
(20) Ibid. p. 7. Through Ashley's efforts in the Commons, the Board was empowered to request returns from all licensed houses in England and Wales. The most obvious and immediate realization was the ignorance of proprietors,

clerks of the peace and visiting magistrates as to their legal obligations. The county asylum superintendents were conscientious in acceding to demands for information however; so much so that the Board was anxious to find more spacious accommodation to house the accumulating records.

(21) Lack of statutory powers did not prevent the Board undertaking to 'advise' and 'exhort' those outside their jurisdiction, adopting the role of agitating informant to the Home Department if their own influence failed.

(22) Ibid. p. 11; Report, 1839 - 40. In one asylum alone, no less than eighty cases were specially investigated, 'some of them at great length.'

(23) Jones, Lunacy, Law and Conscience, pp. 171 - 73. Somerset and Ashley pointed out that large numbers of insane were excluded from the inspection guaranteed by the 1828 legislation: those confined in their own homes, or in separate lodgings, in county asylums, in public hospitals, and in Bethlem and St. Luke's. Somerset's bill aimed at extending the Metropolitan system to the provinces, and included the provision that barrister members of the inspectorate should have a fixed salary (in lieu of the existing hourly payment) and should be allowed to maintain their practises.

(24) 116 institutions were visited by the professional Commissioners, and enquiries 'extended ... to many subjects beyond those ... specifically mentioned in ... (the) Acts.' The county asylums were clogged with incurable paupers, detained cheaply in workhouses until their affliction became irremediable and their conduct unmanageable, whereupon they were transmitted to nullify the curative function of the asylum. The workhouse wards, where they existed, were, of course, unlicensed. The Commissioners were disgusted that so few counties had erected proper receptacles for their insane, and that even where there was provision, it was often defective. Bristol and Nottingham had public institutions, but these were censored for being situated in crowded urban areas. Haverfordwest Asylum, once a gaol, was 'an ill-constructed prison.' The large county Asylums at Hanwell and Lancaster Moor, though well-conceived, and diligently administered, were seen as inadequate to needs. Some places lacked resident medical staff (Bedford, Haverfordwest and Norfolk), whilst some private asylums were often left unattended, and in many institutions 'the provisions of the law were violated.' Metropolitan Commissioners in Lunacy, Report to the Lord Chancellor (London 1844, in octavo) pp. 3-4, 6-7, 12-18, 55.

(25) The Report was a careful piece of work, marred only by Ashley's rambling style, and was based on efficient research. As a propaganda peice it proved effective - and rightly so, as the conditions it exposed, not all of them bad, and some even confidence-inspiring - needed public airing. But not all of the Commissioners' proposals were sound, and some of their wishes hardly beneficial to those they hoped to aid. For example,

their insistence that incurables and chronic patients required less attention and less expensive accommodation, separate from the curables whom they precluded from available asylum space. This was a dangerous assertion: not only was the distinction impracticable, in absolute terms, but most incurables 'require more means of occupation, more space for exercise, greater opportunities for recreation than the curable, and a greater variety of comfortable arrangements to reconcile them to their situation, and to maintain that habitual content and tranquility which distinguish a well-regulated asylum from a miserable madhouse.' Metropolitan Commissioners in Lunacy, Report (1844), p. 92; John Conolly, On the Construction and Government of Lunatic Asylums, p. 5. The influence of the report on public opinion was apparently significant: Jones, Lunacy, Law and Conscience, pp. 185 - 86. The press, at any rate, took up the issue. So well had he and his colleagues aroused the conscience of the Times, that Ashley was chastised for 'humbugging' and 'being humbugged' when he let Graham delay bringing in legislation for a session. Jones seems surprised that public opinion - or at least, newspaper opinion - should reach such a pitch, and especially that the Times should fan it; yet the same paper had performed a similar function in regard to workhouse exposés just two years earlier, fanning anti-Poor Law discontent: Times, 23 July, 1844; Jones, Lunacy, Law and Conscience, p. 188; Edsall, The Anti-Poor Law Movement, pp. 21, 25.

(26) Metropolitan Commissioners in Lunacy, Report (1844) pp. 33, 38, 42, 85, 96, 165, 167, 204 - 208, and passim; Jones, Lunacy, Law and Conscience, p. 187.

(27) Adapted from Harris, British Government Inspection, Chapter One. Factors (i), (iii) to (v) are dealt with in sections III and IV below; factor (ii) in section V; factors (vi) to(x) receive tangential attention throughout this Chapter, and in specific aspects in Chapter Seven.

(28) The Commissioners in Lunacy became restyled as the Board of Control in 1913.

(29) J.B. Sharpe, ed., SC (1815) pp. 233 ff; Jones, Lunacy, Law and Conscience, p. 106.

(30) Robert Greg, The Factory Question, pp. 129 - 30.

(31) M.W. Thomas, 'The Origins of Administrative Centralization,' pp. 224 - 34.

(32) Cp. Roberts, Victorian Origins of the British Welfare State, pp. 109, 129.

(33) S.E. Finer, Chadwick, passim.

(34) 9 Geo. IV c. 41 s. 2; 8 & 9 Vic. c. 100 s. 3.

(35) MacDonagh, A Pattern of Government Growth, pp.91 - 114.

(36) PP (1859) Sess. 1 (75) III, Report from the Select Committee on Lunatics, p. 835.

(37) Entries in the Magistrates' Visiting Book at Lancaster Asylum during the 1830's indicate that visits were usually made by a single person, extraordinarily by three or four, and single-line remarks 'Visited the whole institution' or 'All appears in good order'

indicate the extent and nature of inspection: Lancashire CRO: QAM/1/33/11, passim.

(38) Cp. Roberts, Victorian Origins of British Welfare State, pp. 93 - 94, 114 - 117.

(39) 8 & 9 Vic. c. 100 s. 110.

(40) Sir Frederick Needham noted the role of public opinion in lunacy legislation, especially in the shaping of the 1890 Act: Weatherley, A Plea for the Insane, p. 10.

(41) PRO: MH/50/1 p. 58; 8 & 9 Vic. c. 100 ss. 3 to 5; cp. Burn, Age of Equipoise, pp. 141 - 42. The Commissioners' salaries remained constant throughout the period reviewed.

(42) MH/50/1 p. 7.

(43) 8 & 9 Vic. c. 100 ss. 9, 11, 12; MH/50/1 pp. 30-31. An 'additional clerk' was appointed at £200 p.a.apparently on the Board's initiative, though the issue was complicated by the uncertain status of one clerk, Barlow, whose freedom with the petty cash prompted the Board to pay him his permanent salary, though keeping him on short term notice: ibid. pp. 30.

(44) Commissioners in Lunacy, Sixteenth Annual Report (1862) pp. 72 - 73.

(45) MH/50/11 p. 320.

(46) Ibid. p. 370.

(47) MH/50/1 pp. 99 ff; PP (1877) XIII (1) Report from the Select Committee on the Lunacy Laws, qq. 558,573,574,575

(48) S.C. (1877) q. 555; 8 & 9 Vic. c. 100 ss. 14-17, 61-65, 77.

(49) Commissioners in Lunacy, Sixteenth Report, p. 74.

(50) S.C. (1859) p. 835, and see below, pp. 317 - 26.

(51) S.C. (1877) q. 558.

(52) John Thomas Arlidge (1822 - 99) BA MD (London) MRCS. LSA. FRCP. JP. Son of a doctor. Educ. Chatham and apprenticed to a GP in Rochester. Medical studies completed at Kings College. MO at St. Luke's, where he introduced Conolly's methods. Travel abroad followed by posts at W. London Hospital and Surrey, Chelsea and Farringdon Dispensaries. Physician to North Staffs. Infirmary (1862). Certifying Factory Surgeon to Stoke district. Pioneer in industrial medicine. Mayor of Newcastle-under-Lyme. (1878-79).

(53) J.T. Arlidge, On the State of Lunacy and the Legal Provision for the Insane, (London 1859) p. 194.

(54) Ibid. p. vii.

(55) Arlidge suggested an approximation to coeval inspectorates by separating the professional inspectorate from a newly created central deliberative body, sitting permanently; ibid. pp. 189, 195.

(56) See below, Chapter Seven.

(57) S.C. (1859) p. 4.

(58) The argument was Shaftesbury's, and rested on the one personal link provided by Francis Barlow, one of the statute-named honorary Commissioners of 1845.

(59) S.C. (1859) pp. 2, 11.

(60) Ibid. p. 46. This would have the further advantage of increasing the number of annual visits to Metropolitan asylums from four to six, since Metropolitan magistrates

would then perform for the London area the same tasks already performed by their provincial counterparts. Thus, instead of the existing four visits from the Commissioners-as-magistrates, there would be four actual magisterial visits, and two visits from the Commissioners in their role as inspectors.

(61) Arlidge, On the State of Lunacy, pp. 191 - 92.

(62) Edward Tennyson Conolly, Suggestions for the Amendment of the Laws relating to Private Lunatic Asylums (London 1859).

(63) J.M.Sc. (1859) v. p. 281.

(64) S.C. (1859) p. 46.

(65) Ibid. Shaftesbury's attitude towards institutionalization was equivocal, cf. below, Chapter Eight.

(66) The duties of the honorary Commissioners fell into three categories: Firstly, in conjunction with two professional Commissioners they could visit hospitals and licensed houses on routine circuits; make special visits to order release; regulate the dietaries of paupers in hospital or licensed houses; visit county and borough asylums and gaols (8 & 9 Vic. c. 100 ss. 61, 77, 82, 110). Secondly, individually, they might order a search to be made of an institution's registers, and order the admission of friends or relatives to patients in hospitals or licensed houses; and visit single patients (8 & 9 Vic. c. 100 ss. 34, 85; 16 & 17 Vic. c. 96 ss. 27, 96). Thirdly, in company with one other non-professional Commissioner, they could make night visits to licensed houses and hospitals. Within the Metropolis, they could make special visits to licensed houses with a view to recommending discharge of a patient to the Board; they could sanction the removal of a patient from a hospital or licensed house, and had the right to summon witnesses. They might sanction the transfer of a private patient to an asylum, or the retention of a patient as a boarder after discharge as cured (8 & 9 Vic. c. 100 ss. 71, 76; 18 & 19 Vic. c. 105 ss. 17, 100; 16 & 17 Vic. c. 106 ss. 16, 20) Cp. the evidence of R.W.S. Lutwidge, secretary to the Board: S.C. (1859) p. 46.

(67) The new Examiners were empowered to make daily visitations to licensed houses, if necessary. Their confidential reports were to be made available only to the Commissioners. The proposals were aimed specifically at the private sector - hence the desire to cut out the vested interest of the professional, whose economic interests, even if suspended or potential during the term of his holding office, might colour his attitude towards profit-making establishments with whose proprietors he already shared socio-medical affinities. The fear of stimulated public opinion was further aroused by the apparent hostility of Shaftesbury to the private asylum, which he saw as the principal motivation for legislation, (Tuke, Chapters in the History of the Insane, p. 193), and hence the government's proposals seemed to be consonant with the ideology of the inspectorate.

(68) J.M.Sc. (1859) v. p. 378.
(69) J.M.Sc. (1858) iv. pp. 6, 12 - 13. The self-indulgent rhetoric concluded: 'So great is the contamination and depredation incidental to a connection with the treatment of the insane, and the management of any asylum, that the legislature, in its profound wisdom ... considers two years' purgation ... necessary before the medical man can be qualified to present a clean bill of health, and thereby be fitted to sit at the Board of Commissioners and assist in the administration of the law ... ' Cp. J.M.Sc. (1859) v. p. 381. No physician from the private sector was appointed to the Commission in the nineteenth century.
(70) J.M.Sc. (1859) v. pp. 388 - 89.
(71) Bucknill, The Care of the Insane and their Legal Control, p. xxx.
(72) 8 & 9 Vic. c. 100 s. 3. The named Commissioners were: Lord Ashley, Lord Seymour, Robert Vernon Smith, Robert Gordon, Francis Barlow, Thomas Turner, Henry Herbert Southey, John Robert Hume, Bryan Waller Proctor, James William Mylne and John Hancock Hall. The six present at the first meeting were: Ashley, Gordon, Turner, Proctor, Hall and Mylne.
(73) For the form of the oath: 8 & 9 Vic. c. 100 s. 6. Turner and Mylne had been the first Commissioners sworn, on 6 August: MH/50/1 p. 1. For biographical details of the professional Commissioners see below, section V.
(74) Ibid. p. 7.
(75) Southey resigned and was replaced by James Cowles Prichard, on 27 August.
(76) At the meeting of 26th February, 1846: There were four circuits, the first three divided in two, the fourth into three sections (a) Northern, based on Liverpool/ Manchester and Newcastle/York; (b) Western, based on Bath/Bristol and Salisbury; (c) Midland, based on Birmingham and Norwich; (d) Home Circuit: Surrey/Kent/ Sussex; Hants/Berks/Oxon; Bucks/Beds/Herts/Essex: MH/50/1. 193.
(77) These included all asylums, workhouses and gaols, plus Bethlem, and the naval and military hospitals, brought under the Commissioners' authority by special authority of the Chancellor and Home Secretary respectively: Commissioners in Lunacy, First Report (1846 - 47) p.6.
(78) MH/50/1. 8. The advertisement appeared in the Lancet, Medical Journal, Times, Standard, London Gazette and Morning Chronicle.
(79) The questions covered the age, sex and residence of the applicant, medical qualifications, education, experience with the insane, moral character and financial position, testimonials as to fitness and skill,particulars as to class of patient to be admitted, and fees: First Report, Appendix C, p. 319. The licence revoked was that of Gate Helmsley Retreat, near York.
(80) Hospitals receiving lunatics were to have printed regulations, a resident medical officer and be registered by the Commissioners. Haslar (naval) and Shornecliffe (military) hospitals were doubtfully

included by the Act. The latter soon removed its patients to a permanent hospital at Yarmouth. The military authorities were amenable to inspection; Haslar proved obstinate: MH/50/1. 27; First Report, pp. 16 - 18.

(81) The solicitors eventually made their point, after approaching the President of the Hospital, Mr. Justice Patterson, who persuaded the Treasurer to draw up rules and regulations relating to insane patients, and to arrange the appointment of a medical superintendent of lunatics.

(82) 8 & 9 Vic. c. 100 s. 47. In emergencies, one certificate would suffice to get a confinement, provided reasons were given why the second was lacking, and that a disinterested physician signed a confirmatory certificate within three days of admission.

(83) 8 & 9 Vic. c. 100 s. 60. The Commissioners, however, noted that in some of the best institutions, Case Books had been kept since the commencement of the Act. Medical Visitation Books (s.59) were kept 'with tolerable regularity' - sometimes with 'extreme care': First Report, pp. 19 - 20.

(84) 8 & 9 Vic. c. 100 ss. 71, 83. The night visit was to an unnamed house outside London, and was occasioned by sworn declarations of neglect and brutality: First Report, p. 21.

(85) 8 & 9 Vic. c. 100 s. 86.

(86) 8 & 9 Vic. c. 100 ss. 89, 90: An entirely new function and difficult to implement. The committee was constituted of the chairman and one legal and one medical Commissioner. The Commissioners complained that 'a large proportion of those whom the statute has placed exclusively under its supervision, are dispersed over different parts of the kingdom, at a distance from the capital, and cannot be seen by the Commissioners in the course of their ordinary visitations while on circuit, unless it happens, which is of course seldom, that these are also members of the committee. In all other cases it becomes necessary that one or more of the committee be specially detached for the purpose; and such a step cannot be taken without more or less interrupting and in fact suspending the labours of other Commissioners who are not themselves on the Committee ...' The object of the system was to secure a greater degree of privacy, but since all the Commissioners were sworn to secrecy ('religiously observed by all members'), the function and powers of the private committee could have more efficiently have been entrusted to all the Commissioners - or at least the professional members - indiscriminately.

(87) As the residence of a single patient was likely to vary, there was the probability of great difficulty in procuring the required certificates and fresh orders. The Commissioners were doubtlessly justified in suspecting that the awkwardness of keeping an adequate check in this way permitted 'a general disposition ... among those who earn a livelihood by receiving single

patients, to avoid ... being brought within the operation of the statute.' Thus, under ss. 90, 91, of the Act, the Board should have possessed a complete list of all single patients in the country, but after eighteen months, knew of only two hundred cases. It was not the practice of the private committee to make a visitation, unless the certification proved faulty, or information was received showing the need for investigation. During 1846 - 47, this proved necessary in only twenty cases: First Report, pp. 26, 27.

(88) The Lord Chancellor might direct visitation of any party represented as having a lunatic in charge, and a similar authorisation could be obtained from the Home Secretary.

(89) The Board, through Home Secretary Sir James Graham, communicated their objection to the visitors, in the form of a report. There was no satisfactory amendment of plans until Graham's successor, Grey, strongly 'recommended' the magistrates to accede to the Commissioners' suggestions.

(90) First Report, p. 34; Mortimer-Granville, The Care and Cure of the Insane, pp. 222 - 24.

(91) Cambridge, for example, needed a great deal of threatening suasion before consenting to erect Fulbourne. Plans were not submitted until 1852: Commissioners in Lunacy, Seventh Report (1853) p. 7.

(92) First Report, p. 46.

(93) Ibid. p. 61.

(94) Ibid. p. 34.

(95) First Report, p. 135.

(96) Tuke, Chapters in the History of the Insane, pp.205 ff; Gardiner Hill, A Concise History of the Entire Abolition of Mechanical Restraint, passim.

(97) First Report, p. 153. Registered hospitals did not have to submit their general rules of management to the Home Secretary for approval.

(98) Anon., State of Lincoln Lunatic Asylum, 1846 (London 1846) p. 3.

(99) Ibid. p. 7.

(100) Proceedings of the Lincoln Lunatic Asylum and Communications with Her Majesty's Commissioners in Lunacy (London 1847) pp. i, 3, 84.

(101) State of Lincoln Lunatic Asylum, 1846, p. 9.

(102) Proceedings of the Lincoln Lunatic Asylum, p. 46.

(103) State of Lincoln Lunatic Asylum, 1846, p. 4.

(104) Ibid. p. 5.

(105) Ibid. p. 4.

(106) Ibid. pp. ii, iv.

(107) The Commissioners greeted the Governors' special report as the product of false notions of 'superiority' which allowed 'deviation from the ordinary practice of experienced men.' In their 1847 Report (p.153) they demanded immediate removal of the sources of abuse.

(108) PP 1847 (291) XLIX Further Report of the Commissioners in Lunacy ... relative to Haydock Lodge Lunatic Asylum, p. 1.

(109) Commissioners in Lunacy, Sixteenth Report (1862) p. 25.

(110) Ibid. The licence was exceeded; rooms were overcrowded, damp and ill-ventilated; the drainage was defective; the dietary was poor; clothing and bedding were scanty.
(111) Named simply as Mr. Roberts: MH/50/1. 297.
(112) The attendants had been dismissed by the time of the Commissioners' enquiry.
(113) They would, however, permit the printing of their reports: MH/50/1. 298.
(114) MH/50/2. 27.
(115) The four were Mylne, Prichard, Hume and Campbell, and their inspection lasted 'several days' during which they saw all the patients: PP 1847 (291) XLIX p. 18.
(116) At the time of the visitation there were 29 patients from 12 Welsh unions. There were seven Welsh speakers on the staff. Haydock Lodge, in fact, served a vast catchment area: of 74 unions sending patients, 49 were outside Lancashire. Of 341 paupers in the asylum in October, 1846, 161 were out-county, mainly from the Midlands, the eastern counties, and, of course Wales.
(117) Ibid.p. 13.
(118) Ibid. p. 14.
(119) MH/50/1. 353.
(120) PP 1847 (291) XLIX p. 15.
(121) Sixteenth Report, p. 26.
(122) Commissioners in Lunacy, Seventh Report (1853) p. 4. Sutton had previously been Master of the Manchester workhouse.
(123) Haydock Lodge remained an asylum for over a hundred years. Its somewhat chequered career as a privately-run establishment, with an enduring reputation for eccentricities of management, coming to an end in the 1960's, when it was taken over by Liverpool Regional Hospital Board.
(124) MH/50/1. 297-300, 308, 310, 316-317, 336-53; MH/50/2. 10-11, 22.
(125) Davies had the archetypal attendant's career: sergeant in the 17th Lancers; constable and outdoor porter to St. Martin's workhouse, where he had experience of pauper lunatics; after marriage, he took care of a single lunatic patient; later, attendant in a short-lived hydropathic institution, and thence to West Malling: MH/51/44A. No. 3052. Doc. ii.
(126) Alfred Beaumont Maddock (1816 - 63) MD (Giessen). Proprietor and resident MO, West Malling Retreat, and private practice in Curzon St., Mayfair.
(127) MH/51/44A. No. 3052. Doc. i.
(128) Ibid.
(129) The Commissioners' intention was to keep a record of all attendants in public and private asylums, giving career history, character, reasons for leaving post, etc. See Mercier, Lunatic Asylum, their Organization and Management, p. 290.
(130) Davies had apparently gone to give in his notice, and had been sacked on the spot.
(131) MH/51/44A. No. 3052. Doc. iii.
(132) 8 & 9 Vic. c. 100 s. 59.
(133) Humble Memorial of Alfred Beaumont Maddock and Cres. Perfect.

(134) Lutwidge to Maddock, 21 February 1851: copy in folder with Doc. iii, above.
(135) Loose sheet in folder, handwriting unfamiliar, no initials.
(136) 8th March, 1851. Details in folder as above.
(137) Note from the Commissioners' solicitors, included with Doc. iii.
(138) Letter to Lutwidge, in ibid. dated 10th April, 1851; Commissioners in Lunacy, Seventh Report, p. 5.
(139) Skultans, Madness and Morals, uses Maddock's writings as part of her general argument, but fails to give any indication of his background, thereby giving a false impression of his professional standing at the time of his writing.
(140) Lancaster Gazette, 23 May, 30 May, 1863.
(141) Commissioners in Lunacy, Eighteenth Report (1864) pp. 97 - 99.
(142) MH/51/53. No. 7521.
(143) Ibid. and Eighteenth Report, p. 98.
(144) Letter to Shaftesbury, 27th June, 1863: MH/51/53.loc.cit.
(145) For example, asked Robertson, were the Commissioners aware that the press was excluded from the inquest? Why was the post-mortem conducted by the Asylum's Medical Officer? Why did Broadhurst and the Coroner get together before issuing a press statement?
(146) Robertson wanted it published, but Board secretary Spring-Rice replied that this was not the Commissioners' policy.
(147) Letter from Robert Jackson to the Secretary of the Lunacy Commissioners, 10th August, 1863, in MH/51/53. loc. cit. Perhaps Robertson was a crank. Gaskell, as ex-superintendent of Lancaster might have been aware of the man by previous association.
(148) Note to Spring-Rice, dated 19 July, 1863, from the Royal Station Hotel, York.
(149) Eighteenth Report, p. 99.
(150) Dates in parentheses indicate period of service as a paid Commissioner.
(151) Detailed biographical information lacking.
(152) Campbell (1810 - 81): Barrister, Middle Temple (1836). Honorary Commissioner from 1878 until death: F. Boase, Modern English Biography of the Nineteenth Century (Truro 1892 - 1921).
(153) Procter (1787 - 1874): Born Leeds: Educ. Finchley and Harrow, sub. nom. William Bryan Proct r, Articled to Wiltshire solicitor. Barrister, Grays Inn (1831). Metropolitan Commissioner in Lunacy (1832 - 45). Honorary Commissioner until death. Poet friend of Leigh Hunt, Lamb and Dickens; pseudonym, Barry Cornwall: works incl. Poetical Works (1822), English Songs 1832, Memoir on Lamb (1866) and editions of Jonson and Shakespeare: Boase; T.H. Wade, English Poets (London 1883) vol. iv; Harriet Martineau, Biographical Sketches (London 1876).
(154) Mylne (1800 - 55): Son of Rev. James Mylne, Professor of Moral Philosophy at Glasgow University. Educ. Glasgow GS and Glasgow University and Balliol, Oxford.

Barrister, Lincolns Inn (1827). Metropolitan Commissioner in Lunacy (1832 - 45). Co-author, with Benjamin Keen, of Reports of Cases in the High Courts of Chancery 1832 - 35 (3 vols. 1834 - 37) and with R.D. Craig of the same, 1835 - 48 (5 vols. 1837 - 48): Boase; Joseph Foster Alumni Oxoniensis 1715 - 1886 (London 1887 - 88); I. Addison, The Snell Exhibitioners (Glasgow 1901).

(155) Lutwidge (1802 - 73): Born London, Educ. St. Johns, Cambridge, Barrister, Lincolns Inn (1827). Metropolitan Commissioner in Lunacy (1842 - 45). Secretary to Lunacy Commissioners (1845 - 55). Member of Commission of Inquiry into the State of Lunatic Asylums in Ireland (1856) Remembered by L.S.F. Winslow as 'a kind old gentleman,' he was killed whilst on active duty, on a routine visit to Fisherton House, Salisbury, when a patient attacked him, driving a nail through his skull: Boase; Law Times (1873) iv. p. 127.

(156) Forster (1812 - 76): Son of Robert Forster, cattle dealer, Newcastle. Educ. Newcastle GS and UCL. Barrister, Inner Temple (1843). Dramatic critic of True Sun (1832); editor Foreign Quarterly Review (1842 - 43), Daily News (1846), Examiner (1847 - 55). Collector of paintings and bibliophile: collection bequeathed to South Kensington Museum. Prolific writer, moved in Dickens' circle. Published works incl. Lives of the Statesmen of the Commonwealth (1836 - 39, 5 vols.); Life and Adventures of Oliver Goldsmith (1848); Life of Charles Dickens (1872): Boase; T. Powell, Pictures of Living Authors (London 1851); Illustrated London News (1845) vii p.329; Temple Bar (1876) xlvi; Gentleman's Magazine (1876) xvi; Renton, John Forster, passim. L.S.F. Winslow thought him 'severe and blunt' but 'sympathetic'. (Recollections of Forty Years, p. 38).

(157) Phillips (1822 - 95): Son of William Edward Phillips, Governor of Prince of Wales Island. Educ. Eton and Christ Church, Oxford. Barrister, Lincolns Inn (1846), Chief Secretary to Lord Chancellor Chelmsford (1859). Revising Barrister for City of London (1864). Secretary to Lunacy Commissioners (1864 - 72). Publications incl. The Law Concerning Idiots (1858) and The Law of Copyright (1863): Records of Lincolns Inn (London 1896).

(158) Howard (1836 - 80): Second son of the 17th Earl of Suffolk and Berkshire. Educ. Christ Church, Oxford, Barrister, Lincolns Inn (1863); Boase.

(159) Bagot (1828 - 1906): Born South Australia. Educ.Trinity, Cambridge. Barrister, Inner Temple (1853). Secretary to Lord Justice Selwyn (1868 - 69). Secretary to Lord Justice Hatherley (1870 - 72). Knighted 1903: Who Was Who.

(160) Frere (1840 - 1900): Son of William Edward Frere, civil servant, Bombay. Born Poona. Educ. Harrow (where he won the first fencing prize awarded) and Trinity, Cambridge. Barrister, Lincolns Inn (1865). Revising barrister for North Wiltshire (1877): Boase; Law Journal, 15 Dec,1900, p. 690; Winslow, Recollections, loc. cit.

(161) Urmson (1851 - 1907): Eldest son of George Urmson, Canton, China. Educ. Eton and Oxford (no college assigned). Barrister, Lincolns Inn (1876). Secretary to Commissioners in Lunacy (1889 - 95): Who Was Who.

(162) Giffard (1864 - 1908): Son of J.N. de L. Giffard, County Court Judge, Educ. Merton, Oxford. Barrister, Inner Temple (1887). Private Secretary to Lord Chancellor (1886 - 92, 1895). Secretary to Commissioners in Lunacy (1895 - 1900): Who Was Who.

(163) Hume (1781? - 1857): MD St. Andrews (1816). LRCP (1819). DCL (Oxon)(1834). Physician to Duke of Wellington in the Peninsular War and on his return to England. Inspector General of Hospitals (1818 - 21). Private practice in London: Boase.

(164) Southey (1783 - 1865): Younger brother of Robert Southey. MD Edinburgh (1806). FRCP (1823). FRS (1825). Practice in Durham and London. Physician to Middlesex Hospital (1815 - 27). Physician to George IV (1823) and Queen Adelaide (1830). Censor, RCP (1820, 1832) and Consilarius (1836, 1840 - 42). Metropolitan Commissioner in Lunacy (1836). Gresham Professor of Physic (1834 - 65). Author, Observations on Pulmonary Consumption (1814): Boase; G.H. Brown and R.R. Traill, Royal College of Physicians ... Lives of the Fellows, vol. v.

(165) Turner (1793 - 1873): Medical educ. Guy's and St. Thomas's, London, and Paris. House surgeon, Manchester Infirmary (1817 - 20). Key figure in establishing the Manchester Schools of medicine and surgery. Surgeon to Deaf and Dumb Institution, Manchester (1825) and Royal Infirmary (1830). Professor of Philosophy, Manchester Royal Institution (1843). FRCS (1843): DNB; J.M.Sc. (1873) xix.

(166) Prichard (1786 - 1848): See above, Chapter Four, Note 21.

(167) Gaskell (1807 - 86): See above, Chapter Two,note 116. Sources: Boase; Times 27 March, 1886; J.M.Sc. (1886) xxxii.

(168) Nairne (1804 - 87): Educ. Edinburgh and Trinity, Cambridge. MD (Cantab). FRCP (1838). Physician to St. George's Hospital, London (1839). Private practice in London, with indifferent success, prior to appointment to Lunacy Commission. Like Gaskell, knocked down by a cab, which hastened his death: G.R. Brown, Lives of the Fellows of the Royal College of Physicians of London (London 1955) vol. IV.

(169) Cleaton (18 ? - 1901): MRCS. Resident MO, West Riding Asylum to 1853, and Rainhill Asylum, Lancashire (1853 - 58): Who Was Who.

(170) Williams (1837 - 93): Educ. Merchant Taylors and St. Thomas's Hospital. Assistant to Daventry GP. Assistant MO, Derby County Asylum. Assistant MO, Wyke House Asylum. Assistant MO, Three Counties Asylum. Via Sir W.C. Hood's patronage, Assistant Physician, Bethlem, and Superintendent on breakdown of his superior: J.M.Sc. (1893) xxxix.

(171) Southey (1835 - 99): Youngest son of Henry Herbert Southey. Educ. Westminster and Christ Church. MA (1860). MB (1861). MD (1866). Radcliffe Travelling Fellow(1860).

Assistant Physician, St. Bartholomew's (1865) and Physician (1868 - 83). MRCP (1860). FRCP (1866). Lecturer on Public Health and Forensic Medicine (1868 - 83). Gulstonian Lecturer (1867). Lumleian Lecturer (1881): Boase; Times, 14 Nov. 1899; Lancet, 25 Nov, 1899.

(172) Allbutt (1836 - 1925): See above, Chapter Two, note144. Source: D.N.B.

(173) Needham (d. 1924): MD. MRCP. Educ. St. Peter's, York, and St. Bartholomew's Hospital. Medical Superintendent, York Lunatic Hospital (1858 - 74), and Barnwood Hospital for the Insane, Gloucester (1874 - 92). Member of Royal Commission on the Care and Control of the Feeble Minded: Who Was Who.

(174) Rogers: Detailed biographical information lacking. Medical Superintendent, Rainhill Asylum (1858 - 88).

(175) Wilkes (1811 - 94): See above, Chapter Two, note 154. Source: Boase.

(176) Wallis (1844 - 97): Born Waterford. MD Aberdeen (1875). Resident, Mercers Hospital, Dublin; Medical Superintendent, Hull Borough Asylum; Senior Assistant Physician, Durham County Asylum; Medical Superintendent, Whittingham Asylum (1878 - 93): Boase: Johnson's Roll of Graduates of the University of Aberdeen (1906) p. 572.

(177) Cooke (1852 - 1931): MD London. MRCS. AKC. Educ. privately, and Cholmely's School,Highgate. Medical educ. Kings College Hospital. Medical Superintendent, Worcester County Asylum and the Wiltshire County Asylum. During First World War helped organise conversion of mental hospitals into war hospitals. KBE (1918): Who Was Who.

(178) Coupland (1849 - 1930): Educ. Hove House School, Brighton and UCL. MD. (1874). FRCP (1880). Physician to Middlesex Hospital (1879 - 96): Who Was Who.

(179) Renton, John Forster, p. 186.

(180) Recollections of Forty Years, p. 40. The book in question was Winslow's Manual of Lunacy (London 1874), dedicated to the Commissioners. It received poor reviews in the medical press: J.M.Sc. (1874) xx. p. 126.

(181) Wilkes told the Select Committee of 1877 that 'the general principle ... has been to appoint two of the medical Commissioners who have had practical experience in Asylums, and one who has been in practice as a physician, in London probably' (Q.705).

(182) J.M.Sc. (1857) iv. pp. 127 - 28.

(183) J.M.Sc. (1861) viii. p. 329.

(184) J.M.Sc. (1886) xxxii.

(185) J. Psych. Med. (1850) iii. p. 139. The congratulory address to Gaskell was signed by many public asylum men, but only two from the private sector: Parry-Jones, op. cit. p. 90.

(186) Sources for these statements are the biographical reference works listed above.

(187) John Haslam, Considerations on the Moral Management of Insane Persons (London 1817) pp. 2 - 3.

(188) J.M.Sc. (1858) iv. pp. 6, 12, 13.

(189) J.M.Sc. (1858) iv. pp. 312 - 14.

(190) Cp. J.G. Millingen, Aphorisms, pp. 180-81. Bucknill, when part of the State-supervisory system, averred that 'deprivation of the personal liberty of any of the Queen's subjects is an affair of State, and must only be undertaken by the State.' (The Care of the Insane and their Legal Control, p. 130).

(191) Arlidge, On the State of Lunacy, p. 187.

(192) Quoted in J.M.Sc. (1866) xii. p. 210.

(193) See above, Chapter Four, Section III.

(194) Until 1866, there was only one medical Commissioner with asylum experience. Until 1865, none of the legal Commissioners was a Lunacy specialist.

(195) J.M.Sc. (1866) xii. pp. 213 - 14. The Board, significantly,made no attempt to interfere with medical treatment.

(196) Cp. J.M.Sc. (1880 - 81) xxvi. p. 560.

(197) L.A. Weatherley, A Plea for the Insane, pp. 55 - 66.

(198) A medical Commissioner, according to Weatherley, who gives Clouston. But Thomas Smith Clouston (1840-1915), though a Scottish Commissioner in Lunacy, was never a member of the English Board, and at this date was Chief Physician of Edinburgh's Morningside Asylum. The medical Commissioners at this date were Southey, Wilkes and Cleaton, and it is perhaps the last named that Weatherley mis-named.

(199) Ibid. pp. 58 - 59.

(200) Winslow, Recollections, p. 42.

(201) Cp. Jones, Lunacy, Law and Conscience, pp. 147, 198, for public opinion and illicit confinement; Parry-Jones, Trade in Lunacy, pp. 231, 238.

(202) Cleaton, Wilkes, Williams, Phillips. Howard,having died, was spared direct mention: Louisa Lowe, The Bastilles of England (London 1883) pp. 91 ff.

(203) Lowe, Bastilles, p. 101.

(204) Ibid. Feminine vulnerability to illicit confinement was a topical issue in the United States at the time: E.P.W. Packard, Modern Persecution or Insane Asylums Unveiled (Hartford 1873); cp. Szasz, The Age of Madness, pp. 53 ff; cp. Deutsch, The Mentally Ill in America, pp.307, 424.

(205) 'Doctor' Quail was a quack known to the police as 'unbalanced' and 'dangerous'. He illegally harboured a feebleminded woman for payment and for the offence was prosecuted by the Commissioners. Their First Report recounts their actions, taken in concert with the police, and the account reads as a success story. However, the Commissioners failed to publish the fact that they had known of Quail and his doings for twelve months before the police and local doctors aroused them to action: Quail himself had even made a nuisance of himself at their offices, with a rambling tale of plots and persecutions in which he volunteered the information that he was keeping the unfortunate woman as a 'patient'. Commissioners in Lunacy, First Report pp. 160-65; PRO MH/50/1 pp. 75-76.

(206) Lowe, Bastilles, p. 15.

(207) Ibid. pp. 35-40; Winslow,Recollections of Forty Years,

pp. 116 - 26.

(208) Lowe, p. 61.

(209) Louisa Lowe, *Gagging in Madhouses by Government Servants* (London n.d.)

(210) *S.C.* (1877) qq. 11, 528.

(211) Hodder, *Shaftesbury*, p. 700.

(212) *S.C.* (1859) q. 504.

(213) Ibid. qq. 354, 359, 366, 494, 504, 507, 870, 919; *S.C.* (1860) q. 400.

(214) Hodder, *Shaftesbury*, p. 700.

(215) *S.C.* (1859) qq. 101, 102, 301.

(216) L.A.B. (1875-1976) *Reports of the Superintendent of Prestwich Asylum*. pp. 19, 20; Commissioners in Lunacy: statistics of workhouse visitation in *Reports* for 1849 through 1856.

(217) L.A.B. (1886) *Report of the Commissioners in Lunacy*, Lancaster Asylum, p. 13. My emphases.

(218) Bucknill, *Care of the Insane and their Legal Control*, p. 51.

(219) Ibid. p. 79.

(220) *S.C.* (1877) qq. 635 - 37.

(221) Commissioners in Lunacy, *Further Report*, (1847-48)p.168.

(222) Commissioners in Lunacy, *Fifth Report* (1850) pp. 6-7; *Sixth Report* (1851) p. 12.

(223) A natural step for a Conservative government, out to reduce local taxation, to take. Medical motivation was completely lacking. For attitudes of the PLB inspectorate to pauper lunatics, see *J.M.Sc.* (1859) v. p. 551, and for difficulties in obtaining replies from unions: Commissioners in Lunacy, *Twentieth Report* (1866) p. 23.

(224) Weatherley, *Plea for the Insane*, pp. 73 - 75.

(225) Commissioners in Lunacy, *Thirty-second Report* (1878) pp. 3 - 4.

(226) *Fifth Report* (1850) and *Eleventh Report* (1856).

(227) Exceptionally see Commissioners in Lunacy, *Eighth Report* (1854).

(228) Bucknill, *Care of the Insane and their Legal Control*, p. 66. One is left to assume that 'wide and scientific' views were those which coincided with Bucknill's own: cp. *J.M.Sc.* (1858) iv. loc. cit.

(229) Commissioners in Lunacy, *Thirtieth Report* (1876) p. 22.

(230) *S.C.* (1859) q. 14.

(231) *S.C.* (1877) q. 654.

(232) Mortimer-Granville, *The Care and Cure of the Insane*, p. 325.

(233) Herbert Preston-Thomas, *Work and Play of a Government Inspector* (London 1909) p. 211.

Chapter Seven.

(1) 8 & 9 Vic. c. 100 ss. 42, 111.

(2) Commissioners in Lunacy, *First Report*, pp. 238, 239.

(3) Commissioners in Lunacy, *Further Report*, (1847) p. 42.

(4) The criteria for assessing suitability or otherwise for workhouse confinement were implicit in s. 45 of the Poor Law Amendment Act.

(5) Arlidge, The State of Lunacy, p. 66.
(6) Ibid. pp. 68 - 69; Abel Smith, The Hospitals, p.58-59.
(7) 16 & 17 Vic. c. 97. s. 67.
(8) Arlidge, The State of Lunacy, p. 70; Joseph Rogers, Reminiscences of a Workhouse Medical Officer (London 1889) passim.
(9) Commissioners in Lunacy, Eleventh Report (1857) p.16.
(10) 4 & 5 Wm. IV c. 76 s. 45.
(11) Poor Law Commissioners, Eighth Report, p. 111, Commissioners in Lunacy, First Report, p. 240.
(12) 8 & 9 Vic. c. 126. s. 55.
(13) Commissioners in Lunacy, First Report, pp. 246 - 47.
(14) 9 & 10 Vic. c. 84.
(15) Commissioners in Lunacy, First Report, p. 240, Appendix (A).
(16) Ibid. p. 58 - 59. At an average cost to unions of 3/- per head per week, the Commissioners calculated that pauper lunatics in workhouses were costing a total of £71,440 4s.
(17) Ibid. p. 240.
(18) Commissioners in Lunacy, First Report, pp. 251 - 52.
(19) Commissioners in Lunacy, Supplement to Twelfth Report (1859) p. 4.
(20) Arlidge, The State of Lunacy, pp. 187 - 89; L.A.B. (1854) Report of the Superintendent of Rainhill Asylum p. 60.
(21) Commissioners in Lunacy, First Report, p. 255.
(22) Ibid. p. 259.
(23) Ibid. p. 267.
(24) Commissioners in Lunacy, Supplement to Twelfth Report, p. 14.
(25) Ibid. p. 15.
(26) Commissioners in Lunacy, Eleventh Report, p. 16.
(27) Arlidge, The State of Lunacy, pp. 58 - 59.
(28) J.C. Bucknill, Thirteenth Report of the Superintendent of Devon Asylum, p. 6.
(29) Commissioners in Lunacy, Twenty-first Report (1867)p.24.
(30) Ibid. pp. 23, 25.
(31) Commissioners in Lunacy, Supplement to Twelfth Report, p. 7.
(32) Ibid.
(33) Commissioners in Lunacy, Supplement to Twelfth Report, p.9.
(34) Ibid. p. 10.
(35) Ibid.
(36) Ibid.
(37) Ibid. p. 11.
(38) Ibid. p. 29.
(39) Commissioners in Lunacy, Twenty-first Report, pp. 21-22.
(40) Ruth C. Hodgkinson, 'Provision for Pauper Lunatics' in Med.Hist. (1966) x. pp. 138 ff.
(41) A 'league table' of what the Commissioners considered the best workhouses was drawn up for their 1866 Report. The top ten were: The City of London; Camberwell; St. Saviour's; Bath; Chorlton (Manchester); Crumpsall; Toxteth Park (Liverpool); Ribchester (Preston); Halifax; and Leeds; Twentieth Report, p. 20.

(42) Commissioners in Lunacy, Twenty-first Report, p. 22.
(43) Commissioners in Lunacy, Twenty-fourth Report, (1870) pp. 48 - 49.
(44) Ibid. pp. 49 - 50.
(45) Commissioners in Lunacy, Eighteenth Report (1864) p.77; 25 & 26 Vic. c. 111
(46) 25 & 26 Vic. c. 111. s. 67.
(47) Commissioners in Lunacy, Thirtieth Report (1876) p. 64.
(48) Ibid. p. 65.
(49) Commissioners in Lunacy, Twenty-fourth Report, pp.54-55.
(50) Poor Law Board, Fifteenth Report (1863) pp. 22, 35.
(51) Metropolitan Commissioners in Lunacy, Report (1844)p.92.
(52) Conolly, The Construction and Government of Lunatic Asylums, p. 4.
(53) Commissioners in Lunacy, Twenty-fourth Report, p. 49.
(54) Commissioners in Lunacy, Twentieth Report (1866) p. 19; Twenty-first Report, p. 25; Twenty-fourth Report, p.55.
(55) S.C. (1877) qq. 367 - 69.
(56) J.G. Millingen, Aphorisms, p. 189.
(57) L.A.B. (1854) Report of the Superintendent of Rainhill Asylum, pp. 59 - 60; Commissioners in Lunacy, Twenty-first Report, p. 71.
(58) His district comprised North Wales, Shropshire, Staffordshire, Cheshire (except Stockport and some Ashton parishes) and parts of Derbyshire.
(59) S.C. (1859) I. pp. 131 - 33.
(60) Ibid. p. 73.
(61) Ibid. pp. 124 - 25.
(62) See above, Chapter Three, Table 7.
(63) Commissioners in Lunacy, Supplement to Twelfth Report, pp. 23 - 24.
(64) Ibid. p. 25.
(65) Ibid. Aged paupers were usually appointed as nurses in sick wards of workhouses, since they were likely to remain there for a long period. Employment of this class as attendants to lunatics was a natural extention, cp. Abel Smith, The Hospitals, p. 51.
(66) Ibid. p. 12.
(67) Ibid. p. 21.
(68) Ibid. p. 19.
(69) Ibid. p. 41 - 42.
(70) Ibid. pp. 42 -56.
(71) Ibid. p. 42.
(72) Commissioners in Lunacy, Seventeenth Report, (1863) pp. 156 - 57.
(73) Ibid. p. 157.
(74) Ibid. p. 158.
(75) Commissioners in Lunacy, Twentieth Report (1866) p.19; Twenty-first Report, pp. 23, 71.
(76) F.E. Anstie 'Insane Patients in London Workhouses' in J.M.Sc. (1865) x p. 327.
(77) Ibid. p. 331.
(78) Bruce, The Coming of the Welfare State, p. 119.
(79) J.H. Stallard, Pauper Lunatics and their Treatment (London 1870) p. 45.
(80) Commissioners in Lunacy, Twenty-fourth Report, p. 48.
(81) Stallard, Pauper Lunatics and their Treatment, p. 3.

(82) Ibid. p. 4.
(83) Ibid. p. 6.
(84) Bruce, The Coming of the Welfare State, p. 119; Sir A. Powell, The Metropolitan Asylums Board and its Work, 1867 - 1930 (London 1930) p. 41.
(85) Ibid. pp. 14, 41.
(86) Mortimer-Granville, The Care and Cure of the Insane, p. 263.
(87) Commissioners in Lunacy, Twenty-fifth Report (1871)p.45; A. and C. Reed, Memoirs of the Life and Philanthropic Labours of Andrew Reed DD (London 1863) pp. 404, 414 - 418 and passim; M. Rooff, Voluntary Societies and Social Policy (London 1957) pp. 85 - 86; D.G. Prichard, Education and the Handicapped. pp. 55 - 62.
(88) Mortimer-Granville, The Care and Cure of the Insane. p. 264.
(89) Ibid. pp. 265, 268.
(90) Ibid. p. 263; J. Watson Grice, National and Local Finance, p. 57; Jones, Mental Health and Social Policy, pp. 18 - 19.
(91) Hodgkinson, 'Provision for Pauper Lunatics,' pp. 140-41.
(92) S.C. (1877) qq. 2945 - 47.
(93) Brian Abel Smith, The Hospitals, pp. 49-54; Report from H.B. Farnall Esq. Poor Law Inspector, on the Infirmary Wards of the several Metropolitan Workhouses (1866) passim; Report from Dr. Edward Smith., on the sufficiency of Existing Arrangements for the Care and Treatment of the Sick Poor in 48 Provincial Workhouses ... (1867 - 68) passim.
(94) Abel Smith, ibid. pp. 54, 56.
(95) Edward Smith, ibid. p. 71.
(96) Commissioners in Lunacy, Supplement to twelfth Report, p. 6.
(97) L.A.B. (1856) Report of the Medical Superintendent of the Lancaster County Asylum, Rainhill, pp. 67 - 70; Arlidge, The State of Lunacy, p. 50.
(98) Quoted in Arlidge, The State of Lunacy, p. 61.
(99) Ibid. p. 47.
(100) J.C. Bucknill, 'On the Construction of Public Asylums' in Asylum Journal (1858) iv pp. 188 ff; Mortimer-Granville, The Care and Cure of the Insane, pp. 161-72.
(101) Anstie, 'Insane Patients in London Workhouses', p. 333.
(102) Abel Smith, The Hospitals, pp. 58 - 60.
(103) Ashton-under-Lyne Reporter, 1 April, 1871; Joseph Rogers, Reminiscences of a Workhouse Medical Officer, pp. 64, 139 - 59.
(104) Commissioners in Lunacy, Twentieth Report, p. 19; Thirtieth Report, p. 64.
(105) S.C. (1877) qq. 3862 - 69; 3988; 4018 - 19; 1761 - 64; 7771 - 73.
(106) C.L. Robertson, 'The Care and Treatment of the Insane Poor,' in J.M.Sc. (1867) xiii p. 294.
(107) S.C. (1877) qq. 5773 - 75.
(108) C.M. Vaillant, Historical Sketch of the Emergence of Liverpool Psychiatry, p. 5.
(109) Commissioners in Lunacy, First Report, p. 275.
(110) Hodgkinson, 'Provision for Pauper Lunatics,' p. 142.

(111) Ibid. pp. 142, 149; Prichard, Education and the Handicapped, pp. 57 - 58.
(112) Prichard, op. cit. pp. 58 - 59; Tuke, Chapters in the History of the Insane, pp. 300 - 313.
(113) The Guardian, 23 May, 1972; Szasz, The Age of Madness, pp. 198 - 202.

Chapter Eight.

(1) Roger Bastide, The Sociology of Mental Disorder (Translated by Jean McNeil, London, 1972) p. 186. The quotation from H.Ey is taken from Etudes Psychiatriques (Paris 1948).
(2) Yves Pelicier, Integration des Données Sociologiques (Paris 1964) quoted in Bastide, Sociology of Mental Disorder p. 187.
(3) Sigerist, Civilization and Disease, p. 108.
(4) Shelford, The Law Concerning Lunatics, Vol. I, p. 9; Foucault, Madness and Civilization, p. 7; Kittrie, The Right to be Different, pp. 11, 58 - 60.
(5) Foucault, Madness and Civilization, p. 64.
(6) Halliday, General View, p. 10; Leigh, Historical Development of British Psychiatry, Vol. I, passim; Bastide, The Sociology of Mental Disorder, p. 60.
(7) Solzhenitsyn, quoted in Szasz, 'Undermind', p. 1214.
(8) Ibid.
(9) Perceval, Narrative, passim; W.A. O'Connor, Evidence given before the Select Committee on Lunacy Law (Manchester 1879) passim; Account of a Man's Wrongful Confinement in Haydock Lodge Asylum 1826 - 30 (MS/923/8/REL: Manchester Public Library); Medvedev, A Question of Madness, passim.
(10) Szasz, ibid, p. 1214, and Law, Liberty and Psychiatry (New York 1963) passim.
(11) Hodder, Life and Work of the Seventh Earl of Shaftesbury p. 333, quoting Shaftesbury's diary for 20 August,1845.
(12) E. and J. Cummings, Closed Ranks (Cambridge, Mass.1957) pp. 101 - 102.
(13) Parry-Jones, The Trade in Lunacy, pp. 168-221; cp. Grob, 'Mental Illness, Indigency and Welfare', pp. 252-59, for American parallels.
(14) Jones, Mental Health and Social Policy, pp. 10, 40.
(15) Steven and Hilary Rose, 'The Politics of Neurobiology: biologism in the service of the State,' in Roger Dale et al (eds), Schooling and Capitalism (London 1976), pp. 120 - 26.
(16) Above, Chapter Four. Cp. Skultans, Madness and Morals, pp. 2, 20 - 25; K. Goldstein, 'The Structure of the Organism' cited in Bastide, Sociology of Mental Disorders, p. 89; Foucault, Madness and Civilization, pp. 241 - 54; Thompson, Whigs and Hunters, pp. 258 ff.
(17) Chapter Four, section III. Cp. Glenn, Voices from the Asylum, pp. vii, xii; S. and H. Rose, 'The Politics of Neurobiology,' p. 122; Colin Blakemore in The Listener (16 Dec. 1976).
(18) Kittrie, The Right to be Different, p. 41.
(19) E.B. Sherlock, The Feeble Minded (London 1911) p. 282.

(20) Cure rates in county asylums (1906 - 15) averaged 34% on admissions - roughly the same as in 1866 - 76 (Weatherley, A Plea for the Insane, p. 17). In 1844, the rate had been c. 37% in pauper-only asylums, and c. 47% in mixed asylums: Thurnham, Observations, pp. 29, 137.

(21) Quoted in Weatherley, ibid. p. 10. Cp. Sir George Savage, in Allbutt, System of Medicine, vol. viii, p. 429.

(22) E.J. Ledbitter, The Lunacy and Mental Treatment Acts, 1890 - 1930 (London 1933) p. 34.

(23) T.S. Clouston, quoted in Weatherley, A Plea for the Insane, p. 31.

(24) Donald McI. Johnson, 'Out of Sight; out of Mind' in R.F. Tredgold (ed) Bridging the Gap from Fear to Understanding in Mental Illness (London 1958) p.94.

(25) Thirty Years Administration of the Public Asylums in England and Wales (London 1922) pp. 3 - 4.

(26) Scheff, Being Mentally Ill, p. 74; Nunnally, Popular Conceptions of Mental Health, p. 86; William Hone, The Table Book (London 1864) p.166; Thomas Newbigging, Lancashire Humour (London 1900) pp. 128 - 30; Sir Charles Petrie, Scenes of Edwardian Life (London 1965) pp. 45 - 46.

(27) Hilaire Belloc, Selected Essays (London, Penguin ed. 1958) p. 206. Walker, Crime and Insanity in England, pp. 2 - 3.

(28) W.A. O'Connor, Evidence given before the Select Committee on Lunacy Law (Manchester 1879), and cuttings from Hulme Advertiser and Gazette (undated) attached to a copy of O'Connor's pamphlet in Manchester Central Library.

(29) Hodder, Shaftesbury, p. 315.

BIBLIOGRAPHY

MANUSCRIPT SOURCES

Public Record Office:

MH/50/1 et seq.	Minutes of the Lunacy Commission and Board of Control, 1845 - 1938.
MH/51/1 et seq.	Lunacy Commission, Correspondence and Papers, 1846 - 1960.
MO/OS/74/5488 and 5439	Lunacy Commissioners, Occasional Reports.

County Record Office, Preston:

QAM/1/29.	Admission Registers, Lancaster Asylum (20 Vols.).
QAM/1/30.	Medical Reports, Lancaster Asylum (27 Vols.)
QAM/1/33.	Registers and statutory books, Lancaster Asylum (15 Vols.).
QAM/2/37.	Regulations and orders for guidance of attendants, Rainhill Asylum.
QAM/4/1.	Lunatics' settlements, 1867 - 69.
QAM/4/2.	Lunatics' settlements, 1869 - 93.

Central Library, Manchester:

M4/2/1.	Manchester Union, weekly returns to Poor Law inspector for workhouses at Prestwich, Blackley and Manchester (45 vols.).
MS/923/8/REL.	Account of a man's wrongful confinement in Haydock Lodge Asylum, 1826 - 30.

Brown Library, Liverpool:

353/SEL/1.	Liverpool Select Vestry, Minute Books, 1832 - 1922 (23 vols.).
353/SEL/5.	Liverpool Select Vestry, Workhouse Committee, Minute Books, 1842 - 1911 (17 vols.).
353/SEL/17.	Liverpool Select Vestry, Miscellaneous Documents (3 vols.).
353/WES/1.	West Derby Union, Board of Guardians, Minute Books, 1848 - 1930 (58 vols).

Offices of the Mental After-Care Association:

Collection of annual reports, newspaper cuttings and miscellaneous documents.

PRINTED SOURCES

Principal Statutes:

43 Eliz c. 2.	Poor Law Act, 1601.

12 Anne c. 23.	Act for reducing the laws relating to Rogues, Vagabonds, Sturdy Beggars and Vagrants into one Act of Parliament, 1714.
17 Geo. II c. 5.	Vagrants Act, 1744.
14 Geo. II c. 9.	Act for the regulation of Madhouses, 1774.
39 Geo. III c. 94.	Criminal Lunatics Act, 1800.
48 Geo. III c. 96.	County Asylums Act, 1808.
59 Geo. III c. 127.	Act for making provision for the better care of Pauper Lunatics in England, 1819.
9 Geo. IV c. 40.	Lunatic Asylums and Pauper or Criminals Maintenance Act, 1828.
9 Geo. IV c. 41.	Treatment of Insane Persons Act, 1828.
2 & 3 Will IV c.107.	Care and Treatment of the Insane Poor Act, 1832.
4 & 5 Will IV c. 76.	Poor Law Amendment Act, 1834.
5 & 6 Vic. c. 87.	Lunatic Asylums Act, 1842.
8 & 9 Vic. c. 100.	Lunatics Act, 1845.
8 & 9 Vic. c. 126.	Lunatic Asylums and Pauper Lunatics Act, 1845.
16 & 17 Vic. c. 70.	Lunacy Regulation Act, 1853.
16 & 17 Vic. c. 96.	Lunatics Care and Treatment Amendment Act, 1853.
23 & 24 Vic. c. 75.	Criminal Lunatic Asylum Act, 1860.
25 & 26 Vic. c. 111.	Lunatics Law Amendment Act, 1862.
49 & 50 Vic. c. 25.	Idiots Act, 1886.
51 & 52 Vic. c. 41.	Local Government Act, 1888.
53 Vic. c. 5.	Lunacy (Consolidation) Act, 1890.
54 & 55 Vic. c. 20.	Lancashire County (Lunatic Asylums) Act, 1891.
54 & 55 Vic. c. 65.	Lunacy Act, 1891.

Reports, returns etc:

Metropolitan Commissioners in Lunacy, Annual Reports to Home Department, 1830, 1835 - 41.
Metropolitan Commissioners in Lunacy, Licensed house returns, 1837 - 47.
Metropolitan Commissioners in Lunacy, Report to the Lord Chancellor, 1844.
Commissioners in Lunacy, Annual reports to the Lord Chancellor 1845 - 1900.
Commissioners in Lunacy, Further report to the Lord Chancellor 1847.
Commissioners in Lunacy, Further report to the Home Department relative to Haydock Lodge, 1847.
Commissioners in Lunacy, Correspondence and reports relative to the treatment of lunatics in Haydock Lodge, 1846.
Commissioners in Lunacy, Particulars of travelling expenses etc., 1850.
Commissioners in Lunacy, Expenditure of the secretary, visitations etc., 1851.
Commissioners in Lunacy, Report on the alleged increase of insanity, 1897.

Sharpe, J. ed. Report, together with the Minutes of evidence ... from the Select Committee appointed to consider the provision being made for the better regulation of private madhouses in England, 1815.
Report from the Select Committee on Lunatics, together with the proceedings of the Committee, Minutes of evidence, etc., April 1859, August 1859, July 1860.
Report from H.B. Farnall Esq., Poor Law Inspector, on the infirmary wards of the several Metropolitan workhouses, 1866.
Report from Dr. Edward Smith ... on the sufficiency of existing arrangements for the care and treatment of the sick poor in 48 provincial workhouses, 1867 - 68.
Report from the Select Committee on Lunacy Law, together with the proceedings of the Committee, Minutes of evidence, and Appendix, 1877.
Returns of the lunatic asylums in England and Wales, 1857-58; 1861; 1878; 1888; 1895.
Eccleston, T., Report of the Medical Superintendent, Rainhill Asylum, Newton 1851.
County of Lancaster, Lunatic Asylums, Reports of the Visiting Committee, Commissioners in Lunacy, Medical Superintendent (Lancaster, Rainhill, Prestwich, Whittingham), Preston, 1854 - 1900 (Bound in series as Lancashire Asylums Board Reports).

Books, pamphlets and articles:

A Doctor of Arts, Oxford, Lunatick Asylums: an Essay, Rugby, 1898.
Allbutt, Sir T. Clifford, 'Proposed Hospitals for the Insane' in J.M.Sc. (1891) xxxvii.
Allbutt, Sir T. Clifford and Rolleston, Humphrey Davy, eds., A System of Medicine by Many Writers. 2nd ed. London, 1910, vol. viii.
Alleged Lunatic's Friend Society, Report, London 1851.
Allen, M., Causes of Insanity with Medical, Moral and Philosophical Observations on them. London 1833.
Anon., An Analytical Index to the new Lunatic Act for regulating the Care and Treatment of Insane Persons in England. London 1828.
Anon., Essays on Charitable Institutions. London 1836.
Anon., On the Amendment of the Law of Lunacy. A Letter to Lord Brougham. London 1843.
Archbold, John Frederick, The Law relating to Pauper Lunatics, with Forms in all cases required in practice, also the Law and Practice in appeals against Lunatic Orders. London 1851.
Arlidge, John Thomas, On the State of Lunacy and Legal Provision for the Insane, with Observations on the Construction and Organization of Asylums. London, 1859.
Ashley, Lord, LUNACY. Copy of a Letter to the Lord Chancellor from the Commissioners in Lunacy, with reference to their Duties and Practice under the Act 8 & 9 Vic. c. 100. London 1849.
Bakewell, Thomas, The Domestic Guide in Cases of Insanity, pointing out the Causes, Means of Prevention and Proper Treatment of that Disorder. Newcastle, 1809.

Bakewell, Thomas, A Letter, addressed to the chairman of the Select Committee of the House of Commons, appointed to enquire into the State of Madhouses: to which is subjoined remarks on the Nature, Causes and Cure of Mental Derangement. Stafford, 1815.
Barlow, John, On Man's Power over himself to prevent and control Insanity. London 1843.
Battie, William, A Treatise on Madness. London 1758.
Belgrave, T.B., 'The asylums for the Insane in St. Petersburg and Copenhagen' in J.M.Sc. (1867) xiii.
Black, C. The Insanity of George Victor Townley. London 1865.
Black, William George, Folk-medicine, London, 1883.
Browne, J.M. Balfour, The Medical Jurisprudence of Insanity, London, 1871.
Brown, S., 'Suggestions for the Construction and Organization of Hospitals for the Insane' in J.M.Sc. (1887 - 88) xxxiii.
Browne, W.A.F., What Asylums were, are and ought to be. Edinburgh, 1837.
Bosanquet, B., Aspects of the Social Problem. London 1898.
Boyd, Robert, A Report on the Lunatics charged to the Parish of St. Marylebone. London, 1844.
Bucknill, John Charles, An Inquiry into the proper Classification and Treatment of Criminal Lunatics. London 1851.
Bucknill, John Charles, 'On the Custody of the Insane Poor' in Asylum Journal (1854) iv.
Bucknill, John Charles, and Tuke, Daniel Hack, Manual of Psychological Medicine. London 1858.
Bucknill, John Charles, Notes on Asylums for the Insane in America. London 1876.
Bucknill, John Charles, Habitual Drunkenness and Insane Drunkards. London 1878.
Bucknill, John Charles, The Care of the Insane and their Legal Control. London 1880.
Bucknill, John Charles, 'The Abolition of Private Asylums' in Nineteenth Century (1884) xxvii.
Bucknill, John Charles, The Mad Folk of Shakespeare. London and Cambridge, n.d.
Burnett, C.M., Insanity tested by Science and shown to be a disease rarely connected with permanent organic lesion of the Brain; and on that account far more susceptible of Cure than has hitherto been supposed. London 1848.
Burrows, George Man, An Inquiry into certain Errors relative to Insanity, and their Consequences, Physical, Moral and Civil. London, 1820.
Burrows, George Man, Commentaries on the Causes, Forms, Symptoms and Treatment, Moral and Medical, of Insanity. London 1828.
Campbell, J.A., 'The Local Government Act of 1888 and its probable action on the Treatment of Insanity in England' in J.M.Sc. (1892) xxxiii.
Campbell, J.A., 'Lunacy in Cumberland and Westmoreland' in B.M.J. (1896) ii.
Charlesworth, E.P. Remarks on the Treatment of the Insane and the Management of Lunatic Asylums, Being the substance of a Return from the Lincoln Lunatic Asylum to the Circular of His Majesty's Secretary of State, London, 1828.

Charlesworth, E.P., Considerations on the Moral Management of Insane Persons. London 1830.
Christison, Robert, On some of the Medico-legal relations of the Habit of Intemperance. Edinburgh, 1861.
Conolly, John, The Construction and Government of Lunatic Asylums. London 1847.
Conolly, John, A Letter to Benjamin Rotch Esq., Chairman of the Committee of Visitors, on the Plan and Government of the additional Lunatic Asylum for the County of Middlesex, about to be erected at Colney Hatch. London 1847.
Conolly, John, The Treatment of the Insane without Mechanical Restraints. London 1856.
Conolly, Edward Tennyson, Suggestions for the Amendment of the Laws relating to private Lunatic Asylums. London, 1859.
Coxe, Sir James, Lunacy in its relation to the State: a Commentary on the evidence taken by the Committee of the House of Commons on Lunacy Law in the session of 1877. London 1878.
Coxe, Sir James, 'On the Causes of Insanity and the Means of checking its Growth' in J.M.Sc. (1872) xviii.
Crowther, Bryan, Practical Remarks on Insanity. London 1811.
Dalrymple, Donald, 'Asylum for Drunkards' in Macmillans Magazine (1872) xx.
Davey, J.G., On Dipsomania. London 1872.
Davey, J.G., 'On the Insane Poor in Middlesex' in J.M.Sc. (186 (1867) xiii.
Davey, S., 'The Detention of Lunatics in Workhouses' in Lancet (1901) ii.
Deas, P. Maury, 'Lunacy Legislation and the Lunacy Act of 1890' in B.M.J. (1891) ii.
Defoe, Daniel, A Review of the State of the English Nation. London, 1706. vol. 3.
Dickens, Charles, 'A Curious Dance round a Curious Tree' in Household Words, 17 January 1852.
Eastwood, J., 'On Medico-Legal Uncertainties' in J.M.Sc.(1869) xv.
Ellis, Sir William Charles, A Treatise on the Nature, Causes, Symptoms and Treatment of Insanity. London 1838.
Engels, Friedrich, The Condition of the Working Class in England. Leipzig 1845; London 1892.
Fry, Danby P., The Lunacy Acts: containing all the Statutes relating to Private Lunatics; Pauper Lunatics; Criminal Lunatics; Commissions of Lunacy; Public and Private Asylums; and the Commissioners in Lunacy. 4th edn. London, 1914.
Gairdner, W.T., Insanity: Modern Views as to its Nature and Treatment. Glasgow, 1885.
Gairdner, W.T., Drunkenness and Dipsomania. London 1886.
Gairdner, W.T., Medical and Legal Preventives and Remedies for Drunkenness and Dipsomania. London 1890.
Gaskell, Samuel, 'On the Want of better Provision for the Labouring and Middle Classes when attacked or threatened with Insanity' in J.M.Sc. (1860) vi.
Gerrard, James, and others, Address to the Magistrates of the County of Lancashire on the Situation proposed for an intended Lunatic Asylum. Liverpool, 1810.
Glen, William Cunningham, The Poor Law Orders of the Poor Law Commissioners and the Poor Law Board and the Local Government Board. 9th edn. London, 1883.

Granville, James Mortimer, The Care and Cure of the Insane, being the Reports of the 'Lancet' Commission on Lunatic Asylums, 1875 - 1877, for Middlesex, the City of London and Surrey. 2 vols. London, 1877.
Gray, Jonathan, A History of York Lunatic Asylum, York, 1815.
Greg, Robert, The Factory Question. London 1837.
Halliday, Sir Andrew, A General View of the Present State of Lunatics and Lunatic Asylums in Great Britain and Ireland, and in some other Kingdoms. London 1828.
Halliday, Sir Andrew, A Letter to Lord Robert Seymour, with a Report of the Numbers of Lunatics and Idiots in England and Wales. London 1829.
Harriott, John, Struggles through Life exemplified. 3 vols. London 1815.
Haslam, John, Observations on Madness and Melancholy. London 1817.
Haslam, John, Medical Jurisprudence as it relates to Insanity according to the Laws of England. London 1817.
Haslam, John, Considerations on the Moral Management of Insane Persons. London 1817.
Haslam, John, A Letter to the Right Honorable Lord Chancellor on the Nature and Interpretation of Unsoundness of Mind and Imbecility of Intellect. London 1823.
Hawkes, John, On the General Management of Public Lunatic Asylums in England and Wales. An Essay. London 1871.
Hawkins, Henry., 'Glimpses of Asylum Life' in J.M.Sc. (1869)v.
Hawkins, Henry,, 'A Plea for Convalescent Homes' in J.M.Sc. (1871) xvii.
Hawkins, Henry, 'After-Care' in J.M.Sc. (1879) xxv.
Hawkins, Henry, Treatment of Insanity, Then and Now. London 1901.
Hill, George Nesse, An Essay on the Prevention and Cure of Insanity; with Observations on the Rules for the Detection of Pretenders to Madness. London 1814.
Hill, Robert Gardiner, A Concise History of the entire Abolition of Mechanical Restraints in the Treatment of the Insane and of the Introduction, Success and final Triumph of the Non-Restraint System. Together with a Reprint of a Lecture delivered on the Subject in the year 1838. London 1857.
Hill, Robert Gardiner, Lunacy: its Past and Present. London 1870.
Hill, Matthew Davenport, Suggestions for the Repression of Crime. London 1857.
Hobbes, Thomas, Leviathan, or the Matter, Form and Power of a Commonwealth Ecclesiastical and Civil. London 1651. ed. Michael Oakeshott, 1962.
Holland, Sir Henry, Medical Notes and Reflections. 3rd edn. London 1855.
Hood, William Charles, Suggestions for the future Provision for Criminal Lunatics. London 1854.
Hood, William Charles, Criminal Lunatics. A Letter to the Chairman of the Commissioners in Lunacy. London 1860.
Horsley, J.W. Prisons and Prisoners. London 1898.
Huggard, W.G., 'The Means of determining Causation in Insanity' in J.M.Sc.(1882) xxvii.
Kerr, Norman S., Intemperance and its Remedy. London 1877.

Kirkbride, Thomas, 'Remarks on the Construction and Arrangements of Hospitals for the Insane' in Am.J. Med.Sc. (1847) xiii.

Kirkbride, Thomas, On the Construction, Organization and General Arrangements of Hospitals for the Insane. Philadelphia 1854.

Knight, Paul Slade, Observations on the Causes, Symptoms and Treatment of Derangement of the Mind, founded on an extensive moral and medical practice in the Treatment of Lunatics. London, 1827.

Labbatt, Hamilton, An Essay on the Use and Abuse of Restraint in the Management of the Insane. Dublin, 1847.

Lackington, James, Life of James Lackington. 13th edn. London 1810.

Lane-Poole, S., 'Workhouse Infirmaries' in Macmillans Magazine (1881) iii.

Lincoln Asylum, Proceedings of Lincoln Lunatic Asylum. Lincoln, 1844.

Lincoln Asylum, The State of Lincoln Lunatic Asylum, being the twenty-second Report. Lincoln, 1846.

Lindsay, W. Lauder, 'The Family System as applied to the Treatment of the Chronic Insane' in J.M.Sc. (1870) xvi.

Lindsay, W. Lauder, The Theory and Practice of Non-Restraint in the Treatment of the Insane. London, 1878.

Locke, John, An Essay concerning Human Understanding. London, 1690: 1959 edn.

Lowe, Louisa, Gagging in Madhouses as practised by Government Servants. n.d.

Lowe, Louisa, The Bastilles of England, or the Lunacy Laws at Work. London 1883.

Lushington, S.G., ed., Archbold's Lunacy, 4th edn. London 1895

Madden, The Madden Collection of Broadsides, University Library, Cambridge.

Maddock, Alfred Beaumont, Practical Observations on Mental and Nervous Disorders. London, 1845.

Manchester Lunatic Hospital, Account of the Rise and present Establishment of a Lunatic Hospital in Manchester. Manchester 1771.

Maudsley, Henry, The Physiology and Pathology of Mind. London 1867.

Maudsley, Henry, Body and Mind. London 1873.

Maudsley, Henry, Responsibility and Mental Disease. London 1874.

Maudsley, Henry, Life in Mind and Conduct. London, 1916.

Mental Hospitals Association, Thirty Years' Administration of the Public Asylums in England and Wales. London, 1922.

Mercier, Charles A., Sanity and Insanity. London, 1890.

Mercier, Charles A., Lunatic Asylums, their Organization and Management. London, 1894.

Mill, John Stuart, On Liberty. London, 1859. Everyman edn., 1964.

Millar, John, A Plea in favour of the Insane Poor. London, 1859.

Millar, John, Hints on Insanity. London, 1861.

Millingen, John Gideon, Aphorisms on the Treatment and Management of the Insane; with Considerations on Public and Private Lunatic Asylums, pointing out the Errors of the

present System. London, 1840.
Morison, W.D., Crime and its Causes. London, 1891.
Moseley, G., On Mental Disorders. their Nature, Cause and Treatment. London 1857.
Moseley, William Willis, Eleven Chapters on Nervous and Mental Complaints. London, 1838.
Moss, W., The Liverpool Guide, Liverpool, 1796.
Needham, F., Insanity in relation to Society. London, 1874.
Needham, T., Remarks on the Necessity for Legislation in reference to Habitual Drunkards. London, 1871.
Neison, F.G.P., 'Statistics of Crime in England and Wales' in Statistical Journal (1848) xi.
Nicoll, S.W., An Enquiry into the present State of Visitation in Asylums for the Reception of the Insane and into the Modes by which such Visitation may be improved. London, 1828.
Noble, Daniel, Elements of Psychological Medicine. London,1853.
O'Conor, W.A., Evidence given before the Select Committee on the Lunacy Laws. Manchester, 1879.
Panum, P.L., Observations made during an Epidemic of Measles in the Faroe Islands. New York, 1846. Reprint edn. 1940.
Parchappe, P., Les Principes à suivre dans la Fondation et la Construction des Asiles d'Alienés. Paris, 1853.
Parigot, J. 'The Gheel Question from an American Point of View' in Am.J.Insanity. (1863) xx.
Pashley, Robert, Pauperism and Poor Laws: London, 1852.
Paternoster, R., The Madhouse System. London, 1841.
Peek, Francis, Social Wreckage: A Review of the Laws of England as they affect the Poor. London, 1883.
Perceval, John Thomas, A Narrative of the Treatment experienced by a Gentleman during a State of Mental Derangement; designed to explain the Causes and Nature of Insanity, and to expose the injudicious Conduct pursued towards many unfortunate sufferers under that calamity. 2 vols London, 1838, 1840.
Philips, Charles Palmer, The Law concerning Lunatics, Idiots and Persons of Unsound Mind. London, 1858.
Pierce, Bedford, ed., Addresses to Mental Nurses. A Series of fifteen Lectures delivered to the Nursing Staff of the Retreat, York, by various Authorities. London, 1924.
Pinel, Phillippe, A Treatise on Insanity. Transl. D.D. Davis. Sheffield, 1806.
Pitt-Lewis, George, Smith, R. Percy, and Hawks, J.A., The Insane and the Law. A Plain Guide for Medical Men, Solicitors and Others. London, 1895.
Preston-Thomas, Herbert, Work and Play of A Government Inspector. London, 1909.
Prichard, James Cowles, A Treatise on Insanity and other Disorders affecting the Mind. London, 1835.
Prichard, James Cowles, On the different Forms of Insanity in relation to Jurisprudence. London, 1842.
Purnell, Purnell Bransby, Summary of Suggestions for Additions to the Law of Lunacy. Gloucester. n.d.
Ray, Isaac, A Treatise on the Medical Jurisprudence of Insanity. Boston, 1853.
Rogers, Joseph, Reminiscences of a Workhouse Medical Officer. London, 1889.

Rush, Benjamin, *Medical Inquiries and Observations upon the Diseases of the Mind*. Philadelphia, 1812.

St. Luke's, *Reasons for establishing St. Luke's. Centennial edition*. London, 1851.

Senior, Nassau, *Three Lectures on the Rate of Wages.* London 1830.

Sepharial, *On the Treatment of Criminals and Lunatics*. London 1891.

Seymour, E.J., *A Letter to the Rt. Hon. The Earl of Shaftesbury on the Laws which regulate Private Lunatic Asylums*, London, 1859.

Shaw, James, *Epitome of Mental Diseases*. London and Bristol, 1892.

Shelford, Leonard, *A Practical Treatise on the Law concerning Lunatics, Idiots and Persons of Unsound Mind*. 2 vols. London, 1833.

Sheppard, Edgar, *Lectures on Madness in its Medical, Legal and Social Aspects*. London, 1873.

Sheppard, James, *Observations on the proximate Causes of Insanity*. London, 1844.

Smith, Joshua Toulmin, *Local Self-government and Centralization*. London, 1851.

Smith, Joshua Toulmin, *What is Bureaucracy and what is Local Self-Government*. London, 1855.

Smith, R.P., 'Defects in the working of the Lunacy Act, 1890' in *J.M.Sc.* (1891) xxxvii.

Stallard, Joshua Harrison, *Pauper Lunatics and their Treatment*. London, 1870.

Stark, William, *Remarks on the Construction of Public Hospitals for the Cure of Mental Derangement*. Edinburgh, 1807.

Thompson, G., 'Remarks on the Question of special Hospitals for the early Treatment of the Insane' in *Lancet* (1889) i.

Thurnham, John, *Observations and Essays on the Statistics of Insanity, including an Inquiry into the Causes influencing the Results of Treatment in Establishments for the Insane. To which are added the Statistics of the Retreat, near York*. London, 1845.

Tuke, J.B., 'Lunatics as Patients, not Prisoners' in *Nineteenth Century* (1889) xxv.

Tuke, J.B., 'Habitual Drunkards' in *Nineteenth Century* (1893) xxxiii.

Tuke, Daniel Hack, *The Influence of the Mind on the Body*. London, 1872.

Tuke, Daniel Hack, *Insanity in Ancient and Modern Life. With Chapters on its Prevention*. London, 1878.

Tuke, Daniel Hack, *Chapters in the History of the Insane in the British Isles*. London, 1882.

Tuke, Daniel Hack, *The Past and Present Provision for the Insane Poor in Yorkshire, with suggestions for the future Provision for this Class*. London, 1889.

Tuke, Daniel Hack, *Dictionary of Psychological Medicine*. 2 vols. London, 1892.

Tuke, Samuel, *Description of the Retreat, an Institution near York, for Insane Persons of the Society of Friends*. York, 1813.

Tuke, Samuel, *Practical Hints on the Construction of Lunatic Asylums*. York, 1815.

Tuke, Samuel, A Review of the early History of the Retreat. London, 1846.
Uwins, D., A Treatise on those Disorders of the Brain and Nervous System which are usually considered and called Mental. London, 1833.
Watson, J., and Pritchett, J.P., Plans, Elevations, Sections and Descriptions of the Pauper Lunatic Asylum lately erected at Wakefield. York, 1819.
Weatherley, Leonard A., 'Trials and Troubles and Grievances of a Private Asylum Superintendent' in J.M.Sc. (1894) xi.
Weatherley, Leonard A., A Plea for the Insane. London, 1918.
Webster, J., Notes on Belgian Lunatic Asylums, including the Insane Colony at Gheel. London, 1857.
Weldon, Georgina, The History of my Orphanage; or the Outpourings of an alleged Lunatic. London, 1878.
Wells, A., On the Education of the Working Class. London, 1847.
Williams, Joseph, An Essay on the Use of Narcotics and other remedial Agents calculated to produce Sleep in the Treatment of Insanity, London, 1847.
Williams-Freeman, J.P., The Effect of Town Life on General Health. London 1890.
Wingett, T.T., A Letter to the Rt. Hon. Lord Ashley MP relative to the Case of Nottidge versus Ripley. Dundee, 1849.
Winslow, Forbes Benignus, On Uncontrollable Drunkenness, considered as a form of Mental Disorder, with Suggestions for its Treatment, and the Organization of Sanatoria for Dipsomaniacs. London, 1867.
Winslow, L.S.F., Manual of Lunacy. London 1874.
Winslow, L.S.F., Mad Humanity, Its Forms apparent and obscure. London, 1898.
Winslow, L.S.F., Recollections of Forty Years. London, 1910.
Wood, W., Insanity and the Lunacy Laws. London, 1879.
Worsley, H., Juvenile Depravity. London, 1849.
Wynter, Andrew, The Borderlands of Insanity. London, 1875.
Yellowlees, David, Lunacy and Pauperism. Glasgow, 1884.

Newspapers and Journals:

American Journal of Insanity
Asylum Journal, 1853 - 55.
British Medical Journal.
Edinburgh Review
The Gentleman's Magazine
Journal of Mental Science
Journal of Psychological Medicine and Mental Pathology
Lancet
Macmillans Magazine
Nineteenth Century
Quarterly Review
The Times
Westminster Review

SECONDARY WORKS

Abel-Smith, Brian, The Hospitals, 1800 - 1948. London, 1964.
Addison, I., ed., Prize lists of the University of Glasgow, 1777 - 1833. Glasgow, 1902.

Alexander, Franz G., and Selesnick, Sheldon T., The History of Psychiatry: an Evaluation of Psychiatric Thought and Practice from Prehistoric Times to the Present. London, 1967.
Anderson, J.M., ed., Matriculation Roll of the University of St. Andrew's. 1747 - 1897. Edinburgh, 1905.
Anderson, Michael, Family Structure in Nineteenth-Century Lancashire. Cambridge, 1971.
Anderson, P.J., ed., Roll of Alumni in Arts of the University and King's College of Aberdeen, 1596 - 1860. Aberdeen, 1900.
Arch, Joseph, Joseph Arch: The Story of his Life. London 1898.
Aubrey, John, The Natural History of Wiltshire, 1691. London, 1847.
Baring-Gould, Sabine, Songs of the West. London, 1905.
Bastide, Roger, The Sociology of Mental Disorder. Transl. Jean McNeil. London, 1972.
Bateman, Sir Frederic, and Rye, W., The History of the Bethel Hospital at Norwich. Norwich, 1906.
Bateson, Gregory, Steps to an Ecology of Mind. London, 1972.
Becker, Howard, Outsiders: Studies in the Sociology of Deviance. New York, 1963.
Bell, Sir Charles, Essays on the Anatomy of Expression in Painting. London, 1806.
Bell, Peter S., ed., Victorian Lancashire. Newton Abbot, 1974.
Berke, Joseph, and Barnes, Mary, Mary Barnes. London, 1971.
Belloc, Hilaire, Selected Essays. Penguin edn., London, 1958.
Best, G.F.A., Shaftesbury. London, 1964.
Best, G.F.A., Mid-Victorian Britain, 1851 - 75. London, 1971.
Bett, W.R., The Infirmities of Genius. London, 1952.
Boase, F., Modern English Biography of the Nineteenth Century. 6 vols. Truro, 1892 - 1921.
Booth, William, In Darkest England and the Way Out. London, 1890.
Broadwood, Lucy E., and Maitland, J.A. Fuller, English Country Songs. London, 1893.
Broadwood, Lucy E., Traditional Songs and Carols. London, 1908.
Brebner, J. Bartlett, 'Laissez-faire and State Intervention in Nineteenth Century Britain' in J.Ec.H. (1948) vii.
Briggs, Asa, The Age of Improvement, 1783 - 1867. London, 1959.
Brockbank, E.M., A Short History of Cheadle Royal. Manchester, 1934.
Brockbank, William, Portrait of a Hospital, 1752 - 1948. London, 1952.
Brockington, C. Frazer, A Short History of Public Health. London, 1956.
Bromberg, Walter, Crime and the Mind. New York, 1965.
Bronte, Charlotte, Jane Eyre. London, 1847.
Brown, G.M., ed., Lives of the Fellows of the Royal College of Physicians of London, 1826 - 1925. London, 1955.
Bruce, Maurice, The Coming of the Welfare State. London, 1961.
Buer, M.C., Health, Wealth and Population in the early days of the Industrial Revolution. London, 1926.
Burn, W.L., The Age of Equipoise. London, 1964.
Butterfield, L.M., ed., Letters of Benjamin Rush. Princeton, 1951.
Cadbury, H.C., and Braithewaite, W.C., The Beginnings of Quakerism. Cambridge, 1955.

Carlson, Eric T., and Dain, Norman, 'The Psychotherapy that was Moral Management' in Am.J.Psych. (1960) cxvii.
Chappell, W., A Collection of English National Airs. London, 1840.
Chadwick, William, Reminiscences of a Chief Constable. Longdendale, 1974.
Chevalier, L., Classes Laborieuses et Classes Dangereuses à Paris pendant la première Moitie du 19ème siècle. Paris, 1958.
Christison, R., The Life of Sir Robert Christison, Bart., edited by his Sons. Edinburgh, 1885.
Clark, Sir J., A Memoir of John Conolly MD DCL. London, 1869.
Clay, W.L., Memoir of Rev. John Clay BD. London, 1861.
Clifford, F., A History of Private Bill Legislation. London, 1885.
Coats, A.W., The Classical Economists and Economic Policy. London, 1971.
Cohen, Stanley, ed., Images of Deviance, London, 1971.
Cohen, Stanley, Folk Devils and Moral Panics. London, 1973.
Cohen, Yehudi, A., Social Structure and Personality. New York, 1961.
Comfort, Alex, The Anxiety Makers. London, 1967.
Cockton, H., The Life and Adventures of Valentine Vox, the Ventriloquist. London, 1840.
Collins, Wilkie, The Woman in White. London, 1860.
Conway, M.D., Demonology and Devil Lore. 2 vols. London, n.d.
Cooper, David, The Death of the Family. London, 1972.
Court, W.H.B., A Concise Economic History of Modern Britain from 1750 to Recent Times. Cambridge, 1954.
Cromwell, Valerie, 'Interpretations of Nineteenth Century Administration: An Analysis' in Victorian Studies.(1965 - 66) ix.
Cumming, E. and Cumming, J., Closed Ranks. Cambridge, Mass. 1957.
Curtis, Lewis P., Apes and Angels: The Irishman in Victorian Caricature. Newton Abbot, 1971.
Deutsch, Albert, The Menally Ill in America: a History of their Care and Treatment from Colonial Times.
Dicey, A.V., Lectures on the relation between Law and Public Opinion in England during the Nineteenth Century. London, 1905.
Dickens, Charles, Pickwick Papers. London, 1837.
Dickens, Charles, Barnaby Rudge, London, 1841.
D'Israeli, Isaac, Curiosities of Literature. London. New edn. 1859.
Dictionary of National Biography.
Edsall, Nicholas C., The Anti-Poor Law Movement, 1834 - 44. Manchester, 1971.
Eliade, Mircea, Myths, Dreams and Mysteries. London, 1960.
Ensor, R., England 1870 - 1914. Oxford, 1936.
Fessler, A., 'The Management of Lunacy in Seventeenth Century England. An Investigation of Quarter Sessions Records' in Proc.R.S.Med. (1956) 49.
Finer, Herman, Theory and Practice of Modern Government. New York, 1950.
Finer, S.E., The Life and Times of Sir Edwin Chadwick. London, 1952.
Ford, P., Social Theory and Social Practice. Shannon, 1968.

Foster, Joseph, Alumni Oxoniensis, 1715 - 1886. 6 vols. London, 1887 - 88.
Foucault, Michel, Madness and Civilization. Transl. Richard Howard. London, 1967.
Foulkes, S.M. and Prince, J. Stewart, eds., Psychiatry in a Changing Society. London, 1969.
Freedman, A. ed., Comprehensive Textbook of Psychiatry. New York, 1967.
French, C.N., The Story of St. Luke's Hospital. London, 1951.
Freud, Sigmund, Civilization and its Discontents. Transl. J. Rivière. London, 1953.
Fried, Albert, and Elman, Richard M., Charles Booth's London. A Portrait of the Poor at the turn of the Century. Drawn from his 'Life and Labour of the People of London.' London, 1969.
Friedson, Eliot, ed., The Hospital in Modern Society. New York, 1963.
Fromm, Erich, The Sane Society. New York, 1955.
Gash, N., 'Ashley and the Conservative Party in 1842' in E.H.R. (1938) iii.
Gaskell, Charles G. Milnes, Passages in the History of the York Lunatic Asylum, 1772 - 1901. Wakefield, 1902.
Gissing, George, The Nether World. London, 1885.
Glenn, Michael, ed., Voices from the Asylum. New York 1974.
Glueck, Sheldon, Law and Psychiatry. Baltimore, 1962.
Goffman, Erving, Asylums: Essays in the Social Situation of Mental Patients and other Inmates. New York, 1961.
Goffman, Erving, Stigma. New Jersey, 1963.
Goodwin, Michael, ed., Nineteenth Century Opinion. London, 1951.
Goody, J., and Watt, I., 'Literate Culture: some General Considerations' in Musgrave, P.W, ed., Sociology, History and Education. London, 1970.
Gordon, S., and Cocks, T.G.B., A People's Conscience. London, 1952.
Goshen, Charles E., Documentary History of Psychiatry. London, 1967.
Gray, B. Kirkman, Philanthropy and the State. London, 1908.
Gray, Mrs. Edwin, Papers and Diaries of a York Family, 1764 - 1839.
Gretton, R.M., The King's Government: A Study in the Growth of the Central Administration. London, 1913.
Grob, Gerald N., 'Mental Illness, Indigency and Welfare' in Harevan, Tamara K., Anonymous Americans. New Jersey, 1971.
Grob, Gerald N., Mental Institutions in America: Social Policy to 1875. New York, 1973.
Gutchen, R.M., 'Local Improvements and Centralization in Nineteenth Century England' in H.J. (1961) iv.
Hare, E.H., 'Masturbatory Insanity: the history of an Idea' in J.M.Sc. (1962) cviii.
Hammond, J.L. and Barbara, Lord Shaftesbury. London, 1923.
Harland, John, and Wilkinson, Thomas, Ballads and Songs of Lancashire, Ancient and Modern. London, 1875.
Harland, John, and Wilkinson, Thomas, Lancashire Folklore. London, 1882.
Harris, R.W., Romanticism and the Social Order, 1780 - 1830. London, 1969.

Harris, John S., British Government Inspection. The Local Services and the Central Departments. London, 1955.
Harrison, Brian, Drink and the Victorians. The Temperance Question in England, 1815 - 1872. London, 1971.
Hart, J., 'Nineteenth Century Social Reform: A Tory Interpretation of History' in Past and Present (1965) xxxi.
Hays, Peter, New Horizons in Psychiatry. London, 1964.
Heasman, Kathleen, Evangelicals in Action, An Appraisal of their Social Work. London, 1962.
Hillyer, Richard, Country Boy, London, 1966.
Hodder, Edwin, The Life and Work of the Seventh Earl of Shaftesbury KG. London, Popular edn., 1892.
Hodgkinson, Ruth C., 'Provision for Pauper Lunatics, 1834 - 1871' in Medical History (1966) x.
Hole, Christina, Witchcraft in England. London, 1947.
Holingshead, A.B., and Redlich, F.C., 'Social Stratification and Psychiatric Disorder' in Am.Soc.R. (1953) 18.
Hone, William, The Table Book. London, 1864.
Hone, William, The Every Day Book. 2 vols. London, 1864.
Hoenig, J., and Hamilton, Marian W., The De-segregation of the Mentally Ill. London, 1969.
Horsley, Sir Victor, and Sturge, Mary D., Alcohol and the Human Body. London, 1909.
Hunt, H.C., A Retired Habitation. A History of the Retreat, York. London, 1932.
Hunter, Richard, 'The Rise and Fall of Mental Nursing' in Lancet (1956) i.
Hunter, Richard, and Macalpine, Ida, Three Hundred Years of Psychiatry, 1535 - 1860. A History presented in selected English Texts. London, 1963.
Hunter, Richard, and Macalpine, Ida, Psychiatry for the Poor. 1851 Colney Hatch Asylum, Friern Hospital 1973. A Medical and Social History. London, 1974.
Ilbert, Sir C., Legislative Methods and Forms. Oxford,1901.
Inglis, Brian, Poverty and the Industrial Revolution. London, 1972.
Jackson, J.A., The Irish in Britain. London, 1963.
Jasper, A.S., A Hoxton Childhood. London, 1969.
Jeffries, Richard, Hodge and his Masters. 2 vols. London, 1880. Reprint 1966.
Jones, Kathleen, Lunacy, Law and Conscience, 1744 - 1845. London, 1955.
Jones, Kathleen, Mental Health and Social Policy, 1845 - 1959. London, 1960.
Keir, S., The Royal Albert Institution, Lancaster. Lancaster, 1937.
Kelynack, T.N., ed., The Drink Problem in its Medico-Sociological Aspects, by Fourteen Medical Authorities. London, 1907.
Kittrie, Nicholas N ., The Right to be Different: Deviance and Enforced Therapy. London, 1971.
Kornish, Paul J., Studies in Change and Revolution. London, 1972.
Kraeplin, Emil, One Hundred Years of Psychiatry. Transl. Wade Baskin, New York, 1962.
Laing, R.D., The Divided Self. London, 1959.
Laing, R.D., The Politics of Experience. London, 1967.

Leff, S. and V., The Search for Sanity. London, 1965.
Leigh, Denis, The Historical Development of British Psychiatry. Volume One: 18th and 19th Century. Oxford, 1961.
Lemert, E.M., Social Pathology, New York, 1951.
Lidbetter, E.J., The Lunacy and Mental Treatment Acts., 1890 to 1930. London, 1933.
Lindsay, Jack, ed., Loving Mad Tom. Bedlamite Verses of the XVI and XVII centuries. Welwyn Garden City, 1969.
Linton, Ralph, The Cultural Background of Personality. London, 1947.
Loch, Charles Stewart, A Great Ideal and its Champion. Papers and Addresses by Sir C.S. Loch. London, 1923.
Lomax, Montague, The Experiences of an Asylum Doctor. London, 1921.
Lomax, Montague, and Grant-Richards, R., The Experiences of an Asylum Patient. London, 1922.
McLuhan, Marshall, Understanding Media. London, 1964.
Macalpine, Ida, and Hunter, Richard, George III and the Mad Business. London, 1969.
MacDonagh, Oliver, 'The Nineteenth Century Revolution in Government: a Reappraisal' in H.J. (1958) ii.
MacDonagh, Oliver, A Pattern of Government Growth, 1800 - 60. The Passenger Acts and their Enforcement. London, 1961.
Mackay, Thomas, A History of the English Poor Law, vol. II. 1834 - 98. London, 1898. Reprint, 1967.
Marsh, David C., The Changing Social Structure of England and Wales, 1871 - 1961. London, 1965.
Marshall, J.D., The Old Poor Law, 1795 - 1834. London, 1968.
Mechanic, David, 'Some Factors in identifying and defining Mental Illness' in Mental Hygiene. (1962) 46.
Medvedev, Zhores A., and Roy A., A Question of Madness, London, 1971.
Midwinter, Eric C., ' A Tory Interpretation of History: some Comments' in Past and Present (1966) xxxiv.
Midwinter, Eric, C., Old Liverpool. Newton Abbot, 1971.
Moir, Esther, 'Sir George Onesiphorous Paul' in Finberg, H.P.R., ed., Gloucestershire Studies. Leicester UP, 1957.
Moss, John, 'Inspectorates as a Link between Central and Local Authorities' in Public Administration (1939) xvii.
Nunally, J.C., Popular Conceptions of Mental Health. New York, 1961.
O'Brien, R. Barry, The Life of Lord Russell of Killowen. London, 1901.
O'Donoghue, Edward G., The Story of Bethlem Hospital from its Foundation in 1247. London, 1914.
Oliver, Thomas, Dangerous Trades. The Historical, Social and Legal Aspects of Industrial Occupations as affecting Health. London, 1902.
Owen, David, Philanthropy in England, 1660 - 1960. Cambridge, Mass., 1965.
Parris, Henry, 'The Nineteenth Century Revolution in Government: A Reappraisal reappraised' in H.J. (1960) iii.
Parris, Henry, Constitutional Bureaucracy. The Development of British Central Administration Since the Eighteenth Century. London, 1969.
Parry-Jones, William Ll., The Trade in Lunacy. A Study of Private Madhouses in England in the Eighteenth and Nineteenth

Centuries. London, 1971.
Partridge, Ralph, Broadmoor. A History of Criminal Lunacy and its Problems. London, 1953.
Percy, Thomas, Reliques of Ancient English Poetry. London 1765. Everyman edn. 2 vols. n.d.
Perkin, Harold, The Origins of Modern English Society, 1780 - 1880. London, 1969.
Petrie, Charles, Scenes of Edwardian Life. London, 1965.
Pike, L.O., A History of Crime in England. 2 vols. London, 1876.
Pinker, Robert, Social Theory and Social Policy. London,1971.
Plumb, J.H., The Growth of Political Stability in England, 1675 - 1725. London, 1967.
Pollard, Sidney, The Idea of Progress: History and Society. London, 1968.
Powell, Sir A., The Metropolitan Asylums Board and its Work, 1867 - 1930. London, 1930.
Poynter, J.R., Society and Pauperism: English Ideas on Poor Relief, 1795 - 1834. London, 1969.
Pritchard, D.G., Education and the Handicapped. London, 1963.
Rawes, William, A Short History of St. Luke's Hospital. London, 1901.
Reade, Charles, Hard Cash. A Matter of Fact Romance. London, 1863.
Redford, A., Labour Migration in England, 1800 - 1850. 2nd edn. Manchester, 1964.
Reed, A. and C. eds., Memoirs of the Life and Philanthropic Labours of Andrew Reed DD. London, 1863.
Rennie, T.A.C., and Woodward, L.E., Mental Health in Modern Society. New York, 1948.
Renton, Richard, John Forster and his Friendships. London, 1912.
Ridenour, Nina, Mental Health in the United States: a Fifty Year History. Harvard, 1961.
Ritson, Joseph, Ancient Songs. London, 1790.
Roberts, David, 'Jeremy Bentham and the Victorian Administrative State' in Victorian Studies(1959) ii.
Roberts, David, Victorian Origins of the British Welfare State. New Haven, 1960.
Roberts, Nesta, Cheadle Royal Hospital, A Bicentenary History. Altrincham,
Roberts, Robert, The Classic Slum: Salford Life in the first Quarter of the Century. Manchester, 1971.
Rooff, Madeleine, Voluntary Societies and Social Policy. London, 1957.
Rose, Michael E., The English Poor Law, 1780 - 1930. Newton Abbott, 1971.
Rose, Steven and Hilary, 'The Politics of Neurobiology: Biologies in the service of the State' in Dale, Roger et al, eds., Schooling and Capitalism. London, 1976.
Rosen, George, 'Social Attitudes to Irrationality and Madness in Seventeenth and Eighteenth Century Europe' in J.Hist.Med.& & All. Sc. (1963) 18.
Rosen, George, 'The Philosophy of Ideology and the Emergence of Modern Medicine in France' in Bull.Hist.Med. (1964) xx.
Rosen, George, Madness in Society. Chapters in the Historical Sociology of Mental Illness. London, 1968.

Rosenau, Helen, Social Purpose in Architecture: Paris and London compared, 1760 - 1800. London, 1970.
Rothman, David, The Discovery of the Asylum. Social Order and Disorder in the New Republic. Boston, 1971.
Rows, R.G., The Development of Psychiatric Science as a Branch of Public Health. London, 1912.
Sargant, William, The Unquiet Mind. London, 1967.
Schatzman, Morton, 'Madness and Morals' in Boyers, Robert, and Orrill, Robert, eds., Laing and Anti-Psychiatry. London, 1972.
Schatzman, Morton, Soul Murder. Persecution in the Family. London, 1973.
Scheff, Thomas, 'The Role of the Mentally Ill and the Dynamics of Mental Disorder: a Research Framework' in Sociometry (1963) 26.
Scheff, Thomas, Being Mentally Ill. London, 1966.
Scoffern, J., Stray Leaves of Science and Folklore. London, 1870.
Sherlock, E.B., The Feeble-Minded. London, 1911.
Shepard, Leslie, The History of Street Literature. Newton Abbot, 1973.
Sigerist, Henry E., Civilization and Disease. Cornell UP, 1943.
Skultans, Vieda, Madness and Morals. Ideas on Insanity in the Nineteenth Century. London, 1975.
Smiles, Samuel, Character. London, 1871.
Smith, Paul, Disraelian Conservatism and Social Reform. London, 1967.
Smith, Sydney, Essays of Sydney Smith reprinted from the 'Edinburgh Review'. London, n.d.
Spitzer, S., and Denzin, N., The Mental Patient: Studies in the Sociology of Deviance. New York, 1968.
Staford-Clark, David, Psychiatry To-day. London, 1952.
Stansky, Peter, The Victorian Revolution: Government and Society in Victoria's Britain. New York, 1973.
Stedman-Jones, Gareth, Outcast London. Oxford, 1971.
Sullivan, W.C., Crime and Insanity. London, 1924.
Sutherland, Gillian, ed., Studies in the Growth of Nineteenth Century Government. London, 1972.
Symonds, J.A., Some Account of the Life, Writings, and Character of the late James Cowles Prichard MD FRS. Bristol, 1849.
Szasz, Thomas S., Law, Liberty and Psychiatry. New York, 1963.
Szasz, Thomas S., 'Undermind' in New Society 16 December 1971.
Szasz, Thomas S., The Manufacture of Madness, London, 1972.
Szasz, Thomas S., Ideology and Insanity: Essays in the Psychiatric Dehumanization of Man. London, 1973.
Szasz, Thomas S., The Age of Madness. The History of involuntary Mental Hospitalization presented in selected Texts. London, 1975.
Tawney, R.H., Religion and the Rise of Capitalism. London, 1926. Penguin edn., 1964.
Taylor, Arthur, J., Laissez-faire and State Intervention in nineteenth-century Britain. London, 1972.
Thomas, M.W., 'The Origins of Administrative Centralization' in Current Legal Problems (1950) iii.
Thompson, E.P., Whigs and Hunters. London, 1976.

Thompson, Flora, Lark Rise to Candleford. Oxford, 1939-43. Penguin edn., 1973.
Timms, Noel, A Sociological Approach to Social Problems. London, 1967.
Tobias, J.J., Crime and Industrial Society in the Nineteenth Century. London, 1967.
Tredgold, R.F., ed., Bridging the Gap from Fear to Understanding in Mental Illness. London, 1968.
E.B. Tylor, Primitive Culture. 2 vols. London, 1871.
Venn, J.A., Alumni Cantabrigiensis. Part II. 6 vols. Cambridge 1940 - 54.
Walk, Alexander, 'Some Aspects of the "Moral Treatment" of the Insane up to 1854' in J.M.Sc. (1954) c.
Walk, Alexander, 'The History of Mental Nursing' in J.M.Sc. (1961) cvii.
Walker, Nigel, Crime and Insanity in England. Volume I: The Historical Perspective. Edinburgh, 1968.
Waugh, Edwin, Lancashire Sketches. London, 1869.
Webb, Sidney and Beatrice, English Poor Law Policy. London, 1910.
Wedge, B.M., 'Occurrence of Psychosis among Okinawans in Hawaii' in Psychiatric Quarterly (1954) 28.
Welford, A.T., Argyle, M., Glass, D.V. and Morris, J.N., Society: Psychological Problems and Methods of Study. London, 1968.
Who Was Who.
Woodroofe, Kathleen, From Charity to Social Work. London,1967.
Woodward, E.L., The Age of Reform. Oxford, 1938.
Wrigley, E.A., ed., Nineteenth Century Society. Essays in the Use of Quantitative Methods for the study of social Data. Cambridge, 1972.
Yellowlees, Henry, To Define True Madness. London, 1953.
Zilboorg, Gregory, and Henry, Gregory, History of Medical Psychology. New York, 1941.
Zinberg, Norman, 'The Mirage of Mental Health' in B.J.S. (1970) xxi.
Williams, Charles, Demoniacal Obsession and Possession as Causes of Insanity. London, 1911.

INDEX